QS-9000
Quality Systems
Handbook

QS-9000
Quality Systems
Handbook

David Hoyle

Published on behalf of
Society of Automotive Engineers, Inc.
400 Commonwealth Drive
Warrendale, PA 15096-0001
U.S.A.
Phone: (412) 776-4841
Fax: (412) 776-5760

∞ Recognizing the importance of preserving what has been
written, Butterworth-Heinemann prints its books on acid-free
paper whenever possible.

Library of Congress Cataloging-in-Publication Data

British Library Cataloguing-in-Publication Data
A catalogue record for this book is available from the British Library.

The publisher offers special discounts on bulk orders of this book.
For information, please contact:
Manager of Special Sales
Butterworth-Heinemann
313 Washington Street
Newton, MA 02158-1626
Tel: 617-928-2500
Fax: 617-928-2620

For information on all electronics publications available, contact our World Wide Web
home page at: http://www.bh.com/el

10 9 8 7 6 5 4 3 2 1

Printed in the United States of America

Contents

Appendices

Preface

This handbook has been written for managers, auditors, quality practitioners, students, and tutors as a handy reference book on the requirements, concepts, and ideas which underpin the modern quality system. It is a practical guide for those managing, designing, implementing or assessing quality systems that aim to meet the quality systems standard.

In the period since ISO 9000 was launched, over 95 000 certificates have been awarded[1]. We all know ISO 9000 has its warts and some of them were eradicated in the 1994 revision. It is billed as being generic but generic to what? Most of us take the view that it is generic to manufacturing since it uses the language of the manufacturing industry. Many bodies serving the service sector in particular have issued interpretative guides. Obviously, ISO 9000 was not intended to stand alone in a contractual situation as each customer would need to tailor it to suit particular contracts. This was to be expected and in fact is acknowledged in ISO 9000-1. So it was not surprising that the motor industry should feel it necessary to produce a version of ISO 9000 specifically for their industry.

In 1992 Chrysler, Ford, and General Motors set out to harmonize the fundamental supplier quality system manuals and assessment tools they used and produced QS-9000, a standard that embodied the requirements of ISO 9001 and added some ISO 9000 based requirements, sector specific requirements, and customer specific requirements.

Those who work in such environments will be very familiar with Supplier QA techniques and the plethora of check lists, company standards, and questionnaires that are used. One objective of ISO 9000 was to reduce multiple assessment by customers. Personally I don't believe it has reduced multiple assessments since customers still need assurance that their specific requirements will be met. Customer Supplier QA activities will have changed focus when assessing ISO 9000 registered

---

[1] Figure from *The Mobil Survey* 31 August 1995

suppliers, paying less attention to system elements and more to the contract specific matters. However, I have heard from some customers that they distrust some third party assessments as they have evidence of major gaps in a supplier's quality system going undetected by assessors. Consistency in assessments appears not to be assured by the present controls.

What Chrysler, Ford, and General Motors realized was that their existing supplier QA requirements had a lot in common and that since many of the suppliers supply to one or more of the Big Three (as they have become known), there were many benefits to be gained by all their suppliers meeting a common standard. In the USA, ISO 9000 certification was not as advanced as in Europe. In fact, many American companies did not believe ISO 9000 certification brought any advantages until they realized that to trade with Europe, some of them would need to demonstrate they met ISO 9000. The motor industry soon realized that the passport to European trade would be ISO 9000 certification regardless of there being a European Directive that required formal management systems. The rate of growth (49% from June 94 to March 95) in certification in the USA now equals that of Europe, excluding the UK where it is leveling off.

However, ISO 9000 did not contain the industry specific requirements needed since it was, after all, generic. QS-9000 was first published in August 1994 and is a harmonization of Chrysler's *Supplier Quality Assurance Manual*, Ford's *Q101*, and General Motor's *Targets for Excellence* with some input from the Truck Manufacturers. Section 4 of ISO 9001 1994 has been adopted in its entirety as the foundation for the standard. Some interpretations are included but the greatest differences are presented as supplemental quality system requirements. Unlike ISO 9001, QS-9000 contains mandatory and advisory requirements. The Big Three have chosen not to modify the wording of ISO 9001, an approach I believe is flawed, as the requirements are more easily clarified by rephrasing rather than additional words. The way many of the additions are inserted seems to imply new requirements when in fact they merely clarify a requirement of ISO 9001 for the automotive sector. However, this is a small criticism when viewed against the magnitude of the additional requirements. QS-9000 moves more towards a TQM standard than ISO 9001. Requirements for simultaneous engineering, continuous improvement (covering quality, delivery, and price), zero defects on attribute data, business plans, failure modes analysis, and many more important aspects make QS-9000 a much more stringent standard than ISO 9001. Organizations that achieve QS-9000 registration will be streets ahead of those with ISO 9001 registration.

My *ISO 9000 Quality Systems Handbook* was first published in 1993, with the second edition being published in late 1994, following revision to the ISO 9000 series of standards in July of that year. What I attempted to achieve in the *ISO 9000 Quality Systems Handbook* was a detailed analysis of each individual requirement, of which there are over 300. The feedback I have received has indicated that the handbook has proved to be a very useful tool for quality system implementers and auditors. Although based on ISO 9001, I addressed many of the omissions and in so doing covered much of what was eventually to appear in QS-9000. Whilst the *ISO 9000 Quality Systems Handbook* remains a general text, of use to many industry sectors including the automobile industry, I felt there were several advantages in producing a version that addressed QS-9000 in the same manner. QS-9000 has added a further three elements and 67 clauses which enlarges the number of requirements to over 500. The handbook covers the basic requirements and sector specific requirements but not the customer specific requirements of Section III of QS-9000. It gives an interpretation of the requirements, offers options not boilerplate solutions, and provides strategies rather than typical procedures. Use has been made of the official interpretation of QS-9000 specific requirements issued by the International Auto Sector Group (IASG) and alternative arguments offered when appropriate.

General guidance to meeting QS-9000 is given since correct solutions will depend on particular circumstances. It is therefore recommended that you consult your customer directly or seek advice on specific problems through the IASG.

Although two of the Big Three require certification of first tier suppliers during 1997, second tier suppliers will be subject to QS-9000 assessments by first tier suppliers long after that date. It is therefore hoped that this book will be of benefit to both first and second tier suppliers well into the next century.

The book is divided into two parts. Part 1 gives general background information on QS-9000, its origin, composition, application, the strategies for registration, and other preparatory aspects. Part 2 is divided into chapters that correspond to Sections I and II of the standard both in title and scope. The clauses of the standard are paraphrased and dissected to identify individual requirements. Appendices contain a glossary of over 100 terms and phrases, a bibliography, an index of related standards, and various tables which summarize information in a convenient form.

The interpretations of QS-9000 are those of the author and should not be deemed to be those of the IASG, International Organization for Standardization, or any National Standards Institution.

DH
Monmouth
July 1996

Acknowledgments

The idea for this book came from a discussion I had with Paul Sousa of Delphi Chassis systems, who had purchased over 50 copies of the *ISO 9000 Quality Systems Handbook*. Whilst working on a training course for Delphi it became apparent that those unfamiliar with ISO 9000 and the new requirements of QS-9000 needed more detailed information than was currently available.

I would also like to pay tribute to Michael Forster of Butterworth Heinemann who arranged for the book to be published in the USA, thereby making it more accessible to those in the industries affected by QS-9000.

My thanks to Stephen Morris, my editor, who adapted the original text to produce this QS-9000 version and to the many students of the QS-9000 Lead Auditor courses that I have delivered both in the USA and Europe, whose questions inspired many of the explanations that have been added.

Part 1

Preparation for QS-9000 registration

Foreword

Throughout history mankind has been motivated by the swell of opinion, campaigns, prizes, fashion, and fear. It is fashionable at the present time to focus on quality as a means of increasing one's competitiveness. National campaigns have attempted to motivate industry to improve the quality of their products and services. Prizes are being awarded to those firms who achieve international quality system standards and make breakthroughs in quality performance and many firms live in fear of losing their customers if they don't win these prizes. Quality has been achieved by a hit and miss process in many organizations. Some have had the foresight to achieve it by design and survived several generations and world wars. What is the secret ingredient, one wonders.

Most western businesses were born out of the profit motive – a quest for money regardless of the consequences. After the devastation of the Second World War, there was a great demand for consumer goods and rearmament. Quantity was more important than quality – demand exceeded supply. It was not until Japan showed western companies that exceeding customer expectations would secure continual increases in profits that they directed their full attention to quality and supply started to exceed demand.

The secret behind Japan's economic miracle is believed to be *kaizen*. Kaizen means the relentless pursuit of gradual unending improvements in quality by getting the maximum out of existing resources. Western industrialists believe that to make progress they have to spend more money, replace old equipment, old technology, old buildings. Japan has another word for this; they call it *kairoy*. It means improvement by spending money. While the West throws money at problems, Japan makes improvement by many small changes. Only when they cannot obtain any more improvement is it time for kairoy. Gradual improvement is slow, it doesn't capture the imagination of western managers. Rather than struggle with inefficient resources, they would rather throw them away and introduce a new system, not realizing that it will bring with it a whole new set of problems. By throwing out the old system they may have thrown the baby out with the bath water.

What has this got to do with quality systems and QS-9000? Quality systems should enable companies to maintain control, create stability, predictability, and capability; if you are one of those companies that is always changing then quality systems should enable you to do it under controlled conditions and not as a hit or miss approach. Quality systems enable you to do better what you already do. The first step in developing a quality system is to chart your core processes. You then build in measures that will at first enable you to achieve consistent results and then improve your performance gradually, reducing variation and complexity as you go. In this way you obtain lasting improvement by gradual change – in short, kaizen. However, success is not about using the right tools. A golfer can possess the same clubs as a professional and still not match the professional's performance, so what does the professional have that seems to elude the amateur? In simple terms it is to acquire the knowledge that will enable one to choose the right things to do and to develop the necessary skills that will enable one to do these things right first time. However, one needs to have control over the factors that will affect one's success or at least, as the golfer knows, compensate for the forces outside one's control and act accordingly.

The pursuit of quality is a long-term investment and cannot be equated with improved financial performance. Improvement in quality is totally within a company's control whereas improved financial performance is often at the mercy of competitors, interest rates, and trade barriers. Financial plans can be ruined at a stroke by a fall in share prices, wars or a change in government. QS-9000 has been conceived to cause continuous improvement, defect prevention, and the reduction of variation and waste in the supply chain within the automobile industry.

QS-9000 is only a beginning – it provides a mechanism with which to bring about systematic improvement but it doesn't improve performance by itself. People are motivated by competition, by having something to aim for, not by doing the same mundane things day after day. People want change but only if they believe it is going to be beneficial. Sportsmen perform best when given a target to meet or a record to break; nations perform best when faced with a mortal enemy or a dream of national achievement, such as the Americans' quest to put a person on the moon in the 1960s. Other initiatives have also focussed our attention on quality and provided challenges to industry to succeed. The Malcolm Baldrige National Quality Award, the UK Quality Award, the European Quality Award, and the Deming Prize are giving firms a target to aim for, a prize to be won. QS-9000, however, is only one step on the road to achieving these prizes. Beyond QS-9000 is a world of improvement. Gaining QS-9000 registration should be like being given a new lease of life. With such a system companies should be able to conquer the world.

Assessors have far too little time to carry out a proper assessment. Some look for conformance and stumble across nonconformance, others look only for nonconformance and uncover countless minor errors. They will not have the time to really understand your business, to identify the key factors upon which the quality of your products and services depend. The standard is used to assess your capability of supplying conforming product or service. This does not mean that mistakes are prohibited since anyone can make mistakes, but that a system exists which if followed will ensure that all products and services meet customer requirements. Assessors should therefore determine that suppliers have a system which is capable of supplying conforming product with provisions built in to ensure it is incapable of supplying nonconforming product. Many are trying to prevent problems from occurring which have never occurred before: problems which if solved would add no value, problems which do not reduce the capability of supplying nonconforming product, problems which are trivial when compared to the Space Shuttle, Flixborough, Three Mile Island, Bohpal, and Chernobyl disasters of the Eighties. However, it should not be forgotten that each of these disasters was caused not by man's inability to control events but by man's inability to determine what could cause failure, put in place the measures to prevent it, and then relentlessly ensure they are implemented. This is the secret of the successful companies and what QS-9000 aims to achieve – to prevent problems which may jeopardize customer satisfaction at all stages from conception of the product or service to its disposal or discontinuation.

Don't lose sight of the product or the service. Remember, it is the products and service that you provide that create customers, not your quality system. The quality system is merely a tool to enable you to do this more effectively. Measure your success not by whether you achieve QS-9000 registration but by whether the level of customer satisfaction goes up and stays up.

Chapter 1

Basic concepts

Quality

In supplying products or services there are three fundamental parameters which determine their saleability. They are price, quality, and delivery. Customers require products and services of a given quality to be delivered by or be available by a given time and to be of a price which reflects value for money. These are the needs of customers. An organization will survive only if it creates and retains satisfied customers and this will only be achieved if it offers for sale products or services which respond to customer needs and expectations. While price is a function of cost, profit margin, and market forces, and delivery a function of the organization's efficiency and effectiveness, quality is determined by the extent to which a product or service successfully serves the purposes of the user during usage (not just at the point of sale). Price and delivery are both transient features whereas the impact of quality is sustained long after the attraction or the pain of price and delivery has subsided.

The word *quality* has many meanings: a degree of excellence, conformance with requirements, the totality of characteristics of an entity that bear on its ability to satisfy stated or implied needs, fitness for use, freedom from defects, imperfections or contamination, and (a phrase which is gaining popularity) delighting customers. These are just a few meanings; however, the meaning used in the context of QS-9000 is the one concerned with the totality of characteristics that satisfy needs. The "fitness for use" definition is shorter, more easily remembered, and can be used when making decisions about quality. The specification is often an imperfect definition of what a customer needs and because some needs can be difficult to express clearly, it doesn't mean that by not conforming, the product or service is unfit for use. However, a product which conforms to requirements may be totally useless. It all depends on whose requirements with which it conforms. If a company sets its own standards and these do not meet customer needs then its claim that it produces quality products is bogus. On the other hand, if the standards are well in excess of what the customer needs, the price tag may well be too high for what customers are prepared to pay – there probably isn't a market for a gold-plated mouse trap for instance, except as an ornament perhaps!

A product which possesses features that satisfy customer needs is then a quality product. Likewise, one that possesses features which dissatisfy customers is not a quality product. So the final arbiter on quality is the customer. The customer is the only one who can decide whether the quality of the products and services you supply is satisfactory and you will be conscious of this either by direct feedback or by loss of sales, reduction in market share and, ultimately, loss of business.

There are other considerations in understanding the word *quality*, such as grade and class. These are treated in ISO 8402 but will be addressed briefly here so as to give a complete picture.

Grade

Differences in product or service performance and degrees of refinement are differences in *grade*. Hotels are graded on the number of services they provide such as one star, two star, three star etc. Motor cars are graded on the different features provided, such as the differences between the Buick Skylark, Century, and Le Sabre. If a low-grade service meets the needs for which it was designed then it is of the requisite quality. If a high-grade product or service fails to meet the requirements for which it was designed then it is of poor quality regardless of it still meeting the requirements for the lower grade. There is a market for such differences in products and services but should customer expectations change then what was acceptable as a particular grade becomes no longer acceptable and regrading has to occur.

Where manufacturing processes are prone to uncontrollable variation it is not uncommon to grade products as a method of selection. The product which is free of imperfections would be the highest grade and would therefore command the highest price. Any product with imperfections would be downgraded and sold at a correspondingly lower price. Examples of such practice arise in the ceramics, glass, and textile industries. In the electronic component industry grading is a common practice to select devices which operate between certain temperature ranges. In ideal conditions all devices would meet the higher specification but due to manufacturing variation only a few may actually reach full performance. The remainder of the devices have a degraded performance but still offer all the functions of the top-grade component at lower temperatures. To say that these differences are not differences in quality would be misleading since the products were all designed to fulfill the higher specification. As there is a market for such products it is expedient to exploit it. There is then a range over which product quality can vary and still create satisfied customers. Outside the lower end of this range the product is considered to be of poor quality.

Class

Differences in purpose are differences in *class*. A Cadillac motor car is in a different class to a Chevrolet. They were each designed for a totally different purpose. A Cadillac that constantly fails to start would be of poor quality whereas the Chevrolet that starts every time would be of good quality, assuming all other features to be equal.

Quality and price

Most of us are attracted to certain products and services by their price. If the price is outside our reach then we don't even consider the product or service, whatever its quality, except perhaps to admire it. We also rely on price as a comparison, hoping that we can obtain the same characteristics at a lower price. In the luxury goods market, a high price is often a mark of quality but it is occasionally a confidence trick aimed at making more profit for the supplier. When certain products and services are rare, the price tends to be high and when plentiful the price is low, regardless of their quality. One can purchase the same item in different stores at different prices, some as much as 50% less, many at 10% less than the highest price. You can also receive a discount for buying in bulk and being a trade customer rather than a retail customer. Travelers know that goods are more expensive at the airport than from the country craft shop. However, in the country craft shop, defective goods or "seconds" may well be on sale, whereas at the airport the supplier will want to display only the best examples as a rule. Often an increase in the price of a product may indicate a better service such as free replacement if faulty, free delivery, free telephone support line. The discount shops may not offer such attractions.

The price label on any product or service should be for a product or service free of defects. If there are defects then the label should say as much, otherwise the supplier may be in breach of national laws and statutes. Price is therefore not a feature or characteristic of the product but is a feature of the service. Price is negotiable for the same quality of product. A service that supplies products at a discount price gives better value for money and hence provides a better quality of service. Some may argue that quality is expensive but in reality, the saving you make on buying low-priced goods could well be eroded by inferior service or difference in the cost of ownership.

Unlike ISO 9001, QS-9000 does in fact include price as a factor amongst its require-ments. However, its inclusion is not as a product characteristic but as a driver of improvement. The Continuous Improvement element of the standard requires sup-pliers to continuously improve in quality, service, and price implying that the price the customer pays for the same quality of product or service has to be continually reduced.

Quality and cost

Philip Crosby published his book *Quality Is Free* in 1979 and caused a lot of raised eyebrows among executives because they always believed the removal of defects was an in-built cost in running any business. To get quality you had to pay for inspectors to detect the errors. What Crosby told us was that if we could eliminate all the errors and reach zero defects, we would not only reduce our costs but increase the level of customer satisfaction by several orders of magnitude. In fact there is the cost of doing the right things right first time and the cost of not doing the right things right first time. The latter are quality costs or the cost incurred because failure is possible. If failure of a product, a process or a service is not possible, then there are no quality costs. We could classify the costs as avoidable costs and unavoidable costs. We have to pay for labor, materials, facilities, machines, transport, etc. These costs are unavoidable but we are also paying in addition some cost to cover the prevention, detection, and removal of errors. Should customers have to pay for the errors made by others? There is a basic cost if failure was not possible and the additional costs in preventing and detecting failures and correcting errors because our prevention and detection pro-grams were ineffective. If you reduce complexity, and install failure-prevention meas-ures you will be spending less on failure detection and correction. There is an initial investment to be paid, but in the long term you can meet your customer requirements at a cost far less than you were spending previously. Some customers are now forcing their suppliers to reduce internal costs so that they can offer the same products at lower prices.

High quality and low quality; poor quality and good quality

When a product or service satisfies our needs we are likely to say it is of good quality and likewise when we are dissatisfied we say the product or service is of poor quality. When the product or service exceeds our needs we will probably say it is of high quality and likewise if it falls well below our expectations we say it is of low quality. These measures of quality are all subjective. What is good to one may be poor to another. In the undeveloped countries, any product no matter what the quality is welcomed. When you have nothing, even the poorest of goods is better than none. A product may not need to possess defects for it to be regarded as poor quality – it may not possess the features which we would expect, such as access for maintenance. These are design features which give a product its saleability. Products and services which conform to customer requirements are considered to be products of acceptable quality. However, we need to express our relative satisfaction with products and services and hence use subjective terms such as high, low, good, or poor quality. If a product which meets customer requirements is of acceptable quality, what do we call one that does not quite meet the requirements, or perhaps exceeds the requirements? An otherwise acceptable product has a blemish – is it now unacceptable? Perhaps not. It may still be far superior to other competing products in its acceptable features and characteristics. While not measurable, these subjective terms enable customers to rate products and services on the extent to which they satisfy their requirements and are therefore suitable for their purpose. However, to the company supplying products and services, they need a more precise means of measuring quality and therefore to the supplier, a quality product is one that meets in full the perceived customer requirements.

Quality characteristics

Any feature or characteristic of a product or service which is needed to satisfy customer needs or achieve fitness for use is a *quality characteristic*. When dealing with products the characteristics are almost always technical characteristics, whereas service quality characteristics have a human dimension. Some typical quality characteristics are given in the tables below.

Product Quality Characteristics		
Accessibility	Functionality	Size
Availability	Interchangeability	Susceptibility
Appearance	Maintainability	Storability
Adaptability	Odor	Taste
Cleanliness	Operability	Testability
Consumption	Portability	Traceability
Durability	Producibility	Toxicity
Disposability	Reliability	Transportability
Emittance	Repairability	Vulnerability
Flammability	Safety	Weight
Flexibility	Security	

Service Quality Characteristics		
Accessibility	Credibility	Honesty
Accuracy	Dependability	Promptness
Courtesy	Efficiency	Responsiveness
Comfort	Effectiveness	Reliability
Competence	Flexibility	Security

These are the characteristics which need to be specified and their achievement controlled, assured, improved, managed, and demonstrated. These are the characteristics which form the subject matter of the specified requirements referred to in QS-9000. When the value of these characteristics is quantified or qualified they are termed quality requirements or requirements for quality. ISO 8402 1994 defines requirements for quality as *an expression of the needs or their translation into a set of quantitatively or qualitatively stated requirements for the characteristics of an entity to enable its realization and examination*. While rather verbose, this definition is long overdue and removes the confusion over quality requirements and technical requirements. (I provide an alternative definition in Appendix A.) Technical requirements for a product or service are quality requirements. The requirements of QS-9000 are quality system requirements.

Quality, reliability, and safety

There is a school of thought that distinguishes between quality and reliability and quality and safety. Quality is thought to be a non-time-dependent characteristic and reliability a time-dependent characteristic. Quality is thought of as conformance to specification regardless of whether the specification actually meets the needs of the customer or society. If a product or service is unreliable then it is clearly unfit for use and hence of poor quality. If a product is reliable but emits toxic fumes, is too heavy or not transportable when it is required to be, then it is of poor quality. Also, if a product is unsafe it is of poor quality even though it may meet its specification. In such a case the specification is not a true reflection of customer needs. A nuclear plant may meet all the specified safety requirements but if society demands greater safety standards then the plant is not meeting the quality requirements of society, even though it meets the immediate customer requirements. You therefore need to identify who your real customers are in order to determine the quality characteristics that you need to satisfy. Customers are not only the buyers, they include users, consumers, shareholders, and society in general. It is the needs of all these people that have to be satisfied in order for you to achieve quality. This is born out by ISO 8402 1994 which defines the requirements of society as *the obligations resulting from laws, regulations, rules, codes, statutes, and other considerations* and the standard advises that all requirements of society should be taken into account when defining the requirements for quality.

Quality parameters

Differences in design can be denoted by grade or class but can also be the result of poor attention to customer needs. It is not enough to produce products that conform to the specifications or supply services that meet management's requirements. Quality is a composite of three *parameters*: quality of design, quality of conformance, and quality of use.

- *Quality of design* is the extent to which the design reflects a product or service that satisfies customer needs. All the necessary characteristics need to be designed into the product or service at the outset.

- *Quality of conformance* is the extent to which the product or service conforms to the design standard. The design has to be faithfully reproduced in the product or service.

- *Quality of use* is the extent by which the user is able to secure continuity of use from the product or service. Products need to have a low cost of ownership, be safe and reliable, maintainable in use, and easy to use.

Products or services that do not possess the right features and characteristics either by design or by construction are products of poor quality. Those which fail or are costly to use or in any way fail to give customer satisfaction, are also products of poor quality and, regardless of their conformance to specifications, are unfit for use.

Dimensions of quality

In addition to quality parameters there are three *dimensions of quality* which extend the perception beyond the concepts outlined previously:

- *The business quality dimension*. This is the extent to which the business services the needs of society. Customers are not only interested in the quality of particular products and services but judge suppliers by the general level of quality products they provide, their care of the environment and adherence to health, safety, and legal regulations.

- *The product quality dimension*. This is the extent to which the products and services provided meet the needs of specific customers.

- *The organization quality dimension*. This is the extent to which the organization maximizes its efficiency and effectiveness, achieving minimum waste, efficient management, and good human relations. Companies that do not operate efficiently and meet their employees' expectations will generally find their failure costs to be high and will lose their best people, and this directly affects all aspects of quality.

Many organizations only concentrate on the product quality dimension, but the three are interrelated and interdependent. Deterioration in one leads to a deterioration in the others, perhaps not immediately but eventually.

It is quite possible for an organization to satisfy the customers for its products and services and fail to satisfy the needs of society. Some may argue that the producers of pornographic literature, nuclear power, non-essential drugs, weapons, etc. harm society and so regardless of these products and services being of acceptable quality in themselves, they are not regarded by society as benefiting the quality of life. Within an organization, the working environment may be oppressive, there may be political infighting and the source of revenue so secure that no effort is placed upon waste reduction. Even so, such organizations may produce products and services which satisfy their customers. But we must separate these three concepts, otherwise we will get confused. It is therefore necessary, when talking of quality, to be specific about the object of our discussion. Is it the quality of products or services, or the quality of organization in which we work or the business as a whole, about which we talk? If we only intend that our remarks apply to the quality of products then we should say so.

Achieving, sustaining, and improving quality

Several methods have evolved to *achieve, sustain, and improve quality*; they are quality control, quality improvement, and quality assurance, which collectively are known as *quality management*. This trilogy is illustrated in Figure 1.1. Techniques such as quality planning, quality costs, "Just-in-time", and statistical process control are all elements of these three methods. ISO 8402 1994 separates quality planning from quality control, quality improvement, and quality assurance but by including planning within the domain of each concept, one can focus on the purpose of planning more easily.

Figure 1.1 Quality management

Quality control (QC)

The ISO definition states that *quality control* is the operational techniques and activities that are used to fulfill requirements for quality. This definition could imply that any activity, whether serving the improvement, control, management or assurance of quality could be a quality control activity. What the definition fails to tell us is that controls regulate performance. They prevent change and when applied to quality regulate quality performance and prevent undesirable changes in the quality standards. Quality control is a process for maintaining standards and not for creating them. Standards are maintained through a process of selection, measurement, and correction of work, so that only those products or services which emerge from the process meet the standards. In simple terms, quality control prevents undesirable changes being present in the quality of the product or service being supplied. The simplest form of quality control is illustrated in Figure 1.2. Quality control can be applied to particular products, to processes which produce the products or to the output of the whole organization by measuring the overall quality performance of the organization.

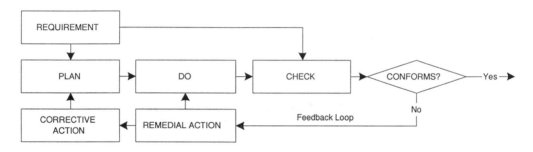

Figure 1.2 Quality control process

Quality control is often regarded as a post-event activity, i.e. a means of detecting whether quality has been achieved and taking action to correct any deficiencies. However, one can control results by installing sensors before, during or after the results are created. It all depends on where you install the sensor, what you measure, and the consequences of failure. Some failures cannot be allowed to occur and so must be prevented from happening through rigorous planning and design. Other failures are not so critical but must be corrected immediately using automatic controls or foolproofing. Where the consequences are less severe or where other types of sensor are not practical or possible, human inspection and test can be used as a means of detecting failure. Where failure cannot be measured without observing trends over longer periods, you can use information controls. They do not stop immediate operations but may well be used to stop further operations when limits are exceeded. The progressive development of controls from having no control of quality to installing controls at all key stages from the beginning to the end of the life cycle is illustrated in Figure 1.3. As can be seen, if you have no controls then quality products are produced

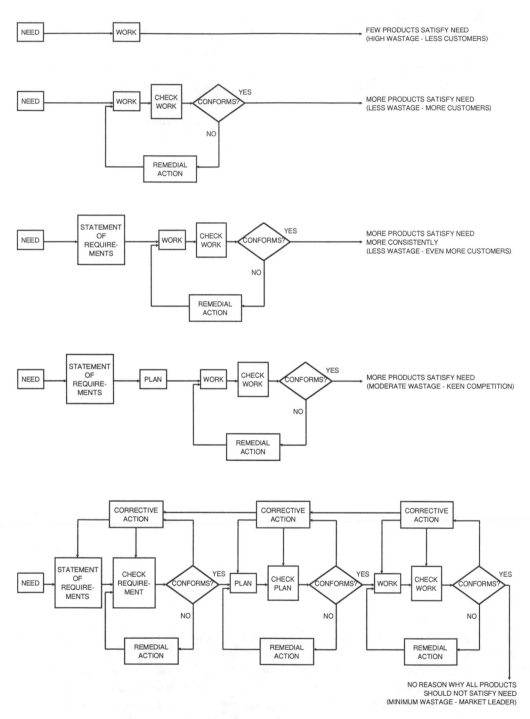

Figure 1.3 Development of quality controls

by chance and not design. The more controls you install the more certain you are of producing products of consistent quality but there is balance to be achieved. Beware of the law of diminishing returns.

It is often deemed that quality assurance serves prevention and quality control detection, but a control installed to detect failure before it occurs serves prevention, such as reducing the tolerance band to well within the specification limits. So quality control can prevent failure. Assurance is the result of an examination whereas control produces the result. Quality Assurance does not change the product, Quality Control does.

Quality Control is also a term used as a name of a department. In most cases Quality Control Departments perform inspection and test activities and the name derives from the authority that such departments have been given. They sort good products from bad products and authorize the release of the good products. It is also common to find that Quality Control Departments perform supplier control activities which are called Supplier Quality Assurance or Vendor Control. In this respect they are authorized to release products from suppliers into the organization either from the supplier's premises or on receipt in the organization.

Since to control anything requires the ability to effect change, the title Quality Control Department is a misuse of the term as such departments do not in fact control quality. They do act as a regulator if given the authority to stop release of product, but this is control of supply and not of quality. Authority to change product usually remains in the hands of the producing departments. It is interesting to note that similar activities within a Design Department are not called quality control but Design Assurance or some similar term. Quality Control has for decades been a term applied primarily in the manufacturing areas of an organization and hence it is difficult to change people's perceptions after so many years of the term's incorrect use.

In recent times the inspection and test activities have been transferred into the production departments of organizations, sometimes retaining the labels and some-times reverting to the inspection and test labels.

Control of quality, or anything else for that matter, can be accomplished by the following steps:

- Determine what parameter is to be controlled.

- Establish its criticality and whether you need to control before, during or after results are produced.

- Establish a specification for the parameter to be controlled which provides limits of acceptability and units of measure.

- Produce plans for control which specify the means by which the characteristics will be achieved and variation detected and removed.

- Organize resources to implement the plans for quality control.

- Install a sensor at an appropriate point in the process to sense variance from specification.

- Collect and transmit data to a place for analysis.

- Verify the results and diagnose the cause of variance.

- Propose remedies and decide on the action needed to restore the status quo.

- Take the agreed action and check that the variance has been corrected.

Quality improvement (QI)

The ISO definition of *quality improvement* states that it is the actions taken throughout the organization to increase the effectiveness of activities and processes to provide added benefits to both the organization and its customers. In simple terms, quality improvement is anything which causes a beneficial change in quality performance. There are two basic ways of bringing about improvement in quality performance. One is by better control and the other by raising standards. We don't have suitable words to define these two concepts. Doing better what you already do is *improvement* but so is doing something new. Juran uses the term *control* for maintaining standards and the term *breakthrough* for achieving new standards. Imai uses the term *improvement* when change is gradual and *innovation* when it is radical. Hammer uses the term *re-engineering* for the radical changes. All beneficial change results in improvement whether gradual or radical so we really need a word which means gradual change or incremental change. The Japanese have the word *kaizen* but there is no English equivalent that I know of other than the word *improvement*.

Quality improvement (for better control) is a process for changing standards. It is not a process for maintaining or creating new standards. Standards are changed through a process of selection, analysis, corrective action on the standard or process, education, and training. The standards which emerge from this process are an improvement from those used previously. A typical quality improvement might be to increase the achieved reliability of a range of products from 1 failure every 1000 hours to meet the specified target of 1 every 5000 hours. Another might be to reduce service call-out response time from an average of 38 hours to the maximum of 36 hours specified. Another might be simply to correct the weaknesses in the registered quality system so that it will pass reassessment.

Quality improvement (raising standards or innovation) is a process for creating new standards. It is not a process for maintaining or improving existing standards. Standards are created through a process which starts at a feasibility stage and progresses through research and development to result in a new standard proven for repeatable applications. Such standards result from innovations in technology, marketing, and management. A typical quality improvement might be to redesign a range of products to increase the achieved reliability from 1 failure every 5000 hours to 1 failure every 10,000 hours. Another example might be to improve the efficiency of the service organization so as to reduce the guaranteed call-out time from the specified 36 hours to 24 hours. A further example might be to design and install a quality system which complies with QS-9000.

The transition between where quality improvement stops and quality control begins is where the level has been set and the mechanisms are in place to keep quality on or above the set level. In simple terms, if quality improvement reduces quality costs from 25% of turnover to 10% of turnover, the objective of quality control is to prevent the quality costs rising above 10% of turnover. This is illustrated in Figure 1.4.

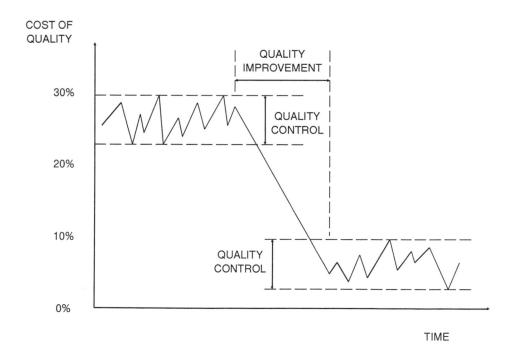

Figure 1.4 Quality improvement and quality control

Improvement by better control is achieved through the corrective action mechanisms described in Part 2 Chapter 14 and ISO 9004-4. Improvement by raising standards requires a different process, a process which results in new standards.

Improving quality by raising standards can be accomplished by the following steps:

- Determine the objective to be achieved, e.g. new markets, products or technologies or new levels of organizational efficiency or managerial effectiveness, new national standards or government legislation. These provide the reasons for needing change.

- Determine the policies needed for improvement, i.e. the broad guidelines to enable management to cause or stimulate the improvement.

- Conduct a feasibility study. This should discover whether accomplishment of the objective is feasible and propose several strategies or conceptual solutions for consideration. If feasible, approval to proceed should be secured.

- Produce plans for the improvement which specify the means by which the objective will be achieved.

- Organize the resources to implement the plan.

- Carry out research, analysis, and design to define a possible solution and credible alternatives.

- Model and develop the best solution and carry out tests to prove it fulfills the objective.

- Identify and overcome any resistance to the change in standards.

- Implement the change, i.e. put new products into production and new services into operation.

- Put in place the controls to hold the new level of performance.

This improvement process will require controls to keep improvement projects on course towards their objectives. The controls applied should be designed in the manner described previously.

Quality assurance (QA)

The ISO definition states that *quality assurance* is all those planned and systematic actions necessary to provide adequate confidence that an entity will fulfill requirements for quality. Both customers and managers have a need for quality assurance as they cannot oversee operations for themselves. They need to place trust in the producing operations, thus avoiding constant intervention.

Customers and managers need to know:

• Whether certain provisions, if implemented, will yield the required results

• Whether the provisions are being implemented

• Whether the provisions have yielded products and services that are fit for their purpose and meet customer needs

The provisions are the policies, practices, specifications, contracts, and other means used to prescribe the requirements that should be met.

You can gain an assurance of quality by either:

a) Testing the product/service against prescribed standards to establish its capability to meet them.

or:

b) Assessing the organization which supplies the products/services against prescribed standards to establish its capability to produce products of a certain standard.

Quality assurance activities do not control quality, they establish the extent to which quality will be, is being or has been controlled. This is borne out by ISO 8402 1994 where it is stated that quality control concerns the operational means to fulfill quality requirements and quality assurance aims at providing confidence in this fulfillment both within the organization and externally to customers and authorities. All quality assurance activities are post-event activities and offline and serve to build confidence in results, in claims, in predictions etc. If a person tells you they will do a certain job for a certain price in a certain time, can you trust them or will they be late, overspent, and under spec? The only way to find out is to gain confidence in their operations and that is what quality assurance activities are designed to do. Quite often, the means to provide the assurance need to be built into the process, such as creating records, documenting plans, documenting specifications, reporting reviews etc. Such documents and activities also serve to control quality as well as assure it (see also ISO 8402).

QS-9000 provides a means for obtaining an assurance of quality, if you are the customer, and a means for controlling quality, if you are the supplier.

Quality Assurance Departments are often formed to provide both customer and management with confidence that quality will be, is being, and has been achieved. However, another way of looking upon Quality Assurance departments is as Corporate Quality Control. Instead of measuring the quality of products they are measuring the quality of the business and by doing so are able to assure management and customers of the quality of products and services.

Assurance of quality can be gained by the following steps:

- Acquire the documents which declare the organization's plans for achieving quality.

- Produce a plan which defines how an assurance of quality will be obtained, i.e. a quality assurance plan.

- Organize the resources to implement the plans for quality assurance.

- Establish whether the organization's proposed product or service possesses characteristics which will satisfy customer needs.

- Assess operations, products, and services of the organization and determine where and what the quality risks are.

- Establish whether the organization's plans make adequate provision for the control, elimination or reduction of the identified risks.

- Determine the extent to which the organization's plans are being implemented and risks contained.

- Establish whether the product or service being supplied has the prescribed characteristics.

In judging the adequacy of provisions you will need to apply the relevant standards, legislation, codes of practices, and other agreed measures for the type of operation, application, and business. These activities are quality assurance activities and may be subdivided into design assurance, procurement assurance, manufacturing assurance etc. Auditing, planning, analysis, inspection, and test are some of the techniques which may be used.

QS-9000 is a quality assurance standard, designed for use in assuring customers that suppliers have the capability of meeting their requirements.

Quality goals

To control, assure, and improve quality you need to focus on certain goals. Let's call them the quality goals:

- Establish your customer needs.

- Design products and services with features that reflect customer needs.

- Build products and services so as to faithfully reproduce the design which meets the customer needs.

- Verify before delivery that your products and services possess the features required to meet the customer needs.

- Prevent supplying products and services that possess features that dissatisfy customers.

- Discover and eliminate undesirable features in products and services even if they possess the requisite features.

- Find less expensive solutions to customer needs because products and services which satisfy these needs may be too expensive.

- Make your operations more efficient and effective so as to reduce costs, because products and services that satisfy customer needs may cost more to produce than the customer is prepared to pay.

- Discover what will delight your customer and provide it. (Regardless of satisfying customer needs your competitor may have provided products with features that give greater satisfaction!)

- Establish and maintain a management system that enables you to achieve these goals reliably, repeatedly, and economically.

ISO 9001 addresses quality goals through the use of the term *quality objectives* but goes no further. QS-9000, however, requires a Business Plan that should include amongst other topics, cost objectives, quality objectives, key internal quality, and operational performance measurables and it also requires key indicators of customer satisfaction and several quality and productivity factors such as machine downtime, scrap, re-work, and quality costs. Therefore, QS-9000 is more improvement oriented than ISO 9001 and although developed for the automobile industry, many of the improvement factors could just as easily apply to any manufacturing industry.

Quality systems

The purpose of a *quality system* is to enable you to achieve, sustain, and improve quality economically. It is unlikely that you will be able to produce and sustain the required quality unless you organize yourselves to do so. Quality does not happen by chance – it has to be managed. No human endeavor has ever been successful without having been planned, organized, and controlled in some way.

The quality system is a tool and like any tool can be a valuable asset (or be abused, neglected, and misused)! Depending on your strategy (see later) quality systems enable you to achieve all the quality goals. Quality systems have a similar purpose to the financial control systems, information technology systems, inventory control systems, and personnel management systems. They organize resources so as to achieve certain objectives by laying down rules and an infrastructure which, if followed and maintained, will yield the desired results. Whether it is the management of costs, inventory, personnel or quality, systems are needed to focus the thought and effort of people towards prescribed objectives. Quality systems focus on the quality of what the organization produces, the factors which might prevent it satisfying customers and the factors which might prevent it from being productive, innovative, and profitable.

Quality systems can address one of the quality goals or all of them, they can be as small or as large as you want them to be. They can be project-specific, or they can be limited to quality control: that is, maintaining standards rather than improving them. They can include Quality Improvement Programs (QIPs) or encompass what is called Total Quality Management (TQM). QS-9000, however, requires a quality system that meets all the above quality goals and many more so that suppliers are left with little choice as to the nature of the quality goals their quality systems must achieve.

Quality systems need to possess certain characteristics for them to be fit for their purpose. QS-9000 specifies functional requirements for quality systems rather than performance requirements. It specifies what a quality system must do but not how well it must do it. The performance required will depend on the environment in which the system will be used however; some of these performance characteristics will be as follows:

Robustness	The ability to withstand variation in the way operations are carried out without system breakdown
Complexity	The number of interconnections, routings, pathways, variations, options, alternatives, etc. which give rise to multiple procedures

Maintainability	The ease and economy with which system changes can be made
Reliability	The extent to which the system produces consistent and predictable results
Flexibility	The ease with which the system can handle changing circumstances
Vulnerability	The extent to which the system is dependent upon certain resources
Consistency	The extent to which the documented system unifies communication both within itself and within the organization in which it is employed
Compliance	The extent to which the system complies with the requirements of QS-9000 or other prescribed requirements
Usability	The ease and economy with which the system enables users to determine the right things to do and to do these things in the right way the first time and every time
Traceability	The ease and economy with which the system enables information to be traceable to the governing requirements and vice versa

The quantitative measure of these characteristics may be difficult if not impractical, but nevertheless they provide a means of judging effectiveness of the system once it is installed. The effectiveness of quality systems is also addressed in Part 2 Chapter 1.

A postscript on definitions

Many of the official definitions of quality terms are verbose, hard to understand at first reading, and often lack the clarity needed to convey the actions and decisions which the terms may imply. They seem to have been constructed so they could withstand the rigors of cross examination in a court of law. One of the perennial problems which faces the quality fraternity is they continually come up with new terms and then spend decades defining them. The only reason for inventing a new term is when we have a new concept or set of concepts that we wish to communicate. The label we give the concepts needs to reflect the concepts without being ambiguous. In reality new terms have emerged and eventually committees have got together to formulate a definition which often disappoints the practitioner. The definition appears after he has built a whole new set of concepts only to find they conflict with what everyone is now labeling them. Sometimes new definitions are found for existing terms which completely change their meaning, such as the change in the concept of quality assurance from being all activities concerned with the attainment of quality (circa 1970) to being limited to the activities which provide confidence that quality has been achieved (circa 1980). I can do no better than quote Juran who said on terminology:

> The prime need is to discover the realities under the labels, i.e. the deeds, activities or things which the other fellow is talking about. Once these are understood accurate communication can take place whether the labels are agreed on or not. In contrast, if communication is purely through labels, it is easy to be deluded into believing there is understanding despite the fact that each of the parties literally does not know what the other fellow is talking about.

Although I have defined terms such as quality control and quality assurance in this chapter, what is important is not the definition but the deeds which it imbues. Whether we call the set of principles I have listed under the heading quality assurance, Quality Assurance, Quality Improvement or Quality Control makes no difference since it does not change the set of principles. We often seem to invent a term then decide what it means rather than invent or discover a set of principles and think of a suitable name which conveys exactly what we intend without confusing people. Instead of saying "Quality control is ..." or "TQM is ..." to which there will be many propositions, we should be asking, what should we call *this* group of principles so that we can communicate with each other more efficiently. As Shakespeare once said: "That which we call a rose/By any other name would smell as sweet."

An extensive range of definitions in the field of quality management is provided in ISO 8402 and there is a glossary in QS-9000 although some of the definitions in QS-9000 are different to those in ISO 8402 (see Part 1 Chapter 2). Appendix A includes over 150 commonly used terms, less verbose but consistent with the definitions found in ISO 8402 and QS-9000.

Chapter 2

What is QS-9000?

QS-9000 contains specific requirements and recommendations for the development of a quality system that meets the expectations of Chrysler, Ford, General Motors, Truck Manufacturers, and other subscribing companies. It harmonizes the approach of the Big Three to quality management.

QS-9000 is not a product standard. It does not contain any requirements with which a product or service can comply. There are no product acceptance criteria in QS-9000 so you can't inspect a product against the standard. You can, however, question whether a particular product has a certain record, an identity, inspection status etc. but any nonconformances are with the quality system not the product. The presence or absence of a record, a document or an inspection label does not alter the characteristics of a product. So where products are being advertised as meeting QS-9000 the consumer is being misled.

> ■ **Products cannot meet QS-9000; organizations can.**

The requirements and recommendations apply to the organizations that supply the product or service, and hence affect the manner in which the products and services are designed, manufactured, installed, delivered etc. They are standards which apply to the management of the organization and only the management can and should decide how it will respond to these requirements and recommendations.

The parts of QS-9000

QS-9000 is fundamentally a suite of documents that include section 4 of ISO 9001 printed in italic type with supplemental and interpretative information printed in normal type. Unlike ISO 9001, QS-9000 contains mandatory and advisory requirements by use of the words "shall" and "should" respectively. Suppliers choosing alternative approaches to those recommended by the "should" statements must be able to show that their approach meets the intent of QS-9000. However there is a minor inconsistency as notes are stated as being for guidance and yet some of the notes contain "shall" statements. The descriptions given in the Glossary to QS-9000 also include a few "shall" statements which can easily be overlooked. Certificates are awarded against QS-9000 as a whole and therefore all relevant requirements have to be met.

The documents in the suite include:

- *Quality system assessment guide* (QSA) (38 pages)

- *Advanced product quality planning and control plan reference manual* (119 pages)

- *Potential failure mode and effects reference manual* (61 pages)

- *Production part approval process manual* (PPAP) (52 pages)

- *Measurement system analysis reference manual* (127 pages)

- *Fundamental statistical process control reference manual* (166 pages)

These are all referenced within QS-9000 and there are other customer specific documents covering a range of topics. One covers quality system assessment for semiconductor suppliers, a variant of the QSA. They are by no means small documents either and include forms for suppliers to use. The beauty of this approach is that all suppliers use the same methods, the same forms, and produce results in the same format. They are excellent documents however and contain a vast amount of experience, well worth reading even for those not in the motor industry. If a particular industry needs consistency and, more importantly, needs to build upon its experiences, then the codification of best practice is indeed an effective way of achieving this.

QS-9000 is a book of 106 pages, several times larger than ISO 9001. In structure it has three sections:

- Section I contains ISO 9000 based requirements. It includes the text of ISO 9001 section 4 and some 58 new clauses.

- Section II contains sector specific requirements and includes three additional elements, namely Production Part Approval, Continuous Improvement, and Manufacturing Capabilities. These add another nine new clauses to the standard.

- Section III contains customer specific requirements for Chrysler, Ford, General Motors, and Truck Manufacturers. These address identification conventions, critical characteristics, audits, heat treatment, material qualification, labeling, and many more.

There are five appendices:

- Appendix A gives an overview of the quality system assessment process.

- Appendix B contains a code of practice for third party registration.

- Appendix C covers special characteristics and symbols.

- Appendix D is a cross reference to national equivalents to ISO 9001 and 9002.

- Appendix E covers the acronyms that are used, of which there are 40.

At the back is a glossary of 37 terms, some of which appear in ISO 8402 but have not been defined in the same way.

It is unclear why there need to be sector specific requirements in a separate section of the standard. All the additional requirements in Section I are in fact specific to the automobile industry. No other industry uses the five reference manuals and yet these are invoked in Section I. The PPAP requirements could just as easily have been incorporated in either element 4.4 or 4.9 of Section I. The requirements on Manufacturing Capabilities would have fitted nicely into element 4.9 and Continuous Improvement would not look out of place in element 4.1. Perhaps at the next revision some refinement will be undertaken.

The origin of ISO 9000

QS-9000 is based upon ISO 9001:1994. However, one cannot be certain when the concepts which underpin ISO 9000 were first derived. The principles of inspection have been around since the Egyptians built the pyramids but quality systems did not appear until the early 1950s. Quality Control, an element of quality management, emerged as a function in industry after WWII and the principles were codified by J M Juran in his Quality Control Handbook of 1951, now in its fourth edition and still the most notable book on the subject today. Progress in this field has always been dominated by the military, starting with the inspection of armaments in WWI. In 1959 the first national standard, Mil Q 9858A, on quality programs was issued by the American Department of Defense and this was followed in 1968 with NATO's Allied Quality Assurance Publications (AQAP). Shortly afterwards in 1970 the UK Ministry of Defence brought out Def Stan 05-08 which was a UK version of AQAP-1 and in 1972 the British Standards Institution (BSI) brought out BS 4891, "A Guide to Quality

Assurance". Def Stan 05-08 was revised in 1973 and several standards were issued to match the AQAP standards. BSI then issued BS 5179 in 1974 to complement the UK MoD standards. This was heavily based on the Defence Standards but was aimed at the non-military market, although it was only a guide. In 1979, BSI published BS 5750 in three parts for contractual purposes, matching the three UK Defence Standards and the three AQAP Standards. Meanwhile the Canadian, Australian, and US standards organizations published standards covering the same ground and by 1983 many more countries had joined the procession but all were slightly different.

By 1984 BSI had drafted a revision to its BS 5750 1979 and in view of the international interest in the subject encouraged the International Organization for Standardization to embark on an International Standard for Quality Systems. Over 26 countries were involved in its development and while the standard still bears evidence of its military pedigree, it did break the mold and set a new world standard for quality management. The first drafts for public comment were published in 1985 and finally approved for publication in 1987. Each country connected with its development then brought out a national equivalent. (The national equivalents differ in language, title, and the forward although the numbering conventions have now been harmonized.) As would be expected from a standard that met with the agreement of 26 countries, one does not achieve a standard which is the state of the art. There had to be compromises and the result is the minimum standard acceptable to the majority.

There followed additional standards and guides in the ISO 9000 series. Now having come of age, ISO 9000 is replacing the military standards which gave it its pedigree. ISO 9000 was conceived as a general standard for quality systems that could be applied to anything from a jobbing shop to the spacecraft industry, from a dry cleaning firm to a multinational insurance corporation, a small catering firm to an international hotel chain. It is sometimes hard to translate the requirements to such diverse industries especially when the requirements are couched in terms more in keeping with hardware manufacturing. It is for these reasons that guides covering software and services have been published, although they are in some respects only a palliative. What is needed is a complete revision so that the requirements are stated in terms that can be applied to any enterprise and this is the goal for achievement by the year 2000. The 1994 version is the first revision since publication of the series in 1987.

The rationale behind publishing three separate standards, ISO 9001, ISO 9002, and ISO 9003 with almost identical requirements where they are common (apart from following the tradition established by the Military), is that they are used for two completely different purposes. The three standards can be used either as assessment standards or as contractual standards. By claiming registration to ISO 9002, you are declaring either that you do not have any design capability or that any you have are not registered. Thus in contractual situations it allows customers to mandate a standard appropriate to the contract (mandating ISO 9002 when design is not required, or final inspection when that is all that is necessary). It can keep down costs if customers don't demand more than they need but it is a somewhat clumsy way of dealing with a problem. QS-9000 is far better in this respect.

Differences between ISO 9000 and QS-9000

ISO 9000 is a family of 19 standards as indicated in Table 2-1.

Standard	Date	Title
ISO 8402	1994	Quality management and quality assurance – vocabulary
ISO 9000-1	1994	Guidelines for selection and use
ISO 9000-2	1993	Guidelines for the application of ISO 9001, ISO 9002 and ISO 9003
ISO 9000-3	1991	Guidelines for the application of ISO 9001 to the development, supply and maintenance of software
ISO 9000-4	1993	Guide to Dependability Program Management
ISO 9001	1994	Model for quality assurance in design/development, production, installation and servicing
ISO 9002	1994	Model for quality assurance in production and installation
ISO 9003	1994	Model for quality assurance in final inspection and test
ISO 9004-1	1994	Quality management and quality system elements – Guidelines
ISO 9004-2	1991	Quality management and quality system elements – Guidelines for services
ISO 9004-3	1993	Quality management and quality system elements – Guidelines for Processed Materials
ISO 9004-4	1993	Quality management and quality system elements – Guidelines for Quality Improvement
ISO 10005	1995	Quality management – Guidelines for quality plans
ISO 10007	1996	Quality management – Guidelines for configuration management
ISO 10011-1	1990	Guidelines for auditing quality systems – Auditing
ISO 10011-2	1991	Guidelines for auditing quality systems – Qualification criteria of quality system auditors
ISO 10011-3	1991	Guidelines for auditing quality systems – Management of audit programs
ISO 10012	1992	Quality assurance requirements for measuring equipment
ISO 10013	1995	Guidelines for developing quality manuals

Table 2-1 ISO 9000 standards

Since QS-9000 is but one standard with six associated guides all of which address different topics to the ISO 9000 family, other than ISO 9001, QS-9000 does not invoke or make reference to any of the other standards in the ISO 9000 family. This is a distinct disadvantage since there are several standards that can be used by the automobile industry particularly ISO 8402, ISO 9004 and all it parts. The only standards in the ISO 9000 family that are referenced are ISO 10011, 10012, and 10013. ISO 9000-3 could be used for the development of software used in the automobile's computerized systems although QS-9000 does not apply to software. ISO 9004-1 should be consulted when developing a quality system even though it does not address the automobile industry directly.

A comparison between ISO 9001 and QS-9000 is given in Table 2-2. The figures for QS-9000 are less precise than those for ISO 9001 due to the differences in style in expressing requirements and hence should be taken as minimums.

	ISO 9001	QS-9000 Sections I, II & Glossary
Elements	20	23
Clauses	59	126
'Shall' statements or equivalents	138	268
'Shall' statements including lists	184	284
Procedures required	20	42
Quality records required	20	25

Table 2-2 Comparison between ISO 9001 and QS-9000

Table 2-3 shows the additional clauses. One of the weakness in the layout is that many of the additional clauses have not been numbered, making referencing difficult.

Differences in style

The authors of QS-9000 have not perpetuated the layout and writing style of ISO 9001. For instance in ISO 9001, the requirements for procedures is expressed as: "Suppliers shall establish and maintain documented procedures for ..." In QS-9000 phrases such as "a documented system, method and process" are used to indicate that procedures may be required but the requirement is not as specific as in ISO 9001.The practice in ISO 9001 of referencing 4.16 to indicate a quality record has not been continued such that the necessity for certain records is not always clear.

Clause	Title	Clause	Title
4.1.2	Organizational interfaces	4.10.3	Defect prevention
4.1.4	Business plan	4.10.4	Layout inspection and functional testing
4.1.5	Analysis and use of data	4.11.3	Inspection, measuring and test equipment records
4.1.6	Customer satisfaction	4.11.4	Measurement system analysis
4.2.3	Advanced product quality planning Use of cross functional teams Feasibility reviews Process failure mode and effects analysis Control plans	4.12	Product layout Supplemental verification
		4.13.1	Suspect product
4.4.2	Required skills	4.13.3	Control of reworked product
4.4.4	Design input supplemental	4.13.4	Engineering approved product authorization
4.4.5	Design output supplemental	4.14.1	Problem solving methods
4.4.7	Design verification supplemental	4.14.2	Returned product test/analysis
4.4.9	Design changes supplemental	4.15.3	Inventory
4.5.1	Reference documents Document identification for special characteristics	4.15.4	Customer packaging standards Labeling
4.5.2	Engineering specifications	4.15.6	Supplier delivery performance monitoring Production scheduling Shipment notification system
4.6.1	Approved materials for ongoing production		
4.6.2	Subcontractor development Scheduling subcontractors	4.16	Record retention Superseded parts
4.6.3	Restricted substances	4.17	Inclusion of working environment
4.9	Government safety and environmental regulations Designated special characteristics Preventive maintenance	4.18	Training as a strategic issue
		4.19	Feedback of information from service
4.9.1	Process monitoring and operator instructions	4.20.2	Selection of statistical tools Knowledge of basic statistical concepts
4.9.2	Preliminary process capability requirements	II-1.1	Production part approval
4.9.3	Ongoing process performance requirements	II-1.2	Engineering change validation
4.9.4	Modified preliminary or ongoing capability requirements	II-2.1	Continuous improvement
		II-2.2	Quality and productivity improvements
4.9.5	Verification of job set-ups	II-2.3	Techniques for continuous improvement
4.9.6	Process changes	II-3.1	Facilities, equipment and process planning and effectiveness
4.9.7	Appearance items		
4.10.1	Acceptance criteria Accredited laboratories	II-3.2	Mistake proofing
		II-3.3	Tool design and fabrication
4.10.2	Incoming product quality	II-3.4	Tooling management

Table 2-3 Additional clauses in QS-9000

Differences in assessment approach

There are several fundamental differences in the approach:

- Third party assessments have to be carried out using the QSA. This reduces variation between different certification bodies.

- Registration to ISO 9000 does not give exemption from QS-9000 requirements.

- Chrysler requires current part suppliers to obtain third party registration to QS-9000 by 31 July 1997 and new suppliers to be registered before being used.

- Ford does not yet require third party registration of their part suppliers but does require compliance by June 1995. This means a self assessment has been conducted, nonconformance issues have been identified, and a work plan is in place to address these issues.

- General Motors requires all suppliers worldwide to obtain third party registration to QS-9000 by 31 December 1997.

- There is no certification requirements on second tier suppliers other than through the first tier suppliers.

- Registrars or Certification Bodies have to be accredited by a customer recognized national body. There are currently 14 acceptable accreditation bodies.[1] QS-9000 is a contractual requirement for all production and service part suppliers.

- Registration to QS-9000 must encompass Sections I and II of the standard.

- Assessments have to cover all elements of a supplier's quality system even when these go beyond QS-9000. However, this practice conflicts with EAC/G3, the guide to EN45012, which states that certification cannot be denied on the grounds that the supplier does not comply with matters not covered by the standard to which it is to be certified.

- Registrars have to conform to EN 45012 and accept a code of practice. There are currently 20 certification bodies approved to conduct QS-9000 audits.

- The entire quality system has to be assessed at least once every three years so rolling audits or continuous assessments are not permitted.

- Each manufacturing location has to be covered by a certificate.

- Each location has to receive a surveillance visit at least every six months.

- The International Auto Sector Group (IASG) sanctions interpretation to QS-9000 and issues agreed interpretations to members. However, these are limited to the additional clauses in QS-9000 and do not address ISO 9001 interpretations, which is the responsibility of the particular registrar or certification body.

- Auditors have to check for effectiveness as well as conformity.

[1] IASG Sanctioned Interpretations, March 1996

- The audit report format has to be based on the RvA (formerly RvC) model.

- Auditors have to identify opportunities for improvement without recommending specific solutions.

- Organizations that have provided consulting services to a particular client are not acceptable as registrars.

- Each auditor has to have completed QS-9000 and QSA training courses approved by the Big Three.

- Registration will not be granted with open major or minor nonconformities.

- A rating system is employed to determine compliance using a pass/fail method or a variable score method. The 23 elements may be classified in one of two ways, either as a "conforms/minor/major nonconformance" status for an element or as a 0 through 3 point rating for an element.

- A pass result will be given when the audit identifies neither any major nor minor nonconformities.

- An open status is given when a major or minor nonconformity exists. This can be converted to a "pass" within 90 days with acceptable evidence of conformity.

- A fail will be given if the audit identifies more than one major nonconformity or there is a lack of nonconformity resolution within the 90 day timeframe.

The nonconformity definitions (see Appendix A) would seem difficult to apply consistently and they do not align with the guidance given in the European Accreditation Committee Guide to EN45012 (EAC/G3) which is recognized by the IASG. There is no definition of what a requirement of QS-9000 is. Is it an element, a numbered clause, a "shall" statement or a part of a "shall" statement? Almost any deviation could result in the probable shipment of nonconforming product. It depends on the attitude of the personnel using the system and the gateways through which the deviation is allowed to pass without being corrected.

If the scoring system is used, then a minimum score of 2 is required on every applicable element. It means that if there is minor inconsistency in implementation then you fail. This makes the scoring method far tougher than the major/minor scoring scheme and open to misapplication by the certification bodies.

Differences in terminology

One of the most significant differences in QS-9000 is that only section 4 of ISO 9001 was embodied and therefore section 3 addressing definitions was omitted. When conducting assessments to ISO 9000, ISO 8402 is a requirement invoked in section 3 of ISO 9001, but when conducting assessments to QS-9000, ISO 8402 is not a requirement. It is unclear as to whether the authors of QS-9000 intended ISO 8402 to be applied to section 4 of ISO 9001 and the Glossary of QS-9000 to only apply to the additional requirements since the Glossary has no introductory remarks.

There are some differences in the terminology that are quite interesting. For instance a *nonconformance* is product or material which does not conform to the customer requirements or specifications whereas a *nonconformity* is a process which does not conform to a quality system requirement. Ironically, the definitions of nonconformity given in the QSA define a nonconformity as a "Noncompliance with ..." but the term *noncompliance* is not defined. Whilst the additional requirements may well use these terms in the same context, the authors seem to have overlooked the fact that the term *nonconformity* is used in clause 4.13.2 of QS-9000 and in this context it does not mean a process which does not conform but a product which does not conform – a slight mix up!

Procedures are defined as documented processes that are used when work affects more than one function or department. Procedures are considered to be level 2 quality system documents. Job instructions describe work conducted in one function in a company and are considered to be level 3 quality system documentation. This perpetuates the departmental approach to quality system design rather than the process approach. Like the 1987 version of ISO 9000, the term *instructions* is used to distinguish between level 2 and level 3 procedures. Calling the documents *control procedures* and *operating procedures* would be a better approach since the ISO 8402 definition of a procedure implies no levels or uses.

The definition given for Quality Manuals requires the manuals to include responsibilities and authorities for each element of the system. This is strange since the elements are topics not processes. As Juran states, one can only be responsible for actions or decisions,[2] therefore defining responsibility for an element would appear to be a futile activity.

The Glossary makes a clear distinction between an assessment and an audit. An assessment is an evaluation including the document review, the on-site audit, the analysis, and the report. An audit is an on-site verification activity used to determine the effective implementation of a supplier's documented quality system. This implies that the document review is not an audit and is conducted off-site. I would agree that an assessment goes beyond an audit but should include four elements: a documentation element, an implementation element, an evaluation element, and a certification element. The Big Three regard the audit as the implementation element only. Therefore what do we call the people who do three out of four of these, Auditors or Assessors?

---

[2] J Juran, *QC Handbook* third edition, Chapter 11-4

Differences in requirements

The most significant additions are the requirements for:

- Customer approval for production deliveries, control plans, FMEAs, acceptance criteria, changes to design and production processes, use of analytical methods, visible rework

- Use of customer prescribed formats for submission data

- Business plans, although the content is not subject to third party audit

- Determining customer satisfaction, trends and indicators, benchmarking etc.

- Failure mode effects analysis

- Compliance with government occupational safety and environmental regulations

- Process capability analysis

- Production part approval

- Measurement system analysis

- Supplier delivery performance monitoring

- Continuous improvement in quality, delivery, and price

- Mistake proofing

- Simultaneous engineering

Many of these requirements are plain common sense rather than specific to the motor industry. The requirement for continuous improvement (which would be better termed *continual improvement* since *continuous* implies no breaks or interruptions) covers quality and service including timing, delivery, and price. The Big Three need suppliers to offer parts at the lowest price and so expect them to seek ways of reducing price as part of their quality efforts. However, element 4.14 of ISO 9001 can be interpreted as a continual improvement requirement when applied to correction and prevention of nonconformities in the quality system. If an organization's quality objectives covered delivery, price, and other objectives for improving efficiency and effectiveness then applying 4.14 would lead to continual improvement.

Production part approval is a sensible technique and practiced not only by the motor industry.

Mistake proofing is the use of process or design features to prevent nonconforming product. This could be used by ISO 9000 registered suppliers to meet clause 4.14.3 on preventive action.

The advanced quality planning requirements extend the quality planning require-ments of ISO 9001 but it seems that the authors have misunderstood the purpose of quality plans as they are more than merely Control Plans. Every instance of the term "quality plan" in ISO 9001 is followed by "(Control Plan)".

Failure modes analysis, whilst being a planning tool, can also be used as a preventive action tool so it is surprising that it is not referred to under that heading also.

Subcontractor development is required but this should not be misinterpreted as it only applies to the development of the subcontractor's quality system.

The presentation of the additional requirements is not in the same style as those of ISO 9001 and hence there are several omissions. For instance:

- Training effectiveness has to be evaluated but there is no requirement for any records.

- There is no cross reference to 4.16 whenever a record is required.

- There are no additional requirements for the supplier to establish and main-tain documented procedures. QS-9000 refers to systems and processes with-out requiring they be documented. It would therefore be helpful if the glossary included definitions of the terms *system* and *process* and indicated they must be documented.

A minor reference to purchase orders under element 4.16 on quality records creates doubt as to what a quality record is. A purchase order is not a quality record. It is a specification governed by element 4.5 not 4.16. The misunderstanding could have arisen because element 4.5 does not contain any requirement for documents to be retained.

Most of the requirements cannot be applied retrospectively except for the requirement for production part approval, design changes, and approved materials for ongoing production. Any parts and materials used in current production will need to exhibit approval as per the new requirements or waiver of such requirements obtained.

The one area of departure from the ISO 9000 mold is the inclusion of occupational safety and environmental requirements, since ISO 9000 only applies to product quality. These are added for the simple reason that as a supplier to the Big Three, you have to be clean as they cannot afford for you to be shut down as a result a law suit.

Duplication of requirement

The additional QS-9000 specific requirements have resulted in duplication of some of the requirements, notably the following:

- Prior approval of changes to production baseline is covered in four places: Sections I.4.4.9, 4.9.6, 4.13.4, and Section II.1.1.

- Use of cross-functional teams is addressed in three places: in 4.1.2 and twice in 4.2.3 under *Cross-Functional Teams* and under *The Control Plan*.

- The requirement for the designation of special characteristics is addressed in three places: 4.2.3, 4.5.1, and 4.9.

- The requirement for all customer requirements to be met is addressed in ISO 9001 clause 4.3.2c and by the new clause 4.3.2d.

- The availability of documents is addressed in four places: in ISO 9001 clause 4.5.2a, in the additional requirements on Reference Documents in clause 4.5.1, in 4.9.1, and in 4.13.3.

- The approval of control plans is addressed twice: in Section I clauses 4.2.3 and 4.9.35.

Why introduce a quality system at all?

There are several benefits to be gained from installing a quality system that meets ISO 9000 or QS-9000, although it depends upon the type of system you actually install. The QS-9000 model of a quality system is built upon the principle of achieving customer satisfaction by preventing nonconformity at all stages in the supply chain.

> ■ **If you are capable of supplying nonconforming products or services, you need a quality system to prevent you from doing so.**

If the right tasks are carried out right first time then there will be no waste, costs will be at a minimum and profit a maximum. Profit is always the result of what you do so by reducing error, remedial action, and waste, you save time, resources, and materials and maximize profits. An effective quality system will:

- Reduce fire-fighting and so free managers from constant intervention in the operations of the business. How? By giving staff the means to control their own operations (clauses 4.2 & 4.9 of QS-9000).

- Provide the means for enabling the rights tasks to be identified and specified in a way that will yield the right results. How? By planning in advance of the work and putting in place procedures, standards, and guidelines which help people choose the right things to do (clauses 4.2 & 4.9 of QS-9000).

- Provide a means of documenting your company's experience in a structured manner that will provide a basis for education and training of staff and the systematic improvement of performance. How? By providing an authorized set of documented practices that reflect your business and that are continually reviewed and maintained (clauses 4.2 & 4.18 of QS-9000).

- Provide a means for identifying and resolving problems and preventing their recurrence. How? By installing measures for detecting deviations from practices and specifications, by discovering the cause of the deviations, and by planning and implementing corrective actions (clauses 4.1.3, 4.10, 4.13, 4.14 & 4.17 of QS-9000).

- Provide the means for enabling people to perform tasks right first time. How? By providing the appropriate resources, training, instructions, and the right environment, motivation, and controls (clauses 4.1.1, 4.1.2, 4.2, and 4.18 of QS-9000).

- Provide objective evidence that can be used to demonstrate the quality of your products and services and to demonstrate that your operations are under control to assessors, customer representatives and, should the situation arise, the lawyers in a product liability claim against you! How? By identifying, producing, and maintaining records of key operations (clauses 4.16 of QS-9000).

- Provide data that can be used to determine the performance of your operating processes, products, and services and for improving business performance and customer satisfaction. How? Through the collection, analysis, and review of the records generated by the system (clauses 4.1.3 & 4.14 of QS-9000).

QS-9000 is the application of common sense through a structured management system that will provide products and services that consistently satisfy customer needs. But it requires the commitment, involvement, and participation of top management for it to function effectively. However, all these benefits will not accrue if you select the wrong strategy.

Many customers of ISO 9000 registered suppliers have not gained the confidence they expected and claim that ISO 9000 permits suppliers to produce rubbish providing it is consistent rubbish. This claim is unfounded but is understandable particularly in cases where auditors concentrate only on documentation and not on the technical issues. Suppliers could write anything in their quality policy since there were no criteria to judge the adequacy of such a policy. Quality is judged by the customer and not the supplier, therefore in the 1994 version of the standard, a new requirement was added for the supplier's quality policy to be relevant to the organizational goals and the expectations and needs of customers. This together with the requirement that the quality system ensure product conforms to specified requirements should overcome this malpractice. QS-9000 is more customer focussed than ISO 9000 and together with the requirement for third party auditors to have automotive experience, similar claims of QS-9000 should not arise.

Applying QS-9000

Currently only the first tier suppliers to the Big Three are required to develop quality systems that meet QS-9000 and only GM and Chrysler require third party certification. First tier suppliers are required to use QS-9000 as a basis for controlling their subcontractors but there is no requirement for the second tier suppliers to be registered to QS-9000. However, second tier suppliers will be required to meet the relevant requirements of QS-9000 by their customers but in so doing, some of these customers may waive certain requirements that are met by themselves such as Advanced Product Quality Planning and Production Part Approval. In other words, these requirements will be implemented by the first tier supplier on behalf of the second tier supplier.

It is interesting to note that QS-9000 does not apply to every contractor to the Big Three. It only applies to internal and external suppliers of:

• Production materials

• Production or service parts

• Heat treating, painting or other finishing services directly to the Big Three or other original equipment manufacturers' customers that subscribe to QS-9000.

QS-9000 does not apply to organizations developing software for the Big Three and the design and servicing requirements of QS-9000 only apply to those organizations with design and servicing responsibility. However, the question of when design applies remains ambiguous. The IASG sanctioned interpretations of March 1996 imply that element 4.4 applies if you are responsible for the design of any product you supply to any customer subscribing to QS-9000. Design responsibility means that you have been delegated, through contract from one of the Big Three, the authority to establish a new product specification or change an existing product specification. Another way of saying this is that you are responsible to one of the Big Three for the design of a certain product. The ambiguity arises because the definition does not contain the words "responsibility to one of the Big Three". If you supply a proprietary product, designed by your organization for general sale, and one of the Big Three decide to purchase it, element 4.4 should not apply but could apply if the IASG interpretation is enforced. If the same product is manufactured by another organization and one of the Big Three purchase that product and not the one you manufacture, then element 4.4 does not apply to the manufacturer of the product. It would seem logical that element 4.4 applies only when products are designed specifically to meet requirements of a customer subscribing to QS-9000 since, in other cases, the customer is purchasing a product of existing design and either it meets their requirements or it does not. The best advice is to consult your customer if you are in any doubt for particular cases.

Scope of registration

Another characteristic of registration is the scope of the business you wish to be registered. The scope describes the products and service for which you require your quality system to be certified. In assessing the quality system, assessors are looking to see that the system is capable of ensuring that the products and services specified in the "scope" meet specified requirements. For example, if you register your system for the manufacture of ignition systems then add to your business the manufacture of electronic components, you cannot claim that you are accredited to QS-9000 for the manufacture of electronic components. The registration is limited only to the scope. When selecting suppliers you cannot rely on the fact that they are registered to a particular standard. You need to know for what products and services they are registered. You also need to know which accreditation body issued the certificate since not all are registered with the national accreditation agency.

The scope of registration is not the same as the scope of your quality system. You may include many functions and processes in the quality system that are not addressed by QS-9000 or which affect product or service quality. If you choose to design a management system which reflects how you conduct your business then you may include finance, legal, medical, catering, personnel, and realty and other management processes. If you do not intend to sell or supply these services to your customer then you would not include them in the scope of registration (see also Part 1 Chapter 3 on *What should be registered*).

The benefits of registration

There are several benefits to be gained by becoming registered. You may request a third party to carry out an assessment of your quality system against QS-9000 and if found compliant you will be recommended to the Registrar for certification and will be granted a Certificate of Registration. The assessment is intended to determine whether your quality system has the capability of enabling you to meet your customers' particular requirements and not whether you are in fact meeting your customers' requirements. Registration, however, does have several benefits:

- The company will be listed in a Register of Companies of Assessed Capability by name and business and therefore any potential customer seeking a qualified supplier may discover you and make contact.

- You will be permitted to advertise that the company has been registered to QS-9000 and this will help your marketing profile and exposure.

- The company will be able to tender for contracts only let to QS-9000 registered organizations.

- Once your company is in the Register and has remained there for over three years it demonstrates to potential customers that you are serious about quality and this will help you create and retain customers. Getting the certificate is easier than keeping it.

In some countries the term *certification* is used in preference to *registration*, the intention being that companies that satisfy the requirements of the assessment standard are *certified* and have their details entered into a *register* of companies of assessed capability. However, the term *certification* implies that all requirements have been met. The nature of the assessment is that no such claim can be made since the assessor is not examining a sample from a homogeneous population. The certificate awarded is therefore a certificate of registration, not a certificate which testifies that the organization's quality system is fully compliant with the standard.

The assessment is intended to determine whether you possess the capability to meet your customer requirements. The results are obtained by sampling activities, documents, and products/services. The assessor tests the sample for conformance and ensures that sufficient samples are taken to show conformance against each requirement of the standard. The granting of a certificate does not mean that you have no noncompliances. It means that no significant ones were found. Neither does it mean that your documented system is fully compliant. The aspects that were examined were found to be compliant and therefore it is likely that the remainder is compliant but this is by no means certain. Assessors will always make a disclaimer that there may be nonconformities in the areas not examined. Hence on subsequent visits, assessors may find new problems that were not found on the first visit even though they existed at that time. (See also Part 1 Chapter 5.)

Self assessment

Before you launch your QS-9000 program you need to know your own performance, your culture, the drivers for change and the barriers against change. It is therefore prudent to carry out a self assessment covering those parts of the organization which contribute to the quality of your products and services. Look at what you do now, using the Quality System Assessment Guide (QSA), compare it with the standard and make a list of the things you will need to change. You may find that you already have in place many provisions which satisfy the requirements of the standard.

For those suppliers that have been doing business with the Big Three for years, many of the additional requirements in QS-9000 will come as no surprise. They are after all a harmonization of previous quality initiatives practiced by the Big Three. It is to be expected therefore that suppliers will have systems for dealing with Advanced Product Quality Planning, Production Part Approval, Potential Failure Modes Effects Analysis, Control Plans etc. Some may have monitoring systems in place based on Ford's Q101 standard, but to many the requirement for a documented quality system will be new. What may also be new are the requirements for documented procedures governing every aspect of the system. A system of internal audits, management reviews, contract reviews, purchasing controls, and design controls is beyond the Advanced Product Quality Planning Manual.

Some organizations make the mistake of redesigning their complete management system when all that was needed was for the existing system to be documented. At the end of Part 1 is a short questionnaire to help you focus on the principal requirements. It covers each element of QS-9000. Answering each question will help develop your quality policies. There is another more detailed questionnaire at the end of each chapter in Part 2. These go further than the QSA and address each clause of the standard separately.

The key requirements

It is easy to lose sight of your objectives when you start to implement QS-9000. The standard presents the requirements as though each is of equal importance. If you analyze the standard you will find that there are more requirements for appraisal (inspection, test, review) than for prevention (specifying, planning, organizing). However, the ratio is more evenly balanced in QS-9000 than it is in ISO 9001. What has to be remembered is that the requirements aim to prevent a nonconforming product from being supplied to customers. To do this you may have to redesign, rework, repair, reorder, and remake the product many times and you could lose money doing so.

The following summarizes the requirements of QS-9000 at three levels: firstly as a single requirement, secondly as a series of generic requirements and thirdly as a series of requirements based on the individual elements of the standard.

The basic requirement

If QS-9000 were to be resolved into a single requirement it would be phrased along the following lines:

> The organization shall establish, document, implement, and maintain a system which will provide confidence to both its own management and the customer that the intended quality of its products and services will be, is being, and has been achieved and which will ensure that its products and services supplied conform to customer requirements.

Generic requirements

If the 300 or so requirements of QS-9000 and the intentions of ISO 9004 were to be condensed into just 10 simple requirements they might read as follows:

Organization purpose and mission

The organization's management shall determine its purpose and mission and develop strategies which safeguard the needs of society and its employees, comply with relevant legislation, satisfy customer expectations, and enable it to grow.

Management system

The organization shall define, document, manage, and implement a management system which ensures that the needs and expectations of its customer are met, its purpose fulfilled and its mission achieved.

Customer requirements

The organization shall determine and document the characteristics which its products and services need to exhibit to satisfy customer needs and expectations.

Management of work processes

The organization shall plan, resource, organize, and control all work processes needed to design, produce, and supply products and services which meet customer needs and expectations and ensure they remain effective.

Process inputs

Inputs to all work processes including materials, documentation, equipment, and personnel shall be defined, approved, and the processes proven capable of delivering the required results before work commences.

Development work processes

The development and introduction of all new products, services, processes, and practices shall be planned, organized, controlled, and demonstrated as meeting the design requirements before they are introduced into service.

Production work processes

All work processes shall be carried out under controlled conditions which ensure that they remain capable of producing the required output, that no product or service is received, delivered or subjected to further processing until verified as compliant with the input requirements and that any noncompliant work is rectified, the cause established, and measures taken to prevent its recurrence.

Process outputs
All finished work shall be protected against damage, cross contamination, deterioration or loss while under the organization's control and all residual materials and obsolete documents removed or otherwise identified to prevent their inadvertent use.

Improving work processes
All work processes shall be analyzed to detect their potential for creating dissatisfied customers or financial loss and measures taken to prevent its occurrence.

Assurance of work processes
Plans and records shall be maintained which demonstrate that the work processes will be, are, and have been under control and the resultant products and services comply with the specified process input requirements.

The principal requirements of QS-9000

These 23 requirements summarize the 500 or so requirements of QS-9000 in layman's terms:

Management responsibility
Management shall define its policies and objectives for quality, specify the responsibilities and authority of all personnel, appoint a person with responsibility for the quality system, manage multidisciplinary activities, set business goals and monitor their achievement, determine customer satisfaction, ensure the quality system is effective and demonstrate its commitment to quality.

Quality system
A system for ensuring that products and services meet customer requirements shall be established, documented, implemented, and maintained, using cross-functional teams, quality planning, and failure prevention techniques. Such systems shall consist of the following elements.

Contract review
Contracts or orders from external customers shall be reviewed to ensure the requirements are adequately defined and that the company has the capability of meeting them.

Design control
Product and service design shall be planned, organized, and controlled so that the design which emerges can be demonstrated to meet agreed design requirements and defined user needs and/or requirements.

Document and data control
Controls shall be employed which ensure the use of valid documents and data and prevent the use of invalid documents and data in operations serving the achievement of customer requirements.

Purchasing
Controls shall be employed which ensure that purchased products and services which directly or indirectly affect the quality of products and service supplied to customers conform to specified requirements including 100% on-time delivery performance.

Customer supplied product
The condition and security of product, tooling and packaging provided by the customer shall be controlled and the customer notified should it be lost or its condition deteriorate.

Product identification and traceability
Products, processes, and services shall be identified by suitable means and when necessary this identity shall be unique to individual product or batches.

Process control
Once processing capability has been assured, the result-producing processes shall be planned, executed, and controlled such that the equipment, environment, personnel, documentation, and material employed delivers a product or service which meets specified requirements consistently within a system that satisfies applicable safety and environmental regulations.

Inspection and testing
Products and services received and produced by the organization shall be verified as meeting the special requirements prior to use, processing, and dispatch.

Inspection, measuring and test equipment
Devices, techniques, and reference standards used to verify that products or services meet specified requirements shall be controlled, calibrated, and maintained within a system that minimizes variation.

Inspection and test status
Products shall be identified such that uninspected product is distinguishable from inspected product and conforming product distinguishable from nonconforming product while under the organization's control.

Control of nonconforming product
Product which fails to meet the customer requirements shall be prevented from inadvertent use and measures employed to control remedial action taken to make such products acceptable for use.

Corrective and preventive action
Action shall be taken to prevent the occurrence and recurrence of nonconformities and ensure these actions are effective using disciplined problem solving methods.

Handling, storage, packaging, preservation, and delivery
Measures shall be taken to detect and prevent damage or deterioration to product while under the organization's control. Inventory and delivery management systems shall optimize inventory and ensure 100% on-time delivery.

Control of quality records
Records shall be established, documented, maintained, and retained which demonstrate achievement of the customer requirements and the effectiveness of the quality system.

Internal quality audits
Audits shall be planned and executed to verify that the quality system is effective in ensuring that the working environment, products, and services conform to customer requirements.

Training
The training needs of personnel whose work affects quality shall be identified, personnel qualified to carry out the work assigned to them, and the effectivess of training evaluated.

Servicing
Controls shall be employed which ensure that servicing operations meet the customers' requirements and which provide for data feedback into design and manufacturing.

Statistical techniques
Measures shall be taken to control the selection, understanding, and application of statistical techniques used in accepting product and determining process capability.

Production part approval
Approval for all production parts and any changes thereto shall be granted before commencing production.

Continuous improvement
Performance on all aspects affecting customer satisfaction shall be continuously improved through use of established improvement methodologies.

Manufacturing capabilities
Plant, facilities, equipment, processes, and tooling shall be planned, organized, and controlled though formal control systems that ensure added value and effectiveness.

Requirements which depend on contract or when appropriate

Some of the requirements only apply when specified in a contract or when appropriate which of course may well be when specified in a contract. There are 16 of these requirements and if your business is such that one or more is unlikely to apply then you need to make no provision for meeting them. It would be prudent, however, to make a declaration in your Policy Manual giving the reasons why certain requirements are not applicable to your business. This makes it clear to any assessor and saves time during the assessment of both the documentation and the practices.

- Verification of purchased product by the customer

- Proposed use or repair of product

- Protection of the quality of product after final inspection and test

- Making quality records available for evaluation by the customer for an agreed period

- Servicing

- Traceability

- Identifying product

- Statistical techniques

- Design control

- Approval of control plans

- Computer aided design and engineering systems

- Comprehensive prototype program

- Identification for special characteristics

- Approved subcontractor list

- Statistical verification of job set-ups

- Supplemental verification and identification

Requirements which assessors focus on

There are some requirements which most organizations fail to satisfy to varying degrees, so you should focus your effort on these. The others are important and you will fail the assessment if there are major deficiencies. The following elements usually require new practices. (Note that the organization may have no existing systems at all that cover these areas.)

4.1	Management responsibility, notably commitment, defined responsibility and authority, and management review
4.2	Quality system, notably documenting and maintaining the system
4.5	Document control, notably change control and document obsolescence
4.9	Preventive maintenance
4.11	Inspection measuring and test equipment, notably what is calibrated, calibration frequency, and the action required following an out-of-calibration result
4.14	Corrective action, notably analyzing records, preventing recurrence of nonconformity, changing procedures
4.16	Quality records, notably what records are produced and maintained and for how long they are retained
4.17	Internal audits, notably planning, implementing the plan and follow-up of corrective actions
II-2	Continuous improvement

A list of do's and don'ts is given at the end of each chapter in Part 2.

Misconceptions

Various misconceptions exist with ISO 9001 and may equally apply to QS-9000. All of the following are untrue:

- The standard requires that you document what you do and do what you document.

- You have to appoint a Quality Manager.

- Job descriptions are required.

- Everyone should be able to recite the quality policy.

- All out of date documents have to be removed.

- All purchases have to be from approved suppliers.

- Purchase orders must be signed.

- Documents have to carry an approval signature.

- There has to be only one index of documentation.

- Work instructions are required for all operations that affect quality.

- All measurements have to be made with calibrated instruments.

- All verification activities have to be performed by staff independent of those responsible for the activities being verified.

- The location of items in stock has to be identified.

- Records of corrective actions have to be retained for a defined period.

- All auditors have to undergo formal training.

- All incoming supplies are to be subject to receipt inspection.

- Storage areas have to be locked at all times.

- The quality record requirements apply to all records.

Chapter 3

Quality system strategies

If your company is considering QS-9000 registration then there are several important decisions to be taken by your top management:

*   What do we mean by quality, quality management, quality improvement, quality control?

*   How many systems do we want?

*   What kind of quality system do we want?

*   When should we go ahead?

*   Which registrar should we choose?

*   Who should be registered?

*   How is it to be funded?

Unifying understanding

Firstly you need to unify understanding on quality amongst the management team. Some may perceive quality as striving for perfection, others may perceive it as inspection, as large quality departments or increasing the overheads. It is highly likely that no one on the management team will regard new product development as quality improvement, market realignment as quality improvement or that you can have quality control in the design office. Some may perceive high grade as high quality, the Cadillac to be superior quality to the Chevrolet (see previously). It may also be likely that management takes the view that the workforce cannot be trusted and that independent inspection is essential to achieve quality. Quality may be perceived only in terms of conformance to procedure, to drawings etc. and not in terms of meeting customer needs. You need to bring these perceptions out into the open before you even decide on the kind of quality system you want, since your perception will determine what you include. Most importantly, staff have to know which strategy top management has chosen – not just the name but the details. When orchestrating a number of people there has to be one piece of music and everyone has to play from the same sheet. You will find that the process of unifying understanding never ceases. There will always be someone with a novel view of quality who is causing havoc. It is better that everyone pulls in the wrong direction than all in different directions. Next time you see a flock of starlings watch how easily they change direction, then work out how you can enable your organization to do the same.

How many systems do we want?

It may seem an odd question but in large organizations it may not be practical to develop one system since the operations of each of its divisions may be quite different. One system can serve an organization in which all its operations contribute to a common purpose and mission and where there is one profit centre. If there are separate profit centres then separate quality systems may be necessary. It would be impractical for each department within a single profit centre to develop its own system, since the departments are not autonomous and will depend on the services of other departments to operate effectively. If the organization is divided geographically then separate quality systems for each region or country may be essential for market, cultural, and language reasons. If divided by market segments, then separate quality systems may be essential because of the wide variation in customer requirements and product operating conditions. In multinational corporations, there may be operational divisions with central marketing, purchasing, personnel, and research divisions. Owing to the desperate nature of these divisions, separate quality systems will be necessary and hence separate certification. Certification applies to a single quality system, not a number of separate quality systems, unless they are integrated and function as one system. A simple rule is to establish where the profit centres are, how business is contracted and subcontracted. The boundaries of the quality systems lie where money changes hands or costs are transferred.

Choosing the type of quality system

You need to decide on the kind of quality system you want. There are three ways of approaching this decision:

- Documenting what you do in response to the requirements of QS-9000.

- Documenting the operational processes limited to the requirements of QS-9000.

- Creating a company wide business management system that covers all processes and where relevant addresses the requirements of QS-9000.

"Documenting what you do" method

With this method you document the activities that are required by the standard and generate a Quality Manual that addresses each element of the standard in the sequence in which they are presented, regardless of their relevance to your business. This is a minimal approach and will provide the evidence needed to demonstrate compliance with the standard. However, this approach tends to be rather limiting as it does not place within the quality system aspects that may ensure understanding of the system, the reasons for the policies and procedures or their relationship. It will also omit aspects that are not directly related to QS-9000 but which follow naturally in operating the management and operational processes employed in the organization. It will also not build a coherent and consistent system since this is not a requirement of the standard. It can often lead to a "bolt-on system", a system that consists of a series of related but unconnected parts. A system is an integration of interconnected business processes which collectively cause the supply of conforming product/service and prevent the supply of nonconforming product/service. It is likely that if you merely document what you do you will not create an effective system.

QS-9000 contains a series of related requirements but they are not presented in any particular sequence. Producing a procedure for each element or clause of the standard, whilst meeting the requirements, will not in fact provide a system that adds value to the organization. Employees may not easily relate to the manuals and procedures as they are based on QS-9000 and not on the business.

It is a mistaken belief that auditors prefer a manual that follows the elements of the standard and procedures that cover each element. Auditors need to understand your business if they are to establish that you have your operations under control. A manual and set of procedures that mirrors the standard does not provide the necessary information. QS-9000 does not require suppliers to describe their business and the interrelationship between processes and hence many suppliers omit this information from their manuals and have to supply it separately so that auditors can understand how business is carried out. But nonetheless this solution to QS-9000 is the one most commonly adopted.

"QS-9000 operational process" method

With this method the focus is on the processes that convert customer input into customer output rather than on addressing the elements of the standard. With the "document what you do" method you respond to the requirements of the standard. With the operational process method you firstly define the processes that convert inputs into outputs and map the requirements of the standard onto the process model that has been created, omitting those that are not relevant to your business and adding activities that are needed to meet the standard. With this method you create a Quality Manual that addresses the operational processes in the sequence they are executed. In the former methodology, you merely produce documents that the standard requires.

In the operational process methodology you produce documents that reflect what you do and in doing so meet the requirements of the standard. It is a reverse of the "document what you do" method. It produces documents that are more readily understood by the employees. A matrix cross referencing the requirements of QS-9000 with the documented system provides auditors and customers with a route map to the system and it is a method that is accepted by the IASG.

In order to design an operational management system you have to understand how business is conducted in your company. It will be obvious from looking at the management tree that business is not actually conducted from the top down through each department but across the departmental boundaries. Orders are received in the Sales Department, routed to the Production Department that produces the product from materials supplied by the Purchasing Department and following inspection by the Inspection Department the product is routed back to Production for rework and after again being handled by the Inspection Department is passed to the Shipping Department for delivery to the customer. For many companies the interdepartmental transactions will be far more complex than this simple example. To design an operational management system you have to forget who does what and concentrate on the functions that convert inputs into outputs of added value. A *function* in this context is not a department of the company but a group of processes which serve the fulfillment of the business purpose and mission. In some texts the term *business process* is used to define both the processes and groups of processes. I prefer to call groups of processes *functions* as one would in system design. The functions of a computer, for instance, are different from the physical arrangement of its hardware and software. These equate to departments of a company whose physical arrangement differs from the way they operate.

In creating an operational management system the basic sequence of steps is as follows:

- Create a system model depicting the result-producing functions (not departments) which convert customer inputs into outputs that meet customer requirements. Such functions might be business planning, marketing, research, new product planning, design, sales, production planning, manufacture, inventory control, procurement, installation, customer service.

- Add all the supporting functions (again not departments) which provide personnel, material, equipment, documentation, utilities etc.

- Draw the principal paths connecting each function along which either product or information passes and the net result should be a schematic flow diagram depicting how the company operates.

- Now assign each element of QS-9000 to the appropriate functions. You will find that there are some functions that cannot be assigned an element of the standard. You will now see which requirements each function has to satisfy.

- The next step is to analyze each function and identify the processes which together provide that function and draw in the principal paths connecting each process. At this stage you can refine the allocation of QS-9000 elements to individual processes.

- Once the processes are identified you can now chart the tasks in the sequence they occur to execute each process, again ignoring who does what. Some tasks may be decisions so you need to show the feedback loops. Any new tasks required as a result of analyzing the appropriate elements of QS-9000 should now be added, such as Design Reviews, Process Change Control, Corrective and Preventive Action etc.

- Each task may be broken down further as a flow chart depicting the actions and decisions involved, again in the sequence they occur.

- The last step is to draw boundaries around groups of activities or tasks to define where the procedure boundaries are drawn. A list of procedures to be developed can now be established.

This strategy builds a more coherent system as it focuses on what the business does first and foremost and then, as a means of confirmation or improvement, addresses QS-9000. The operational system methodology is a means to an end and not an end in itself. Having designed and documented the system, you can then apply the quality improvement techniques given in QS-9000 to make the functions and processes more effective in delivering customer satisfaction. A term gaining in popularity is *business process re-engineering* or BPR. BPR is in principle quality improvement but not improvement by gradual change; it is improvement by radical change to make a quantum leap in process effectiveness.

An important consideration with this strategy is that the scope of the system will not necessarily be the scope of QS-9000 registration (see later).

"Company wide integrated business management" method

This is an extended version of the operational process method, covering all functions of the business and resulting in a company wide integrated business management system. It would include all activities that serve the business and not only those covered by QS-9000. Included would be strategic planning, research, marketing, information technology, finance, human resources, administration, legal, and real estate functions etc. The system would also address health, safety, and environmental management, not just the compliance aspects covered in clause 4.9 of QS-9000, but cover ISO 14000 as well.

Selecting an appropriate strategy

Introducing a QS-9000 quality system while management is under pressure to introduce other major programs has a demotivating and retarding effect. This can be totally uneconomic. Management has to be relatively free to devote the required time and resources. Organizational change has to be minimal whichever strategy is chosen.

Should there be no other pressures to detract from a total commitment to QS-9000 then any of the other strategies can be pursued. Choosing the minimal approach can be followed by each other strategy when resources allow. Doing it in phases may result in some redesign of the existing quality system when you attempt to introduce a different strategy. It may also cause staff confusion and may create apathy for the system.

Another approach is to choose the operational management system strategy and in doing so address all the requirements of QS-9000. This is by far the more robust approach and provides a system which benefits the business rather than a system which merely meets the requirements of the standard.

The more complex approach is an integrated management system covering a scope much wider than QS-9000. This type of system can be difficult to develop due to conflicting priorities and cultural differences. However, an integrated management system be can more easily developed from an operational management system than a QS-9000 focused quality system since the foundation for the system will have been laid, leaving other components to be added when required.

These are just a few of the approaches you can take. There could be many more variations on a theme, but the ultimate decision rests with top management.

By the time you read this book, it may be already too late to adopt the operational process method and you may have to settle for the minimal approach, although the development time may not be significantly shorter.

When should we go ahead?

The next decision is to determine when to commence quality system development. Doing nothing is always a possible option and can be taken as do nothing ever or do nothing just at the present time. The pressure from your customers may suggest that doing nothing ever is out of the question. But, is the time right for change? It is important that the introduction of a quality system is carried out at a time when no other major changes are intended. One of the main reasons for failure in quality programs is that too many other things are changing at the same time. So you have to ask yourself, are any other major changes likely over the next 12 months or so? If so, do nothing now.

If your customers are requiring QS-9000 certification right now, then it is already too late for you to beat your competitors. You need to establish not what customers want now, but what will they want in 1 to 5 years from now since it will take you that long to get the quality system up and running and mature enough to be certified to QS-9000. You also need to know in which markets you will be trading in 1 to 5 years time so that you can prepare to be ready to meet the requirements of such markets should the trading regulations require QS-9000 certification.

■ Quality system development is a long term matter not a short term matter.

Which registrar?

You need to obtain a list of the accredited registrars from your national standards association. Some registrars are not accredited to perform QS-9000 registration audits and therefore the certificates they issue are not recognized nationally or internationally. Most informed customers will ask who your registrar is and unless they are accredited will discount any certificate they have issued to you.

Regarding the assessors who will perform the assessment, you need to determine whether they are employed by the firm on a permanent basis or are associates, and whether or not the same person will examine your quality manual as will carry out the site visit. This is important for continuity reasons. If they are different you could find that there is conflict between the two or you may have to explain all over again the way your business operates.

The other element is the cost. There are few set fees; each registrar will vary the charges, so you need to obtain quotations. To be able to compare quotations you need to know the fees for the pre-assessment, the formal assessment, and the annual surveillance visits including expenses. (See also Part 1 Chapter 5.)

The final element is the timescale. Some registrars have a long waiting list and as a result use associates to discharge the assignments. Others may well be able to fit the assessment in to suit your plans, a useful benefit if your program overruns the target.

What should be registered?

You will need to establish the scope of the quality system and the scope of registration. These are not the same since QS-9000 may not address every operation in your business, as is illustrated by Figure 3.1.

The scope of registration should include all the operations that directly or indirectly affect the products and services for which you require your quality system to be certified. Your quality system may include the accounting, advertising, public relations, employee welfare, site maintenance operations etc., but you do not need to gain

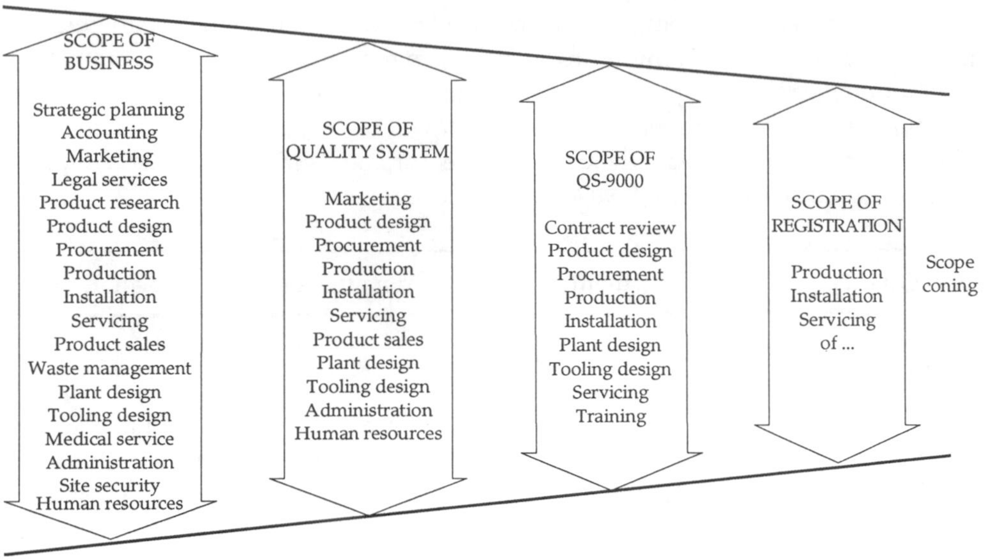

Figure 3.1 The scoping effect

registration for these unless you offer such services to your customer. You may have some product lines for which registration is not important or necessary or some services that are so insignificant that you would rather exclude them from the registration process. Some companies seek registration for one division at a time or one site at a time. Registration is normally site oriented so that if the operations of the site change or you add a new site to the scope, you will need to seek a re-assessment for those areas affected by the change. An advantage of individual site registration is that the performance of one site does not affect the others, whereas if seeking company-wide registration, the performance of all sites is considered. If a few minor nonconformities against the same requirement of the standard were observed at several sites it may be deemed to be a major nonconformity and you may not be recommended for registration. On individual site registrations this cannot happen. Another consideration with multi-site operations is that you don't have to have one quality system. If you register individual sites, they could be independent of one another. If you seek company-wide registration you have to establish and maintain one quality system. The choice is yours. You can always extend the scope later. (See also Part 2 Chapter 2.)

How is it to be funded?

Although the cost of installing a quality system will be a factor in deciding whether to install one, it should not be a primary factor since you cannot afford not to pay attention to quality. However, you need to ensure that funds are not wasted building a system that is too complex or continuing with a program that has clearly lost direction or support. Severe overspend can indicate these conditions and alert management to the crisis. The mechanisms you use to collect costs will have a bearing on whether you can allocate a budget and monitor spend. In some organizations, nobody does anything without a cost collection number against which to charge their time. Such disciplines can be a barrier to gaining commitment unless you provide a means for staff to escape being pressurized for under utilization. In such organizations there is always pressure to devote effort to funded programs. Fund the quality program and thereby make the work legitimate.

Chapter 4

Managing quality system development

Once you have decided which strategy to pursue you need to plan, organize, and control the development of the quality system – in other words you have to manage the program. No program will succeed unless the resources and activities are orchestrated, coordinated, and directed towards a common goal, and this requires the art of management. However, the first step is to decide what you want the quality system to do; for what purpose is it being created? Without a clearly defined purpose you will not be able to establish whether the system you have developed is fit for its purpose and hence of adequate quality.

Establishing the requirements

In order to establish the purpose of the system you need to find out where you are at present. Many companies start out by documenting what they do now and merely add the additional tasks needed to meet the minimum requirements of QS-9000. This takes no account of their current performance and so after the system has been in operation for some months there is concern that it has not changed anything. In fact all it seems to have done is to increase the amount of paperwork, create bottlenecks where none existed before and divert scarce resources. Unless you establish your current position before you start you will have no means of measuring improvement as a result of installing a quality system.

To establish the requirements you need to do several things:

- Establish your current position.

- Identify current documented practices.

- Identify strengths, weaknesses, opportunities, and threats in the business.

- Define the purpose of the quality system and the objectives you want to achieve.

The current position

To determine your current position you need to assess your performance in a number of key areas such as new product development timescales, post development modifications, customer complaints, receipt rejects, assembly rejects, test failures, service response times, time to process product or information through the key processes. One way of establishing the current position is to compute the quality costs but this may be difficult if the accounting mechanisms are not in place. Most business accounting systems do not measure the cost of doing the wrong things or doing the right things wrong so you may have to estimate these costs. Whichever method you choose it is essential to stick to the same cost categories throughout the program otherwise your conclusions will be invalid. It is the relative change that is important not the absolute expenditure. Having identified where you are you can then see what you want to change.

Identifying current documented practices

Make a list of all the documented procedures that are in use, the official ones and the unofficial ones. Establish their status and whether they reflect current practice. You may also have to search the memo files to establish management policy as, without a formal system in existence, managers will have probably communicated their policies by memos, notices, minutes of meetings, standing orders, directives or by any other similar method. Only collect the documented statements as the validity of any verbal instructions will be suspect. If possible get management to review the information so as to discard any that have clearly become obsolete. You will probably find quite a lot that can be used as input data to the development process.

Identifying strengths, weaknesses, opportunities, and threats (SWOT)

Assessing your strengths, weaknesses, opportunities, and threats is a common method for companies to find out where they are and where they want to be. It does not indicate how they might get to where they want to be but the provision of a map is the function of planning! Your company must be good at something; in fact there are probably many areas in which you excel – make a note of these. Also identify where you are weakest. The following presents some of the areas you should consider with respect to strengths and weaknesses:

- Management style: is it a barrier or a driver, does it help or hinder the process of change?

- Technology: is it old and inappropriate for today's needs or are you applying the best that will produce the desired results?

- Values: do you value relationships with suppliers, customers, employees, unions, is there integrity in decisions and in the treatment of employees or is money the only driver?

- Quality: is there a uniform understanding or is it fragmented, misdirected, and compromised?

- Policy: is it documented and honored or is it given lip service only, unwritten, and autocratically enforced?

- Organization: do you build teams, is there flexibility or is there demarcation, restrictive practices, and work rules?

- Communication: are staff kept in the picture or in the dark, does everyone know where the company is going or is it only the CEO and his team who know?

- Measuring performance: are standards set and is performance measured or are you totally unaware of how the business is performing, how the processes are performing and how you are performing?

- Handling problems: is it constant firefighting or are problems dealt with at the earliest opportunity and prevented from recurrence?

The situation may not be wholly positive or negative. Some areas may be positive and others negative. Analyze your organization to know the difference and identify the innovators, conservatives, and inhibitors. There will be some who want to change, others who can be persuaded, and some who won't change unless threatened.

The threats may come from your competitors in terms of what initiatives they are taking, or from your suppliers who may be less concerned about quality than you are. Threats may also come from the unions or from government in the form of legislation, trade barriers, and cartels. The opportunities are the results of the above. Every threat and weakness presents an opportunity but so does new business, new markets, new technologies.

This analysis will help you derive the drivers and barriers to successful implementation. Knowing these helps you to identify what you need to change for the program to be successful. Changing everything is not a priority for success. Identify the change priorities and address those that will retard initial progress. When managers see the benefits of change they will often follow rather than be left behind.

Defining purpose and objectives

When you have established what needs to be changed you can determine what you want the quality system to do. Some reasons for establishing a quality system are given in Part 2 Chapter 2. They range from ensuring that products and services satisfy customer requirements to improving efficiency within the organization. Whatever the reasons they need to be based on the facts revealed from the foregoing analysis. Producing a wish list will probably result in you being over ambitious. You don't need to go for zero defects at first (other than for attribute data) or include all operations of the business. Quality improvement can be taken a step at a time. Some of the steps will be quite small ones, others may be quite radical and involve a major reorganization.

The measure of your current performance will indicate what needs to be improved and what needs to be maintained. There may well be some aspects of your performance that you want to remain at the current level because you are particularly good and competitive in that area. The quality system needs to sustain that performance even if in such areas you don't satisfy all the requirements of the standard. Formalizing the controls should not result in a reduced performance but in sustained performance. You will therefore come up with two types of objectives, some for control and others for improvement. (See also Part 1 Chapter 1.)

Planning development

Preparing the development plan

You need to prepare, agree, and issue a quality system development plan as a means of showing how you are going to develop a quality system that fulfills the agreed purpose and meets the agreed objectives. The plan should define the key activities to be carried out, who is to perform them and when they are to commence and be completed. The bar chart shown in Figure 4.1 is a typical example of such a plan. However, you should also add some text to explain the roles of those involved and to record the agreed purpose and objectives.

Communicating the message

If you found that certain things need to be changed before commencing the development program, then the changes should be made before committing staff to the program. The climate has to be right, other major changes need to be either far off or nearing completion before launching a quality system development program. It is extremely important to gain commitment from top management before going ahead (see also Part 2 Chapter 1). You need to agree on the communication program, how the messages will be put over, when, by whom, and to whom. If you have a company newsletter, then this vehicle could be used to announce the program. You will need to replay the messages periodically throughout the program, changing the emphasis where necessary. One problem you may face is the information gap which often

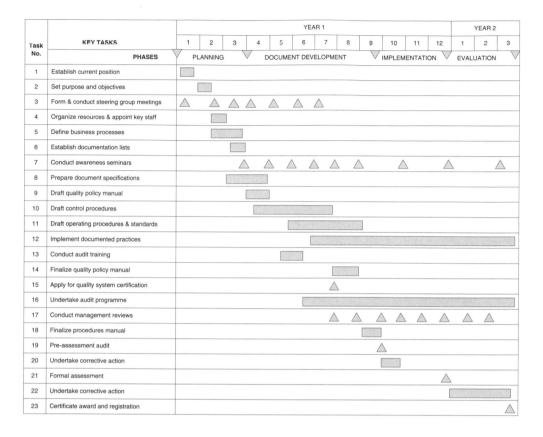

Figure 4.1 Quality system development programme

follows the launch. You announce to everyone that you are going for QS-9000, appoint the project leader and key players and then a long period of silence follows. By doing all the analysis and planning beforehand you can prevent this; however, there may well be a delay while resources are assembled, people trained etc. Keep sending out positive signals. Management must keep demonstrating their commitment, their support, their interest. You may well need an awareness and alignment program before you start so that everyone involved is prepared for the task ahead and any doubtful individuals are reassigned. Some people are innovators, some conservatives, and some just plain inhibitors. Don't have any inhibitors on your team as they can destroy the morale of the others, but an unconvinced manager can sometimes have a change in attitude when amongst peers who demonstrate enthusiasm.

Determining timescales

In choosing the timescales there are no rules except that you should run the system for at least three months before bringing in the external assessors. Also allow three months between the pre-assessment and the formal assessment so that you can put right any problems and demonstrate not only that the paperwork has been changed but the problem has been fixed.

Organizing the resources

The development budget
Once you have a plan of activities you need to determine what resources will be required in terms of the funds, people, equipment, materials, and space. A development budget should be established and means provided for staff to charge their time to the program. Use the principles of quality management to run the quality system development program and, if the budget is exceeded, establish the cause before proceeding further.

The project manager
You shouldn't start out on the road to QS-9000 unless you intend to succeed so you clearly need someone who has the necessary skills, knowledge, and personal attributes to make the project a success. The person who develops the quality system does not necessarily have to be the same as he who will maintain it but he should primarily understand the standard sufficiently well enough to guide both upper management and staff. Ask yourself, would you appoint a non-financial person to run your finance function, a non-engineer to run your engineering function? So one of the attributes is that the person must be a quality professional. He doesn't have to be an expert but should have an adequate knowledge of quality management and the QS-9000 series of standards. If you don't have one hire one for the job! You don't have to place him on staff, he can be retained under contract. It's a good way of selecting the right person, since another important attribute is his ability to inspire people to do the right things right. The person must represent quality in his actions and behavior and hence must set an example to his colleagues.

The steering committee
Managers ensure success by defining what they want, making sure their requirements are understood, providing the necessary resources and monitoring progress so as to detect and correct problems before they jeopardize the success of the project. Hence you should set up a steering group or committee comprising your upper management. They should agree on strategy, funding, policies, and the project plan, allocate resources and resolve policy, procedure, and resource issues. This will need a commitment from the management to meet regularly and steer the project towards completion.

Process owners

Each function or process should be assigned an owner: a person who has the authority to change the process should it be required either to meet the standard or to improve its performance. The process owners may be the line managers or their representatives. These people should form the quality system development team together with the project manager. It is not a full-time job. Their role is to help determine the process models and identify the associated documentation. They may produce the procedures themselves or nominate suitable authors.

Quality system controller

Quality system development is initially paper intensive while the policies and practices are documented. During this phase, draft documents need to be reviewed, changed, reviewed again, approved, and issued. As the system is progressively implemented, policies and procedures will in all probability require change as knowledge of use is gained. You need to keep control of the documents throughout this turbulent period and this is a role for a quality system controller. For a small project the project manager may perform the role but on larger projects, you may need someone else.

Materials and equipment

To begin with the only materials you will need are paper and binders to contain the procedures. However, you may decide to use computers to produce the documentation or have a paperless system using a computer network. You can prepare your procedures using a typewriter but desktop computers are now inexpensive and a good investment as they save time and effort. You should obtain several software packages, a word processor for text production, a spreadsheet or database package for document control and a drawing package that can produce diagrams and flowcharts. The simpler the system the less tools you will need. As you develop the procedures and standards you may find that you need other materials and equipment to control the operating processes, but these should be budgeted separately as part of the implementation program.

Developing the system

Faced with the task of applying QS-9000, it is not surprising to find many firms bewildered by the terminology, the apparent complexity of the requirements and the prospect of having to do everything immediately! This book should help explain the terminology and clarify your understanding. You don't have to do everything at once.

When all the preparation has been accomplished you can commence development. The way you proceed with development will depend on the strategy you have chosen. If you have chosen to develop an operational management system then the first place to start is with the system model and then develop the process models and identify the procedures to be prepared. You should not start by producing the quality manual.

The policies in the quality manual need to align with the procedures. By deriving the objectives for the procedures you form the policies that will be included in the quality manual. As you identify which elements of the standard apply to which processes you can derive the policies that address these requirements. So the procedures and the quality manual proceed in parallel.

However, there are some procedures that should be developed first. Those which will be used to control the preparation and maintenance of quality system documents should be produced first, followed by the audits and management review procedures. Next should be the customer feedback, purchasing, and contract review procedures so that the procedures at the customer and supplier interface can be used to collect data on the effectiveness of the system at the earliest opportunity. Thereafter, develop those procedures dealing with the core activities and follow with those dealing with the support activities. Since the quality system should be designed to ensure that only products and services which satisfy customers are supplied, the first place to start implementation is with your customers. Follow these 10 steps to help you identify where to focus your efforts and develop your system:

1   Discover your customer's opinion of your products/services.

2   Establish your customer's requirements.

3   Set up a customer complaints procedure to log and identify the errors which escape undetected.

4   Install final inspection prior to delivery of product/service to sort the good from the bad.

5   Examine the bad products to discover why they are bad.

6   Establish what controls are needed to prevent bad products reaching final inspection further upstream and put them into effect.

7   Examine the upstream controls and discover why they let through errors.

8   Establish what controls are needed to prevent errors reaching downstream controls and put them into effect.

9   Trace through the process back to purchasing, sales, and design and repeat the exercise to eliminate errors in these processes.

10 Adjust all the controls so that an economic balance is achieved. It is sometimes more costly to eliminate errors than to detect and correct them (the law of diminishing returns) so balance the preventive and corrective provisions such that errors are eliminated at the most expedient point in the process prior to delivery.

Controlling development

As you develop the documentation you should convene regular meetings of the team to establish progress, identify any problems, and agree on a course of action. The steering committee should meet periodically to review the policies and procedures that have been documented and adjust the funding and resources if necessary. The development plan should be used as the primary vehicle for monitoring progress. The list of documents to be developed should identify the process owners, the authors, and the dates by which the draft documents are required. This can then be used to monitor the progress of documentation development and implementation. The audit program should commence as soon as the auditors have been trained. When sufficient data has been gathered from the audits, the first management review should be held. The management review may be conducted by the same people that attend the steering committee but their role has now changed to that of determining if the system is effective. It is at this stage that the data gathered on past performance becomes most useful in detecting whether there has been any beneficial effect. In many cases the real benefits will not be visible for several years.

It is most important that you keep control over what documents are produced since you need to develop a coherent system, one in which all the interfaces match. For this reason, you should include in your documentation development procedures a means by which staff can apply to develop new documents (see Part 2 Chapter 2). On receipt of the request you can establish where it fits in the process model, ensure there is a need and that the interfaces with other procedures match. As documents are approved they should be listed in a Master Document Record (see Part 2 Chapter 5) and the issue status controlled.

Chapter 5

The assessment

The purpose of the assessment is to determine whether your quality system provides the capability for you to meet customer requirements. It is therefore important to commence a dialog with your certification body early in the program so as to obtain their interpretation of the standard to your business. The assessment itself is only as good as the assessor who conducts the assessment. Assessors are subject to annual appraisal by an independent council but the process in no way guarantees that high standards are maintained. You need to determine whether the assessors appointed will be fair and reasonable and that they have an adequate understanding of your business. Further information on how the assessment will be carried out is given in ISO 10011. The certification process is illustrated in Figure 5.1. The process will vary slightly with each registrar. Some carry out the documentation review on site followed by the conformance audit. Others conduct it off site with the conformance audit being carried out some time later. Some conduct reassessments every three years, others reassess parts of the system at each surveillance visit.

Assessment by the customer is addressed in Appendix A to QS-9000. This chapter covers the assessment by the third party certification body or registrar.

The initial visit

The initial visit enables the assessor to plan the formal assessment and so they will want to look around the plant, determine the key processes, key personnel, and examine your documentation, although not in depth. At this stage you can agree on the scope of the assessment, what is to be included, what excluded. The assessor may well find several areas where improvement is necessary. These need to be corrected before you submit your quality manual for assessment.

```
┌─────────────────────────┐
│  CONSULT QS-9000 REGISTER │
│      OF REGISTRARS        │
└─────────────────────────┘
            │
            ▼
┌─────────────────────────┐
│  OBTAIN APPLICATION FORMS │
└─────────────────────────┘
            │
            ▼
┌─────────────────────────┐
│    SUBMIT APPLICATION     │◄───────────────────────────────────────┐
└─────────────────────────┘                                          │
            │                                                         │
            ▼                                                         │
┌─────────────────────────┐                                          │
│   OBTAIN & EVALUATE       │                                         │
│      QUOTATIONS           │                                         │
└─────────────────────────┘                                          │
            │                                                         │
            ▼                                                         │
┌─────────────────────────┐                                          │
│     SELECT REGISTRAR      │                                         │
└─────────────────────────┘                                          │
            │                                                         │
            ▼                                                         │
┌─────────────────────────┐                                          │
│     INITIAL SITE VISIT    │                                         │
└─────────────────────────┘                                          │
            │                                                         │
            ▼                                                         │
┌─────────────────────────┐   ┌──────────┐   ┌──────────────────┐    │
│ PRELIMINARY ASSESSMENT    │──▶│  REPORT  │──▶│ CORRECTIVE ACTION │    │
│      (OPTIONAL)           │   │ SUBMITTED│   └──────────────────┘    │
└─────────────────────────┘   └──────────┘            │               │
            │                                          │               │
            ▼                                          │               │
┌─────────────────────────┐◄──────────────────────────┘               │
│ SUBMIT QUALITY SYSTEM     │◄─────────────────────────┐               │
│    DOCUMENTATION          │                          │               │
└─────────────────────────┘                           │               │
            │                                          │               │
            ▼                                          │               │
┌─────────────────────────┐   ┌──────────┐   ┌──────────────────┐     │
│  QUALITY SYSTEM           │──▶│  REPORT  │──▶│ CORRECTIVE ACTION │     │
│  DOCUMENTATION AUDIT      │   │ SUBMITTED│   └──────────────────┘     │
└─────────────────────────┘   └──────────┘                            │
            │                                                          │
            ▼                                        ┌──────────────┐  │
┌─────────────────────────┐                         │     FAIL      │──┘
│ INITIAL IMPLEMENTATION    │                        └──────────────┘
│      AUDIT                │                            ▲
└─────────────────────────┘                         YES │
            │                                            │
            ▼                                            │
        ◇ NONCONFORMITY? ◇──YES──▶◇ 2 MAJOR        ◇──NO──▶ CORRECTIVE ACTION ◄──┐
                                   NONCONFORMITIES?                             │
            │ NO                                                                │
            ▼                                                                   │
┌─────────────────────────┐    YES  ◇ CONFORMITY? ◇         ┌──────────────────┐│
│    RECOMMENDATION         │◄───────                        │  NONCONFORMITY    ││
└─────────────────────────┘                                 │  FOLLOW-UP ACTION │┘
            │                          │ NO                  └──────────────────┘
            ▼                          ▼
┌─────────────────────────┐      ◇ SUSPENSION ◇──NO
│  ISSUE/RENEWAL OF         │        CRITERIA MET?
│    CERTIFICATE            │            │
└─────────────────────────┘            │ YES
            │                           ▼
            ▼                   ┌──────────────────────┐
┌─────────────────────────┐    │ WITHDRAW CERTIFICATION │
│ PERIODIC DOCUMENTATION    │   └──────────────────────┘
│ & IMPLEMENTATION AUDITS   │
└─────────────────────────┘
```

Figure 5.1 The certification process

The preliminary assessment

It is prudent to arrange a preliminary assessment (or pre-assessment) so that you can test your readiness for the formal assessment. The preliminary assessment is not mandatory and does not have to be carried out by the registrar. You could employ the services of a consultant in order to obtain a view and advice as to what action would remove the problems detected. Assessors are not permitted to give advice on the assessment as there may be a conflict of interest. You can arrange the preliminary assessment before inviting the registrar for an initial visit or afterwards.

The formal assessment

The formal assessment is in three parts:

- The assessment of your documented system to determine whether it addresses the requirements of the standard (Documentation Audit)

- The assessment of practices to establish that the documented system is being implemented and that the practices satisfy the requirements of the standard (Implementation Audit or Site Audit)

- The evaluation of the results and issue of a report

It is in this area that there may be some difference in the approach each assessor takes. You only have to meet the requirements of the standard even though your documented quality system may go beyond these requirements.

Quality system documentation audit

The quality system *documentation audit* is sometimes referred to as a *system audit*, *adequacy audit* or a *documentation review*.

A copy of your documented quality system should be provided to the assessor for review prior to an implementation audit being performed. Whether you submit all the policies and procedures will depend upon its size and complexity. It is normal practice for organizations to submit only the policy manual (sometimes called the Quality Manual; see Part 2 Chapter 1). As a minimum, the documentation provided will need to include the policies and a list of the quality system procedures. Many of the requirements in the standard cannot be addressed at the policy level. Some will only be addressed in the control procedures and others much lower down in the tiers of documentation, in operating procedures, instructions, and forms. If the relationship between policies and procedures is vague then the assessor may well request copies of the procedures. Writing the manual around the requirements of the standard makes the assessor's job easier but may well not provide a system which reflects the way you conduct your business. A manual written around the standard is often not user friendly and hence is likely to been seen as only serving the needs of the assessor. As a compromise, you could include a cross-reference matrix showing the relationship between your manual and the standard. (See Part 2 Chapter 2.) IASG do accept this approach.

In assessing the documentation the assessor is looking for conformance, although some assessors may appear to be only concerned with nonconformance. It is therefore of no interest that you may have included aspects outside the scope of the standard. The documentation should reflect a system with elements which fit together. The outputs from one process should be inputs to other processes. There should be no loose ends, conflict, gaps, unnecessary overlaps and ambiguities. The assessor should therefore look for coherence. The assessor may well request further information in order to gain an adequate understanding of your system. Should an element of the standard have not been addressed then the assessor will proceed no further until it has been resolved. Should a clause of the standard have not been addressed then this may be resolved by providing documented procedures for review. Should a requirement of a clause have not been addressed then the assessor may add this to the check list and establish whether the practice is compliant during the implementation audit.

Implementation audit

The *implementation audit* is sometimes referred to as a *compliance audit, conformance audit*, or *site audit*.

Condition	Requirement of QS-9000	Provision of registration	Practice documented	Practice implemented	Example	Result
Activity outside scope of business	Yes	No	No	No	Design or servicing	No nonconformity
Activity outside scope of quality system	No	No	No	Yes	Finance, Security, Medical	No nonconformity
Activity outside scope of quality system	Yes	No	No	Yes	Design or servicing	No nonconformity
Activity outside scope of registration	No	No	Yes	No	Advertising, Public relations	No nonconformity
Activity outside scope of registration	Yes	No	Yes	No	Marine products	No nonconformity
Pertinent activity	Yes	Yes	No	No		Nonconformity
Pertinent activity	Yes	Yes	No	Yes		Nonconformity
Pertinent activity	Yes	Yes	Yes	No		Nonconformity

Figure 5.2 Determining validity of nonconformities

In assessing the practice, the assessor is looking for evidence that you are implementing the documented system. If you are not implementing those parts of the system that are outside the scope of the standard or the scope of registration, the assessor may or may not regard this as a nonconformance by virtue of the requirements of clause 4.2.2b ("The supplier shall effectively implement the quality system and its documented procedures"). If your practices are compliant with the requirements of the standard but the practices are not addressed in your documented system, then this should be deemed a minor nonconformity (see later). Figure 5.2 should help to distinguish between valid and invalid nonconformities. The table clearly shows that the only nonconformities that are valid are those where the requirements of QS-9000 and the scope of registration match.

Audit process

The site visit will take the following form:

- There will be an opening meeting to introduce the assessment team, confirm the scope and timetable, outline the assessment process and reporting method, and clarify any unclear aspects.

- During the assessment the assessors interview members of your staff to determine how work is carried out in certain areas, establish if it conforms with your policies and procedures, seek objective evidence of the facts, and compare the facts with the requirements of the standard. Any observations will be documented and the assessor may seek confirmation of the facts and request that you endorse the observation report before proceeding further.

- At the end of the assessment the assessor will prepare a report detailing the observations and identifying those which are nonconformities with the re-quirements of the standard. The lead assessor will draw conclusions from the results and formulate the recommendations.

- There will be a closing meeting to thank the participants, emphasize the good points, explain the nonconformities and observations, and make recommen-dations as to whether or not the company will be recommended for registra-tion. The assessor may leave the assessment report with you or it may be issued later following a review by the registrar.

- If there is more than one assessor there will be a lead assessor who will manage the assessment.

- If the assessment takes more than one day the lead assessor may call a daily meeting with the company to convey the results thus far.

Results

If the auditors use the Pass/Fail method to summarize the findings there are only three possible results of the assessment: Pass, Open, or Fail.

- A pass verdict means that no major or minor nonconformities were detected.

- An open verdict means that the auditors found no more than one major and several minor nonconformities and that you have 90 days in which to eliminate them.

- A fail verdict means that the auditors found two or more major nonconformities.

Should you fail the assessment or fail to correct the nonconformities to the auditors' satisfaction within the 90 days, you will have to make a new application for registration and go through the whole process again. With an open verdict, the auditors return to conduct a follow-up audit on the specific areas where nonconformities were detected.

If the auditors use the Variable Score method then to pass, a minimum score of two is required on every applicable element of QS-9000. This is based on answers to the questions in the QSA. The criteria are shown in the table below. The final score is calculated by dividing the total element score by the number of elements answered and multiplying the result by 50. There are 151 numbered questions and another 50 question marks as some questions are subdivided. The maximum score you could achieve is 150 with meaningful improvement or 100 with no nonconformities. Few registrars use this method and Ford prefers it to the Pass/Fail method; however, it is useful as a diagnostic tool in self assessment.

Question Scoring	Code	Element Scoring	Score	Result
This requirement is not met at all, or there are major inconsistencies in implementation	O	One or more questions with this result	0	Fail
This requirement is met but there are minor inconsistencies in implementation	M	One to three questions with this result	1	Fail
		Four or more questions with this result	0	Fail
This requirement is met and effectively implemented	C	All questions with this result	2	Pass
This requirement is met, effectively implemented, and shows improvement over the past 12 months that is meaningful to the customer	CI	All questions with this result	3	Pass

Nonconformities

The definitions of major and minor nonconformities are given in the QSA. The definitions given rely on there being unified understanding on what a requirement of the standard is. All nonconformities should be identified with the element and clause of the standard which has not been met. The nonconformity statement should be concise, accurate, and supported with objective evidence. It should enable you to take remedial action to eliminate the nonconformity. Vague statements should be challenged. Nonconformity statements should therefore specify:

- The object of the nonconformity

- The location of the object

- The requirement of the standard which has not been met

As the detection of a nonconformity can be cause for refusal to award certification, it is extremely important that there is agreement on the nature of such nonconformity. If the provisions in place have not been followed in one instance then the assessor should look for more objective evidence. If compliance is established in some cases but not others then a judgement needs to be made as to whether it signifies that the system has broken down. The assessor needs to establish whether the nonconformity is the result of random error or indicative of operations being out of control. The assessor should establish if the system is incapable of stopping the supply of nonconforming product or service.

Existing nonconformities

If you know of nonconformities and have in fact put in place corrective action plans which have not yet been implemented, then whether the nonconformities would be deemed sufficient cause for refusing certification will depend on their magnitude. Failure to address an element or clause of the standard, regardless of your plans to remedy the situation, will be cause for refusal of certification, simply because your system is incomplete. You may however, have commenced a program of change which is only partially complete. Providing there is evidence of conformance to the standard in some cases, then you will be deemed compliant. The assessor will want to check progress at the subsequent surveillance visit. If no progress has been made, then this may indicate that the system is not in place.

Challenging nonconformities

If you believe the nonconformity to be invalid then challenge the assessor to demonstrate its validity by showing you the requirement of the standard that has not been met and showing you the evidence of nonconformity. If you are still not satisfied, ask the assessor to explain how the nonconformity can effect quality. Remember you are paying for the assessment, although if you withdraw on the basis that you are dissatisfied then you may have to pay another registrar to repeat the assessment. It is prudent only to challenge the assessor when you are on firm ground and when the corrective measures may well be costly and, in your view, add no value. Minor nonconformities are best accepted if their correction is trivial. You do not want to give the impression that you are not committed to quality by dismissing errors in the paperwork. The smallest error in paperwork has been known to result in severe penalties. Assessors should note that:

■ **You are only taken as seriously as your most insignificant nonconformity.**

Since the standard is for use where a supplier's capability needs to be demonstrated, it follows that if a purchaser or assessor has confidence in the supplier's capability, regardless of all the requirements being met, then the supplier need do no more. If more is required, the supplier should ascertain the effect that meeting the requirements will have on its capability to supply conforming product and its capability of preventing the supply of nonconforming product.

Correcting nonconformities

The standard requires that you take timely corrective action on deficiencies found during internal quality audits and the same is expected (but not required) of external audits. The assessor will request proposals from you concerning the remedial action and corrective action you intend to take and the dates by which these actions will be completed. The remedial action is intended to correct the error and the corrective action to prevent it from recurring. (See also Part 2 Chapter 14 for the subtle distinction between these terms.) The assessor will not normally agree to timescales in excess of 90 days to correct the nonconformities as it indicates that the assessment was premature. In some cases the nonconformity can be closed by letter or submission of changed pages to the manual or procedures. In other cases the new procedures need to be in place for several months before sufficient evidence has been generated to show that the system is effective.

In correcting the nonconformities you should:

• Correct the specific nonconforming item.

• Seek out and correct any other similar instances.

• Recall product containing suspect nonconforming product (if applicable).

• Correct that which caused the nonconformity to prevent recurrence.

Chapter 6

Beyond QS-9000 certification

After registration to QS-9000, you have made a major achievement, but you have just started on the road to a quality culture. Meeting the requirements at the assessment is like passing a school exam. You know the syllabus and could be asked any questions. You did your homework and you are fortunate that you could give the right answers to the questions. But passing the exam doesn't mean you have become educated. You weren't tested on the whole syllabus, only a sample. You could have failed if other questions had been asked. And so it is in the QS-9000 assessment. QS-9000 certification implies that you have reached the minimum standard but this may not be sufficient to win business from your competitors. You will need to do three things: maintain, improve, and innovate; *maintain* your standards, *improve* on the efficiency and effectiveness with which you meet these standards and *innovate* occasionally to set new standards. This was also covered in Part 1 Chapter 1 under *Quality improvement*. The MII cycle can be illustrated as shown in Figure 6.1. In this cycle, routine activities should be moving between Maintenance and Improvement with periodic excursions into Innovation when the routines have exhausted improvement potential.

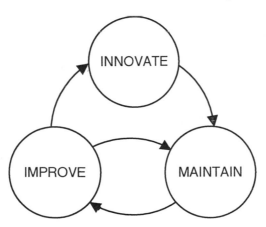

Figure 6.1 The MII cycle

The payback

The investment to achieve QS-9000 certification may be considerable and therefore top management will be looking for the payback. When should you expect to reap the dividends? Well, it depends on the state of your organization before you started on the road to QS-9000 certification. It was for this reason that I recommended you measure your performance in key areas before commencing quality system development (see Part 1 Chapter 4). If you have done this and installed the necessary provisions to capture the relevant performance data, then you will be able to detect when performance starts to improve. It is not unusual for performance to decline slightly during system development as effort is diverted to building the quality system and more efficient means of collecting data emerge. One of the significant differences between an ISO 9001 quality system and a QS-9000 quality system is the requirement for continuous improvement. It should therefore be expected that improvements will be made immediately on installing the system. If improved performance is not attained by the first surveillance visit then you will be noncompliant with the standard. However, the degree of improvement will vary depending on the level of performance at the start.

One of the most significant findings as a result of installing a quality system should be that performance becomes less erratic and less sensitive to changes in organization or customer requirements. A factor which will distort the picture is the effect of any new technology that you have introduced in the same period.

There will of course be short-term gains such as:

- The decline in reactive management as staff employ the documented procedures

- The decline in overtime as fewer products are found nonconforming before delivery

- The decline in design modifications as customer requirements are established before commencing design

- The increase in orders as customers apply selection policies based on QS-9000

If performance remains persistently poor even though you remain compliant with QS-9000, it is a sign that the problem is much deeper routed than can be resolved by management systems. What is often needed is a breakthrough in attitudes, management behavior, and staff motivation (see later).

Continuing development

There will be many areas where development of the system needs to be completed. If your organization is one that is constantly changing to respond to market forces, then quality system development never ceases. The initial assessment only took a sample of your operations to test for conformity against the standard. Subsequent audits will reveal more nonconformities and if you do not continue with the development of your system, these audits may find major nonconformities which, if not corrected promptly, will lead to the withdrawal of your certificate.

At the time of the assessment you do not need to have implemented every policy, every procedure etc. If, for example, you embarked on the program of upgrading equipment, documentation, training programs, recording measures etc. then it is important that you continue with these activities. Every policy and requirement of every procedure needs to be tested over the range of operations to which it applies. This may well yield opportunities for improvement which should be followed.

Improvement within QS-9000

The certification body will conduct periodic audits to verify that you remain compliant with the requirements of QS-9000. These audits only establish that you have retained the capability of meeting your customers' requirements and that the quality system is being implemented effectively. The audits are not intended to address standards other than the one against which you were certificated. However there are many areas of QS-9000 where the auditors will search for evidence of improvement action. There are five areas in which improvement is addressed in ISO 9001 and several additional requirements for improvement in QS-9000.

Quality objectives (4.1.1 of QS-9000)
You should be achieving your defined quality objectives and setting new objectives as opportunities for improvement arise.

Management review (4.1.3 of QS-9000)
You should continue with the management review process, reviewing all data generated by the quality system to establish whether there are opportunities for improvement.

Business plan (4.1.4 of QS-9000)
You should be tracking achievement of the goals specified in the business plan and using the data to drive improvement plans.

Analysis and use of company level data (4.1.5 of QS-9000)
You should be monitoring quality performance in key areas, comparing with competitors, and actioning improvement.

Subcontractor development (4.6.2 of QS-9000)

You should be assessing subcontractor performance, tracking delivery performance, and ensuring improvement.

Process capability (4.9.3 of QS-9000)

You should be conducting process capability studies and achieving specified C_{pk} and P_{pk} values and, regardless of demonstrated capability, seeking continuous improvement particularly on special characteristics.

Measurement system analysis (4.11.4 of QS-9000)

You should be reducing variation in the results of each type of measuring system.

Control of reworked product (4.13.3 of QS-9000)

You should be quantifying and analyzing nonconforming product and implementing prioritized reduction plans.

Corrective actions (4.14.2 of QS-9000)

Periodically you should be collecting and analyzing detected nonconformities and determining their root cause, devising corrective action programs and monitoring their effectiveness.

Preventive actions (4.14.3 of QS-9000)

You should be analyzing performance data to determine whether nonconformities will be generated if current trends continue.

Delivery performance (4.15.6 of QS-9000)

You should be monitoring delivery performance and implementing improvement plans to improve performance.

Internal quality audit program (4.17 of QS-9000)

You should be analyzing audit data, detecting trends, and adjusting the program periodically to address areas where nonconformities are concentrated. Where appropriate you should be also extending auditing periods where nonconformities are reducing.

Continuous improvement (II-2.1 of QS-9000)

You should be deploying a comprehensive continuous improvement philosophy and improving quality, service, and price for all customers and extending continuous improvement to all business processes and support services.

With ISO 9001 suppliers do not have to improve internal efficiency and effectiveness. Suppliers can reject 90% of all products purchased or produced and remain compliant as long as corrective action plans are initiated and implemented. Developments and deliveries could be late and projects overspent. With QS-9000, however, the picture is dramatically different, as illustrated by the above clauses that address improvement.

There are four key areas where change can be initiated: areas where you can Reduce, Increase, Stabilize, and Keep factors which impinge upon the ability of the business to satisfy its customers. They are RISK factors, factors which if not addressed will increase the risk of failure.

Some of the following factors are covered by QS-9000 and provide opportunities for improvement within QS-9000, others may provide opportunities for improvement outside QS-9000.

Reduction measures

In any organization there is always too much of something (except profit!) and so there are usually ample opportunities for reduction. There follow some pointers to areas where reduction may yield considerable benefits.

- Reduce complexity so that there are fewer ways of doing something, fewer interfaces, and fewer things to go wrong.

- Reduce variation so that processes produce results of consistent quality.

- Reduce waste so that resource costs can be kept low.

- Reduce time through the process so that bottlenecks are avoided.

- Reduce error in products, services, documents, decisions, and communication so that costs decline.

- Reduce job classifications so that you are not reliant on particular individuals.

- Reduce inspection so that costs decline.

- Reduce anti-quality attitudes which will jeopardize the program.

Increasing measures

For some factors any reduction would only make things worse and so you have to increase the amount of it to gain any benefit. Here are some which can yield considerable benefits.

- Increase utilization of material, machines, tools, equipment, personnel, and facilities.

- Increase training of management and staff.

- Increase discipline and adherence to policy and practices.

- Increase tidiness and cleanliness.

- Increase availability and retrievability of information.

- Increase motivation of management and staff.

Stabilizing measures

Before you had a quality system, performance may have been erratic; now it should be less erratic but you may need to apply further effort to make it stable. Aspects you can address are as follows:

- Stabilizing the controls so that less correction is needed to maintain quality standards

- Stabilizing methods so that once a good method is found it is used throughout the organization

- Stabilizing materials so that the effects of variation in materials are reduced

- Stabilizing suppliers so that you depend on fewer but more reliable suppliers

- Stabilizing processes so that variation is predictable

- Stabilizing the environment to reduce the effect that variations might have on operations

Keeping measures

While the introduction of a quality system may have resulted in you throwing away many obsolete documents, there are several things you need to keep and they are not all documents. Here are some of the more important things to keep.

- Keep commitments to signal to the workforce that you are serious about quality.

- Keep records so that you don't have to rely on opinions.

- Keep measuring performance so that you know where you are at any time.

- Keep analyzing results so that you know what to fix, what is about to happen, and what has happened.

- Keep auditing to determine the health of the organization.

- Keep questioning the status quo as nothing stands still.

- Keep reducing, increasing, and stabilizing.

- Keep maintaining, improving, and innovating.

Total quality management (TQM)

Total quality management is a concept which goes beyond ISO 9001 although within QS-9000 there are a number of aspects that could be classified as being part of a TQM program. The term is in fact a misnomer as the term *quality management* does not by itself imply any range of application. The term is probably derived from the term *total quality control*, which was conceived by Feigenbaum in the 1950s. At this stage in the evolution of quality management, quality control was limited to the manufacturing operations of a business and therefore to indicate that other parts of the business contribute to end product quality such as marketing, engineering, purchasing, and shipping, the word *total* was added. The focus was still on the product and those operations that directly contributed to the supply of product. Meanwhile in Japan the term *total quality control* was also being used and for a time had the same meaning as that given to it by Feigenbaum. The Japanese perception of quality control began to change as it was recognized that to compete they had to improve quality standards. Merely maintaining standards wasn't good enough. Their notion of quality control was that it involved everyone in the business in a totally integrated effort toward improving performance at every level. TQC therefore meant both maintaining and improving standards of performance. Rather than change the term, the Japanese changed its meaning. While this may be all right in Japan, changing meaning without changing the label causes untold confusion in the West.

In the West there was a need to change the dimensions of QC in three plains: the first so that it extended throughout the supply chain, the second so that it impacted upon everyone in the organization and the third so that it included people, processes, and management. Hence the birth of TQM. Since quality management was perceived as a combination of quality control, quality assurance and quality improvement the word *total* was added to indicate that it went beyond paying customer satisfaction and addressed internal customers and suppliers, the customer as shareholder, stakeholder, society etc.

There remains much confusion over what TQM really is. Some would argue that it focuses only on people and not on systems, others would say it focuses on processes and people and others might say it does all of this. There are definitions of quality management, TQM, and quality improvement in ISO 8402 but no guidance on how the concepts differ. The problem with TQM is that it is what you say it is. Quality management does not need the word *total* to be added providing you do not limit your perception of quality only to the products and services you sell. Quality can pertain to anything: the quality of products, services, organizations, management, decisions, documents, environment, and in the final analysis the quality of life itself. If you wish to limit quality management to one of these entities, then you should prefix the term *quality management* with the specific entity, such as *product* quality management.

Regardless of what it might be called there is a need for businesses to pursue improvement in at least three dimensions. They are improvement in the organization, in the processes, and in the employee since it is believed that these three elements are at the core of all business activity. Align these towards the purpose and mission of the business and sustained quality will result.

- Organization alignment creates the conditions that enable systems and resources to be developed and maintained to yield continuous improvement in quality. This should focus on business purpose and mission, the organizational goals, and management issues such as management style, communications, commitment, and leadership.

- Process alignment creates coherent processes across organizational boundaries from which product quality is predictable and dependable. This should focus on business processes, looking at all activities that contribute to the purpose and mission of the organization and building a hierarchical management system using system design techniques.

- Employee alignment gives employees the power, tools, and knowledge to improve the quality of their work. This should focus on team-building and problem-solving using quality improvement teams.

You can launch specific improvement projects targeted at key areas in the business. Providing you have designed a quality system that possesses the policies and practices for improvement as well as control, the system can be employed to push through improvement programs which create gradual change and those which create more radical changes. If you have given your quality system these attributes then it will be recognized by all personnel to be of tremendous benefit to the organization and they will defend it, resource it, and improve it.

Quality awards

There is no hierarchy in the QS-9000 certification process. QS-9000 is one level. One cannot graduate from QS-9000 to QS-10000 to QS-11000 etc. In some respects a hierarchy has its merits as it would allow organizations that were able to exceed the requirements of QS-9000 to obtain some recognition for their efforts. Currently, the organization that does the minimum and the one that goes beyond the requirements receive the same certificate. Even the entries in the Register of Companies of Assessed Capability would not discriminate between such organizations. So how can an organization be measured beyond QS-9000? The only route open in 1994 is the quality award system. The Deming Prize, Baldrige Award, UK Quality Award, European Quality Award are just a few and there may well be others. Each of these awards is given to organizations that meet very demanding assessment criteria. Having an effective quality system is only one aspect. Many of the other aspects address the culture, the treatment of employees, customers and suppliers, product innovation, quality improvement, education and training, and many more aspects of business management. This, at present, is the only award you can get beyond QS-9000 other than awards within particular multinational corporations, such as the Philips Quality Award, which is rated higher than any of the national and international award schemes.

QS-9000 primary questionnaire

This questionnaire addresses all the key requirements of QS-9000 and reflects the type of questions your management should answer when embarking upon a program to introduce QS-9000. It will help them determine their quality policies. If your business is the provision of services rather than products then replace the word *product* with *service* in the following questions.

1 How do you ensure that your policy for quality is understood, implemented, and maintained at all levels in the organization?

2 Where do you define the responsibility, authority, and interrelation of all personnel who manage, perform, and verify work affecting quality?

3 How do you ensure that resources are adequate for management, performance of work, and verification activities?

4 How do you organize and control the various disciplines assigned to the design, development, prototyping, and production phases of a product?

5 Who have you appointed to ensure that the requirements of QS-9000 are implemented and maintained and for reporting on quality system performance?

6 How does your management ensure the continuing suitability and effectiveness of the quality system?

7 How do you conduct business planning and ensure the defined goals are achieved?

8   How does your performance compare with that of your competitors and what systems are employed to ensure the validity of the data used?

9   What methods are used to plan and control the development, prototyping, and production phases of a product?

10 Which documents constitute the system you employ to ensure that product conforms to specified requirements?

11 How do you ensure that customer requirements are adequately defined and that you have the capability to meet them?

12 How do you control, verify, and validate product design?

13 How do you ensure that customer approval of production parts is obtained before shipping production product and introducing any changes?

14 How do you control documents and data that relate to the requirements of QS-9000?

15 How do you ensure that purchased product conforms to specified requirements?

16 How do you verify, store, and maintain customer supplied product?

17 What means are used for identifying the product?

18 How do you ensure that production, installation, and servicing processes that directly affect quality are identified, planned, and carried out under controlled conditions?

19 How do you ensure that production processes are capable of yielding products of consistent quality?

20 How do you ensure that manufacturing plant, facilities, tooling, techniques, and equipment are effective in optimizing the utilization of resources?

21 How do you ensure that product is not used, processed or dispatched until verified as conforming with specified requirements?

22 How do you control, calibrate, and maintain devices used to demonstrate conformance of product with specified requirements?

23 How do you minimize the variation present in each type of measurement process?

24 How do you identify product in a way which indicates its conformance or nonconformance with regard to inspections and tests performed?

25 How do you ensure that product which does not conform to specified requirements is prevented from inadvertent use or installation?

26 How do you prevent the recurrence of nonconformities?

27 How do you detect and eliminate potential causes of nonconformance and prevent their occurrence?

28 How do you prevent damage or deterioration of product in handling, storage, and delivery?

29 How do you ensure 100% on-time delivery to customers?

30 How do you verify whether quality activities comply with planned arrangements and determine the effectiveness of the quality system?

31 How do you identify training needs and ensure that personnel performing specific assigned tasks are qualified on the basis of appropriate education, training, and/or experience?

32 How do you ensure that servicing is performed, reported, and verified in a way that meets the specified requirements?

33 How do you control the selection and application of statistical techniques required for verifying the acceptability of process capability and product characteristics?

34 What philosophy is employed to ensure continuous improvement in quality, service, and price for all customers and how are improvement projects identified and implemented?

Part 2

Satisfying QS-9000 requirements

Foreword

This part of the book addresses each subsection of section 4 of QS-9000 and analyzes the principal requirements, each taking a separate chapter, 23 in total. Within each chapter there is an explanation of the scope of the requirements in terms of what they apply to, their purpose and meaning. Where the requirements omit aspects that should be considered, these are also addressed. Each chapter then addresses the individual requirements of each subclause of the standard by dissecting them into their component parts. The subheadings act as indicators to the subject of the requirement. Recommendations are given for implementation of each individual requirement, the procedures to be produced, the aspects which are important, and problems to look out for. Examples are given for both products and services in most cases, but as the size of the book is somewhat limited, it has not been possible to cover a wide range of examples. The principle adopted has been to interpret the requirements as they are stated and not as one might like them to be stated. Much may be implied by the standard but if it is not stated it is not a requirement and no competent Assessor should insist on a company taking corrective action against nonconformities that do not exist.

At the end of each chapter is a task list which summarizes the main tasks that need to be carried out to fulfill the requirements. Where a task list is given within the chapter this is not repeated. Care should be taken when using the task list as it is not exhaustive and does not list tasks in any particular sequence. It is admitted that these lists focus on hardware, since the vast majority of applications for QS-9000 are in the hardware sector.

Next is a questionnaire which only covers the specific requirements of the standard. This breaks down the requirements into their individual components where it is likely that the solutions for each part will be different. It can be used as a basic check list for verifying that the quality system you have designed addresses all of the requirements, or as a means of creating policy or of assessing conformity.

At the end of each chapter is a list of do's and don'ts, which attempts to identify some of the principal things that you should and should not do. Again it summarizes much of the advice given within the chapter but often includes aspects that have not been covered.

Doing all the things that are listed will not guarantee QS-9000 registration, but not doing any of them will almost certainly guarantee failure.

Quality management is not an exact science. There are no hard and fast rules. Each situation in each organization will produce new problems which demand perhaps different solutions to those that are presented here. The knowledge that has enabled this book to be produced was gained over a period of 25 years in industry, mainly in the "high tech" field but subsequent consultancy and training assignments in a range of industries in Europe, USA, the Middle East, India, and South East Asia has added greatly to this knowledge. When management is receptive and unquestioning, you may wonder what all the fuss is about. But there will be many out there who are having difficulty in convincing their managers of the need for some of the things that have to be done to meet the requirements of QS-9000. It is hoped that the following chapters will provide solutions to those who have problems and forearm those who do not.

Chapter 1

Management responsibility

Scope of requirements

The requirements for management responsibility do not prescribe any particular organization but are rules that govern the management and allocation of work. They apply to all levels of management and supervision although where the organization is divided into separate divisions, groups, or departments, there may be justification for limiting some of the requirements to specific levels. The requirements should not be seen as all embracing as there are many other rules that ought to be followed if an organization is to become a world leader. They apply only to quality responsibilities and not to other responsibilities, although it may be difficult to separate them. These requirements are amongst the most important in the standard. Without management's acceptance of responsibility for quality, its achievement, control, and improvement, quality will remain an illusive goal.

Unlike other sections of the standard, section 4.1 does not contain any requirement for documented procedures. It is not mandatory that you have documented procedures for forming the quality policy and the quality objectives, defining the responsibility of personnel, identifying resources, or conducting management reviews. However, section 4 of the standard is titled *Quality System Requirements* and section 4.2 requires that a quality manual be prepared covering the requirements of the standard. It follows therefore that you have to address the requirements of section 4.1 in your quality manual. You have a choice of how you address the requirements providing they are documented.

The requirements in element 4.1 are linked with other elements of the standard even when there is no cross reference. This relationship is illustrated in Figure 1-1.

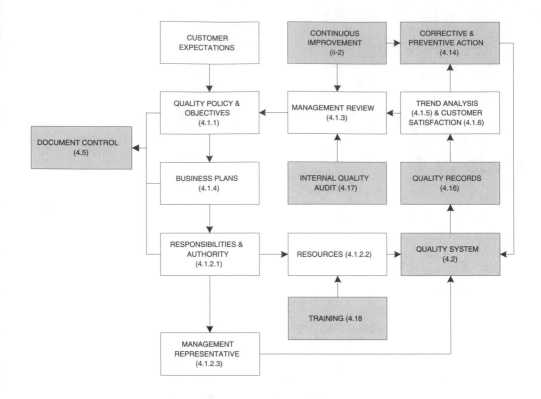

Figure 1.1 Element relationships with the management responsibility element

Quality policy

Although under a single heading of *Quality Policy*, this clause in fact contains three quite different requirements: one concerning policy, another concerning objectives, and a third on commitment. You can have policies on setting objectives but commitment is not something for which you can legislate (more on this later).

Defining policies

The standard requires that *the supplier's management with executive responsibility define and document its policy for quality*.

Executive responsibility
Before examining what is meant by policy, QS-9000 specifically refers to management with executive responsibility. Management is such a general term that it could apply to almost any group of persons with staff reporting to them. Those managers with executive responsibility sit at the top of the tree. These are the people who make policy decisions affecting the whole organization and may include the person with the title Quality Manager, but will not and should not be exclusive to this position. One reason

for specifically requiring management with executive responsibility to define the quality policy is that if it is defined at some other level there may well be conflict with the organization's other goals (see later).

In order to clarify who in the organization has executive responsibility, it will be advantageous to specify this in the quality manual. It is then necessary to ensure that the positions of the personnel appointing the Management Representative and reviewing the quality system are those persons with executive responsibility. In some organizations, there are two roles, one of Management Representative and another of Quality Manager, with the former only having executive responsibility.

Types of quality policy

You will note that the heading of this section of the standard is *Quality Policy*, and not *Quality Policies*, as if there should be only one policy. Many companies do have a single quality policy statement at the front of their quality manual, but this is more of a quality philosophy than a policy which will guide conduct (see also *Commitment*).

Any statement made by management at any level which is designed to constrain the actions and decisions of those it affects is a policy. QS-9000 could therefore be requiring policy on quality at all levels to be defined. It is only by consulting ISO 8402 that the level of policy required is clarified.

ISO 8402 defines quality policy as the overall quality intentions and direction of an organization with regard to quality, as formally expressed by top management, and it adds that the quality policy forms one element of corporate policy and is authorized by top management. The quality policy that is required to be defined is therefore the corporate quality policy and not lower level policies. However, there are different types of policy and it is important that they are not confused so that a policy purporting to be a quality policy is actually an operational policy, marketing policy etc.

- Government policy, which applies to any commercial enterprise

- Corporate policy, which applies to the business as a whole and may cover, for example:

  * Environmental policy – our intentions with respect to the conservation of the natural environment

  * Financial policy – how the business is to be financed

  * Marketing policy – to what markets the business is to supply its products

  * Investment policy – how we are to secure the future

* Expansion policy – the way in which we are to grow, both nationally and internationally

* Personnel policy – how we are to treat our employees and the labor unions

* Safety policy – our intentions with respect to hazards in the work place and to users of our products

* Social policy – how we are to interface with society

* Quality policy – our intentions with respect to meeting customer requirements

- Operational policy, which applies to the operations of the business, such as design, procurement, manufacture, servicing, quality assurance etc. and may cover, for example:

* Pricing policy – how the pricing of products is to be determined

* Procurement policy – how we are to obtain the components and services needed

* Product policy – what range of products the business is to produce

* Inventory policy – how we are to maintain economic order quantities to meet our production schedules

* Production policy – how we determine what we make or buy and how the production resources are to be organized

* Servicing policy – how we are to service the products our customers have purchased

- Department policy, which applies to one department, such as the particular rules a department manager may impose to allocate work, review output, monitor progress etc.

- Industry policy, which applies to a particular industry, such as the codes of practice set by trade associations for a certain trade

In the context of QS-9000, the quality policy referred to in clause 4.1.1 is one of the corporate policies. It is characterized by a single policy statement which declares the organization's commitment to quality and the strategy adopted to discharge this commitment.

Does QS-9000 require the other types of policies to be defined and documented? There is no requirement in clause 4.1.1 but in clause 4.2.2 there is a requirement to prepare a quality manual covering the requirements of the standard and this is where you should document your operational policies. While the quality manual could simply contain the quality system procedures, the guidelines given in ISO 10013 clearly indicate that whether or not this is the case, the manual should describe the organization's policies for meeting the requirements of the standard. These aspects are addressed in Part 2 Chapter 2.

Subject matter of corporate quality policy

The following are some typical quality policy statements:

* *We will perform exactly like the requirement or cause the requirement to be officially changed.*

* *We will satisfy our customers' requirements on time, every time, and within budget.*

* *Our aim is to give customer satisfaction in everything we do.*

* *We shall not knowingly ship defective products.*

Some quality policy statements are as simple as these, others are much longer (see below) but all seem to be accommodated by a single page. Very short statements tend to become slogans which people chant but they rarely understand their impact on what they do. Their virtue is that they rarely become outdated. Long statements confuse people because they contain too much for them to remember. Their virtue is that they not only define what the company stands for but how it will keep its promises.

NISSAN UK's Quality Policy

We will comply with NML's policies and procedures for quality assurance activities. In addition we will develop our own ideas to improve upon NML requirements. We will set quality targets and objectives in line with corporate standards. In support of achieving customer satisfaction we will seek to achieve product conformity by carrying out quality assurance activities at all stages of vehicle manufacture – from planning through to vehicle sales.

These activities will involve all relevant departments based on the concepts of the Plan, Do Check, Action Cycle, Right First Time, and that each employee has a role to play in achieving product quality.

NISSAN UK's Quality Philosophy

We aim for total customer satisfaction. Customers are those who buy our products; our suppliers, our staff and all people with whom we have contact. We will treat each other with care and respect and strive for excellence in all we do to provide a high level of service to all customers, internal and external. We will thereby provide finished products and services to the highest standards of quality, safety, reliability, and durability.

Delphi Chassis Systems Quality Policy

Delphi Chassis Systems will provide products and services to global markets that will meet or exceed customer expectations through people, teamwork, and continuous improvement.

Whilst these and many other contemporary quality policies would not have been publicized ten or so years ago, policy statements are not something new to the automobile industry. The General Motors of the 1920s under the direction of Alfred P Sloan used corporate policy as a means of coordinating the efforts of several divisions. GM's quality policy was to build quality products sold at fair prices and in setting up an Executive Committee Sloan wrote on the subject of quality, "A carefully designed policy should be enunciated that will convey to each division a complete understanding of the general quality of product that should be attained or maintained and all major alterations of design should be submitted to the Executive Committee for approval from this standpoint". He goes on to state: "In general, the activity of the Executive Committee should be guided along the lines of establishing policies and laying the same down in such clear cut and comprehensive terms as to supply the basis of authorized executive action ..." Clearly, this strategy focuses on the key purpose of the Executive Management in policy matters and is fundamental to creating the direction in which the organization is to pursue its business.

The purpose of corporate quality policies is to direct everyone in a particular direction regarding quality, to give them a sound basis for their actions and decisions. In the above cases, if you cannot meet the requirement then get it changed or hand the job to someone else. If by taking a particular action you will upset your customer then don't do it. One of the problems with such statements is that there will always be occasions when you can't adhere to the policy. When something goes wrong, as it always does, you may have to exceed the budget to put things right, to deviate from one requirement in order to meet another. It is no use management having a vision of a perfect world while having to work with imperfect people and materials. They have to accept human imperfections and compensate for them. Remember, the policy is only a guide. It is not a law, a rule that must not be broken. There is no penalty for not meeting the policy in one instance. However, if the policy is frequently not followed then slowly but surely the company will decline.

There is no guidance in QS-9000 on the subject matter of corporate quality policies. The wording of these corporate statements varies but they do seem to have certain characteristics. The organization's corporate quality policies may address some or all of the following:

- Declare the intention to satisfy customer requirements.

- Define who the customers are.

- Declare the position regarding the treatment of customers, employees, suppliers.

- Declare the intentions regarding investment in training, new technology, continuous improvement, and best practice.

- Declare the intentions regarding the law, national and international standards, industry practices, human safety, reliability, natural resource conservation, and the environment.

- Declare the intentions regarding the use of a documented quality system and its certification to national standards.

- Declare the scope of the policy and the quality system if applying to all operations of the business.

- Declare management commitment to the policy.

There are several things the policy should not include:

- Quantitative targets or limits, as these need to change and also tend to signal near enough is good enough

- The responsibilities of any particular manager, since implementation of the policy will become the burden of this manager rather than all the managers

- Any method for deviating from the policy, since it signals management flexibility and reduces the original intent

While it is important that management show commitment towards quality, these statements can be one of two things: worthless or obvious. They are worthless if they do not reflect what the organization already believes and is implementing and obvious if they do reflect the current beliefs and practices of the organization. It is therefore foolish to declare in your quality policy what you would like the organization to become. You have to be already doing it and publishing it merely confirms that this is your policy. If the organization does not exhibit the right characteristics then change the culture first before publishing the policy, otherwise you may create an impossible goal. Commitment and understanding are extremely important aspects in making the quality policy work and these are dealt with later in this chapter.

Defining quality objectives

The standard requires that the management with executive responsibility *define and document its objectives for quality*, but what are objectives for quality? The term is not defined in ISO 8402. QS-9000 requires you to define your policy for quality including your objectives for quality, implying that the objectives be included in your quality policy. If a separate statement of quality objectives is not required, the wording would have been "which shall include objectives for quality". However, ISO 9004 defines quality objectives as key elements of quality, such as fitness of use, performance, safety, and reliability. It also mentions the calculation and evaluation of costs associated with all quality objectives. It goes on to suggest that specific quality objectives be documented and be consistent with quality policy as well as other objectives of the organization. The guidance in ISO 9004-1 therefore indicates that quality objectives are not intended to be included in the quality policy statement. In fact the QS-9000 requirements for a Business Plan include among the typical contents "quality objectives". Reducing nonconformances, improving customer feedback, skill training, improving product reliability, reducing quality costs, TQM, and "Just-in-time" (JIT) programs are all quality objectives. They all aim to improve the ability of the organization to satisfy customer needs, but they are not limited to these subjects. Section II of QS-9000 includes a fairly comprehensive list of topics that could form the basis of quality objectives.

The requirement for defining objectives is one of the most important requirements. Without quality objectives there is nothing to aim for, the system becomes stagnant, there is no improvement and no indication of how well you are doing. There are two types of quality objectives, those serving the control of quality and those serving the improvement of quality.

The objectives for quality control should relate to the standards you wish to maintain, to prevent from deteriorating. At the corporate level these will be phrased in similar terms to the principal requirements given in Part 1 Chapter 2 and possibly some lower level requirements pertaining to specific characteristics such as safety and reliability or customer care.

Quality improvement objectives are often limited to reducing errors and reducing waste, but if we ask why a company develops new products and services, or breaks into new markets, we find that it is to create new customers and satisfy new needs and therefore they are setting quality objectives. You can improve the quality of your products and services in two ways: remove nonconformances in existing products (improving control) or develop new products with features that more effectively satisfy customer needs (improving performance). A product or service that meets its specification is only of good quality if it satisfies customer needs. Eliminating all errors is not enough to survive – you need to have the right products and services to put on the market.

There are five types of quality objectives:

- Objectives for business performance, addressing markets, the environment, and society

- Objectives for product or service performance, addressing customer needs and competition

- Objectives for process performance, addressing the capability, efficiency, and effectiveness of the process, its use of resources and its controllability

- Objectives for organization performance, addressing the capability, efficiency, and effectiveness of the organization, its responsiveness to change, the environment in which people work etc.

- Objectives for worker performance, addressing the skills, knowledge, ability, motivation, and development of workers

Whether you address all five of these subjects for quality objectives depends on your strategy. Many quality systems only address process performance and worker performance. Quality objectives for business performance and product/service performance are often known by different names. They should be contained in the Business Plan, the Marketing Plan or the New Product/Service Development Plan. They remain quality objectives wherever you put them.

Although ISO 9001 does not actually require you to plan and organize for meeting these objectives or in fact monitor their achievement, QS-9000 does. The subsequent requirement in clause 4.1.1 for the policy to be understood, implemented, and maintained does not apply to quality objectives or to commitment but this is not critical since other requirements on business plans and continuous improvement adequately overcome this inconsistency.

The key difference between setting policies and setting objectives is that policies remain in force until changed whereas objectives remain in force until achieved. You then go on to set new objectives. In this way a quality system can drive you forward towards world class quality. It is not a static system but a dynamic one if properly designed and implemented.

■ **Objectives are results to be achieved by a certain date.**

Commitment

The standard requires that *management with executive responsibility define and document its commitment to quality.*

As stated above, commitment is not something for which you can legislate. The management has to be committed to quality, in other words it must not knowingly ship defective products or give inferior service. It must do what it says it will do and no less. A manager who signs off waivers without customer agreement is not committed to quality, whatever the reasons. However, it is not always easy for managers to honor their commitments when the chips are down and the customer is screaming down the phone for supplies that have been ordered. The standard only requires that commitment is defined and documented. It does not require that it is honored or tested but that will emerge as objective evidence is gathered over a period of time. The proof that managers are committed to quality will be self evident from their actions and decisions. When they start spending time and money on quality, diverting people to resolve problems, motivating their staff to achieve performance standards, listening to their staff and to customers, then there is commitment. It will also be evident from the customer feedback, internal and external audits, and sustained business growth. Increasing profits do not necessarily show that the company is committed to quality. Profits can rise for many reasons, not necessarily because of an improvement in quality. Managers should not just look at profit results to measure the program's success. Profits may go down initially as investment is made in quality system development. If managers abandon the program because of short-term results, then it shows not only a lack of commitment but a lack of understanding. Every parent knows that a child's education does not bear fruit until he or she is an adult.

A commitment is an obligation that a person (or a company) takes on in order to do something. It very easily tested by examination of the results.

■   **Commitment means doing what you say, not saying what you do.**

A commitment exists if a person agrees to do something and informs others of their intentions. A commitment that is not communicated is merely a personal commitment with no obligation except to one's own conscience.

Commitment can be defined and documented either through the quality policy statement or through a Vision and Values Statement that defines management values with respect to:

* Doing what you say you will do

* Not accepting work below standard

- Not shipping product below standard

- Improving processes

- Honoring plans, procedures, policies

- Listening to the workforce

- Listening to the customer

Once communicated, a commitment can be tested by:

- Establishing if resources have been budgeted for discharging the commitment

- Establishing that resources are allocated when needed

- Establishing that performance of the tasks to which the person has given their commitment is progressed, monitored, and controlled

- Establishing that deviations from commitment are not easily granted

In managing a quality system such tests will need to be periodically carried out even though it will be tedious to both the person doing the test and the person being subjected to it. It is less tedious if such tests are carried out at each stage in the program and are a feature of the program that the management has agreed to, thereby making it impersonal and of mutual consent.

Many organizations document their commitment to quality by issuing a Corporate Policy Statement of the form described previously. These statements are really the creed or philosophy of the company and thereby a statement of the company's commitment to quality. However, any policy statement agreed by management is a commitment by the company, for example the principal managers signing the documents containing the corporate and operational quality policies. There does not have to be a single statement but if management declare their quality philosophy and display it in a prominent place, it can help focus attention.

A signed statement by management without its approval to the quality system documented policies and procedures will indicate that it is not committed to honoring the policies and procedures. Managers need to approve the documents within the quality system that prescribe activities for which they are responsible as a demonstration that they agree with the manner in which the policy has been interpreted and are prepared to provide the resources needed to implement the documented practices.

Ensuring the relevance of quality policy

The standard requires that *the quality policy be relevant to the supplier's organizational goals and the expectations and needs of its customers.*

The goals of the organization may be driving it in one direction and the quality policy in another. This situation can arise when the organizational goals are defined by top management and the quality policy by a lower level of management, as indicated previously. The only way to ensure there is no conflict is for the management that defines the organizational goals to either define the quality policy or ensure that it is not promulgated without their written permission.

Ensuring that the policy is relevant to the expectations and needs of the organization's customers is a little more difficult. The quality system need only ensure that product conform to specified requirements as stated in clause 4.2.1 of QS-9000. It does not require product to conform to customer expectations and needs but clearly if the specified requirements do not match customer expectations and needs then they are deficient. Companies have to predict what their customer expectations and needs are. They may be beyond what they specify in contracts although they may in fact be identical to such specifications. For companies to create satisfied customers they not only have to meet requirements specified by the customer but meet national and international legislation and have consideration for society's needs and expectations. As explained in Part 1 Chapter 1 on *Quality Characteristics*, customers are not only the buyers but comprise several other interested parties. You need to provide a means of determining what the customer expectations and needs are and then subject the written quality policy to a review against those expectations and needs to determine if there is any conflict. Although not a requirement of ISO 9001, the method of determining your customer expectations is a requirement of QS-9000 and is covered in clause 4.1.4. The management review (see later in this chapter) should perform this role but in addition any change to published quality policy should be reviewed by the same management that approved the original policy using the document control procedures (see Part 2 Chapter 5).

Ensuring that the policy is understood

The standard requires that the supplier *ensure that its quality policy is understood at all levels of the organization.*

This is perhaps the most difficult requirement to achieve. Any amount of documentation, presentations by management, and staff briefings will not necessarily ensure that the policy is understood. Communication of policy is about gaining understanding but you should not be fooled into believing that messages delivered by management are effective communication. Effective communication consists of four steps: attention, understanding, acceptance, and action. It is not just the sending of messages from one source to another. So how do you *ensure* (i.e. make certain) that the policy is understood?

Within your quality system you should prescribe the method you will employ to ensure that all the policies are understood at all levels in the organization, but it is not mandatory since all you have to document and define is the quality policy, the quality objectives, and your commitment to quality.

One method is for top management to do the following:

* Debate the policy together and thrash out all the issues. Don't announce anything until there is a uniform understanding among the members of the management team. Get the managers to face the question, "Do we intend to adhere to this policy?" and remove any doubt before going ahead.

* Announce to the workforce that you now have a quality policy that affects everyone from the top down.

* Publish the policy to the employees (including other managers).

* Display the quality policy in key places to attract people's attention.

* Arrange and implement training/instruction for those affected.

* Test understanding at every opportunity, at meetings, when issuing instructions/procedures, when delays occur, when failures arise, when costs escalate.

* Audit the decisions taken that affect quality and go back to those who made them if they do not comply with the stated policy.

* Take action every time there is misunderstanding. Don't let it go unattended and don't admonish those who may not understand the policy. It may not be their fault!

* Every time there is a change in policy, go through the same process. Never announce a change and walk away from it. The change may never be implemented!

* Give time for the understanding to be gained. Use case studies and current problems to get the message across.

The audit program is another method of testing understanding and is a way of verifying whether the chosen method of ensuring understanding is effective.

In determining whether the policy is understood, auditors should not simply ask "What is the quality policy?" All this will prove is whether the auditee remembers it. The standard does not require that everyone know the policy, only that it be understood. To test understanding therefore, you need to ask, for example:

- How does the quality policy affect what you do?

- What happens if you can't accomplish all the tasks in the allotted time?

- What would you do should you discover a nonconformity immediately prior to delivery?

- How would you treat a customer who constantly complains about your products and services?

- What action would you take if someone requested you to undertake a task for which you were not trained?

- What action would you take if you were requested to perform an important task on the day you were committed to carry out an internal audit?

- What action would you take if you noticed that someone was consuming food and drink in a prohibited area?

- What action would you take if you noticed that product for which you were not responsible was in danger of being damaged?

Ensuring that the policy is implemented

The standard requires that the supplier *ensure that its quality policy is implemented at all levels of the organization.*

Publishing the quality policy alone will not ensure it is implemented. People don't use such documents to carry out their duties. As stated previously, policies set boundary conditions for the actions and decisions and therefore it is through procedures that actions and decisions are taken. However, jumping from a corporate quality policy statement directly to procedures is often too large a step to take and most organizations introduce an intermediate level which we will call the operational policies. These are often documented in a quality manual (see Part 2 Chapter 2). Some procedures will implement a policy directly, other procedures may be constrained by many policies. It is therefore necessary to trace policies through to the procedures which serve to control work processes and in the review of these procedures ensure that the applicable policies have been complied with. In some cases no procedure may be necessary to implement a policy, its implementation being met by the existence of a record, a post in the management structure, a piece of equipment etc.

The quality system should be designed to implement the corporate quality policy and hence the operational policies need to be consistent with the corporate policy. Often the operational policies are merely a paraphrasing of the requirements of QS-9000 and in such cases there can be no direct relationship between the two. Care should be taken to ensure that there is traceability from corporate quality policy to operational policy and in doing so you may need to deviate from a strict paraphrasing of QS-9000. In fact paraphrasing QS-9000 is often not a suitable approach to take (see Part 2 Chapter 2).

■ *Ensuring* means *making certain* and you can't make certain without having control over that which causes the results.

Ensuring that the policy is maintained

The standard requires that the supplier *ensure that its quality policy is maintained at all levels of the organization*.

Maintenance is concerned with retaining something in or restoring something to a state in which it can perform its required function. However, the standard does not require that the maintenance of policy is to be preventive or corrective. In other words it does not require that maintenance of the quality policy should be carried out before or after it is changed. Even so, it is advisable to maintain documented policies in line with your beliefs and to do this:

- Don't change the policy by any other means than by changing the quality manual. Having declared that your quality policy is documented in the quality manual, you have imposed limits on what you can do. If you want to allow changes ahead of changing the manual, you will need to do it formally through a written procedure. It is unwise to permit the use of memoranda to promulgate policies as they are uncontrolled: much better to use a formal change notice. It should take no longer to produce, is official, and can be more easily controlled.

- Review the policy periodically to ensure that it remains current and relevant to the business (see later under *Management review*).

- Don't allow any deviations from the policy unless authorized in writing by those who sanctioned the original policy. By allowing deviations you are not maintaining the status quo. The requirement applies to defining and implementing as well as documenting the policies so the three have to be in concert.

The standard does not require you to document how you maintain your quality policy but the requirements of clause 4.5.1. place the quality policy into the category of documents which have to be governed by documented control procedures and hence all changes must be reviewed and approved.

Responsibility and authority

The requirements on responsibility and authority are in two parts: one general and the other relating to people with particular roles. Each is treated separately.

Identifying work that affects quality

The standard requires that *the responsibility, authority, and interrelation of personnel who manage, perform, and verify work affecting quality be defined and documented.*

The key to this requirement is determining what work affects quality, for if you can identify any work that does not affect quality, you are not obliged to define in your quality system the responsibilities and authority of those who manage, perform or verify it.

In principle, everyone's work affects the quality of the products and services supplied by the organization, some directly, others indirectly. Work can be divided into result-producing, support and housekeeping activities. All are essential to the business but only the result-producing and support activities affect the quality of the products and services supplied. The result-producing activities are those which directly bring in revenue and which contribute to results, such as sales, marketing, development, manufacture, and maintenance. The support activities are usually those which set standards, create vision, produce information needed by the result-producers, provide teaching, training, and advice, such as research, computer services, quality assurance, training, and personnel. Housekeeping activities are those which do not contribute to results but their malfunction could harm the business, such as health and safety, security, catering, travel, medical, general maintenance etc. Clearly some of these issues need to be addressed by the quality system since compliance with health, safety, and environment regulations are a requirement of clause 4.9 of QS-9000. If there are personnel involved with the identification, interpretation, promulgation, and verification of such regulations then their responsibilities and authority will need to be defined in the quality system.

What is "responsibility and authority"?

Defining the responsibility and authority of personnel can be achieved in several ways but first let's look at what we mean by *responsibility and authority*.

Responsibility is in simple terms an area in which one is entitled to act on one's own accord. It is the obligation of subordinates to their superiors for performing the duties of their jobs. It is thus the obligation of a person to achieve the desired conditions for which they are accountable to their superiors. If you caused something to happen then you must be responsible for the result just as you would if you caused an accident – so to determine a person's responsibility, ask "What can you cause to happen?"

Authority is in simple terms the right to take actions and make decisions. Authority in the management context constitutes a form of influence and a right to take action, to direct and coordinate the actions of others, and to use discretion in the position an individual occupies, rather than in the individual personally. The delegation of authority permits decisions to be made more rapidly by those who are in more direct contact with the problem.

It is necessary for management to define who should do what in order that the work to be done is assigned to someone to carry out. It is not cost effective to have duplicate responsibilities or gaps in responsibility since it leads to conflict or tasks not being done at all.

A person's job can be divided into two components: actions and decisions. Responsibilities and authority should therefore be described in terms of the actions assigned to an individual to perform and the discretion delegated to an individual: that is, the decisions they are permitted to take. In defining responsibilities and authority there are some simple rules that you should follow:

- Through the process of delegation, authority is passed downward within the organization and divided among subordinate personnel, whereas responsibility passes upwards.

- A manager may assign responsibilities to a subordinate and delegate authority; however, they remain responsible for the subordinate's use of that authority.

- When a manager delegates responsibility for something, they remain responsible for it. When a manager delegates authority they lose the right to make the decisions they have delegated but remain responsible and accountable for the way such authority is used. Accountability is one's control over the authority one has delegated to one's immediate subordinates.

- It is considered unreasonable to hold a person responsible for events caused by factors that they are powerless to control.

- Before a person can be in a state of control they must be provided with three things:

  i) Knowledge of what they are supposed to do: i.e. the requirements of the job, the objectives they are required to achieve.

  ii) Knowledge of what they are doing, provided either from their own senses or from an instrument or another person authorized to provide such data.

iii) Means of regulating what they are doing in the event of failing to meet the prescribed objectives. These means must always include the authority to regulate and the ability to regulate both by varying the person's own conduct and by varying the process under the person's authority.

- The person given responsibility for achieving certain results must have the right (i.e. the authority) to decide how those results will be achieved; otherwise, the responsibility for the results rests with those who dictate the course of action.

- Individuals can rightfully exercise only that authority which is delegated to them and that authority should be equal to that person's responsibility and not more or less than it. If a person has authority for action without responsibility, it enables them to walk by problems without doing anything about them. Authority is not power itself and it is quite possible to have one without the other. A person can exert influence without the right to exert it.

- In the absence of the delegation of authority and assignment of responsibilities, individuals assume duties that may duplicate those duties assumed by others. Thus jobs that are necessary but unattractive will be left undone. It also causes decisions to be made only by top management, resulting in an increasing management workload and engendering a feeling of mistrust in the workforce.

Defining responsibilities and authority

QS-9000 requires responsibilities and authority to be documented in addition to being defined, since one can define such things in dialog with one's subordinates without documenting them. This is indeed a common way for staff to discover their responsibilities. Sometimes you may not be aware of the limits of your authority until you overstep the mark. By documenting the responsibility and authority of their staff, a manager should be able to avoid such surprises.

There are four principal ways in which responsibilities and authority can be documented:

- In an organization structure diagram, or *organigram*

- In job descriptions

- In terms of reference

- In procedures

The standard does not stipulate which method should be used. In very small companies a lack of such documents defining responsibility and authority may not prove detrimental to quality provided people are adequately trained. However, if you are going to rely on training, then there has to be some written material which is used so that training is carried out consistently.

Organigrams are a useful way of showing interrelationships (see below) but imprecise as a means of defining responsibility and authority. They do illustrate the lines of authority and accountability but only in the chain of command. Although organigrams can define the area in which one has authority to act, they do not preclude others having responsibilities within the same area; for example, the title "Design Manager – Computer Products" implies the person could be responsible for all aspects of computer product design when in fact they may not have any software, mechanical engineering or reliability engineering responsibilities. Titles have to be kept brief as they are labels for communication purposes and are not usually intended for precision on the subject of responsibilities and authority. Organigrams are also an imperfect way of showing the true relationships of people within the company as they rarely show horizontal relationships. They should therefore not be used as a substitute for policy.

Job descriptions or job profiles are useful in describing what a person is responsible for; however, it rather depends upon the reason for having them as to whether they will be of any use in managing quality. Those produced for job evaluation, recruitment, salary grading, etc. may be of use in the quality system if they specify the objectives people are responsible for achieving and the decisions they are authorized to take.

Terms of reference are not job descriptions but descriptions of the boundary conditions. They act as statements that can be referred to in deciding the direction in which one should be going and the constraints on how to get there. They are more like rules than a job description and more suited to a committee than an individual. They rarely cover responsibilities and authority except by default.

Procedures are probably the most effective way of defining people's responsibilities and authority since it is at the level of procedures that one can be specific as to what someone is required to do. Procedures specify individual actions and decisions. By assigning a person to the action or decision you have assigned to them a responsibility or given them certain authority. Procedures do present problems however. It may be difficult for a person to see clearly what their job is by scanning the various procedures as procedures often describe tasks rather than objectives. One should not use names of individuals in procedures as they will inevitably change. The solution is to use position titles and then have a description for a particular position that covers all the responsibilities assigned through the procedures. Individuals only need to know what positions they occupy, and their responsibilities and authority are clarified by the procedures and the position descriptions.

There is a requirement in the Glossary of terms of QS-9000 for the quality manual to include responsibilities and authority for each element of the quality system. This is rather a futile requirement since elements are not necessarily processes, functions, or departments of an organization. For some elements, the assignment of responsibility may appear possible as in the case of element 4.4 on design control and 4.6 on purchasing, but when you come to look at it more closely you will find that it is not so easy. If we look at purchasing we find that it is made up of many actions and decisions, such as defining the technical requirement, evaluating the supplier, choosing the supplier, placing the order, monitoring the supply, inspecting the goods on receipt etc. No one person other than the CEO is responsible for all of these actions unless it is a small company. The Purchasing Manager may place the order on the subcontractor but may not accept responsibility for errors in the technical specification that was invoked in the order if he/she did not prepare or approve it. When auditors ask "Who is responsible for purchasing?" ask them to specify the particular activity they are interested in since you have an integrated system which delegates authority to those qualified to do the job. Providing the responsibility and authority for actions and decisions is defined and documented and the documents controlled through the quality system, then it matters not where they are defined.

Defining the interrelation of personnel

Defining individual responsibilities and authority alone will not define how personnel relate to one another. Interrelation means to place in mutual relationship, so what is needed is a definition of the relationships between staff with quality responsibilities. The primary reason for defining interrelationships is to establish channels of communication so that work proceeds smoothly without unplanned interruption. Staff need to know from whom they will receive their instructions, to whom they are accountable, to whom they should go to seek information to resolve difficulties, and to whom information or product should be submitted when complete.

Personnel within a company are related in several ways:

- By position in a reporting hierarchy

- By position in a chain of operations as internal customers and suppliers of information or products or service

- By position in a salary-grading structure

- By job title, profession, type of work

- By location, i.e. being on the same site but not in the same department, group, or division

In order for personnel to achieve a common objective (product or service quality) they must relate to one another – they must interact. Work passes from one person to another, from one department to another and often this relationship is quite different from the hierarchical relationship of personnel in the company. In order to meet this particular requirement it is therefore necessary to:

- Define the structure of the company, preferably in diagrammatic form showing each department and section whose work affects quality. You don't have to define all parts of the company.

- Define the location of work, departments, groups, and divisions.

- Define the processes that manage, specify, achieve, and control product/service quality and who performs each stage in the process, preferably in the form of flow diagrams.

An organization may respond to these requirements in several ways, so in managing the quality system a list of the documents needs to be produced that contains the definition of people's responsibilities and authority. The difficulty arises in keeping all such documents compatible and so it is often better to limit the documents to the three types above, if possible.

Personnel with organizational freedom

The second part of the responsibility and authority requirement requires the supplier to *define the responsibility, authority, and interrelation of personnel who need the organizational freedom and authority to*:

a) *Initiate action to prevent the occurrence of any nonconformities relating to product, process, and quality system.*

b) *Identify and record any problems relating to the product, process, and quality system.*

c) *Initiate, recommend or provide solutions through designated channels.*

d) *Verify the implementation of solutions.*

e) *Control further processing, delivery or installation of nonconforming products until the deficiency or unsatisfactory condition has been corrected.*

Who are these personnel who need organizational freedom and why do they warrant a special mention? This is not meant to imply that you should set up a separate quality department. The standard does not in fact require any personnel to have organizational freedom but it suggests that some people will *need* organizational freedom to do certain things.

Personnel who initiate action to prevent nonconformity

Initiating action to prevent something is not the same as preventing something from taking place. You can prevent something from happening either by not starting the process or by stopping it before a nonconformance has occurred. The only people who should prevent the occurrence of product or process nonconformity are those in control of the process – those operating the machines, producing the results, doing the work – or those people who manage or supervise such people. It would not be right for anyone not responsible for the process to exert power over it, such as stopping the process, or changing the material, the documentation, the instructions, or the personnel. In addition to the managers of the process, the management representative and the quality auditors should be given the authority to initiate action to prevent nonconformity (i.e. the organizational freedom) but if you do this, such authority should override that of those in control of the process. In other words if the auditor requires some action to be taken to prevent the recurrence of nonconformity, then he has to do more than notify those in control of the process, otherwise such notification could be ignored or any agreement abandoned. The reason for doing this is so that the management representative can discharge responsibility for *ensuring* that the requirements of the standard are met (see later in this chapter). Authority to initiate means authority to cause someone to take action. It does not give the initiator the right to specify what action to take. However, the receiver of the instruction must obey it or escalate it to higher management.

Regarding nonconformities relating to the quality system, anyone should be permitted to request a change to the quality system documentation to prevent the occurrence of nonconformities, however only a person's manager should be permitted to issue instructions to their staff enforcing compliance with the documented quality system. The management representative can and should, however, instruct other managers to comply with the agreed policies and practices.

Personnel who identify and record problems

A problem is the difference between the way things are and the way things ought to be, as perceived by the one identifying it. A problem relating to the product, process, or quality system (or quality problem) is therefore a difference between what has been achieved and what is required. There is no requirement in this clause for you to actually identify and record such problems (see below). You are only required to define the responsibilities and authority of those personnel in your organization who need to identify and record such problems.

Should anyone *need* organizational freedom and authority to identify and record problems? Any organization should provide an environment which encourages all employees to contribute to the business, but unfortunately this is not so in many organizations. There may well be some merit in limiting such freedom in order that management is not swamped with fictitious problems. It all comes down to deciding who is in a position to be able to tell whether a situation is a problem and whether it affects quality. Certainly managers and professional staff should be free to identify problems since they should have the knowledge to report only problems that can be resolved.

To provide staff with the necessary organizational freedom you will need one or more problem-reporting procedures and some policies that give staff the freedom to identify, record, and report problems relating to the product, process, and quality system.

The requirement does not cross refer to clause 4.16 on Quality Records clearly indicating that there is no requirement in this clause for problems to be recorded, as other clauses such as 4.10, 4.13, and 4.14 cover this. However, these clauses only relate to problems in not meeting the specified requirements and therefore may exclude types of problems not governed by specified requirements. So having identified the responsibilities of these personnel there may be no compulsion to provide a means for such problems to be documented, resolved, and prevented from recurrence.

Personnel who initiate, recommend or provide solutions
There is no requirement to implement solutions, only to initiate, recommend, provide, and verify them. Initiating, recommending, and providing have three quite different meanings. Initiating in this context means causing a solution to be implemented and has more power than a recommendation, which can be ignored, as can solutions provided by others. Managers of the functions concerned should have authority to initiate solutions to problems arising in their areas of responsibility. Experts and other personnel used in an advisory capacity should also be given authority to make recommendations and provide solutions. However, you may wish to limit such powers. You will not want just anyone to influence those resolving the problems. Those not qualified to give advice on certain subjects should not have authority to do so. There have been many cases where a person has taken unqualified advice to find that they should not have done so. Hence the requirement that solutions be provided through *designated channels*. You will therefore need some policy to ensure that the credentials of those giving advice are checked before the advice is accepted. Likewise, there should be a policy that ensures staff take the advice given by qualified personnel unless they can justify otherwise. There is no point in an organization employing experts and then allowing their advice to be ignored. If the experts are no good it is better to replace them!

Personnel who verify the implementation of solutions
The person resolving the problem should be the person who caused it or, if this is not possible or appropriate, it should be the person responsible for the result. This person should also verify that they have implemented the solution correctly, but there may be a need for others to verify that the solution resolves the problem. The person detecting the problem may be a customer. Quite often the solution implemented may not in fact resolve the original problem. This could be due to poor communication or to politics. In addition, the designer of the solution may decide to take the opportunity to change things that were perhaps not perfect but found them less costly to change in conjunction with other changes. Where such changes may result in the problem not

being solved it becomes more important that the verification be carried out by someone other than the designer. You will need to define who has the authority to verify certain types of solutions, such as new products, design changes, policy changes, planning changes, procedures changes, or process changes. They may be the same people who verified the original designs, plans, procedures etc. but could be different if you have a product support, maintenance, or post-design organization.

Personnel who control further processing, delivery or installation of nonconforming product

There are three separate requirements here. Control of further processing involves stopping the process and, as explained previously, should be carried out only by those responsible for the process. Controlling further delivery is somewhat different, as the authority to deliver may not be vested in the same person who performed the processing.

Delivery decisions are more than decisions about conformance to specification. They are about conformance to contract and those responsible for the production processes may not be able to determine whether contractual conditions have been met. Much more may hang on the resolution of a problem than mere conformance to specification. The decision in some circumstances may be taken by the CEO. There may have been a safety problem or a product liability problem so your system needs to recognize these fine distinctions. Those making the delivery decisions need possession of all the information required to protect the company as well as meet customer needs.

Installation decisions are similar to process decisions and the decision to start or stop further installation work should rest with those responsible for installation. If the materials have not been delivered they cannot be installed, so the key decision in this case is the delivery decision.

Resources

Identifying and providing adequate resources

The standard requires that the supplier *identify resource requirements for management, performance of work and verification activities and provide adequate resources.*

The term *resource* is often used to imply only human resources when there are in fact other types of resources. The standard is not specific although resources would normally include time, manpower, machines, materials, finance, plant, facilities: in fact, any means available to the supplier for implementing the quality system. So when QS-9000 requires that you provide adequate resources it requires that you provide all the human, finance, and material resources necessary to implement your quality system including the allocation of sufficient time.

Resource management is a common feature of all organizations and while it may be known by different titles, the determination and control of the resources to meet customer needs is a fundamental requirement and fundamental to the achievement of all other requirements. There are two types of resource requirements. Those needed to run the business and those needed to execute particular contracts or sales. The standard is not specific, but a glance at ISO 9004-1 will reveal that it is more than just the particular contract and less than needed to run the business. ISO 9004-1 limits the resources to those needed to implement the quality policy and meet quality objectives. It will be very difficult for companies to distinguish between those resources which serve quality and those which serve other objectives. There may be some departments that can be eliminated, such as the legal, insurance, catering, medical, or publicity departments, but in a company-wide quality culture all departments etc. will be included.

The way many companies identify resource requirements is to solicit resource budgets from each department covering a 1 to 5 year period. However, before the managers can prepare budgets they need to know what requirements they will have to meet. They will need access to the corporate plans, sales forecasts, new product development plans, marketing plans, production plans etc. as well as the quality policies, objectives, and procedures.

The standard does not require the resource requirements to be documented or that documented procedures be established and maintained for resource management, or that records of resource utilization be kept. However, without such documentation it will be difficult to demonstrate that you have allocated adequate resources to implement your quality system. Whilst clause 4.1.2.2 does not require resource plans to be documented, clause 4.1.4 does by implication that a business plan without a statement on resource provisions wouldn't be a business plan.

A practical way of ensuring that you have adequate resources to implement the quality system is to assign cost codes to each category of work and include the management and verification activities among these. Quality system management activities are often deemed as an overhead, but the costs may be difficult to identify among all the other overheads. Unless you can identify what you spent on internal audits, for instance, how can you allocate sufficient resources for future programs? Allocating and collecting costs does not inhibit you from moving resources around to resolve immediate problems and gives you more effective control of the business. Providing a means for staff to charge their time is often a practical way of overcoming resistance to the policies and procedures (see Part 1 Chapter 4 on the quality system development budget).

It is quite normal to provide sufficient resources to produce product. However, when it comes to verifying that you have done what you say you will do, there is a tendency to under estimate or to cut verification resources when costs escalate. These cuts are often seen as a risk worth taking. Another common weakness is defining requirements that are desirable rather than essential and then not verifying that they have been implemented. Being able to demonstrate provision of adequate verification resources is another sign of commitment to quality (see *Defining commitment to quality* above).

Assigning trained personnel

The standard requires that *trained personnel be assigned for management, performance of work and verification activities including internal quality audits*.

Training is covered by section 4.18 of the standard where it requires the training of all personnel performing activities affecting quality. However, the clause on resources gives a certain perspective to the identity of these personnel. They have to include management and verification personnel including internal auditors (further clarification is given in section 18 of ISO 9004-1). You are free to determine the training necessary for such personnel but it should be commensurate with the level of responsibility, the complexity of the task, and the experience and qualifications of the person.

It should be recognized that there is no requirement for auditors to be trained as Lead Assessors or Registered Internal Quality Auditors. Staff need only to be trained sufficient to carry out the task given to them.

Management representative

The standard requires that the supplier's management with executive responsibility *appoints a member of its own management with responsibility for ensuring that quality system requirements are established, implemented, and maintained*.

The requirements of QS-9000 do not apply solely to one department. Since everyone in some way contributes to the quality of the products and services provided by the supplier, everyone shares the responsibility for the quality of these products and services. Every manager within an organization makes a unique contribution towards the organization's purpose and mission. The achievement of quality, however, is everyone's job but only in so far as each person is responsible for the quality of what they do. You cannot hold each person accountable for ensuring that the requirements of QS-9000 are implemented and maintained, since the requirements apply to the organization as a whole and not to any specific individual. It is a trait of human nature that there has to be a leader for an organization to meet an objective. It does not do it by itself or by collective responsibility – someone has to lead; hence the purpose of this requirement.

Appointing a management representative

In the standard the term *management representative* appears only in the title of the requirement. The emphasis has been put on management appointing a member of its own management, indicating that the person should have a managerial appointment in the organization. This implies that the role cannot be filled by a contractor or external consultant. It also implies that the person should already hold a managerial position and be on the payroll. However, it is doubtful that the intention is to exclude a person from being promoted into a managerial position as a result of the appointment or in fact preclude the authority of the management representative being delegated to a contractor, providing responsibility for the tasks is retained within the company.

There are four issues here. What kind of person is needed? For how long is the person needed? Who makes the appointment? To what level in the organization should they report?

What kind of person?

If you can afford it, there are very good reasons for appointing a quality professional, someone who understands the standard and has held previous "quality" appointments at a professional level in your industry sector (see Part 1 Chapter 4). Opinions vary but it is often far easier to educate a quality professional in your business, providing the person has experience in your sector of industry, than to educate a non-quality professional in quality management. After all, you really need someone to guide you, to steer the design of the quality system, to identify problems and to offer solutions, not a helper but a leader. Someone who has no previous experience in this area is unlikely to be able to offer the right kind of guidance. When the size of the job doesn't warrant a full-time appointment it may be more practical to train an existing member of your management in quality management. There are several training courses and books which may provide the requisite skills and knowledge.

For how long?

You will need someone to manage the development, maintenance, and evaluation of the quality system. The person who manages the development may be someone different from the person who maintains and evaluates the system. As the quality system develops you can change horses to one more suited to the role. Initially you will need a person with project management skills, a leader of men, a driver, one who can manage change. Later you may only need a person who will keep things stable, under control. However, as your system will continually evolve to meet new challenges, it is never a job for a person without some project management and innovative skills. It is a permanent position. As long as you have a quality system you will need someone to take charge of it.

To what level should the person report?

The position needs to report at a level that will avoid conflicting responsibilities and enable the incumbent to exert some authority over every other manager, otherwise the person is an adviser and cannot ensure that the quality system requirements are established, implemented, and maintained. The person should report to the CEO, whatever the size of organization; however, it will depend on the management's perception of quality (see Part 1 Chapter 3). If quality is a big issue then the person should report to the CEO. If quality is a small issue then it is likely they will report to the manufacturing manager, customer service manager or development manager. The level to which they report tells you something about how the company views quality. It could, however, also reveal something about the style of management; for example, management may be too weak or benevolent to get rid of the present incumbent and prefer to wait until that person retires before making the appointment that would truly reflect the company's perception towards quality. The initial job may be small, just putting in a quality system for manufacturing. When it is decided to enlarge the function you can elect to give it a higher profile. But if someone is appointed without the necessary influence, quality will remain a small issue.

Who makes the appointment?

The appointment has to be made by top management since this person will be their representative. The decision should be made by the board of directors or their equivalent and the letter of appointment signed by the CEO. This gives it the required status and recognition.

Responsibilities and authority of the management representative

The standard requires that this person have *defined authority for ensuring that a quality system is established, implemented, and maintained in accordance with QS-9000, and for reporting on the performance of the quality system to management for review and as a basis for improvement of the quality system.*

Primarily, the person is the system designer for the quality system. This person may not produce the policies and procedures but operate as a system designer. This person lays down the requirements needed to implement the corporate quality policy and verifies that they are being achieved. It is also necessary to have someone who can liaise with customers on quality issues, who can coordinate the assessment and subsequent surveillance visits, who can keep abreast of the state of the art in quality management. The person should be an adviser to the top management who can measure the overall performance of the company with respect to quality.

To meet this requirement the management representative needs the right to:

- Manage the design, development, implementation, and evaluation of the quality system including the necessary resources (the management role)

- Determine whether proposed policies and practices meet the requirements of the standard, are suitable for meeting the business needs, are being properly implemented, and cause noncompliances to be corrected (the regulatory role)

- Determine the effectiveness of the quality system (the analysis role)

- Report on the quality performance of the organization (the scorekeeper role)

- Identify and manage programs for improvement in the quality system (the innovative role)

- Liaise with external bodies on quality matters (the role of ambassador)

Organizational interfaces

The standard requires *systems to be in place to ensure management of appropriate activities during concept development, prototype, and production using multidisciplinary approach for decision making and providing the ability to communicate information and data in the customer prescribed format.*

Reference is made in this requirement to the *Advanced Product Quality Planning and Control Plan* reference manual. What this implies is that the organization has to set up a product oriented team comprising staff from each of the disciplines that will be involved (a list of typical disciplines is given in the standard). These teams should be formed during the conceptual phase of product development and operate throughout the development and production phases. What is required is *project management* through development and *product management* through production. What is interesting about this list of disciplines is that it goes beyond product and process design. It also includes those disciplines involved with plant and facility design and maintenance and this is necessary because, in Section II, the requirements on manufacturing capability indirectly require a *Simultaneous Engineering* approach to development.

The standard requires *a system in place*, but what would constitute such a system? The organization maintains its line and staff departments and allocates staff to each product. Where the products of the organization cover several ranges then it is often practical to divide the staff into divisions each equipped with its own set of disciplines. Such a system would include:

- Policies that govern the allocation of work to the divisions.

- Policies that govern the allocation of work to staff in these divisions.

- Job descriptions for each role stating responsibilities, authority, and accountability.

- Procedures that identify the roles responsible for each task and for ensuring that information is conveyed to and from these staff at the appropriate time.

- Procedures that consolidate information from several disciplines for transmission to the customer when required.

- Monitoring procedures to track progress and performance.

- Procedures that ensure the participation of all parties in decisions affecting the product and its development and production.

- Procedures for setting priorities and securing commitment.

- Procedures that include the management of subcontractor programs during development and deal with the transmission of information to and from the subcontractors, what is to be transmitted, by who, in what form, and with whose approval.

Management review

Ensuring the continuous effectiveness of the system

The standard requires that *the quality system be reviewed at defined intervals sufficient to ensure its continuing suitability and effectiveness in satisfying the requirements of QS-9000 and the supplier's stated quality policy and objectives*.

Although termed a management review the requirement is strictly referring to a review of the quality system and not the Corporate Plan.

A review is another view of something. There is a need for the supplier's management with executive responsibility, as the sponsors of the system, to look again at the data the system generates and determine whether the system they installed is actually doing the job they wanted it to do. These are big issues and most of the time management only wants to be told of the exceptions. One of the reasons that the management review may not work is when it is considered something separate to management's job, separate to running the business, a chore to be carried out just to satisfy the standard. This is partially due to its perceptions about quality (see Part 1). If managers perceive quality to be about the big issues, like new product or service development, major investment programs for improving plant, for installing computerization etc., then the management review will take on a new meaning. If on the other hand it looks only at audit results it will not attract a great deal of attention, unless of course the audits also include the big issues.

The requirement for the review to ensure that the quality system satisfies the quality policy and objectives emphasizes that compliance with QS-9000 alone is insufficient and that the system has to meet business needs as well. However, the effectiveness of the system is dependent upon what you defined as its purpose. If the purpose of the system is merely to ensure customers are supplied with products and services which meet their requirements, then its effectiveness is judged by how well it does this and not how much it costs to do it. If on the other hand you develop a quality system with the purpose of minimizing waste, improving efficiency, reducing operating costs etc. (see Part 2 Chapter 2) then its effectiveness will be judged by how well it does these things. The standard does not simply require the system to be effective. It requires the system to be effective in satisfying the requirements of the standard and your stated policies and objectives. This is measurable, whereas the former statement is not. (See also Part 1 Chapter 1 for a means of measuring system effectiveness.)

As stated at the beginning of this chapter, there is no requirement for you to have a documented procedure for management review. However, you have to ensure that certain information is brought before the review and the review produces certain results. As you are going to conduct these reviews frequently you may want to ensure they follow a repeatable process and an obvious way to achieve this is through a documented procedure. There are three references to the management review in other sections of the standard: preventive action information (clause 4.14.3), internal audit results (clause 4.17), and changes to procedures (clause 4.14.1) are required to be submitted for management review.

The additional requirement in QS-9000 for the management review to include all elements of the entire system, rather than being limited to those specifically required in clause 4.14.3d and Note 20 does seem unnecessary. Its inclusion appears as a result of an ambiguity arising out of there being only two cross references to input data for management review in ISO 9001. The ISO 9001 requirement clearly states that the quality system has to be reviewed, not part of it, and if readers consult ISO 8402 for the definition of a quality system, then any ambiguity would be quickly overcome. ISO 8402 states that a quality system is the organizational structure, procedures, processes, and resources for implementing quality management. It therefore follows that in reviewing the quality system one needs to review each of these aspects.

The management review is not a meeting, although there may be a meeting to discuss the results and decide on any actions necessary. Management review is an activity aimed at assessing information on the performance of the quality system. The review therefore commences long before the meeting. A typical review process is illustrated in Figure 1.2.

The management review should do several things:

- Establish whether the system is being used properly.

  You can determine this by providing the results of all quality audits of the system, of processes and of products.

- Establish whether the audit program is effective.

  You can do this by providing the evidence of previous audit results and problems reported by other means.

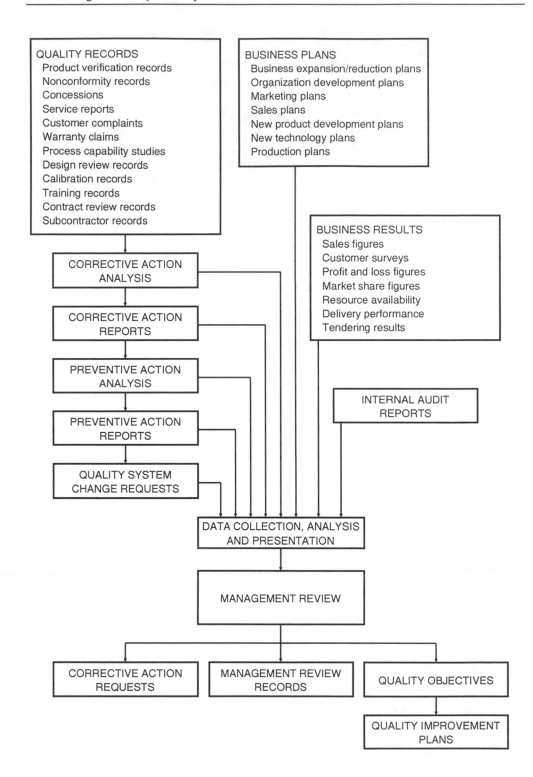

Figure 1.2 Management review process

- Establish whether customer needs are being satisfied.

  You can determine this by providing the evidence of customer complaints, market share statistics, competitor statistics, warranty claims etc.

- Establish whether the defined quality objectives are being met.

  Analysis of the data the system generates should reveal whether the targets are being achieved.

- Establish whether there is conflict between the stated quality policy, the quality objectives, and the organizational goals and expectations and needs of your customers.

- Establish whether the quality philosophy is being honored.

  An analysis of managerial decisions should reveal whether there is constancy of purpose or lip service being given to the policy.

- Establish whether the system requires any change to match changing business needs.

  You can do this by assessing the proposed changes in business against the known capability of the system.

- Establish whether the system provides useful data with which to manage the business.

  This can be done by providing evidence showing how business decisions have been made. Those made without using available data from the quality system show either that poor data is being produced or management is unaware of its value.

The key questions to be answered are: "Is the system effective?" and "Is it suitable to continue without change?" At every meeting of the review team these questions should be answered and the response recorded.

What are defined intervals?

The periodicity of management reviews should be matched to the evidence that demonstrates the effectiveness of the system. Initially the reviews should be frequent, say monthly, until it is established that the system is effective. Thereafter the frequency of reviews can be modified. If performance has already reached a satisfactory level and no deterioration appears within the next three months, then extend the period between reviews to six months. If no deterioration appears in six months extend the period to twelve months. It is unwise to go beyond twelve months without a review as something is bound to change which will affect the system. Shortly after a reorganization, the launch of a new product/service, breaking into a new market, securing new customers etc., a review should be held to establish if performance has changed. After new technology is planned then a review should be held before and afterwards to measure the effects of the change. Your procedures need to state the criteria for scheduling the reviews. Don't set them at a specific period, other than a maximum interval, since it limits your flexibility. You can define the interval between reviews in the minutes of the review meeting, thereby giving you the flexibility to change the frequency when desirable.

Maintaining records of management reviews

The standard requires that *records of management reviews be maintained*.

The standard does not specify what should be recorded. A note from the CEO stating when the review was held, who attended, and what the conclusion was meets the standard providing it is identified, indexed, filed, and stored etc. in accordance with clause 4.16. However, to demonstrate that the review of the quality system has been effective you have to do more than this. Such records need to identify the matters reviewed, the results, the actions, and the decisions taken together with the names of those responsible and the date by which actions are to be completed. The records should also contain the data used to conduct the review as the basis upon which the decisions have been made and so that comparisons can be made at later reviews when determining progress. Finally, the records should declare the extent to which the quality system is meeting its objectives and is effective in maintaining control.

Business planning

Business plan utilization

The standard requires that *a formal, documented, comprehensive business plan be utilized* and lists several aspects which should be included.

Whilst the plan itself is not auditable by third parties, it may be auditable by second parties i.e. customers. The third party or registrar is entitled to examine the plan to ascertain that it is what it proclaims to be. The particulars are of no concern except those aspects relating to quality such as the resources, quality objectives, customer satisfaction plans, performance metrics. Whatever is stated on these aspects, the auditor will expect to see evidence that they are not merely wish lists and have substance by being implemented through the quality system.

It should be noted that the business plan is a document that relates to the requirements of the standard and therefore should be under document control although you may want to provide different document control procedures to those used for other documents.

Determination of goals and plans

The standard recommends that *goals and plans cover short-term and longer term and be based on analysis of competitive products and on benchmarking inside and outside the automotive industry and the supplier's commodity.*

Although only a recommendation, you have to meet the intent of the clause whether or not you perform benchmarking. To demonstrate intent, you need to define how you set the goals and formulate the plans. Such a description could be included in a business planning procedure covering the topics listed in the standard and stating how each is to be determined.

Determination of customer expectations

The standard requires *the determination of current and future customer expectations using an objective and valid process to collect information at a defined frequency.*

As part of your business planning procedure you should indicate how you determine your customer expectations. As was mentioned under the *relevance of quality policy*, you cannot ensure the policy is relevant unless the customer expectations are documented and there is a formal method in place to define them. One method of establishing customer's current expectations is to conduct customer surveys coupled with an analysis of complaints. Asking questions that reveal their priorities, their preferences, their desires, their unsatisfied wants will provide the necessary information. Information on the distribution of the ultimate customers with respect to location, occupation, life style, spending power, leisure pursuits etc. will enable the size of market to be established. Asking questions about their supplier preferences and establishing what these suppliers provide that you don't provide is also necessary.

Customers will expect more than they will require. Expectations are brought about by experience. One experiences what features are currently available and begins to expect them in every automobile. Knowing what the customer will pay more for is also necessary since many will expect features that were options to be provided as standard. The procedure needs to provide for the analysis to be continual, i.e. performed at regular intervals.

Adhering to the business plan

The standard requires *methods to track, update, revise, and review the business plan to ensure it is adhered to and communicated throughout the organization.*

A plan is more than a list of goals, a bar chart, or schedule of activities. For the business plan to be effective it needs to define how the measures it covers are to be achieved and the resources to achieve them obtained. There may well be supplementary plans for this purpose. The plan or plans also need to define who is to be responsible for achieving the goals and implementing the plans. Once this is done and the provisions communicated to those affected, a method of tracking achievement can be put in place. To track performance effectively the implementation of the plan needs to be phased such that target dates are set for the determination and acquisition of resources, the issue of detail implementation plans, the organization of work and completion of individual tasks.

It is often the case in business that strategic plans remain unchanged even though circumstances may change and that business planning is an annual event rather than a continual event. QS-9000, however, does not permit this approach as it requires the plan to be updated, revised, and reviewed. Suppliers therefore need to schedule regular reviews of the plan and progress of its implementation. Most organizations will already perform monthly or quarterly business reviews so this requirement will not be onerous apart from that of updating and revising the plan. The terms *update* and *revise* may appear to be one and the same requirement. However, update means keeping current so that it reflects current circumstances, whereas revise means to change for whatever reasons some of which may not arise out of current circumstances, such as extending the scope of the plan, correcting errors, refining objectives and goals as more accurate data emerges.

Communicating the plan throughout the organization may call for some prudence. The standard does add the rider "as appropriate" so you do not have to send copies of the plan to everyone – only those who have a responsibility to implement it. Where staff are assigned responsibilities for implementing parts of the plan through other directives, then they only need that which is essential to their needs and no more. This does require, however, that should data be taken from the plan and conveyed to staff in another form, e.g. in a task directive, then you have to maintain control of the data so that, if as a result of the business planning review, the data changes, the data in the task directives needs to be also changed. This is governed by clause 4.5.1 of the standard.

Company level data

Analysis and use of company level data

The standard requires *trends in quality operational performance and current quality levels for key product and service features to be documented.*

This requirement is similar to that in clause 4.14.3 under preventive action since the data collected for preventive action serves a similar purpose. In one case an analysis of company level data serves to identify overall trends and predict potential failures that will affect achievement of the goals. In the preventive action case, the data serves to identify local and overall trends and predict potential failures that will affect achievement of specified requirements for the product, process, and the quality system. It would be sensible to develop a data collection and analysis system that served all levels in the organization with criteria at each level for reporting data upwards as necessary. You should not treat this requirement totally separate from that for preventive action since the same data should be used. Using different procedures may create conflicting conclusions. A general plan of action would cover the following:

• Identify the key parameters to be measured.

• Locate where in the process they are achieved.

• Install data collection method in relevant procedures.

• Collect and analyze the data.

• Use suitable presentation techniques to draw attention to the results.

• Determine priorities.

• Get management buy-in to action.

In collecting the data care should be taken to avoid data paralysis (see Part 2 Chapter 14). The various quality tools can be used to prioritize the identified problems and corresponding decisions. As with all data collection tasks, you should show a direct correlation between what you are collecting and the goals to be achieved and all conclusions should lead to positive action otherwise the effort has been futile.

Customer satisfaction

Determining customer satisfaction

The standard requires *a documented process for determining customer satisfaction, including frequency of determination and how objectivity and validity are assured.*

One way of meeting this requirement is to do the following:

• Seek the opinions of customers about the products and services provided through questionnaires.

• Seek opinions from the people within the customer organization such as Marketing, Design, Purchasing, Quality Assurance, Manufacturing etc.

• Target key product features as well as delivery, price, and relationships.

• Collect and analyze customer feedback over the intervening period, particularly complaints to target areas for improvement.

- Conduct customer focus meetings to gather opinion and recommendations for action using data gathered from questionnaires and periodic feedback.

- Report back the findings to particular customers to secure understanding.

- Summarize the data to identify trends and conditions that indicate improvement opportunities.

- Compute customer satisfaction indices as an aid to measuring change.

- Use the data to derive the business, product development, and quality plans for current and future products and services.

To document this process you should develop a customer satisfaction procedure that details:

- The sources from which information is to be gathered and the forms and questionnaires to be used

- The actions and decisions to be taken and those responsible for the actions and decisions

- The methods to be used for computing the customer satisfaction index

- The records to be created and maintained

- The reports to be issued and to whom they should be issued

A customer satisfaction index that is derived from data gathered by independent organizations would indeed be more objective than that created by the organization it measures. Such schemes are in use in North America, Sweden, and Germany. A method developed by a Professor Claes Fornell has been in operation for eight years in Sweden and is now being used at the National Quality Research Center of the University of Michigan Business School. Called the American Customer Satisfaction Index (ACSI) it covers seven sectors, 40 industries, and some 200 companies and government agencies. It is sponsored by the ASQC and the University of Michigan Business School with corporate sponsorship from AT&T, General Motors, and others. Using data obtained from customer interviews, sector reports are published indicating a CSI for each listed organization thereby providing a quantitative and independent measure of performance of use to economists, investors, and potential customers.

Customer dissatisfaction indicators

The standard requires *trends in customer satisfaction and key indicators in customer dissatisfaction to be documented and supported by objective documentation.*

To determine trends in customer satisfaction you will need to make regular surveys and plot the results preferably by particular attributes or variables. The factors will need to include quality characteristics of the product or service as well as delivery performance and price. The surveys could be linked to your improvement programs so that following an improvement and allowing sufficient time for it to be observed by the customer, customer feedback data could be secured to indicate the effect of the improvement.

Customer dissatisfaction will be noticeable from the number and nature of customer complaints collected and analyzed as part of your corrective action procedures (see Part 2 Chapter 14). This data provides the objective documentation or evidence and again can be reduced to indices to indicate trends.

The note following this requirement refers to both intermediate and final customers. Most of your data will emanate from your immediate customers, one of the Big Three. By targeting the final customer using data provided by your customers, you will be able to secure data from the users but it may not be very reliable. A nil return will not indicate complete satisfaction so you will have to decide whether the feedback you get is significant enough to warrant attention. Using statistics to make decisions may not be a viable approach since you will not possess all the facts.

Task list

1   Define, agree, and publish your corporate quality policy.

2   Define, agree, and publish operational policies for meeting each of the requirements of the standard and publish them in a Policy Manual.

3   Define your quality objectives, document and publish them in the Business Plan.

4   Initiate seminars and meetings to gain understanding of the policies and objectives.

5   Define management values.

6   Audit commitment and understanding of the policies and objectives periodically.

7   Establish customer needs and expectations and define organizational goals and record them in the business plan.

8   Introduce a procedure for changing and deviating from the agreed policies.

9   Conduct periodic reviews of your policies and objectives.

10   Create, agree, and publish rules for the assignment of responsibilities and delegation of authority.

11   Produce, agree, and publish organization charts.

12   Produce, agree, and issue to those concerned job descriptions for each defined position.

13   Ensure responsibilities are clearly understood and documented and clarify who is accountable for the resolution of quality problems.

14   Check that authority matches responsibility.

15   Produce, agree, and publish flow diagrams of the processes that contribute to the achievement of quality and identify the interfaces and responsibilities.

16   Produce and agree resource budgets for management, productive work, and verification activities.

17 Assign trained personnel to all tasks.

18 Create staff lists that indicate competency to perform tasks and use techniques within a job.

19 Create team management procedures that define interfaces with line departments, customers, and suppliers.

20 Appoint a management representative to manage the quality system and define, agree, and publish the responsibilities and authority.

21 Provide for assignment of staff to cross-functional teams and monitor their performance.

22 Collect and analyze data on quality performance.

23 Conduct periodic reviews of the quality system using the collected data.

24 Carry out corrective actions to improve the effectiveness of the quality system.

25 Maintain records of the management reviews.

26 Prepare business plans for each aspect of the business where performance is critical to its success.

27 Carry out competitor analysis and benchmarking inside and outside the company.

28 Create procedures for determining customer expectations.

29 Create procedures for developing and maintaining business plans.

30 Create procedures for determining customer satisfaction.

Management responsibility questionnaire

1   In what document is your corporate policy for quality and your commitment to quality defined?

2   In what document do you define your quality objectives?

3   How do you ensure that the corporate quality policy is relevant to your organizational goals and the expectations and needs of your customers?

4   How do you ensure that your corporate policy for quality is understood at all levels in the organization?

5   How do you ensure that your corporate policy for quality is implemented at all levels in the organization?

6   How do you ensure that your corporate policy for quality is maintained at all levels in the organization?

7   In what document do you define the responsibility and authority of personnel who manage, perform, and verify work affecting quality?

8   How do you ensure that, when needed, personnel have the organizational freedom to identify and record product, process, and quality system problems, provide solutions and initiate action to prevent the occurrence and recurrence of any nonconformities?

9   How do you ensure that those responsible for results have the organizational freedom necessary to control processing, delivery, or installation of product?

10 In what document do you define the interrelation of all personnel who manage, perform, and verify work affecting quality?

11 How do you identify resource requirements?

12 How do you ensure that adequate resources are provided?

13 How do you ensure that trained personnel are assigned for management, productive work, and verification activities?

14 Whom have you appointed to ensure that a quality system is established, implemented, and maintained?

15 How do you ensure your management representative remains a member of your own management?

16 In what document is the management representative's authority and responsibility defined?

17 What system is used for management of concept development, prototype, and production phases?

18 Which functions participate in decision making?

19 How does your management ensure the continuing suitability and effectiveness of the quality system?

20 What information is used to determine the effectiveness of the quality system?

21 What evidence demonstrates that your quality system is suitable and effective in satisfying QS-9000 and your stated quality policy and objectives?

22 In what documents are your business plans, goals, and objectives defined?

23 How do you determine the current and future expectations of your customers?

24 What methods are used to communicate, track, review, update, and revise your business plans?

25 In what documents are trends in operational performance and quality levels defined?

26 How do you determine customer satisfaction and dissatisfaction?

27 In what documents are trends and key indicators of customer satisfaction and dissatisfaction defined?

Do's and don'ts

* Do ensure everyone knows their responsibilities and what decisions they are permitted/not permitted to take.

* Do ensure the managers know their objectives and have plans to meet them.

* Do ensure signatures are legible and traceable to those with the necessary authority.

* Do ensure that job descriptions and procedures are compatible.

* Do ensure your staff know where to find the quality policies.

* Do ensure everyone knows the source of their requirements.

* Do ensure that everyone knows what to do if they can't meet the requirements.

* Do ensure there is no conflict between the responsibilities and authority of different managers.

* Do ensure staff know who has the right to stop the process.

* Do ensure you have sufficient resources to carry through your plans.

* Do give your management representative the teeth to get things done.

* Do keep the management reviews separate from other meetings.

* Don't issue edicts or directives that violate the declared policies.

* Don't write procedures that violate published policies.

* Don't publish policies that your managers cannot or will not abide by.

* Don't grant concessions without giving time limits and valid reasons.

* Don't sign documents unless you have the necessary authority to do so.

* Don't allocate funds for managing the quality system without providing a means of collecting the costs or time spent.

* Don't let your management reviews degenerate into a talking shop.

* Don't let the action list from the management review become a wish list!

Chapter 2

Quality system

Scope of requirements

Although there are only two basic requirements in QS-9000 for the establishment and maintenance of a quality system, they are perhaps the most important requirements of all. The quality system is a tool to enable you to achieve, sustain, and improve quality. It implements your quality policy and enables you to achieve your quality objectives either for control or for improvement. Quality systems, like any other system, have to be managed and so quality system management is a function of the business. This function consists of four principal processes:

- Quality system design and development, addressed by clauses 4.2.1 and 4.2.2

- Quality system implementation, addressed by clauses 4.2.2 and 4.18

- Quality system evaluation, addressed by clauses 4.1.3 and 4.17

- Quality system maintenance, addressed by clauses 4.2.1, 4.5, and 4.16

These elements of QS-9000 are linked together as shown in Figure 2.1. In the figure, Document Control and Management are functions common to other elements of the business, and the Education and Training process is shown separate since it operates in both the implementation and the design phase.

The standard does not require you to demonstrate that you meet all the requirements of the standard. It only requires a quality system to be documented, implemented, and maintained. While clause 4.16 on quality records does in fact require you to demonstrate the effective operation of the quality system, it does not dictate how you should do this. Since the purpose of the system is to ensure that product conforms to specified requirements, an unblemished record of zero customer complaints and a healthy order book would appear to indicate that your quality system is effective.

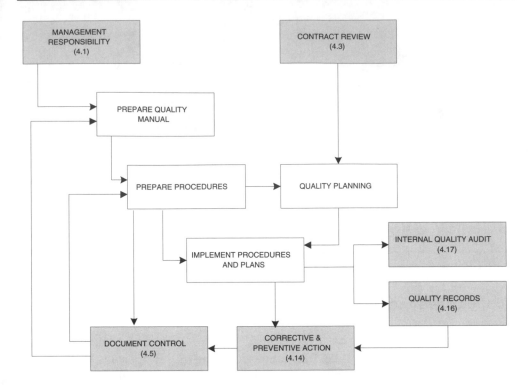

Figure 2.1 Element relationships with quality system element

Establishing a documented quality system

The standard requires suppliers to *establish and document a quality system as a means of ensuring that product conforms to specified requirements.*

To *establish* means to set up on a permanent basis, and the requirement therefore emphasizes that the quality system should not be temporary.

This requirement clearly defines the purpose of a quality system, that of ensuring that products conform to specified requirements. One of the principal differences between ISO 9000 and QS-9000 is the emphasis QS-9000 places on internal efficiency and effectiveness. The requirements covering continuous improvement, manufacturing capability, business plans etc. all drive improvement in efficiency and effectiveness making the purpose of a QS-9000 quality system much more than merely that of ensuring that product meets specified requirements.

One of the first decisions to take should be to define the purpose of the quality system, what you want it to do, why you want to create it. Your reasons for creating a documented quality system may be to:

- Ensure products and services satisfy customer requirements

- Maintain the standards which you have been successful in achieving

- Improve standards in those areas where performance is wanting

- Harmonize policies and practices across all departments

- Improve efficiency

- Create stability and minimize variance

- Eliminate complexity and reduce processing time

- Benchmark current performance

- Focus attention on quality

- Ensure products and services are delivered on time

- Reduce operating costs

These are only some of the reasons for creating a quality system. Whatever your reasons are, define and document them and review them often. When you evaluate the system these reasons will help determine whether your system is effective (see Part 2 Chapter 17).

A system is an ordered set of ideas, principles, and theories or a chain of operations that produces specific results; to be a chain of operations, the operations have to work together in a regular relationship. A quality system is not a random collection of procedures (which many quality systems are) and therefore quality systems, like air conditioning systems, have to be designed. All the components have to fit together, the inputs and outputs have to be connected, sensors have to feed information to processes which cause change in performance and all parts have to work together to achieve a common purpose: i.e. to ensure that products conform to specified requirements. You may in fact already have a kind of quality system in place. You may have rules and methods which your staff follow in order to ensure product conforms to customer requirements, but they may not be documented. Even if some are documented, unless they reflect a chain of operations that produces specific results consistently, then they cannot be considered to be a system.

Many suppliers to the Big Three will already have methods in place that cover most of the requirements of QS-9000. What they may not have done, however, is integrate these methods into a system that will cause conformity and prevent nonconformity. The ISO 8402 definition of a quality system makes it clear that a quality system is not just a set of procedures but the organization structure, processes, and resources to manage the achievement, control, and improvement of quality.

Preparing the quality manual

The standard requires the supplier to *prepare a quality manual covering the requirements of the standard* and also requires *the quality manual to include or make reference to the quality system procedures and outline the structure of the documentation used in the system.*

The structure of the quality manual

If we look at ISO 10013 which is referenced for guidance in preparing a quality manual, we will see that it shows that the quality manual is a top-level document containing the stated quality policy, the quality objectives, and a description of the quality system (see Figure 2.2). The definition in ISO 8402 supports this concept and the requirement aligns with this definition. However, ISO 8402, ISO 10013, and the above requirement from ISO 9001 provide a choice as to whether the manual contains or refers to procedures.

For a quality manual to be a manual it should contain the procedures and instructions as does a computer manual or a car maintenance manual, so whether one volume of the manual contains or refers to other documents does not prevent the collection of documents being referred to as the quality manual. Manuals tend to include operating instructions, hence the word *manual*. The quality manual should therefore contain all the policies and procedures but not necessarily in one volume.

Some organizations divide their quality system documentation into three levels, a quality manual, a set of operating procedures, and the support documentation. The manual would contain the policies, the procedures would prescribe the interdepartmental activities, and the support documentation would include work instructions, codes of practice, technical documents, and any other documents that are needed. This

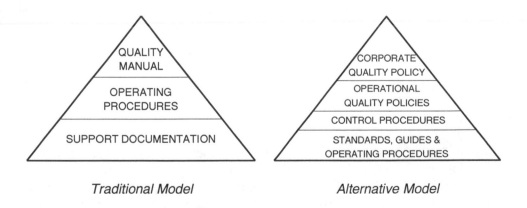

Traditional Model   *Alternative Model*

Figure 2.2 Levels of quality system documentation

is illustrated in Figure 2.2 as the Traditional Model. The Alternative Model is more realistic when the quality manual only contains the policies. In the alternative model, the complete model represents the quality manual.

The model given in QS-9000 is slightly different to that above (see Figure 2.3). If the corporate quality policy is included as a level (as it is the alternative model), then this becomes Level 0 in the QS-9000 model, although it can be confusing when mixing documentation levels and documentation manuals as they are not one and the same thing. The ISO 8402 definition of a quality manual is that it is a document stating the quality policy and describing the quality system of an organization. Clearly the description of the quality system is not complete unless it includes Levels 0, 1, 2, and 3.

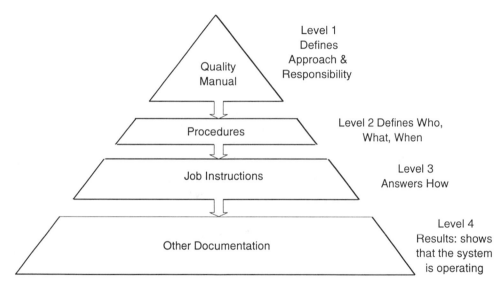

Figure 2.3 QS-9000 quality system documentation model

The QS-9000 model does possess some anomalies. Responsibility is not only defined in the quality manual but in the procedures. The quality manual should define more than an approach, it should define the operational policies for implementing the requirements of the standard.

Policies define *what* and procedures define *how* although it depends on the level of procedures. Control procedures will define what to control and in doing so will define how to control.

Job instructions will define how to perform specific jobs but will also define who, what, when, and how depending on the type of instruction (see under *What are the differences between procedures and instructions?* later in this chapter).

The term "Other Documentation" is rather vague since it is unclear whether it includes both prescriptive and descriptive documents. Anything that is produced by implementing a policy or procedure is a result, some of which are input documents to processes and others output documents from processes and some of these are prescriptive and others descriptive. (See also Part 2 Chapter 5.)

The 1987 version of ISO 9001 required the quality policy and the quality system procedures and instructions to be documented, clearly identifying three levels of documents; in practice organizations produced an intermediate level between the quality policy statement and the procedures which addressed the requirements of the standard and cross-referenced the associated procedures. This intermediate level together with the quality policy statement was often referred to as the quality manual. However, some manuals merely paraphrase the requirements of the standard, some describe the quality system, and others confine the manual to the organization's operational policies. The guidance given in clause 5.3.1 of ISO 9004-1 suggests that the quality system documentation consists of policies and procedures. Clearly these policies are of a somewhat lower level than the corporate quality policy addressed in Part 2 Chapter 1.

There is no requirement for you to state the policies to meet each clause of the standard but many organizations in fact do just this. QS-9000 requires the manual to cover the requirements of the standard and ISO 10013 gives an example of how this may be done. ISO 10013, however, points you in the direction of producing a quality manual which is structured in the sequence of the key elements of the standard rather than the operations of your business. This is fine for assessors but not for your staff, who will probably want to know your policy on some aspect of your operations in order to make a certain decision. This is where you need operational quality policies organized around the operations of the business – such an approach is deemed acceptable in ISO 10013.

It would be sensible to document your quality policies separately from your quality objectives and make these separate from the quality system itself. One way of achieving this is to have:

- A Policy Manual containing the corporate and operational quality policies

- A Business Plan containing the quality objectives (see Part 2 Chapter 1)

- A Quality System Manual containing a description of the system

- A Procedures Manual containing the documented procedures

The reason for a separate quality system manual is so that there is a description of the system showing how it works and how it controls the achievement of quality. This is different from the policies and procedures. The policies are a guide to action and decision and as such are prescriptive. The procedures are the methods to be used to carry out certain tasks and as such are task related. They need to be relatively simple and concise. A car maintenance manual for example tells you how to maintain the car but not how the car works. Some requirements such as those on traceability and identification cannot be implemented by specific procedures although you can have specific policies covering such topics. There is no sequence of tasks you can perform to achieve traceability and identification. These requirements tend to be implemented as elements of many procedures which when taken as a whole achieve the traceability and identification requirements. In order that you can demonstrate achievement of such requirements and educate your staff, a description of the system rather than a separate procedure would be an advantage.

Contents of the quality manual

* Introduction covering purpose, scope, applicability, and definitions

* Business overview describing the nature of the business (not required but extremely useful)

* Corporate policy covering the mission, vision, values, objectives, and quality policy

* Operational management covering planning, organization, and management control including quality system management, audits, reviews, and improvement

* Operational policies structured to align with the sequence of key processes from receipt of customer enquiry through to delivery and after sales support, referencing the implementing control procedures

* Cross reference matrix between manual and QS-9000

Operational policies

As stated in Part 2 Chapter 1, any statement made by management at any level which is designed to constrain the actions and decisions of those it affects is a policy. Policies serve to guide the actions and decisions required to achieve objectives and are not therefore objectives in themselves. Policies set boundary conditions so that actions and decisions are channeled along a particular path in pursuit of an objective. Many see policies as requirements to be met. They are requirements but only in so far as an enabling mechanism. Policies enable management to operate without constant intervention and once established enable others to work within a framework without seeking decisions or guidance from above.

Staff do not work to policies but in fact work in accordance with procedures which themselves direct actions and decisions within the framework of the stated policies. In order to make the decisions required of the procedures, staff will often need to know the company policy on a particular subject, such as procurement, recruitment, release of product, licencing agreements, agreeing design changes etc. Can they or can they not do something and if so what criteria would they satisfy?

When one deviates from procedure one may not in fact be violating a policy since the procedure may describe one of several ways of doing something. Should top management dictate that all work be conducted in accordance with certain procedures they have put themselves in a position of having to authorize deviations when the procedures cannot be followed. It is therefore more effective use of their time if top management prescribe the policies to be met by their direct subordinates rather than for all levels.

There are many sound reasons for documenting your operational policies:

- To translate corporate policy into practical terms which can be implemented through procedures.

- Every job has constraints surrounding it – without written policies people would be left to discover them by trial and error, the organization would become a disorganized mess, its managers lacking any means to direct and harmonize their staff's activities.

- Policies enable managers and their subordinates to be left in no doubt about what they are actually responsible for, the boundaries within which they have to work, and the demands upon them to which they can expect to respond.

- Policies set clear boundaries for people's jobs so that everyone knows in advance what response they will get from others when making decisions.

- Policies create a baseline to which subsequent change can be referred and enable changes in the way things are done to be clearly defined.

- Policies enable managers to determine whether a subordinate's action or decision was simply poor judgment or an infringement of the rules. If no rule existed, subordinates cannot be criticized for using their judgment, however poorly it is used. If a rule exists, one has to establish whether it was accidentally or deliberately broken, for the latter is a disciplinary offence. Without written policy no one knows where they stand and any decision may create an unwanted precedent.

- Policies provide freedom to individuals in the execution of their duties to make decisions within defined boundaries and avoid over-control by managers. If people are uncertain about where the limits of their job lie they cannot feel free to act. Without a clearly defined area of freedom there is no real freedom.

- Policies enable management to exercise control by exceptions rather than over every action and decision of their subordinates and therefore enable self-control by subordinates.

- Policies enable managers to control events in advance. Before the action begins, people know the rules and so are more likely to produce the right result first time. Without policies, one is forced to control events in arrears, after something has happened to cause dissatisfaction. Alternatively, one has to be on the scene of the event to respond as soon as the situation approaches the limits. This is a costly use of managers' time.

However, one does not need to write *everything* down, since policies are needed only for important matters where the question of right or wrong does not depend upon circumstances at the time, or when circumstances only rarely come into the picture.

■ Policies that don't cause action are not policies.

In documenting your operational policies to meet QS-9000 you need to address each requirement in the standard where it is relevant to your business in terms that enshrine the above principles. Procedures implement policies – therefore the policies do not have to stipulate *how* things are carried out. In order to be effective, the policies should state *what* is to be done and the rules which constrain the actions and decisions connected with it.

A common practice is to paraphrase the requirements of QS-9000 as operational policy statements. Whilst this approach does provide direct correlation with QS-9000 it does not by itself add any value since users can read the same things by referring to QS-9000. Operational policies should respond to the requirements not paraphrase them and they should provide solutions appropriate to the organization as given in the following examples.

- On responsibility and authority: "The responsibility and authority of all personnel shall be defined and documented within the procedures that apply to the operations they perform. In addition, the responsibilities, authority, and accountabilities for those holding specific positions or carrying out a particular trade or profession shall be defined in Job Profiles".

- On resources: "The manpower, material, facilities, and plant needed to execute a particular contract shall be established, documented, and agreed with senior management prior to submission of any tender, bid, or offer. The estimate shall include the resources to manage and carry out the work required and in addition that required to verify that the work has been completed in accordance with the contractual requirements".

- On the quality system: "The quality assurance authority shall establish that all quality system procedures, standards, and guidelines satisfy the requirements of QS-9000 and the quality policy prior to their release for use. Prior to introducing a new policy or practice those who will be affected by it shall be notified as to what will be expected of them and appropriate training provided".

- On nonconformance control: "All products shall be subject to the planned inspections and tests and those found nonconforming with the requirements identified with a reject label and retained under the control of the inspection authority until their release has been authorized".

- On documentation control: "Any document and data for which its development, approval, issue, revision, distribution, maintenance, use, storage, obsolescence, or disposal needs to be controlled, shall be defined in company procedures and the appropriate control measures specified. All company documents shall be assigned an Owner who may be the author or the sponsor. The Owner will be responsible for controlling such documents".

These examples illustrate only one policy in each area. In order to address all aspects of the business and all the requirements of the standard many more policies will be required.

■ **Policies limit choice where choice is available.**

While procedures implement policies there will be occasions when one level of procedure contains policies that are to be implemented by a lower level, as may be the case with large companies with several divisions.

It is often difficult to separate quality policies from other policies such as finance, personnel, and marketing. To avoid duplication, overlap, and possible conflict (as well as simplify maintenance) a single policy manual would be preferable.

Referencing procedures in the quality manual

There are a number of ways to show traceability between policy and procedures:

- Number the procedures so that they relate to the section of the quality manual that has been implemented.

  The limitations with this method are that you can only add new sections to the end of the quality manual, otherwise the procedure numbers would have to change. Also you cannot relate a procedure to a specific policy unless the section contains only one policy.

- List the procedures at the end of the appropriate section of the quality manual.

  The limitations with this method are that you cannot relate a procedure to a specific policy unless the section contains only one policy. However, it is the most common solution.

- Produce a matrix showing the relationship between procedures and policies.

  To make this method better than the others, you would need to number all your policies.

- Cross-reference the procedures within the text of the quality manual.

  This is the only method that matches specific policies with specific procedures, other than numbering each policy. Note that this is not practical for policies that are implemented through many procedures.

Once you have matched the policies with the procedures (a one-off activity), implementation is assured by verifying that the procedures are being adhered to by those to whom they apply. Simply auditing procedures will not ensure that policies are implemented unless you verify that the procedures themselves comply with the appropriate policies.

What documents should form part of the quality system?

As stated previously, the quality system is a tool for achieving, sustaining, and improving quality and so should be relatively static once it has been proven fit for use. You don't want to keep changing it for every product and every contract. If you include *all* the technical documents then it will be constantly changing. This can have some profound effects.

For several reasons it is important to define which documents constitute your quality system:

- Any procedures which specify controls for quality system documents apply to all quality system documents. Procedures which govern the preparation and maintenance of policies and procedures may not be appropriate for all technical documents if you include these in your definition of the quality system.

- Anywhere you define responsibilities for the quality system you are giving that person responsibility for the documents within it. Making the quality system encompass all technical documents may create conflict with the responsibilities of other managers.

- You may be required to lodge a copy of all or part of the quality system with your registrar. If your system includes all technical documents your system is much larger than the single manual which bears the title "Quality system".

- You may be required to provide to the registrar prior notice in writing of variations to the quality system. They may make special visits to assess changes that significantly affect conformance with ISO 9000. If you include all technical documents you put yourself in a straitjacket.

- Your management representative will be required to sign a declaration to the effect that any changes in the quality system have been notified to the accreditation body. If you include all technical documents you put yourself in an even tighter straitjacket!

- Your customer may request a copy of your quality manual and if you have included all the documented policies and practices in one volume, you could be disclosing confidential information by providing such a copy.

So limit your quality system to the documents which remain relatively static from one contract to the next and keep the policies separate from the practices. Do not include the documents you create as a result of implementing the quality system such as drawings, specifications, test procedures etc. You may need to adjust the system to meet special contract requirements and this can be achieved through a quality plan.

In QS-9000 the quality plan is called a *control plan*; however, this is somewhat different to a true quality plan. Quality plans are dealt with later in the chapter under *Quality planning*.

Such a plan would invoke all the elements of your quality system that applied to the contract and specify any new policies and procedures which are unique to that particular contract. In addition the plan should particularize what the procedures generalize, such as specifying the actual reviews, audits, inspections, and tests that will be conducted and the criteria for acceptance. However, the quality plan should not be used as a means of changing company policies and procedures, as it may create conflicting requirements for operations staff. You cannot expect staff to operate reliably if you keep changing their practices from one product to another. If the requirements are essentially different, such as between GM and Ford, then you should set up separate lines, separate departments or separate groups so that all in that group use common procedures.

Handling non-applicable requirements

It is required that the *quality manual cover the requirements of the standard*. However, not all requirements may apply to your business so how should you proceed? There are several ways of handling requirements that are not applicable. You can include a cross-reference matrix showing the relationship between the sections of the manual and QS-9000 and indicate which elements of the standard are not applicable. This method is the simplest but is only a rough guide as one can only identify complete elements such as 4.20 or clauses such as 4.6.4.1. One cannot identify individual requirements such as those pertaining to test software in element 4.11. Another method is to refer to the non-applicable requirements within the introductory sections of the manual, either in the statement defining the scope of the quality system or in the section profiling the organization. Alternatively you can refer to non-applicable requirements in the relevant sections of the policy manual but this may not be practical, especially if you have structured your manual around your business rather than the standard. Of course you can omit any reference to those requirements which are not applicable but you will in all probability receive enquiries from the assessor so it is advantageous to have your answers prepared. A more robust solution is to prepare a separate document which provides a response to each of the requirements. The questionnaires included at the end of each chapter in Part 2 of this book provide the questions you need to address. Alternatively, a version of the QSA could be produced. Where the requirements do apply, your response could be a cross reference to the policy manual and/or procedures manual. Where the requirements do not apply, an explanation can be given to justify its exclusion from your system.

Quality systems which go beyond QS-9000

The standard only requires the documentation covering the requirements of the standard to be defined in a quality manual. If your quality system covers areas outside the scope of QS-9000, as it may if you have used ISO 9004 as the basis for designing the system, or if you have included more functions of the business than addressed in QS-9000, then this raises several questions.

* Where should you put such documentation, in the quality manual or in a separate manual?

- Will the assessment of the system extend to such documents?

- If the assessment does extend to such documents, should the assessor find nonconformities in the areas outside the scope of the standard, will they count?

- If such nonconformities count, could they be deemed major nonconformities and thus result in failure to achieve certification or re-certification?

These are questions you need to put to the selected certification body and if such nonconformities will count against you ask the assessor to justify the rationale. It may seem a somewhat negative approach to take, since anything you do to improve your performance should be encouraged. However, for the certification to mean anything it has to be awarded on an equitable basis. A company that does more than required and fails in the areas outside the scope of the standard is clearly better than one that does the minimum and passes. Assessors should stay within the scope of the standard as well as within the scope of the assessment.

Maintaining a quality system

The standard requires suppliers to *maintain a quality system as a means of ensuring that product conforms to specified requirements*.

As stated in Part 2 Chapter 1, maintenance is concerned with retaining something in or restoring something to a state in which it can perform its required function. Quality systems comprise the organization, resources, and processes as well as the documentation needed for achieving quality, so you need to maintain more than the documentation.

In maintaining a quality system you need to:

- Keep the quality system documents updated with the needs of the business.

- Keep copies of the documents updated with the latest amendments.

- Keep the policies and procedures up to date with the latest industry practices and technologies.

- Keep staff training up to date with current policies and procedures.

- Change policies and procedures to prevent the recurrence of problems.

- Keep the description of the organization including the associated responsibilities and authority compatible with the actual staff relationships and their responsibilities and authority.

- Keep the resources required to implement the policies and procedures compatible with the actual resources available.

Why should all this be necessary to maintain the quality system? The answer can be found in ISO 8402 which defines a quality system as *the organizational structure, responsibilities, procedures, processes, and resources needed to implement quality management*. In maintaining the quality system you are therefore doing more than maintaining pieces of paper.

Business changes

In order to keep the system up to date with the needs of the business you will need to review the system when changes occur in the business. This review may be carried out at the same time as the management reviews described in Part 2 Chapter 1; however, since these reviews may be scheduled on a periodic basis, you should not allow the system to become outdated. The system should always reflect what you do and should remain ahead of actual practice rather than lag behind it. You should therefore integrate your system review with the business review so that changes in the business are implemented through the quality system rather than as an afterthought.

Amendments

It is a fact of life that people don't put a high priority on installing amendments to documents in their possession. Some will carry out the amendments immediately on receipt while others will allow them to pile up in the pending tray. To keep copies of your documents up to date you should adopt a method of issuing changes that minimizes the effort required to amend copies of documents. There are several options:

- Reissue documents in their entirety instead of employing manuscript amendment or page replacement techniques.

- Task one individual with updating all the manuals.

- Place the manuals in the custody of secretaries or clerks instead of the users.

- Limit the number of copies to those who need regular access, with a library copy for casual users.

- Structure your documentation so that it consists of a number of volumes, each addressing a particular department or phase of operations. Limit the distribution of the relevant volume to staff affected and only keep one complete set.

Each of these options has advantages and disadvantages depending on the type, size, and dispersal of staff in the organization.

State of the art changes

To keep your policies and procedures up to date with the latest industry practices you should provide a means of identifying new developments. This can be done by scanning journals, attending seminars and conferences, and generally maintaining an awareness of developments in quality management and technologies relevant to your business.

Staff changes

When you set up your quality system as part of its implementation you should train staff in the application and use of the various documents. The system may not change as frequently as the staff so as new staff enter the organization or change roles, they need to be trained to carry out their jobs as well as possible. This training needs to be a continuous process if the standards of quality are to be maintained with a fluid workforce. You will therefore need a means of identifying when staff changes occur so as to schedule their training. These training plans are as much a part of quality system maintenance as staff induction and development. Therefore, provision needs to be made in your procedures to ensure this occurs.

Improvement changes

Internal audits, corrective action plans, and management reviews may all indicate a need for the documented policies to be changed or staff to be trained in order to prevent the recurrence of problems. This is by far the most frequent cause of change – certainly until your system has stabilized. You will need a method of making such changes promptly if the problems are not to recur. Often the change control system may be too bureaucratic and inject delays while management procrastinates over policy and procedure changes. As a result, a manager may issue a memo instructing a change in practice to overcome a particular problem and possibly at the same time initiate a formal change to the system documentation. This method should be prohibited by the system since the memo is an uncontrolled vehicle which may set unwanted precedents as well as cause your documented system to diverge from the system in operation. Your change procedures should be such that they are the quickest way to change the system. It should be possible to issue a Change Note within a working day (see Part 2 Chapter 5). Walk it around the managers if the internal mail takes too long, call a meeting, or invoke the manager's deputy if the manager is unavailable. If the managers cannot agree then no change should be made anyway and certainly not by a memo.

Organization changes

A common failing of many quality systems is that the organization structure, job titles, and responsibilities are out of date shortly after the documentation is issued. Managers often believe that the organization charts in the quality manual are there simply as a publicity aid and not as a definitive statement. Managers also prefer to be free to change their organization when it suits them and not to be constrained by a bureaucratic system. Most managers will announce a change in their organization, then rely on the quality manager to change the charts in the quality manual. To avoid conflicts you need a method whereby managers change the charts then announce the changes in their organization, and not vice versa. Again, if you employ a quick change procedure such as that described above, managers will find no advantage in bypassing the system. One way of limiting the effects that organization changes have on the quality system is to make the system immune to such changes. By avoiding job titles, locations, department names, and other labels that are prone to change you can minimize the impact of organizational change on the documentation. To achieve such immunity you need to use terms such as design authority, manufacturing authority, inspection authority etc. instead. If you need to be specific then you can do so in a Quality Plan or Organization Manual which translates the authorities into department names or job titles. Thus in the case of reorganization you need only change one document instead of many. Processes often remain the same after a reorganization as only the names and positions may have changed.

Resource changes

Policies and procedures, including the processes they define, require human, material, and financial resources to implement. When you introduce the policies and procedures for the first time you need to take into account the resources that will be needed. It is of no use to issue a new procedure that requires new equipment, new skills, and many more people if no one has made provision for them. Likewise, when procedures change you need to consider the impact on resources and when resources are reduced you need to consider the impact on the procedures. Managers may inadvertently dispose of old equipment or acquire new equipment without giving consideration to the procedures or instructions which specify the equipment. Some procedures may be designed around a certain facility or around a particular department, section or even a particular person or skill, although every attempt to make them immune to such changes was taken. In times of a recession certain pruning may have to occur which may affect the implementation of the procedures. You therefore need to be vigilant and identify the effects of these changes on your procedures and take prompt action to maintain them in line with current circumstances. Rather than dispose of procedures that have become obsolete due to such changes, archive them because you may be able to resurrect them when circumstances improve.

Quality system procedures

Preparation of documented procedures and instructions

The standard requires the supplier to *prepare documented procedures consistent with the requirements of this International Standard and the supplier's stated quality policy.*

What are procedures?

A procedure is a sequence of steps to execute a routine task. ISO 8402 defines a procedure as *a specified way to perform an activity*. It prescribes how one should proceed in certain circumstances in order to produce a desired result. Sometimes the word can imply formality and a document of several pages but this is not necessarily so. A procedure can be five lines, where each line represents a step to execute a task.

Quality system procedures are a certain type of procedure. They implement the operational policies and regulate processes that produce an output, the quality of which is essential to the business. Procedures do not in fact achieve quality, it is people who do that. Procedures do not take decisions, it is people who do that. So you could have the best procedures in the world and still not achieve quality. It has to be a combination of both for you to achieve the desired quality.

The standard only refers to procedures as the category of quality system documentation. If we use the term *documented practices* we have a wider choice as to the types of documents we put into the quality system. Many documents are not procedures. They do not tell us how to proceed or specify a way to perform an activity. They specify criteria we must meet or provide guidance in conducting a task. They may, however, give examples or define rules to follow.

The documentation model in QS-9000 shows two categories of prescriptive documentation (procedures and job instructions), whereas in practice there are other types.

Types of documented practices

There are various types of documented practices:

- Divisional procedures apply to more than one division of a company and regulate common activities.

- Control procedures control work on product as it passes between departments or processes. These should contain the forms which convey information from department to department and reference the operating procedures that apply to each task.

- Operating procedures prescribe how specific tasks are to be performed. Subcategories of these procedures may include test procedures, inspection procedures, installation procedures etc. These should reference the standards and guides (see below) which are needed to carry out the task, document the results and contain the forms to be used to record information.

- Standards define the acceptance criteria for judging the quality of an activity, a document, a product, or a service. There are national standards, international standards, standards for a particular industry and company standards. Standards may be in diagrammatic form or narrative form or a mixture of the two. Standards need to be referenced in control procedures or operating procedures and be a part of the quality system. These standards are in fact your quality standards. They describe features and characteristics which all your products and service must possess. Some may be type-specific, others may apply to a range of products or types of products and some may apply to all products whatever their type. These standards are not the drawings and specifications that describe a particular product but the standards that are invoked in such drawings and specifications and are selected when designing the product.

- Guides are aids to decision-making and to the conduct of activities. They are useful as a means of documenting your experience and should contain examples, illustrations, hints, and tips to help staff perform their work as well as possible. Customer reference manuals such as the *Advanced Product Planning Manual* are guides even though they are referenced in QS-9000.

- Work instructions define the work required in terms of who is to perform it, when it is to commence and be completed, what standard it has to meet, and any other instructions which constrain the quality, quantity, delivery, and cost of the work required. Work instructions are the product of implementing a control procedure, an operating procedure or a document standard (see further explanation below).

The relationship between these documents and the policies described in Part 2 Chapter 1 is illustrated in Figure 2.4.

By having several types of quality system document you can place the mandatory provisions in the control and operating procedures, select the standards that are appropriate to the task, and place all the other material in the guides. You will then not be committed to doing things that are not essential. The assessors should assess you only against the mandatory procedures and the appropriate standards and not the guides unless the guides are invoked in QS-9000 when you will have to justify to your customer any alternative approach taken.

What are the differences between procedures and instructions?

In the 1987 version of ISO 9001 it referred to procedures and instructions and in section 4.9.1 on process control it referred to work instructions. All other references were to procedures. Work instructions are now identified in a Note to clause 4.2.2 of ISO 9001. Here it implies that work instructions define how an activity is performed but in ISO 8402 a procedure is a specified way to perform the activity. There isn't enough

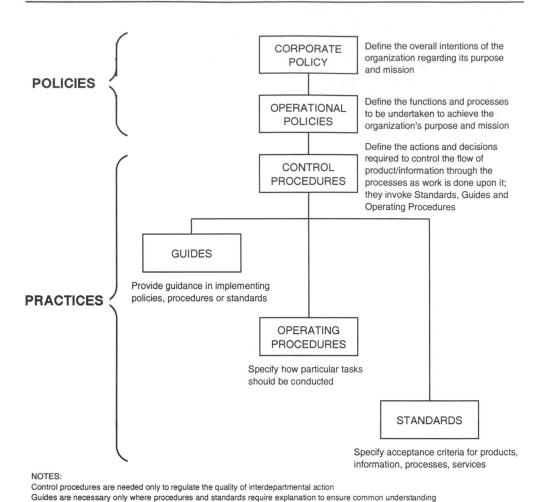

POLICIES

CORPORATE POLICY

Define the overall intentions of the organization regarding its purpose and mission

OPERATIONAL POLICIES

Define the functions and processes to be undertaken to achieve the organization's purpose and mission

CONTROL PROCEDURES

Define the actions and decisions required to control the flow of product/information through the processes as work is done upon it; they invoke Standards, Guides and Operating Procedures

PRACTICES

GUIDES

Provide guidance in implementing policies, procedures or standards

OPERATING PROCEDURES

Specify how particular tasks should be conducted

STANDARDS

Specify acceptance criteria for products, information, processes, services

NOTES:
Control procedures are needed only to regulate the quality of interdepartmental action
Guides are necessary only where procedures and standards require explanation to ensure common understanding
Operating Procedures may be common or unique to a department and are necessary only for ensuring the quality of repetitive tasks
Standards are necessary where the removal of subjectivity is essential in judging the quality of product, information, processes or services

Figure 2.4 Relationship between policies and practices

difference between these two defintions to warrant a change in the term and its inclusion may well create much confusion, especially since ISO 9004-1 does not refer to work instructions or any other type of instructions.

QS-9000 refers to job instructions and defines these as documents that describe work conducted in one function in a company: e.g. set-up instructions, inspection instructions, rework instructions, operator instructions. This definition is a little ambiguous since the term *function* is not defined and might be a function such as design or production. However, the model states that they answer "how" which implies they are tasks and not functions. The examples are certainly unrepresentative of functions; they are more like tasks, except for inspection which could be a department or a task. The intention is thought to be that job instructions describe how a particular task is to be carried out and therefore equate with the term *operating procedures* in Figure 2.4.

Differentiating between procedures and instructions implies that there is a difference. Procedures are practices, work instructions are not. They merely contain instructions to do work, and although many organizations produce documents they call work instructions they are in fact procedures because they specify a particular way to perform an activity. An instruction conveys knowledge, information, or directions for the purpose of performing work. Procedures also convey knowledge, information, and directions but they relate to how certain tasks are to be performed and specify who is to perform them. For example, you may issue an instruction for certain goods to be packed in a certain way on a particular date and the package marked with the contents and the address to which it is to be delivered. So that the task is carried out properly you may also specify the methods of packing in a procedure. The procedure would not contain specific details of the particular package – this is the purpose of the instruction. Procedures by themselves do not cause work to be carried out. This is the role of instructions. For instance, a purchase order is an instruction to a supplier and the method of producing one would be defined in a purchasing procedure. Similarly, Change Requests, Amendment Instructions, Engineering Orders, and Print Requisitions are all instructions that cause people to do work and hence are work instructions rather than procedures. Work instructions cause work to commence or to stop, procedures define how such work should be performed.

Another use of the term *instructions* is in the performance of activities relating to a specific task: for example, Assembly Instructions, Maintenance Instructions, Operating Instructions, Cleaning Instructions etc. These prescribe the activities to be performed by a person in carrying out a specific task and as such define how the task is to be carried out. They do not define when, who, or how the activities are to be performed. For example an assembly instruction may state that panel A is to be fixed to panel B using the screws provided. It will not tell you how to use a screwdriver but it may tell you to be careful not to damage the outer surface or to overtighten the screws.

The quality system should not include all these instructions. If it were to do so it would be in a state of continual change. These instructions result from implementing procedures and therefore the standard need only specify where procedures are required.

What should be documented?

The standard advises that *the range and detail of the procedures that form part of the quality system depend upon the complexity of the work, the methods used, and the skills and training needed by personnel involved in carrying out the activity.*

Clause 4.9 of the standard requires procedures only where the absence of such procedures would adversely affect quality. This phrase is often taken out of context and used as a valid reason for not documenting aspects of the quality system. There has to be a limit on what you proceduralize. At school we are taught reading, writing, and arithmetic, so procedures should not attempt to define these functions. The procedures need only detail that which would not be covered by education and training. A balance should be attained between training and procedures. In order to provide training of consistent quality, it too should be documented in the form of training manuals, training aids and facilities. If you rely on training rather than employing documented procedures then you will need to show that you have control over the quality of training to a level that will ensure its effectiveness. We expect staff to know how to do the various tasks that comprise their trade or profession, how to write, how to design, how to type, how to answer the telephone, how to paint, how to lay bricks etc. You may feel it necessary to provide handbooks with useful tips on how to do these tasks more economically and effectively and you may also use such books to bridge gaps in education and training but these are not your procedures. The quality system has to be documented either in your procedures, standards, guides, or manuals.

Not everything you do can be proceduralized. Some policies can be implemented without a procedure. The following are examples of such policies:

- All communication with suppliers shall be with the approval of the purchasing authority.

- Positive feedback from customers shall be recorded, filed with client data, and posted on the company noticeboard.

- No deviations from the policies stated in the policy manual will be permitted without written authorization of the Managing Director.

In many organizations, procedures for such policies would not be necessary as the policy is concise enough for effective implementation. In other organizations procedures may well be required to limit the number of possible variables in carrying out such simple tasks.

As a minimum you should document your response to the requirements of the standard – the general requirements as well as each individual requirement. Some requirements will be addressed in your policy statements, others will be addressed directly in your procedures. It is within the framework of systematic procedures that experience and judgment produce successful results and a reputation for managerial excellence. Procedures can only work, however, where judgment is no longer required or necessary.

How many procedures and how big do they need to be?

The standard requires documented procedures to be prepared consistent with the requirements of this international standard, but what does this mean? "Consistent with" implies that where the standard specifies that the supplier shall prepare a documented procedure one shall be prepared. The standard requires 40 documented procedures directly. The table below identifies these procedures indicating the clause numbers, with the * denoting those which are applicable only when the requirement applies. In Appendix B are a further 129 topics which your procedures need to address in order to demonstrate that you have *documented* your quality system.

Procedures requirements	Clause
Project management	4.1.2
Customer expectation determination	4.1.4
Business planning procedure	4.1.4
Customer satisfaction determination	4.1.6
Advanced product quality planning	4.2.3
Contract review procedures	4.3.1
Design control procedures	4.4*
Document and data control procedures	4.5.1
Control of customer engineering standards	4.5.2
Purchasing procedures	4.6.1
Subcontractor delivery performance monitoring	4.6.2
Control of restricted substances	4.6.3
Product identification procedures	4.8*
Traceability procedures	4.8*
Production procedures	4.9*
Installation procedures	4.9*
Servicing procedures	4.9*
Safety procedures	4.9
Environmental procedures	4.9
Preventive maintenance procedures	4.9
Process monitoring instructions	4.9.1
Operator instructions	4.9.1
Inspection and test procedures	4.10
Control of inspection, measuring, and test equipment	4.11
Calibration of inspection, measurement, and test equipment	4.11
Maintenance of inspection, measuring, and test equipment	4.11
Control of nonconforming product	4.13
Corrective action procedures	4.14.1

Procedures requirements	Clause
Preventive action procedures	4.14.1
Handling procedures	4.15.1
Storage procedures	4.15.1
Inventory management procedures	4.15.3
Packaging procedures	4.15.1
Preservation procedures	4.15.1
Delivery procedures	4.15.1
Delivery performance monitoring procedure	4.15.6
Control of quality records	4.16
Internal quality audits	4.17
Identification of training needs	4.18
Servicing management procedures	4.19*
Application of statistical techniques	4.20.2
Continuous improvement	II-2.1
Facilities planning	II-3.1
Tooling management	II-3.4

The standard doesn't require a procedure for Management Review and while it does require procedures for Design Control it does not specify that a Design Review Procedure is required. The phrases "consistent with" and "in accordance with" have the same meaning as both imply compatibility and agreement. If you restrict yourself to a literal interpretation of the standard, then you need produce no more than 40 documented procedures – possibly less if some aspects do not apply to your business. You can combine several procedures in one document, the size of which depends on the complexity of your business. The more complex the business the larger the quality system. The more variations in the ways that work is executed, the larger the quality system will need to be. So if you have a small business and only one way of carrying out work then your system will tend to be small. Your quality system may be described in one document of no more than 30 pages. On the other hand a larger business may require several volumes and dozens of procedures of over 10 pages each to adequately describe your system.

Control procedures need to be user friendly and so should be limited in size. Remember you can use other documents, such as guides, standards, and operating procedures, to extend what you have written in the control procedures. However, the procedures should not be so short as to be worthless as a means of controlling activities. They need to provide an adequate degree of direction so that the results of using them are predictable. If you neglect to adequately define what needs to be done and how to do it then don't be surprised that staff don't know what to do or constantly make mistakes. It is also important to resist the desire to produce manuals that are impressive rather than practical. Printing the documents on expensive paper with colored logo does not improve their effectiveness and if they not written simply and understood by a person of average intelligence, they will not be used.

To determine the procedures you need you should design the system from the top down. The following sequence of activities is one way of doing this:

- Analyze your business, identify the functions you perform, and draw up a system model with the major interfaces between the system and other systems, together with the interfaces external to the business.

- Analyze each function and identify the processes which when combined together provide the function and draw up flowcharts which show how the processes relate to one another, with interfaces to other functions and processes.

- Analyze each of the processes to identify the tasks that are carried out to execute a process and again draw flowcharts showing the sequence of tasks and the interfaces.

- Analyze each task to identify the discrete activities that accomplish a task and draw flowcharts showing the interfaces.

When you have reached this stage you can draw boundaries around groups of processes, tasks or activities to identify the procedures you will need (see Part 1 Chapter 3). Remember, the sequence of activities is unlikely to follow the order of either the requirements in QS-9000 or your policies. You will need to build into your procedures those elements which implement the QS-9000 requirements and the policies. Some requirements will apply to many operations such as document control, corrective action, and quality records whereas other requirements may apply to only one operation such as auditing and management review. A matrix showing this relationship is given in Appendix E.

Why are documented procedures needed?

All references to "procedures" in the 1987 version of ISO 9000 were changed to "documented procedures" since the requirement for procedures does not by itself stipulate that they be documented. One can have a common way of doing something without it being documented.

In QS-9000, however, the same style as used in ISO 9000 has not been adopted and therefore the customer may expect a documented procedure even though the standard does not expressly state that a process or system or method has to be documented.

Although not mandatory, it would be prudent to document all procedures that relate to requirements of the standard.

There are, however, several good reasons for documenting the organization's procedures:

- To encourage the people involved into thinking a problem through

- To convert solved problems into recorded knowledge so as to avoid having to solve them repeatedly

- To maximize company performance rather than departmental performance

- To cause people to act in a uniform way and so make processes predictable

- To provide freedom for management and staff to maximize their contribution to the business

- To free the business from reliance on particular people for its effectiveness

- To provide legitimacy and authority for the deeds needed

- To make responsibility clear and to create the conditions of self-control

- To provide coordination for interdepartmental action

- To enable the effects of potential process changes to be assessed

- To minimize variance and eliminate bottlenecks

- To improve communication and to provide consistency and predictability in carrying out repetitive tasks

- To provide training and reference material for new and existing staff

- To provide evidence to those concerned of your intentions

- To provide auditable criteria for execution against authorized practices

- To provide a basis for studying existing work practices and identifying opportunities for improvement

- To demonstrate after an incident the precautions which were taken or which should have been taken to prevent it or minimize its occurrence

Reasons for not documenting procedures

If you can't predict the course of action or sequence of steps you need to take then you can't write a procedure. You can't plan for unforeseen events and since the unexpected will happen sooner or later, it would be wasteful of resources to produce procedures for such hypothetical situations. So if you do not use statistical techniques for instance, it is a waste of time writing a procedure that will not be used even though the standard requires one.

There are several other good reasons for not documenting procedures. Management may have no objection to doing many sensible things but may well resist declaring them as policy or prescribing them in published procedures. Management may take this attitude for several reasons:

- Customers may use evidence of noncompliance, no matter how trivial, to terminate a contract or decline a tender.

- There may be many instances where the policy or procedure doesn't apply.

- Management may wish to safeguard against over zealous auditors or assessors.

- Managers may wish to choose the most appropriate action for given circumstances.

- Managers may wish to avoid overkill, avoid doing more than is necessary.

- The practices may not have any effect on product or service quality.

- The practices rely on skills acquired through training where judgement is necessary to produce the desired result.

Content of procedures

In deciding what should go into procedures you should limit them to defining the activities and decisions to be carried out and only prescribe how actions and decisions should be carried out where:

- The method is critical to the result.

- Too much choice can be bad for efficiency.

- It would be unreasonable, unsafe or unreliable to expect staff to commit the knowledge required to memory.

An effective procedure would contain some or all of the following elements:

- A flowchart of the process that depicts the sequence of actions and decisions, inputs, outputs, and interfaces with other procedures

- Paragraphs describing the actions and decisions required, indicating the role responsible by matching the flowchart in the sequence in which they occur

- The minimum information and equipment needed to perform each activity or make each decision

- The criteria for decisions as a list of aspects to be considered or a statement of requirement which the decision should satisfy

- The criteria for choosing optional routes and the sequence of steps to be taken

- The entry conditions for starting the process, in terms of the minimum inputs and approvals to be satisfied before the procedure may commence

- The exit conditions for ending the process or task, in terms of the minimum outputs and approvals to be satisfied for successful completion of the process

- The source of information or product needed, in terms of from what process, what procedure, what person (role) or organization it comes

- The routing instructions for information or product emerging from the procedure

- Any precautions needed to prevent incident, accident, error, problems etc.

- Any recording requirements to provide evidence of actions or decisions or to enable traceability in the event of subsequent problems

- Any rules that have to be followed in order to ensure that the task is carried out in a uniform manner and satisfies statutory obligations

- Controls needed to verify the quality of any products with feedback loops

- Controls needed to verify that the process or task achieves its purpose and to verify that critical activities and decisions occur when required

- Any forms to be completed, together with form-filling instructions and responsibilities, the numbering system to be used, and the registers to be maintained

- Cross reference to other documents in which essential supplementary information can be found

Control procedures may be represented by flowcharts and forms with notes on the charts and form-filling instructions on the back of the forms. For simple quality systems this method has many advantages. It is concise, easy to produce, easy to understand, and easy to use. The main vehicle for transmitting information is the form, both in simple and in complex quality systems. Information passes from one department to another by use of forms so it makes sense to write your control procedures around the forms you use. You probably won't be able to do this for operating procedures that require instruction on how to operate a piece of equipment, how to perform a test, or how to carry out a calibration.

Preparing procedures

The preparation of procedures takes time and careful planning to get right. A common approach is to assign the writing to one person but this has its drawbacks:

- No person will understand *everything* about the organization.

- There will be a mismatch between procedure and practice.

- Staff will not own the system, as they didn't contribute towards it.

- The system may meet the requirements in the standard but may not be workable.

A better method is to nominate several key staff in the organization to join a quality system development team and arrange for them to produce the documentation with guidance from an expert. With this approach you will need a procedure which contains:

- The document application process

   This is to authorize the preparation of new documents, nominate authors and owners, and determine the procedure's scope and objectives. This mechanism prevents staff duplicating effort and ensures that the system remains under control.

- The documentation standard

   This should specify the format, numbering, layout, typing, issue notation, dating, and content conventions to which you wish to adhere.

- The preparation process

   This should describe the routine that authors and typists should follow to produce drafts, forms, tables, charts, and flow diagrams.

- The review and approval process

  This should detail the method for obtaining comment on the drafts and gaining approval of those responsible for its implementation.

- The publication process

  This should cover the copying and distribution of quality system documents.

- The implementation process

  This is for bringing new and changed procedures to the attention of staff and for proving the new methods before full-scale application.

- The change process

  This is for proposing, reviewing, approving, and issuing changes to quality system documents.

- Filing and storage provisions

  This should cover the master material, computer disks, paper copies, current and obsolete issues.

QS-9000 does not, however, make these demands of you. To comply with QS-9000 you only need to provide for the document review, approval, distribution, and change processes.

It is important that all procedures interface properly with one another. The outputs of one procedure should lead into the inputs of others. Control of these interfaces can be maintained by using the procedure application routines mentioned above. You should not allow uncontrolled generation of procedures; every one should be carefully planned as you would plan the design of a product. Every procedure must have a purpose and a place in the system so that the system remains coherent.

Forms

Forms are very much part of the control procedures, in fact together with a flow diagram they may be the control procedure. You will need to create a mechanism for the control of forms, their numbering system, application, and related procedures. Every form should be related to a particular procedure. A form without a procedure is not part of the quality system. However, it is the content of the blank form that you should control rather than the piece of paper. If you have a large stock of existing forms it would seem uneconomic to destroy these simply because they are not traceable to the quality system. You have a choice:

- Scrap existing forms and produce new forms on computer using a word-processing or database package and network the computers.

- Scrap the existing forms and create new paper forms with form number and revision status.

- Include the existing form in the procedure and apply a form number and revision status on each blank using an ink stamp.

- Provide form content requirements in the procedure, use the specific form name, and deregulate the forms.

In the case of the last option, control is not as robust but one can check forms against procedures at any time to verify conformance. It also allows forms to be laid out to suit the amount of information provided. There are some drawbacks, however. Where forms pass between departments, allowing individuals to vary the layout may cause processing delays and staff irritation. The layout of forms which pass between divisions and companies should remain uniform to avoid unnecessary disruption. Too much flexibility will almost certainly increase the likelihood of error.

Many of the Reference Manuals contain forms for suppliers to use. However their inclusion does not mean that you have to take copies and use only these copies. The information on the forms can be organized in a manner to suit your own method of operation providing its substance is not changed. You will need to control the forms and may wish to add your company logo. Don't add more boxes on the forms that are intended to convey data to customers as they often prefer standard forms to make processing easier.

Making the system effective

The standard does not in fact require you to design an effective system. It does require the system to be reviewed to ensure its continuing effectiveness but if the system was not designed properly in the first place, the review may simply result in a series of minor improvements that are never ending and do not deal with the system as a whole. Many initiatives for quality improvement attack parts of the system but not the whole system. Improvement in processes is often made without considering the effects on other processes. This is certainly true with document changes where the effects of changes on other documents are not usually considered before authorizing the change.

How do you then design an effective system? There are several techniques you can use. Failure Modes and Effect Analysis (FMEA), Fault Tree Analysis (FTA), and Theory of Constraints (TOC) are but three. The FMEA is a bottom up approach, the FTA a top down approach, and TOC a holistic approach.

One way of applying the FMEA technique to the quality system is to take each procedure objective and establish the probability of it not being achieved, the likely cause and effect on the system, and the probability of the failure being detected by the downstream controls. The analysis may show up key activities for which there are no safeguards, activities that rely on one person doing something for which there are no checks that it has been done. The quality system is a collection of interrelated processes; therefore by chasing the effect along the chain you may find single point failures, parts of the system which affect the performance of the whole system.

The FMEA approach is a bottom up approach, looking at component failures and establishing their effect on the system. An alternative approach is to use a top down approach such as Fault Tree Analysis to postulate system failure modes and establish which processes, procedures, or activities are likely to causes such failures.

The third method is relatively new. The Theory of Constraints developed by Eliyahu M. Goldratt in the 1980s examines the system as an interconnection of processes and focuses on the one constraint that limits overall system performance. The theory is founded on the principle that if all parts are performing as well as they can, the system as a whole may not be. Each process links with others in a chain and therefore by improving one process you may degrade the performance of another. It looks for the weakest link in the chain of processes that produce organizational performance and seeks to eliminate it. Once eliminated, it looks for the next constraint on the system. Many of the constraints may not be physical. There may well be policy constraints that govern many of the actions and decisions being made. What may have to change is the policy for improvement in system performance to be achieved. In this way TOC is similar to FTA but goes beyond the physical boundaries of the system.

Ensuring effective implementation

The standard requires the supplier to *effectively implement the quality system and its documented procedures.*

The 1994 version of the standard has changed the emphasis of this requirement. The standard previously required the procedures and instructions to be implemented but not the policies. Since the operational policies form part of the quality system and are documented in the quality manual, policies now have to be implemented.

Unless practice follows procedure, the procedures are not being implemented. One only implements by following what is stated, not by changing your procedures after changing your practice. However, one can argue that effective implementation is trying out the new practice first and then documenting it but it is stretching a point to bring your procedures in line with your current practice as a regular event, since they should not be out of line in the first place.

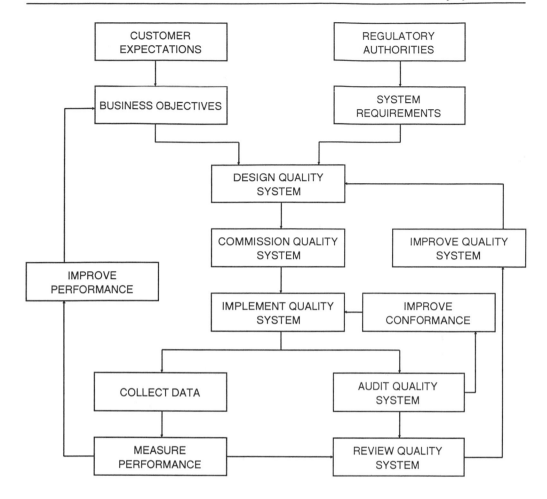

Figure 2.5 Quality system life cycle model

A common failing with the implementation of procedures is that they are not sold to the workforce before they become mandatory. Also, after spending much effort in their development, procedures are often issued without any thought given to training or to verifying that practices have in fact been changed. As a result, development is often discontinued after their release. It then comes as a shock to managers to find that all their hard work has been wasted. A managed program of introducing new or revised procedures is a way of overcoming these shortfalls.

The process of implementing a new procedure or one that requires a change in practice is one that is concerned with the management of change. It has to be planned and resourced and account taken of attitudes, culture, barriers, and any other resistance there may be. One must not forget that those who are to implement the procedure may not have participated in its development and may therefore be reluctant to change their practices. The process of introducing a new or revised practice consists of Preparation, Commissioning, Implementation, and Qualification. Once the qualification exercise has proved that the procedure fulfills its purpose effectively one may resort to periodic auditing to confirm continued effectiveness.

The quality system life cycle

The way in which these phases of quality system development are related is illustrated in the quality system life cycle model shown in Figure 2.5 above.

Preparing for implementation

The following are some of the activities that should be carried out when preparing for the introduction of new or revised practices:

- Establish who is affected by the procedure and verify that they know what is expected of them.

- Identify the areas where resistance is likely and develop the appropriate responses.

- Choose the timing of the change and identify the champions for each department.

- Decide whether to conduct trial installation in one area, progressive installation across all areas, or big bang approach, and who is to be involved.

- Determine the extent of staff training necessary.

- Consider the preparation of staff awareness bulletins (Advertising).

- Advise managers on the approach they should take in announcing the changes to their staff and making them aware of their new responsibilities.

- If a major change affects many areas (or if it greatly affects one particular area) the procedure should be added to the Improvement Program and detailed plans drawn up on how the practices will be gradually changed.

- Determine what other procedures have to be in place for the new procedure to work effectively.

- Determine how commitment is going to be tested.

- Decide what communication links are necessary for reporting problems, dealing with priorities and disputes, and processing changes.

- Decide when the old practices are to be discontinued. (It may be wise to leave the old system in place until the new one is working effectively.)

Commissioning new practices

Either during or after the preparation process and depending on the type of procedure to be introduced, several activities may be necessary before full implementation is possible:

- New forms should be introduced and the old ones removed from circulation.

- New files should be established for holding the new data and existing files should be re-identified.

- The communication links should be set up and verified, as those supplying or receiving information associated with the procedure may be unaware of their new responsibilities.

- New registers of records should be created if required.

- New distribution lists may be required.

- New equipment, tools, and facilities should be acquired and commissioned.

- The awareness briefings prepared previously should be put into effect.

- The training plans prepared previously should be put into effect.

Commissioning is finished when everything is in place ready for implementation.

Implementing new practices

Following the Commissioning phase everything should be in place to effect a smooth implementation. During this phase the actions and decisions required by the procedure are carried out and initially this may demand considerable effort.

- New documents may have to be produced and old ones may have to be revised or reformatted. This may mean a major upheaval until all have been completed and the process stabilized.

- Staff performing new activities for the first time will reveal problems with the procedure or the training and these will need to be resolved.

- Difficulties may emerge at the interfaces.

- The procedure or parts of it may not be activated for some time.

During this phase the activities should be closely monitored to ensure that the new practices remain in place and staff do not revert to the old practices. Care should be taken to ensure that the intent of the procedure is understood and that any resistance to change is overcome.

Qualification/validation of new practices

At some suitable stage during implementation, the new procedure should be qualified or validated; i.e. it should be thoroughly tested to verify that it fulfills its purpose. The implementation of every requirement of the procedure should be verified in every area to which it applies to determine the following:

- Which areas are applying the procedure

- The extent to which the procedure is being followed

- The extent of variation between different departments, if more than one department implements the procedure

- Whether the procedure, if followed as stated, will produce the required results, consistently and predictably

- Whether the required results are still valid in light of changing circumstances

- Which changes are needed to make it effective

If, as a result of the above, no changes are necessary either in the procedure or in the practice then the procedure is qualified for its application. If at some later stage the procedure is applied in new areas a similar review should be undertaken after commissioning. If changes are necessary then procedure implementation should be re-examined after the changes have been implemented.

In ensuring the effective implementation of the quality system you should continually ask:

- Does the quality system fulfill its purpose?

- Do the results of the audits indicate that the system is effective?

- Are procedures being used properly?

- Are policies being adhered to?

- Are the customers satisfied with the products and services we provide?

If the answer is "Yes" your system is operating effectively. If your answer is "No" to any of these questions, your quality system is not being effectively implemented.

Quality planning

Defining how requirements for quality will be met

The standard requires the supplier to *define and document how the requirements for quality will be met.*

The quality system developed to meet the requirements of QS-9000 is likely to be a generic system, not specific to any particular product, project or contract other than the range of products and services which your organization supplies. By implementing the policies and procedures of the documented quality system, product, project, or contract specific plans, procedures, specifications etc. are generated. QS-9000 contains quality system requirements not product quality requirements. For a given product, project, or contract there will be specific product, project, or contract requirements and it is these requirements to which this clause of the standard refers.

The term "requirements for quality" is defined in ISO 8402 as *an expression of the needs or their translation into a set of quantitatively or qualitatively stated requirements for the characteristics of an entity to enable its realization and examination.*

Quality requirements are not the requirements contained in QS-9000. These are quality system requirements; they apply to quality systems, not to products and services. A product cannot conform with QS-9000 as it contains no product requirements. (See also Part 1 Chapter 1.)

The requirements for quality are the objectives which the organization is committed to achieve through the contract. They may relate to products, services or both. The vehicle for you to define and document how these objectives will be met is called a quality plan but may be known by other names such as a project plan or contract plan. In some cases the requirement may be met in the form of a technical proposal by the supplier to the customer.

The *Advanced Product Quality Planning Manual* refers to a Product Quality Plan which includes a Product Assurance Plan but does not prescribe the content of the Product Quality Plan; neither is it an input nor output of any of the phases in the product quality planning cycle. However, whatever the document that is produced as a result of product quality planning, such a document should be considered the response to this requirement. ISO 10005 provides further clarification.

Ensuring consistency with other quality system requirements

The standard requires that *quality planning be consistent with all other requirements of the quality system*.

The quality system you have developed should have made all the necessary provisions to enable the products and services you normally supply to conform with customer requirements. It is therefore essential that the provisions made for any particular product, service, project, or contract do not conflict with the authorized policies and procedures. There is often a temptation when planning for specific contracts to change the policies and procedures where they are inflexible, invent new forms, change responsibilities, by-pass known bottlenecks etc. You have to be careful not to develop a mutant quality system for specific contracts. If the changes needed are good for the business as a whole then they should be made using the prescribed quality system change procedures. This is another good reason for having a fast method of making authorized changes to approved documents. Changes to meet specific contractual requirements should be made without causing ,conflict with existing practices. If special procedures are needed which replace existing procedures in the quality system, then a mechanism needs to be developed which authorizes staff to deviate from the existing procedures.

Documenting quality planning

The standard requires *quality planning to be documented in a format to suit the supplier's method of operation*.

Although the standard does not specifically require a quality planning procedure, to ensure that such planning is carried out in a manner which avoids conflict with existing practices and in a format which suits your operations, you will need to prescribe the method to be employed in a procedure. Some contracts may stipulate a particular format for contract-specific procedures, especially when they are to be submitted to the customer for approval. If these procedures are only used by the project team then this may not cause any conflict. However, if they are to be used by staff in the line departments then you may have to reach a compromise with the customer so that any differences in format do not create implementation problems.

Planning to meet specified requirements

The standard requires that *the supplier gives consideration* to a number of activities as appropriate but does not define when such consideration should be given. If you intend submitting a fixed price tender to a customer, then preparing detailed plans of what you are going to do for the price *before* you submit your bid is giving "appropriate consideration" to planning. Likewise, identifying controls, ordering equipment and materials etc. in good time before you need them is giving "appropriate consideration"; i.e. anticipating what you may need and initiating its acquisition beforehand will prevent you from having delays and problems when you embark upon the work.

Preparing quality plans

Quality plans are needed when the work you intend to carry out requires detailed planning beyond that already planned for by the quality system. The system will not specify everything you need to do for every job. It will usually specify only general provisions which apply in the majority of situations. You will need to define the specific documentation to be produced, tests, inspections, and reviews to be performed, and resources to be employed. The contract may specify particular standards or requirements that you must meet and these may require additional provisions to those in the quality system. Guidance in preparing quality plans is given in ISO 9004-6, but these guidelines are based on the structure of ISO 9001 and your quality system may not in fact be structured in this manner. However, the guidance given in ISO 9004-6 is indeed sound advice and it identifies many of the aspects which need to be planned when applying your quality system to a specific product, project, or contract. The note at the end of section 4.2.3 in the standard recognizes that a quality plan may in fact be no more than a list of procedures which apply to a particular product, project, or contract. If your system is structured so that you can select the appropriate procedures then this is by far the simplest method. However, in addition to the procedures, you may need to specify when particular reviews, inspections, and tests etc. are to be carried out and in what sequence. Where a procedure provides an option, an alternative route or for activities and decisions to be based on particular contract, product, or project requirements, then these aspects need to be addressed in your quality plan.

QS-9000 creates an ambiguity regarding quality plans since the term "control plan" is inserted at every mention of the term "quality plan". If one examines each such reference to control plans one will find that the control plans described in the *Advanced Product Quality Planning and Control Plan Reference Manual* specify product characteristics, tolerances, and measurement methods. There are three types: prototype, pre-launch, and production control plans. They do not make provision for controlling any design and development activities, neither do they describe how activities should be performed; that is the purpose of operating procedures or operator instructions. They also do not describe provisions that may need to be varied to suit a particular contract. The focus is on manufacturing processes and not other processes addressed by the quality system. To resolve the ambiguity you may need to prepare three types of quality plan:

- System quality plan that tailors the quality system to particular projects. (This will meet the requirements of clause 4.2.3.)

- Product development quality plan that describes the advanced product quality planning provisions. (This will double as the design and development plan required under clause 4.4.2.)

- Control plan which defines the characteristics to be measured, the measurement method, and reaction plan for prototype, pilot production, and production models. (This will meet the requirements of all references to quality plan in the ISO 9001 italic text of QS-9000 other than in clause 4.2.3.)

Advanced product quality planning

The standard requires *the use of the Advanced Product Quality Planning and Control Plan reference manual* and under the heading of Cross-Functional Teams requires *an advanced product quality planning process to be established and implemented.*

Why these two requirements were separated in the standard is unclear as both references relate to quality planning. The manual does include mandatory requirements by use of the words "shall", "will", and "must" as well as an advisory approach indicated by the word "should". However, use of the word "will" is not consistent since in some cases it has a future implication such as "there will be assumptions ..." Other styles are also used such as "is responsible" and whilst many of the provisions are advisory, the lists of inputs and outputs, having no preceding instruction, are neither mandatory nor advisory so you should consult your customer if in doubt. Certain topics in QS-9000 are also covered in the APQP manual and thus convert advice into mandatory requirements. However, in the final analysis, the auditor will judge so be prepared to justify why you have not done something that is addressed in the manual. There is much good advice in the manual which is commended to readers. It is not the purpose of this handbook to cover the detail of the supplementary manuals, as they speak for themselves. The development cycle shown as a bar chart is illustrated in Figure 2.6.

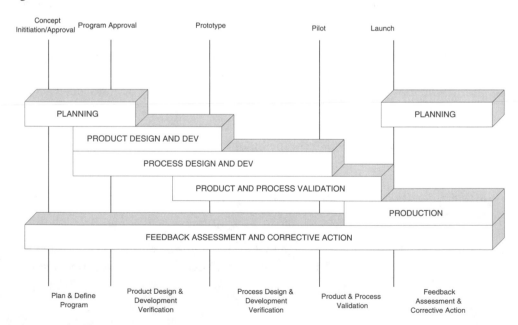

Figure 2.6 Product quality planning timing chart

Finalizing special characteristics

The standard requires *special characteristics to be finalized during the product quality planning process and appropriate process controls to be established.*

During the planning phase, a preliminary list of special product characteristics should be produced (see section 1 of the APQP manual). Special characteristics are those characteristics of products and processes designated by the customer and/or selected by the supplier through knowledge of the product and the process. They are special because they can affect the safe functioning of the vehicle and compliance with government regulations such as flammability, occupant protection, steering control, braking, emissions, noise, EMC etc. During the product design and development phase, the list should be refined, reviewed, and consensus reached. The output is required to be documented in the prototype control plan. During process design and development, the list should be converted into a matrix which displays the relationship between the process parameters and the manufacturing stations and this documented in the production control plan.

Identifying and acquiring controls

In planning for a contract or new product or service, the existing quality system needs to be reviewed against the customer or market requirements. One can then identify whether the system provides an adequate degree of control. Search for unusual requirements and risks to establish whether an adjustment to procedures is necessary. This may require you to introduce new forms, provide additional review, test, and inspection stages and feedback loops, or prepare contingency plans.

One technique you can use to identify the new controls is to establish a list of critical items or areas by analyzing the design. Such items may include:

*   Long lead items, i.e. items that have to be procured well in advance of the main procurement

*   Risky suppliers, i.e. single source suppliers or suppliers with a poor quality record for which there is no alternative

*   High reliability items and single point failure items

*   Limited life items, fragile items, or hazardous items

For each item you should:

*   Provide a description.

*   State the nature of criticality.

- Identify the failure modes and the effects.

- Determine the action required to eliminate, reduce, or control the criticality.

New controls may also be needed if there are unusual contractual relationships, such as overseas subcontractors, international consortia, or in-plant surveillance by the customer. There may be language problems, translation work, harmonization of standards, and other matters arising from international trade.

Once the criticality has been eliminated or reduced by design, choosing the right quality controls is key to the achievement of quality. You need to:

- Analyze the items or activities to determine the key characteristics the measurement and control of which will ensure quality.

- Install provisions that will ensure that these characteristics are achieved.

- Define methods for evaluating the selected characteristics.

- Establish when to perform the measurements and what to do if they are not achieved.

Another method of identifying the controls needed is to describe the result-producing processes in flow diagram format. This will enable you to identify where the verification stages need to be added and the feedback loops inserted. All processes have inputs and outputs and a model process control diagram is shown in Figure 2.7. At the detail level, each of the factors shown in the figure needs to be identified for each process that is critical to the achievement of quality. Some will already be well documented in your quality system, others may have to be developed for specific projects.

Identifying and acquiring processes

You need to identify very early in the program any new processes and one way is to establish a list of processes. The list would identify:

- The process by name

- The process specification

- Manufacturer, if relevant

- Existing qualification data for required application

- Required qualification for the application

Such items may be allocated to several different departments or suppliers and if their acquisition is not coordinated you may find that all the right materials, equipment, resources, processes etc. are not available when you need them.

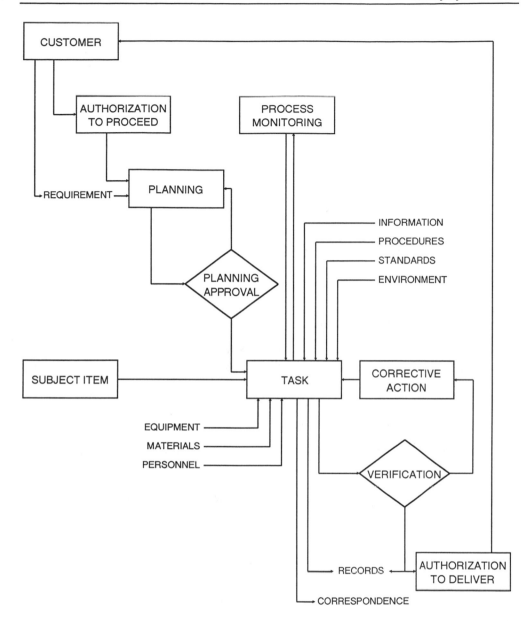

Figure 2.7 Work process control

Identifying and acquiring equipment

You will need to review the requirements and the resultant design to identify any special equipment, tools, test software, and test or measuring equipment required. Once identified, plan for its design, manufacture, procurement, verification, and certification. One way of doing this is to produce a list which contains the following details:

- Nomenclature of the equipment or software

- What it is to be used for

- Reference to its specification

- The location of any design data

- Manufacturer

- The date it was proven fit for use

- Reference to any release certificates

In the service industries, you may need to install new information controls for management to determine whether the services are giving customer satisfaction. This may require new equipment to record, collect, and transmit the data.

Identifying and acquiring fixtures

Fixtures, jigs, and other tools required can be identified in a similar manner. One advantage in producing separate lists is that they serve as a coordination and tracking tool.

Identifying and acquiring resources

Resources are an available supply of equipment, environment, machines, materials, processes, labor, documentation, and utilities, such as heat, light, water, and power etc. that can be drawn upon when needed. This therefore requires detailed planning and logistics management and may require many lists and subplans so that the resources are available when required.

Identifying skills needed to achieve quality

You need to identify any new skills required to operate the processes, design new equipment, perform new roles; for example, if the company hasn't carried out a military project before, you may need to train a project manager specifically for the job. If the project language is not limited to your own language you may need to provide language courses for your staff. Remember, any additional staff need to be trained and qualified before work commences if quality problems are to be minimized. You will also need to identify those skills upon which the success of the project depends and ensure they are not lost to other work. No one is indispensable but a key player leaving at a critical point in the program because of dissatisfaction with working conditions is avoidable!

Ensuring the compatibility of the design, the production process, etc.

It is necessary to verify that all the documentation needed to produce and install the product is compatible; that you haven't a situation where the design documentation requires one thing and the production documents require another or that details in the design specification conflict with the details in the test specification. Incompatibilities can arise in a contract which has been compiled by different groups. For example, the contract requires one thing in one clause and the opposite in another. Many of the standards invoked in the contract may not be applicable to the product or service required. Production processes may not be qualified for the material specified in the design – the designer may have specified materials that are unavailable!

In order to ensure compatibility of these procedures, quality planning reviews need to be planned and performed as the new documentation is produced. Depending on the type of contract, several quality planning reviews may be necessary, each scheduled to occur prior to commencing subsequent stages of development, production, installation, or servicing. The quality planning reviews during product development can be held in conjunction with the design stage reviews required in section 4.4.7 of QS-9000. At these reviews the technical and program requirements should be examined to determine whether the existing quality system provisions are adequate, compatible, and suitable to achieve the requirements; if necessary, additional provisions should be put in place.

Updating quality control and inspection and testing techniques

You should review the contract and the detail specifications to identify whether your existing controls will regulate quality within the limits required. You may need to change the limits, the standards, the techniques, the methods, the environment, and the instruments used to measure quality characteristics.

Development of new instrumentation

Should you need any new instrumentation, either for monitoring processes or for measuring quality characteristics, then you need to make provision for its development. You will need to develop detail specifications of the instrumentation, and design, manufacture, inspect, and install the instruments under controlled conditions which meet the requirements of the standard.

Identifying new measurement capabilities

By assessing the specifications, you may come across a parameter that cannot be measured using state of the art instrumentation. You have three choices: to change the design, renegotiate the contract, or develop some new measurement techniques. The customer should be informed, as he may well be able to relax or change the parameters. Should this not be possible, then you will need to develop a new measurement capability. This may require a separate contract with all the attendant coordination problems of ensuring that the supplier comes up with the goods when you need them. More often than not, as with all new endeavors, there will be unforeseen problems, so keep your customer informed and ensure you are covered contractually when you hit trouble.

Identifying verification requirements

Identifying verification requirements are an important aspect of quality planning. Often all that needs to be defined in a quality plan are the verification requirements such as the inspection and tests to be performed on a particular product. While clauses 4.4.7 and 4.10 deal with verification procedures during design, production, installation, and servicing, a vital aspect of quality planning is the application of these procedures to determine what the verification requirements are, when, and on what size and nature of sample the verification activities are to be carried out. The verification procedures are unlikely to define these aspects for a specific product or service so they have to be determined in the planning phase. However, this requirement does not take into account the validation process in clause 4.4.8. It would appear that this requirement is also partially addressed in section 4.11.2 on *Inspection, measuring, and test equipment*. In this section you are required to determine the measurements to be made to demonstrate the conformance of product to the specified requirements. Clearly you can't do this without having identified what you need to verify.

To give this appropriate consideration you have to do two things: define the requirements the product/service has to meet and define how these requirements are to be verified.

If all the key features and characteristics of your product or service can be verified by a simple examination on final inspection or at the point of delivery, then the requirement is easily satisfied. On the other hand if you can't do this, while the principle is the same, it becomes more complex.

Generically there are two types of requirements: defining requirements and verification requirements. *Defining requirements* specify the features and characteristics required of a product, process, or service. (Within the standard these are termed *specifying requirements*.) These may be wholly specified by the customer or by the supplier or a mixture of the two. *Verification requirements* specify the requirements for verifying that the defining requirements have been achieved and again may be wholly specified by the customer or by the supplier or a mixture of the two. With verification requirements, however, other factors have to be taken into consideration, depending on what you are supplying and to whom you are supplying it. In a contractual situation, the customer may specify what he wants verified and how he wants it verified. In a non-contractual situation, there may be legal requirements, compliance with which is essential to avoid prosecution. Many of the national and international standards specify the tests which products must pass rather than performance or design requirements, so identifying the verification requirements can be quite a complex issue. It is likely to be a combination of:

- What your customer wants verified to meet the need for confidence (the customer may not demand you demonstrate compliance with all customer requirements, only those which he judges as critical)

- What you need to verify to demonstrate that you are meeting all your customer's defining requirements (you may have a choice as to how you do this, so it is not as onerous as it appears)

- What you need to verify to demonstrate that you are meeting your own defining requirements (where your customer defines the product/service in performance terms, you will need to define in more detail the features and characteristics that will deliver the specified performance and these will need to be verified)

- What you need to verify to demonstrate that you are complying with the law (product safety, personnel health and safety, conservation, environmental, and other legislation)

- What you need to verify to obtain confidence that your subcontractors are meeting your requirements

Verification requirements are not limited to product/service features and characteristics. One may need to consider who carries out the verification, where, and when it is carried out and under what conditions and on what quantity (sample or 100%) and standard of product (prototype or production models).

You may find that the only way you can put your product on the market is by having it tested by an independent test authority. You may have to have a license to manufacture it or to supply it to certain countries and this may only be granted after independent certification. Some verification requirements only apply to the type of product/service, others to the process or each batch of product, and others to each product or service delivery. Some requirements can only be verified under actual conditions of use. Others can be verified by analysis or similarity with other products that have been thoroughly tested (see Chapter 4). The range is so widespread it is not possible in this book to explore all examples, but as you can see, this small and innocuous requirement contains a minefield unless you have a simple product or unless the customer has specified everything you need to verify.

There are a number of ways of documenting verification requirements:

- By producing defining specifications that prescribe requirements for products or services and also the means by which these requirements are to be verified in-house in terms of the inspections, tests, analyses, audits, reviews, evaluations, and other means of verification

- By producing separate verification specifications that define which features and characteristics of the product or service are to be verified and the means by which such verification is to be carried out

- By producing a quality plan or a control plan that identifies the verification stages from product conception to delivery and further as appropriate, and refers to other documents that define the specific requirements at each stage

- By route-card referencing drawings and specifications

- By inspection and test instructions specific to a production line, product, or range of products

In fact you may have to employ one or more of the above techniques to identify all the verification requirements. The standard does not limit the requirements to production.

Clarification of standards of acceptability

In order to verify that the products or services meet the specified requirements you will need to carry out tests, inspections, assessments etc. and these need to be performed against unambiguous standards of acceptability. You need to establish for each requirement that there are adequate criteria for judging compliance. You need to establish how reliable is "reliable", how safe is "safe", how clean is "clean", how good is "good quality". Specifications often contain subjective statements such as good commercial quality, smooth finish etc., and require further clarification in order that an acceptable standard can be attained. The secret is to read the statement then ask yourself if you can verify it. If not, select a standard that is attainable, unambiguous, and acceptable to both customer and supplier.

Identification and preparation of quality records

While procedures should define the quality records that are to be produced, these are the records that will be produced if these procedures are used. On particular contracts only those procedures that are relevant will be applied and therefore the records to be produced will vary from contract to contract. Special conditions in the contract may make it necessary for additional quality records. Records represent the objective evidence with which you are going to demonstrate compliance with the contractual requirements. It would therefore be expedient, although not essential, to list all the records that will be produced and where they will be located. The list does not need to detail every specific record, providing it identifies types of records and all new records to be produced.

Use of cross-funotional teams

The standard recommends that *internal cross-functional teams be convened to prepare for production of new or changed products* and suggests that *they may include customer personnel and subcontractors*. Another requirement for cross-functional teams appears under the heading of Control Plans where they are required *to be established to develop the control plans*.

A cross-functional team is another term for a multidisciplinary team or a project team. Such teams comprise representatives from each line and staff department so that decisions are taken close the development work by those who will have to implement them or verify them. They facilitate communication and overcome delays that often occur when reliant upon line-staff relationships. Advice on setting up such a team is given in the APQP manual. The project organization has been used for several decades as an effective means of organizing knowledge based staff, pooling ideas, obtaining consensus, and making decisions that don't have to be sold to the line departments since they are usually well represented. They do have some disadvantages as several project teams may call upon a single resource at the same time and this is where upper management need to prioritize projects. Also if standards for each project differ, errors can occur as staff juggle with different requirements for the same piece of work. (See also Part 2 Chapter 1 under *Organizational interfaces*.)

Feasibility reviews

The standard requires that *the manufacturing feasibility of proposed products be investigated prior to contracting to produce such products*.

This is a very sensible requirement and should have been included in ISO 9001 (see Part 2 Chapter 9). However, it should have been placed either under the heading *Design control* or under *Process control* since the feasibility review in this context is not concerned with the feasibility of the project before commencing design, but the feasibility of manufacturing the product following completion of design.

Details on what is required are given in section 2 of the APQP manual. However, the design reviews carried out at strategic stages during development should address manufacturability and so rather than conduct one feasibility review, you should plan a review as part of each design review.

Process Failure Mode and Effects Analysis

The standard requires *process FMEAs to consider all special characteristics and recommends that effort is taken to improve the process to achieve defect prevention rather than defect detection*.

The interesting aspect of this requirement is that is does not actually require process FMEAs to be carried out and that it is limited to process FMEAs and does not address product or design FMEAs although these are required in clause 4.4.5 of the standard. It is also interesting that these requirements appear under the heading *Quality planning* and not *Preventive action* or *Design control*. A Failure Mode and Effects Analysis (FMEA) is a systematic analytical technique for identifying potential failures in a design or a process, assessing the probability of occurrence and likely effect and determining the measures needed to eliminate, contain, or control the effects. Action taken on the basis of an FMEA will improve safety, performance, reliability, maintainability, and reduce costs. The outputs are essential to balanced and effective quality plans for both development and production as it will help focus the controls upon those products, processes, and characteristics that are at risk. It is not the intention here to give a full appreciation of the FMEA technique and readers are advised to consult the *Potential Failure Mode and Effects Analysis Manual*. A Microsoft Excel based application has been developed called FMEA Pro containing templates and macros to help engineers perform FMEAs more efficiently.

The FMEA is presented as a table or spreadsheet and contains the following information:

- Function of the item or process

- Potential failure mode (the manner in which the item or process could potentially fail to meet the design intent)

- Potential effects of failure in terms of what the customer might notice or experience

- Severity in the range 1 to 10, 10 being hazardous without warning and 1 having no effect

- Classification in terms of critical, key, major, significant

- Potential cause(s)/mechanism(s) of failure

- Occurrence (the likelihood that a specific cause/mechanism will occur in the range 1 to 10 with 10 being almost inevitable and 1 being unlikely)

- Current design/process controls in terms of the prevention, verification, or other activities to assure design/process adequacy

- Detection in the range 1 to 10 with 10 meaning that the control will not detect the potential failure and 1 meaning that the control will almost certainly detect the potential cause of failure

- Risk priority number: this is the product of the severity, occurrence, and detection factors

- Recommended actions, prioritizing action on the highest ranked concerns

- Responsibility for actions

- Actions taken

- Resulting severity, occurrence, detection ranking, and risk priority number

Control Plans

The standard requires *control plans to be developed at system, subsystem, component, and/or material level as appropriate covering prototype, pre-launch, and production phases.*

The purpose of the control plan is to ensure that all process outputs will be in a state of control by providing process monitoring and control methods to control product and process characteristics. The control plan is covered in section 6 of the APQP manual and consists of forms containing data for identifying process characteristics and helps to identify sources of variation in the inputs that cause product characteristics to vary. The APQP manual provides excellent guidance on the compilation and use of the control plan so no further guidance is given here. However, the control plan defined in the APQP manual does not fully meet the definition of a quality plan in ISO 8402 so additional plans may be needed as discussed previously in this chapter.

Three types of control plan are required. During the product design and development phase, a prototype control plan is required to be produced; during the process design and development phase a pre-launch or pilot production control plan is required; and during the product and process validation phase the production control plan is to be issued.

Pre-launch occurs after prototype testing and prior to full production. Additional inspections and tests may be needed until the production processes have been validated and process capability assured. The additional checks serve to contain nonconformities until variation has been brought within acceptable limits for production.

Maintenance of control plans

The standard requires *controls plans to be reviewed and updated* when a number of situations occur.

This requirement should have been unnecessary since clause 4.2.1 requires the quality system to be maintained. However, what it does do is limit the occasions when the control plan has to be updated and therefore in other circumstances, the plan need not be revised.

Task list

1 Define what you want your quality system to do – define its purpose.

2 Create a plan of how you intend to design, develop, introduce, and evaluate the quality system.

3 Determine the resources required to design, develop, introduce, and evaluate the quality system.

4 Determine training needs for developing, implementing, and evaluating the quality system.

5 Determine the operational policies needed to implement the corporate quality policy and place these in a policy manual with the corporate quality policy.

6 Create a system manual which describes your quality system, how it works and references all the procedures, standards etc. that implement your quality policies.

7 Determine the hierarchy of documentation which you intend to produce to define your quality system: the number and content of the volumes of procedures etc.

8 Define what types of document constitute your quality system.

9 Design the quality system from the top down by analyzing your business functions and processes and then implement from the bottom up, starting with customer complaints.

10 Produce a glossary of terms covering the concepts, documents, and activities to be used in developing and implementing the quality system.

11 Identify the control procedures you need to control what you do now and prepare a document development plan.

12 Compare what you do now with the requirements of QS-9000 and identify additional procedures and changes to your existing procedures.

13 Set up a quality system development team.

14 Determine methods for authorizing the preparation of new quality system documents.

15 Produce procedures for preparing, reviewing, approving, publishing, and distributing quality system documents.

16 Produce procedures for introducing, commissioning, qualifying, changing, filing, and withdrawing quality system documents.

17 Implement the document development plan.

18 Determine how you intend to maintain the system.

19 Determine how you intend to capture potential changes that will affect your quality system.

20 Install the procedures, standards, and guides into the business operations on a progressive basis.

21 Monitor the introduction of new practices.

22 Commence change control practices.

23 Qualify quality system documents for their application.

24 Remove all obsolete documents from operational use.

25 Launch the internal audit program.

26 Collect and analyze the data which the system generates.

27 Use the data for improving the effectiveness of the system.

28 Create procedures for performing advanced product quality planning

29 Create a mechanism for preparing quality control plans if your quality system has to be tailored to suit each product, contract, or project.

30 Produce and agree resource budgets for implementing the quality plan.

31 Create procedures for organizing resources into cross functional teams

32 Review quality plans at each stage of the product/project life cycle for continued suitability.

Quality system questionnaire

1 What is the purpose of the quality system and where is it defined?

2 What is the scope of the quality system and where is it defined?

3 In what document are the requirements of QS-9000 addressed?

4 In what document are the quality system procedures either contained or referenced?

5 In what document is the outline structure of the documentation used in the quality system described?

6 How do you prepare the quality system procedures?

7 How is the degree of documentation required determined?

8 How do you ensure your quality system procedures are consistent with the requirements of QS-9000 and your quality policy?

9 How do you ensure that the documented quality system is implemented effectively?

10 How is the quality system maintained?

11 In what manner do you define and document how the requirements for quality will be met?

12 How do you ensure that quality planning is consistent with other requirements of the quality system?

13 How is the development, prototyping, and production of products planned and managed?

14 How do you identify and acquire any controls, processes, equipment, fixtures, resources, and skills that may be needed to achieve the required quality?

15 How do you ensure that the design, production process, installation, servicing, inspection and test procedures, and applicable documentation are compatible with the specified requirements?

16 How do you identify whether any quality control, inspection and testing techniques, and instrumentation requires updating to meet specified requirements?

17 How do you identify measurement requirements involving a capability that exceeds the known state of the art in sufficient time for the capability to be developed?

18 How do you identify verification requirements and plan their implementation at the appropriate stages?

19 How do you ensure that standards of acceptability for all features, including those containing a subjective element, are clarified before work commences?

20 How do you identify and prepare any new quality records that are needed to meet specified requirements?

21 How are the resources required to develop new products organized?

22 How do you ensure the manufacturability of product prior to contracting for their production?

23 What methods are employed to detect potential failures during product and process design and how are the results used to effect improvement?

24 In what documents are the provisions defined for monitoring processes during prototype, pre-launch, and production phases?

Do's and don'ts

* Don't attempt anything unless you have the commitment and the funding to carry it through.

* Don't start by defining new ways of doing things.

* Do document what you do now before considering new practices.

* Don't let your consultants write all the documents.

* Don't abdicate the preparation of documents to others.

* Do keep it simple and avoid unnecessary complexity.

* Do set targets for developers to aim for.

* Do review progress often.

* Don't let the standard dictate what you must do – let the business do that.

* Don't use cross-referencing between documents unless it is to the whole document.

* Don't put people's names, titles, and locations in your procedures.

* Don't divorce the quality system documents from other documents of your business – develop an integrated system.

* Don't accept any application for a new procedure until you have determined where it fits in the system and how it will interface with other procedures.

* Do publish a glossary of terms to those involved before you commence procedure preparation.

* Do depict the system by diagrams and flowcharts as well as by text.

* Don't try to anticipate everything – if it fits 80% of situations publish it.

* Do obtain prior approval before issuing new procedures for use.

* Do circulate draft documents for comment before submitting for approval.

* Don't ignore people's comments – you may need their support in implementing the procedure later.

* Don't stop development after registration.

* Don't produce project/product specific procedures that conflict with the established quality system.

Chapter 3

Contract review

Scope of requirements

This chapter deals with contracts placed on the supplier by customers, rather than contracts placed by the company on its suppliers. This can be a source of confusion for those unfamiliar with marketing and sales functions.

If you don't have contracts then you can't have a record of contract reviews. However, if the organization being certified to QS-9000 is part of a larger organization, then it may receive orders from other divisions of the same organization and these transactions can be interpreted as "contracts" for the purpose of QS-9000 certification. In such cases you will need Service Agreements with the other divisions which will be governed by the requirements of this clause of the standard. If you obtain services from other divisions of the same organization then these will need to be treated as "subcontractors" and governed by the requirements of clause 4.6 of the standard.

The purpose of the requirements is to ensure that you have established the requirements you are obliged to meet before you commence work. A literal translation of this clause may therefore cause some difficulty.

Many organizations do business through purchase orders or simply orders over the telephone or by mail. However, a contract does not have to be written and signed by both parties to be a binding agreement. Any undertaking given by one party to another for the provision of products or services is a contract whether written or not. An example of how these requirements can be applied to a simple over-the-counter transaction is given at the end of the chapter.

In this competitive environment, product design may well be carried out during the tendering phase and yet QS-9000 does not require the tendering phase to be performed under controlled conditions. Customers need confidence that the supplier's tender was produced under controlled conditions. That is, there is more to the words in the tender than mere promises – the facts have been checked and validated; any proposed solution to the requirements will if implemented actually satisfy all the accepted requirements.

The requirements in element 4.3 are linked with other elements of the standard even when there is no cross reference. This relationship is illustrated in Figure 3.1.

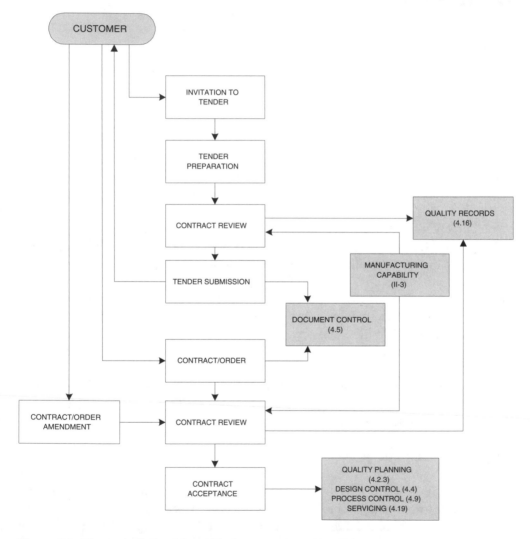

Figure 3.1 Element relationships with the contract review element

Procedures for contract review

The standard requires firstly that the supplier *establishes and maintains documented procedures for contract review*.

Contract review is but one of the tasks in the contract acquisition process. These are marketing, prospect acquisition, tendering, contract negotiation, contract award, and then contract review. However, in a sales situation, you may simply have a catalog of products and services and a sales office taking orders over the telephone or over the counter. The contract review element of this operation takes a few seconds while you determine if you can supply the item requested. In an organization that produces products to specific customer requirements you may in fact carry out all the tasks in the contract acquisition process. Rather than isolate the contract review task and produce a procedure for this, your business may benefit more from a procedure or series of procedures that covers the contract acquisition process as a whole.

Your contract acquisition procedures need to define as appropriate:

- How potential customers are persuaded to place orders or invitations to tender

- How invitations to tender and customer orders are dealt with

- How proposals and quotations are generated, reviewed, and approved

- How contracts are negotiated

- How contracts are accepted, promulgated, and communicated to those concerned

- How changes to contract are initiated

- How changes to contract are agreed, promulgated, and communicated to those concerned

- What channels of communication should be established between supplier and customer

- The authority and responsibility of those who are permitted to interface with the customer

The standard specifies when contract reviews should be undertaken; before submission of a tender or acceptance of a contract. However, having reviewed it once, there is an ongoing requirement for you to ensure you remain capable of satisfying the requirements to which you have agreed. For contracts of short duration this will not be necessary. However, where the contract duration extends over several months or years, then it is necessary to review periodically the requirements and your capability of meeting them. In project work these are known as *project reviews* and may be held at planned stages: monthly, quarterly, yearly, or when the nature of the subsequent work is to change; for instance:

*   At the end of conceptual design prior to commencing detail design

*   At the end of detail design prior to commencing production

*   At the end of production prior to commencing installation

*   At the end of installation prior to handover into service

Coordinating contract review activities

The standard requires that the supplier *establishes documented procedures for coordinating contract review activities*.

In over-the-counter sale situations there is nothing to coordinate. However, in the contracting business, where several departments of the organization have an input to the contract and its acceptability, these activities do need coordinating. When you enter into contract negotiations, the activities of your staff and those of your customer will need coordinating so that you are all working with the same set of documents. You will need to collect the contributions of those involved and ensure they are properly represented at meetings. Those who negotiate contracts on behalf of the company carry a great responsibility. A sales person who promises a short delivery to win an order places an impossible burden on the company. A company's capability is not increased by accepting contracts beyond its current level of capability. You need to ensure that your sales personnel are provided with reliable data on the capability of the organization, do not exceed their authority and always obtain the agreement of those who will execute the contractual conditions before accepting them on their behalf.

One aspect of a contract often overlooked is shipment of finished goods. You have ascertained the delivery schedule, the place of delivery, but how do you intend to ship it: by road, rail, ship, or air. It makes a lot of difference to the costs. Also delivery dates often mean the date on which the shipment arrives not the date it leaves. You therefore need to build into your schedules an appropriate lead time for shipping by the means agreed to. If you are late then you may have to employ speedier means but that will incur a premium for which you may not be paid. Your financial staff will therefore need to be involved in the contract review.

Having agreed to the contract, you need to convey all the contractual requirements to their point of implementation in sufficient time for resources to be acquired and put to work.

Ensuring that the requirements are adequately defined and documented

The standard requires that *before submission of a tender, or acceptance of a contract or order (statement of requirement) the tender, contract, and order is reviewed to ensure that the requirements are adequately defined and documented*.

There will be some organizations that deal with such predictable orders that a formal documented review before acceptance will be an added burden. But however predictable the order it is prudent to establish that it is what you believe it to be before acceptance. Many have been caught out by the small print in contracts or sales agreements such as the wording: "This agreement takes precedence over any conditions of sale offered by the supplier".

If the customer is choosing from a catalog or selecting from a shelf of products, you need to ensure that the products offered for sale are properly described. Such descriptions must not be unrepresentative of the product, otherwise you may be in breech of national laws and statutes. In other situations you need some means of establishing that the customer requirements are adequate.

Although ISO 8402 defines quality as the totality of characteristics of an entity that bears on its ability to satisfy a stated or implied need, QS-9000 does not require the required characteristics to be specified. Note 2 of clause 4.3.4 defines a contract and accepted order as agreed requirements but not specified requirements as used elsewhere in the standard. It would have made for less ambiguity if the term "customer requirements" had been used throughout and then there would be no doubt as to what requirements and whose requirements these clauses refer to.

You could be forgiven for restricting your quality system to the products or services you supply since all the requirements in the standard except clause 4.3 focus on an end product or service conforming to specified requirements. Contract or order requirements will go beyond end product or service requirements. They will address delivery, quantity, warranty, payment, and other legal obligations. With every product one provides a service; for instance one may provide delivery to destination, invoices for payment, credit services, enquiry services, warranty services etc. The principal product may not be the only product either. There may be packaging, brochures, handbooks, specifications etc. With services there may also be products such as brochures, replacement parts and consumables, reports, certificates etc. The definition given in ISO 8402 for product provides for a product being a combination of products and services; therefore, when conducting your contract review you should be addressing all products and services you provide to your customer.

■ **Each product has associated services and each service associated products.**

In ensuring that the contract requirements are adequately defined you should establish where applicable that:

- There is a clear definition of the purpose of the product or service you are being contracted to supply.

- The conditions of use are clearly specified.

- The requirements are specified in terms of the features and characteristics that will make the product or service fit for its intended purpose. A list of typical features and characteristics is given in Part 1 Chapter 1 for both products and services.

- The quantity and delivery are specified.

- The contractual requirements are specified, including: warranty, payment conditions, acceptance conditions, customer supplied material, financial liability, legal matters, penalties, subcontracting, licenses, and design rights.

- The management requirements are specified, such as points of contact, program plans, work breakdown structure, progress reporting, meetings, reviews, interfaces

- The quality assurance requirements are specified, such as quality system standards, quality plans, reports, customer surveillance, and concessions.

An adequately documented requirement would be a written contract, schedule of work, and/or specification. However simple the requirement, it is wise to have it documented in case of a dispute later. The document needs to carry an identity and if subject to change, an issue status. In the simple case this is the serial numbered invoice and in more complicated transactions, it will be a multi-page contract with official contract number, date, and signatures of both parties.

The standard allows for undocumented verbal orders but requires that the order requirements are agreed before their acceptance. The assessor cannot confirm conformity with this requirement as there will be no objective evidence to substantiate the transaction other than the payment invoice. If the supplier confirms the agreement in writing then a written statement of requirement exists. The standard does not stipulate that the agreement has to be documented only that the requirements have to be documented whoever produced them. The only evidence that the requirements were adequately defined is therefore the payment from the customer against the supplier's invoice.

Resolving differences

The standard requires that *before submission of a tender, or acceptance of a contract or order (statement of requirement) the tender, contract, and order is reviewed to ensure that any contract or accepted order requirements differing from those in the tender are resolved.*

There is a slight conflict in this clause as it requires that before acceptance of an order, you have to ensure that any differences between your tender and the accepted order requirements are resolved. Clearly if you have not accepted the order you don't have any accepted order requirement. But this small error doesn't detract from the essence of the requirement.

Whether or not you have submitted a formal tender, any offer you make in response to a requirement is a kind of tender. Where a customer's needs are stated and you offer your product, you are implying that it responds to your customer's stated needs. You need to ensure that your "tender" is compatible with your customer's needs otherwise the customer may claim you have sold a product that is not fit for purpose. If the product or service you offer is in any way different than the requirement, you need to point it out to your customer in your tender or in negotiations and reach agreement. Always record the differences in the contract. Don't rely on verbal agreements as they can be conveniently forgotten when it suits one party or the other.

Ensuring that the supplier has the capability to meet contractual requirements

The standard requires that *before submission of a tender, or acceptance of a contract or order (statement of requirement) each tender, contract, and order be reviewed to ensure that the supplier has the capability to meet contract or accepted order requirements.*

You must surely determine that you have the necessary capability before accepting the contract as to find out afterwards that you haven't the capability to honor your obligations could land you in deep trouble. It is important that those accepting a contract are in a position to judge whether the organization has the capability of executing it. You have to consider that:

- You have access to the products and services required.

- You have a license to supply them if appropriate.

- You have the technology to design, manufacture, or install the product.

- You have the skills and knowledge to execute the work required in the time required and to the specified standards.

- There is sufficient time to accomplish the task with the resources you have available.

- You have access to appropriate subcontractors and suppliers.

- There is a secure supply of the necessary materials and components.

- You can meet the terms and conditions imposed by your customer.

- You are prepared to be held to the penalty clause (if specified).

If you don't have any of the above, you will have to determine the feasibility of acquiring the relevant license, the skills, the technology etc. within the timescale. Many organizations do not have staff on waiting time, waiting for the next contract. It is a common practice for companies to bid for work for which they do not have the necessary numbers of staff. However, what they need to ascertain is from where and how quickly they can obtain the appropriate staff. If a contract requires specialist skills or technologies that you don't already possess, it is highly probable that you will not be able to acquire them in the timescale. It is also likely that your customer will want an assurance that you have the necessary skills and technologies before the contract is placed. No organization can expect to hire extraordinary people at short notice. All you can rely on is acquiring average people. With good management skills and a good working environment you may be able to get these average people to do extraordinary things but it is not guaranteed!

In telephone sales transactions or transactions made by a sales person without involving others in the organization, the sales personnel need to be provided with current details of the products and services available, the delivery times, prices, and procedures for varying the conditions.

An additional sentence has been inserted in QS-9000 requiring suppliers to review contracts to ensure that all customer requirements including those in Section III of QS-9000 can be met. This addition was in fact unnecessary as the ISO 9000 requirement for suppliers to have the capability to meet contract requirements is sufficient. Contracts from the Big Three will invariably specify additional requirements to those in QS-9000 Sections I & II and will invoke the appropriate parts of Section III. It is therefore important that those staff reviewing such contracts are familiar with these additional requirements and their impact on the existing quality system. In some cases, special instructions will be necessary to tailor your procedures to meet the specific customer requirements. Merely accepting requirements without ensuring that the means to convey them to the point of implementation are in place will undoubtedly result in noncompliances.

Amendments to contract

The standard requires suppliers to *identify how an amendment to a contract is made and correctly transferred to the functions concerned.*

There may be several reasons why a customer needs to amend the original contract. Customer needs may change, your customer's customer may change the requirement or details unknown at the time of contract may be brought to light. Whatever the reasons you need to provide a procedure for changing the contract under controlled conditions. On contracts where liaison with the customer is permitted between several individuals – e.g. a project manager, contract manger, design manager, procurement manager, manufacturing manager, quality assurance manager – it is essential to establish ground rules for changing contracts, otherwise your company may unwittingly be held liable for meeting requirements beyond what was originally funded. It is often necessary to stipulate that only those changes to contract that are received in writing from the contract authority of either party will be legally binding. Any other changes proposed, suggested, or otherwise communicated should be regarded as being invalid. Agreement between members of either project team should be followed by an official communication from the contract authority before binding either side to the agreement.

Having made the change to the contract officially, a means has to be devised to communicate the change to those who will be affected by it. You will need to establish a distribution list for each contract and ensure that any amendments are issued on the same distribution list. The distribution list should be determined by establishing who acts upon information in the contract and may include the technical or design managers, the production and procurement managers, the test, commissioning and installation managers, and the quality manager or management representative. Once established, the distribution list needs to be under control since the effect of not being informed of a change to contract may well jeopardize delivery of conforming product.

Maintaining records of contract reviews

The standard requires *records of contract reviews to be maintained.*

Each order or contract should be signed by a person authorized to accept orders or contracts on behalf of the organization. You should also maintain a register of all contracts or orders and in the register indicate which were accepted and which declined. If you prescribe in your contract acquisition procedures the criteria for accepting a contract, the signature of the contract or order together with this register can be adequate evidence of contract review. If contract reviews require the participation of several departments in the organization, then their comments on the contract, minutes of meetings and any records of contract negotiations with the customer represent the records of contract review. It is important, however, to be able to demonstrate that the contract being executed was reviewed for adequacy, differences in the tender and for supplier capability before work commenced. As stated previously, if you don't have written contracts you can't have records of contract reviews. The minimum you can have is a signature accepting an assignment to do work or supply goods but you must ensure that those signing the document know what they are signing for.

Application of requirements

Consider, for example, the transaction made between a person purchasing a replacement lamp for a motor vehicle. How might these requirements apply in such a case?

- The customer inquires whether the supplier has a lamp for a motor vehicle.

- The supplier obtains details of the type, model, and year of the vehicle and which lamp in which position and accesses the stock computer to identify the part number.

- The supplier then confirms with the customer that the correct lamp has been located. (The supplier is ensuring that the requirements are adequately defined. There is no document unless the customer makes the transaction by mail and there is no tender since the customer did not request one. These requirements are therefore not applicable.)

- The supplier then establishes that the identified part is in stock. (The supplier is now establishing the capability of meeting the requirement.)

- Having determined that the item is in stock and informed the customer of the price, the supplier presents the lamp together with an invoice to the customer for payment. (The invoice is the record of the contract review.)

- Should the customer then change the requirement, a new transaction will commence. (This new transaction is the method by which amendments to contract are made.)

Task list

1   Define what constitutes a contract for your organization.

2   Determine when a formal review of a contract is necessary.

3   Determine what constitutes a review of a contract.

4   Prepare a procedure for conducting formal contract reviews.

5   Determine which functions in the organization should participate in contract reviews.

6   Decide how you will obtain input, comment, and participation in contract reviews.

7   Determine who should receive copies of the contract.

8   Establish criteria for determining whether sufficient information has been provided in the contract.

9   Establish a means for the reviewers to determine whether your organization has the capability to meet the contract requirements.

10   Prepare a contract amendment procedure covering incoming and outgoing amendments.

11   Establish who will hold the records of contract reviews, where they will be filed, and who will have access to them.

Contract review questionnaire

1   How do you review tenders, orders, and contracts?

2   How do you coordinate contract reviews?

3   In what documents are the channels of communication and interface with the customer defined?

4   How do you ensure that requirements are adequately documented before they are accepted?

5   How do you ensure that requirements differing from those in the tender are resolved before contract or order acceptance?

6   How do you ensure that you have the capability to meet the contractual requirements before accepting a contract or order?

7   How are amendments to contracts made and correctly transferred to the functions concerned?

8   In what documents do you record the results of contract reviews?

Do's and don'ts

* Don't accept any contract unless you have established that you have the capability to satisfy its requirements, and you have agreement on the payment to be made on completion and when completion is required.

* Do establish what constitutes acceptance by the customer.

* Do ensure that those determining compliance with contracts have access to current versions of the contract.

* Do read the small print and any reference documents before you accept the contract.

* Do declare any areas where your offer differs from that required and state the reasons in terms advantageous to the customer.

* Do establish the boundaries affecting what you and the customer are responsible for.

* Don't make promises to your customer that your staff will not be able to honor.

* Do check your sources of data, prices, technical specification etc., and that they are current and applicable to the specific terms of the contract.

* Do issue contract amendments on the same distribution list as the original contract.

* Don't imply acceptance of a change to contract in any communication other than a formal contract amendment.

Chapter 4

Design control

Scope of requirements

This chapter deals with requirements for the control of any design activities carried out by the supplier, whether it be the design of products or services. It is not specified whether the requirements also apply to the design of items which support the core business, such as test equipment, tools, computer networks, maintenance services, library services etc. It is only from examining ISO 9004 that it becomes clear that the products and services in question are only those which will be supplied to customers with the intention of satisfying their "stated or implied needs". As installation is likely to be a service offered to the customer, the design of the installation should be governed by these design control requirements even though the standard is not specific.

Design can be as simple as replacing the motor in an existing vehicle with one of a different specification, or as complex as the design of an entirely new type of vehicle powered by replenishable organic fuel. Design can be of hardware, software (or a mixture of both), or of services that include a product such as maintenance, communications, processing customer supplied material etc. It can also include services that do not directly include a product, such as cleaning, consultancy, mathematical modeling services. All services have some tangible outcome that can be measured and therefore there is something that can be designed to meet a given need.

Before design commences there is either a requirement or simply an idea. Design is a creative process that creates something tangible out of an idea or a requirement. The controls specified in the standard apply to the design process. There are no requirements that will inhibit creativity or innovation. In order to succeed, the process of converting an idea into a design which can be put into production or service has to be controlled. Design is often a process which strives to set new levels of performance, new standards or create new wants and as such can be a journey into the unknown. On such a journey we can encounter obstacles we haven't predicted, which may cause us to change our course but our objective remains constant. Design control is a method of keeping the design on course towards its objectives and as such will comprise all the factors that may prevent the design from achieving its objectives. It controls the process not the designer; i.e. the inputs, the outputs, the selection of components, standards, materials, processes, techniques, and technologies.

The principles outlined in the standard can be applied to any creative activity and while the standard primarily addresses the design of products and services for onward sale to customers, the principles can be applied to internal systems such as an information technology system, an inventory control system and even the quality system.

The requirements in element 4.4 are linked with other elements of the standard even when there is no cross reference. This relationship is illustrated in Figure 4.1.

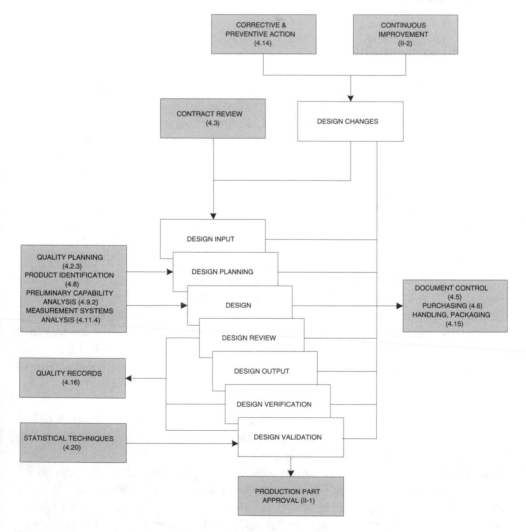

Figure 4.1 Element relationships with the design control element

Design procedures

Procedures to control the design

The standard requires the supplier to *establish and maintain documented procedures to control the design of the product in order to ensure that the specified requirements are met*.

To control any design activity there are ten primary steps in the design process:

- Establish the customer needs.

- Convert the customer needs into a definitive specification of the requirements.

- Conduct a feasibility study to discover whether accomplishment of the requirements is feasible.

- Plan for meeting the requirements.

- Organize resources and materials for meeting the requirements.

- Conduct a project definition study to discover which of the many possible solutions will be the most suitable.

- Develop a specification which details all the features and characteristics of the product or service.

- Produce a prototype or model of the proposed design.

- Conduct extensive trials to discover whether the product or service which has been developed meets the design requirements and customer needs.

- Feed data back into the design and repeat the process until the product or service is proven to be fit for the task.

Procedures need to be produced that address each of these stages. However, control of the design process requires more than procedures. You will need standards and guides or codes of practice, since design is often a process of choosing solutions from available technologies. You may require two types of design control procedures, standards, and guides: those for controlling all designs and those for controlling individual designs. You should either use national and international standards and industry guidelines or develop your own, the latter course being more costly but often the only course if you are operating at the edge of technology. You may need to develop lists of parts, materials, and processes that have been proven for your application and from which designers may select with confidence.

This general requirement for procedures introduces uncertainty into what particular procedures are actually required. The standard does not require the design control procedures to address each requirement of this clause but were they not to, then you would need to demonstrate that the absence of such procedures had no adverse affect on the quality of design.

You need to develop a design strategy that sets out rules for designing your products and services. If your products are grouped into various ranges, you will need standards for each range to ensure that any product added to a particular range is compatible with other products in the range. In other cases you may have modular designs which build designs from existing modules, where the only new design is the "glue" that holds it all together.

Procedures to verify the design

The standard requires the supplier to *establish and maintain documented procedures to verify the design of the product in order to ensure that the specified requirements are met*.

Design verification in particular should address all the activities identified in clause 4.4.7 of the standard. However, procedures that verify the design should be part of the set of procedures used to control the design. Design verification is not something separate from design control. You cannot control the design without verifying that it meets the requirements. The requirement for procedures to control the design should also be interpreted as including design validation, since it is not specifically stated otherwise.

Design and development planning

Preparing the plans

The standard requires the supplier to *prepare plans for each design and development activity which describe or reference these activities and define responsibility for their implementation*.

You should prepare a design and development plan for each new design and also for any modification of an existing design that radically changes the performance of the product or service. For modifications that marginally change performance, control of the changes required may be accomplished through your design change procedures.

Design and development plans need to identify the activities to be performed, who will perform them and when they should commence and be complete. One good technique is to use a network chart, which links all the activities together. Alternatively a bar chart may be adequate. In addition there does need to be some narrative, as charts rarely convey everything required.

It is strange that QS-9000 does not make any reference to Advanced Product Quality Planning under this heading, implying that a development plan is required in addition to the Product Quality Plan generated as a result of implementing the APQP manual. The manual does not require a design and development plan specifically but does require a Product Assurance Plan which in part satisfies the requirements of clause 4.4.2.

Design and development is not complete until the design has been proven as meeting the design requirements, so in drawing up a design and development plan you will need to cover the planning of design verification and validation activities. As the requirements for this are in clauses 4.4.7 and 4.4.8 this aspect will be dealt with later.

The plans should identify as a minimum:

- The design requirements

- The design and development program showing activities against time

- The work packages and names of those who will execute them (work packages are the parcels of work that are to be handed out either internally or to subcontractors)

- The work breakdown structure showing the relationship between all the parcels of work

- The reviews to be held for authorizing work to proceed from stage to stage

- The resources in terms of finance, manpower, and facilities

- The risks to success and the plans to minimize them

- The controls (quality plan or procedures and standards) that will be exercised to keep the design on course

In drawing up your design and development plans you need to identify the principal activities and a good place to start is with the list of ten steps detailed previously. Any further detail will in all probability be a breakdown of each of these stages, initially for the complete design and subsequently for each element of it. If dealing with a system you should break it down into subsystems, and the subsystems into equipments, and equipments into assemblies, and so on. It is most important that you agree the system hierarchy and associated terminology early on in the development program, otherwise you will create both technical and organizational problems at the interfaces. The ten steps referred to previously can be grouped into four phases, a phase being a stage in the evolution of a product or service:

- Feasibility Phase

- Project Definition Phase

- Development Phase

- Production Phase

Planning for all phases at once can be difficult, as information for later phases will not be available until early phases have been completed. So, your design and development plans may consist of four separate documents, one for each phase and each containing some detail of the plans you have made for subsequent phases.

Your design and development plans may also have to be subdivided into plans for special aspects of the design, such as reliability plans, safety plans, electromagnetic compatibility plans, configuration management plans. For services you may separate your home market development plans from your overseas development plans.

With simple designs there may be only one person carrying out the design activities. Since the design and development plan needs to identify all design and development activities, even in this situation you will need to identify who carries out the design, who will review the design and who will verify the design. The design and design verification activities may be performed by the same person. However, it is good practice to allocate design verification to another person or organization as it will reveal problems overlooked by the designer. On larger design projects you may need to employ staff of various disciplines, such as mechanical engineers, electronic engineers, reliability engineers etc. The responsibilities of all these people or groups need to be identified and a useful way of parceling up the work is to use work packages which list all the activities to be performed by a particular group. If you subcontract any of the design activities, the subcontractor's plans need to be integrated with your plans and your plan should identify which activities are the subcontractor's responsibility. While purchasing is dealt with in clause 4.6 of the standard, the requirements apply to the design activities.

The standard requires that the design and development plans describe or reference design and development activities. Hence where you need to produce separate plans they should be referenced in the overall plan so that you remain in control of all the activities.

Assigning design and verification activities

The standard requires that *the design and verification activities be assigned to qualified personnel equipped with adequate resources.*

Once identified, you need to assign the activities and this requires that you identify competent personnel in adequate numbers. Your plans up to this point may only have identified the department or group. You now have to ensure that those carrying out the tasks are competent to do so by virtue of their qualifications and experience. You also need to establish that these groups can provide the staff in adequate numbers to fulfill their responsibilities. Again by using the work package technique you can specify not only what is to be done but the hours, days, months, or years to do it and then obtain the group's acceptance and hence commitment to the task.

Resources are not limited to human resources, as stated in Part 2 Chapter 1. You need to ensure that the design groups are equipped with the necessary design tools, equipment, and facilities with which to execute the tasks. Once you have asked each group to propose how they are to meet the requirements, you then need to ensure that they have the capability of doing so. This is less of a problem in-house as with subcontractors. Due to their remoteness and the keen competition, they may make claims they cannot fulfill. In controlling the design you need to ensure that adequate resources are deployed by the subcontractors and to do this pre-contract surveys and assessments need to be performed. This is implied in clause 4.6.

You also have to be careful that work is not delegated or subcontracted to parties about whom you have little knowledge. In subcontracts, clauses that prohibit subcontracting without your approval need to be inserted, thereby enabling you to retain control.

Ensuring that plans are updated as the design evolves

The standard requires that *the design and development plans be updated as the design evolves.*

Some design planning needs to be carried out before any design commences, but it is an iterative process and therefore the design plans may be completed progressively as more design detail emerges. It is not unusual for plans to be produced and then as design gets underway, problems are encountered which require a change in direction. When this occurs the original plans should be changed. The assessor will be looking to see that your current design and development activities match those in the approved plans. The design and development plan should be placed under document control after it has been approved. When a change in the plan is necessary you should use the document change request mechanism to change your design and development plan and not implement the change until the request has been approved. In this way you remain in control.

Required skills

The standard recommends that *the supplier's design activity should be qualified in several named skills as appropriate.*

Appropriate in this context means appropriate to the nature of the work to be undertaken to meet the contract requirements. It does not mandate that the staff of design departments are competent in all of these skills. However, there is a customer expectation that if possession of one of these skills would lead to a more effective design in a particular case, then the supplier should be employing that skill. Failure to do so requires the supplier to show that it would not be appropriate to the particular design.

Whilst many of these skills are relatively new, i.e. the latter part of the last 100 years, geometric tolerancing has been around for some time. Henry Leland, head of Cadillac, was responsible for bringing the techniques of interchangeable parts into automobile manufacturing around 1900, and the technique goes even further back to Eli Whitney in connection with the manufacture of guns.

An explanation of some of the techniques is given in Appendix A.

Design interfaces

Identifying and documenting organizational interfaces

The standard requires that *organizational interfaces between different groups which input to the design process be identified and the necessary information documented.*

This may well be covered by your design and development plan. In your design procedures you should identify where work passes from one organization to another and the means you use to convey the requirements, such as work instructions. Often in design work, the product requirements are analyzed to identify further requirements for constituent parts. These may be passed on to other groups as input requirements for them to produce a design solution. In doing so these groups may in fact generate further requirements in the form of development specifications to be passed to other groups and so on. For example, the systems engineer generates the system specification and subsystem specifications and passes the latter to the subsystem engineers. These engineers design the subsystem and generate equipment specifications to pass on to the equipment engineers. To meet the equipment specification new parts may be necessary and so these engineers generate part specifications and pass these to the parts engineers. Some of these transactions may be in-house but many will be subcontracted. Some systems houses only possess systems engineering capabilities and subcontract most of the hardware or the software to specialists. In this way they concentrate on the business they are good at and get the best specialist support through competitive tenders. These situations create organizational interfaces that require contractual arrangements, documented requirements, and careful control.

In documenting the organizational interfaces you will need to:

- Define the customer and the supplier.

- Define the work that the supplier is to carry out in a statement of work or list of tasks.

- Define the requirements that the supplier is to meet in a controlled specification.

- Define the means used to convey the requirements and conditions governing the work, and either use a formal contract if external or a work instruction if internal.

- Define the reporting and review requirements for monitoring the work.

- Define the quality management requirement for assuring the quality of the work.

Identifying and documenting technical interfaces

The standard requires that *technical interfaces between different groups which input to the design process be identified and the necessary information documented*.

Technical interfaces and organizational interfaces are often inseparable as the detail specification may have been written around a particular supplier. However, within each development specification the technical interfaces between systems, subsystems, equipments etc. should be specified so that when all these components are integrated they function properly. In some situations it may be necessary to generate separate interface specifications, defining requirements that are common to all components of the system. In a large complex design, minor details of a component may be extremely important in the design of another component. Instead of providing designers with specifications of all the components, it may be more economical (as well as more controllable) if the features and characteristics at the interface between components are detailed in separate interface specifications.

Transmitting interface information

The standard requires that *organizational and technical interface information be transmitted*.

Having documented your organizational and technical interfaces you will need to convey it to those who need it. This may seem an obvious and unnecessary requirement; however, many designs have failed because information was not conveyed in the right form at the right time. You need to provide a mechanism for listing all the documentation that the designers require and making this accessible to them. Some standard interface data can be promulgated in data sheet form, which designers retain in manuals. For other data you may need project-specific listings.

One mechanism of transmitting this design information is to establish and promulgate a set of baseline requirements that are to be used at commencement of design for a particular phase. Any change to these requirements should be processed by a change control board which, when approved, results in a change to the baseline. This baseline listing becomes a source of reference and if managed properly ensures that no designer is without the current design and interface information.

Reviewing interface information

The standard requires that *organizational and technical interface information be regularly reviewed*.

Interfaces should be reviewed along with other aspects of the design at regular design reviews, scheduled prior to the completion of each phase or more often if warranted.

Where several large organizations are working together to produce a design, an interface control board or similar body may need to be created to review and approve changes to technical interfaces. Interface control is especially difficult with complex projects. Once under way, an organization, like a large ship, gains momentum and takes some time to stop. The project manager may not know of everything that is happening. Control is largely by information and it often has a tendency to be historical information by the time it reaches its destination. So it is important to control changes in the interfaces. If one small change goes unreported, it may cause months of delay when an attempt is made to join the two components together and it is discovered that they don't fit – such as two tracks of a railway or a tunnel.

Design input

Identifying and documenting design input requirements

The standard requires that *design input requirements relating to the product be identified and documented*.

This requirement appears low down in the list of requirements and should ideally have been the first requirement that the standard addressed under design control. Until you have a design input you cannot carry out your design and development planning.

Your initial tasks are to establish what the customer requires and what the expectations are, then convert this into a definitive specification or a design brief.

Design input requirements may in fact be detailed in the contract. The customer may have drawn up a specification detailing the features and characteristics product or service needs to exhibit (see Part 1 Chapter 1 on *Quality characteristics*). Alternatively, the customer needs may be stated in very basic terms; for example:

- *I require a decorative finish for automotive fenders that is of the same appearance as the bodywork.*

- *I require a durable fabric for interior seating that will retain its appearance for the life of the vehicle and is not electrostatic.*

- *I require an electronic door locking system with remote control and manual override that is impervious to unauthorized personnel.*

- *We need a car that will do 100 miles per gallon, carry five passengers, cruise at 65 mph, meet all current safety and pollution laws, and cost no more than $12 000.*

From these simple statements of need you have to gather more information and turn the requirement into a definitive specification. Sometimes you can satisfy your customer with an existing product or service, but when this is not possible you have to resort to designing one to meet the customer's particular needs, whether the customer be a specific customer or the market in general.

You should note that these requirements do not require that design input requirements be stated in terms which, if satisfied, will render the product or service fit for purpose – nor does it state when the design input should be documented. Design inputs should reflect the customer needs and be produced or available before any design commences.

To identify design input requirements you need to identify:

- The purpose of the product or service

- The conditions (or environment) under which it will be used, stored, and transported

- The skills and category of those who will use and maintain the product or service

- The countries to which it will be sold

- The special features and characteristics which the customer requires the product or service to exhibit (see Part 1 Chapter 1 for a list of typical features and characteristics)

- The constraints in terms of timescale, operating environment, cost, size, weight, or other factors

- The standards with which the product or service needs to comply

- The products or service with which it will directly and indirectly interface, and their features and characteristics

- The documentation required of the design output necessary to manufacture, procure, inspect, test, install, operate, and maintain a product or service

As a supplier you have a responsibility to establish your customer requirements and expectations. If you do not determine conditions that may be detrimental to the product and you supply the product as meeting the customer needs and it sub-sequently fails, the failure is your liability. If the customer did not provide reasonable opportunity for you to establish the requirements, the failure may be the customer's liability. If you think you may need some information in order to design a product that meets the customer needs, you must obtain it or declare your assumptions. A nil response is often taken as acceptance in full.

In addition to customer requirements there may be industry practices, national stand-ards, company standards, and other sources of input to the design input requirements to be taken into account. You should provide design guides or codes of practice that will assist designers in identifying the design input requirements that are typical of your business.

The requirement in Section II 2.1 of QS-9000 for continuous improvement on price creates an additional design constraint that should be specified in the design input documents. A guideline price for production units should be established with a requirement that the product be designed so as to meet that price.

The design output has to reflect a product which is producible or a service which is deliverable. The design input requirements may have been specified by the customer and hence not have taken into account your production capability. The product of the design may therefore need to be producible within your current production capability using your existing technologies, tooling, production processes, material handling equipment etc. There is no requirement in the standard for designs to be economically producible and therefore unless such requirements are contained in the design input requirements, producibility will not be verified before product is released into pro-duction (see later under *Design verification*).

Having identified the design input requirements, you need to document them in a specification that, when approved, is brought under document control. The require-ments should not contain any solutions at this stage, so as to provide freedom and flexibility to the designers. If the design is to be subcontracted, it makes for fair competition and removes from you the responsibility for the solution. Where specifications contain solutions, the supplier is being given no choice and if there are delays and problems the supplier may have a legitimate claim against you.

Identifying and documenting statutory and regulatory requirements

The standard requires that *the design input requirements include applicable statutory and regulatory requirements.*

Statutory and regulatory requirements are those which apply in the country to which the product or service is to be supplied. While some customers have the foresight to specify these, they often don't. Just because such requirements are not specified in the contract doesn't mean you don't have to meet them.

Statutory requirements may apply to the prohibition of items from certain countries, power supply ratings, security provisions, markings, and certain notices.

Regulatory requirements may apply to health, safety, environmental emissions, and electromagnetic compatibility and these often require accompanying certification of compliance. In cases where customers require suppliers to be certified to QS-9000 it imposes a regulatory requirement on the design process.

If you intend exporting the product or service, it would be prudent to determine the regulations that would apply before you complete the design requirement. Failure to meet some of these requirements can result in no export license being granted as a minimum and imprisonment in certain cases if found noncompliant subsequently.

Having established what the applicable statutes and regulations are, you need to plan for meeting them and for verifying that they have been met. The plan should be integrated with the design and development plan or a separate plan should be created. Verification of compliance can be treated in the same way, although if the tests, inspections, and analyses are integrated with other tests etc., it may be more difficult to demonstrate compliance through the records alone. In some cases tests such as pollution tests, safety tests, proof loading tests, electromagnetic compatibility tests, pressure vessel tests etc. are so significant that separate tests and test specifications are the most effective method.

Reviewing the selection of design input requirements

The standard also requires that *the selection of design input requirements be reviewed by the supplier for adequacy.*

Adequacy in this context means that the design requirements are a true reflection of the customer needs. It is prudent to obtain customer agreement to the design requirements before you commence the design. In this way you will establish whether you have correctly understood and translated customer needs. It is advisable also to hold an internal design review at this stage so that you may benefit from the experience of other staff in the organization. Any meetings, reviews, or other means of determining the adequacy of the requirements should be recorded so as to provide evidence later if there are disputes. Records may also be needed to demonstrate that you have satisfied the requirements of this clause of the standard.

Resolving incomplete, ambiguous or conflicting requirements

The standard requires that *incomplete, ambiguous or conflicting requirements be resolved with those responsible for drawing up these requirements*.

The review of the design requirements needs to be a systematic review, not a superficial glance. Design work will commence on the basis of what is written in the requirements or the brief, although you should ensure there is a mechanism in place to change the document should it become necessary later. In fact such a mechanism should be agreed at the same time as agreement to the requirement is reached.

In order to detect incomplete requirements you either need experts on tap or check lists to refer to. It is often easy to comment on what has been included but difficult to imagine what has been excluded. It is also important to remove subjective statements (see Part 2 Chapter 2 on *Clarifying standards of acceptability*).

Ambiguities arise where statements imply one thing but the context implies another. You may also find cross-references to be ambiguous or in conflict. To detect the ambiguities and conflicts you need to read statements and examine diagrams very carefully. Items shown on one diagram may be shown differently in another. There are many other aspects you need to check before being satisfied they are fit for use. Any inconsistencies you find should be documented and conveyed to the appropriate person with a request for action. Any changes to correct the errors should be self-evident so that you do not need to review the complete document again.

Impact of the results of contract reviews on design input

The standard requires that *design input take into consideration the results of any contract review activities*.

In cases where the contract includes a design requirement, then in establishing the adequacy of such requirements during contract review, these requirements may be changed or any conflicting or ambiguous requirements resolved. The results of these negotiations should be reflected in a revision of the contractual documentation, but the customer may be unwilling or unable to amend the documents. In such cases the contract review records become in effect a supplement to the contract. These records should therefore be passed to the designers so they can be taken into account when preparing the design requirement specification or design brief.

Computer-aided design, engineering, and analysis

The standard requires the supplier to have *appropriate resources and facilities to utilize computer-aided product design, engineering, and analysis and if subcontracted, technical leadership has to be provided.* Such systems are also required to be *capable of two way interface with customer systems.*

Computer-aided systems are not mandated for all design activities since the requirement can be waived by the customer. When it is a contractual requirement it is likely that your customer will require design information to be transmitted electronically to their location. The standard, however, does not require that these resources be used under controlled conditions, that is that there be documented procedures covering their use, application, maintenance, modification, and improvement, but clearly it would be sensible to employ such controls in order to guard against substandard output produced as a result of inferior facilities. If the facilities are used to establish and verify product characteristics the need for them to be controlled is covered by clause 4.11.

If the computer-aided engineering activities are to be subcontracted then you need to convey the appropriate requirements of your contract to your subcontractor (especially the requirements for special characteristics), impose the controls established to meet element 4.6 and devise a means of verifying that the subcontractor has met your requirements. As the data stored in the CAE system is vital to your business, you need to ensure its protection and control. You need to ensure that the systems used by the subcontractor are not unique and that the data can be migrated to another subcontractor. Also insist on duplicate copies as a safeguard against the subcontractor terminating his business. Where such data is transmitted directly to your customer, you need to verify its integrity including computer virus protection prior to its transmission.

The bit between design input and design output!

Design occurs between receiving the input requirements and producing the output. There are no requirements to govern the very important process of design between the two. During this process several activities are carried out which can be controlled. These are some concerning product design:

* Selection and use of parts, materials, processes

* Selection and use of standards

* Selection and use of tolerances on dimensions

* Performance predictions and analyses covering reliability, maintainability, and safety

- Trade-off studies

- Computer aided engineering

- Production of laboratory prototypes and qualification models

- Value engineering tasks

- Evaluation of new techniques, components, materials, and processes

- Stress calculations, fault tree analysis, failure modes analysis, and worst case analysis

- Use of field data on similar designs

Should you carry out any of these design activities you should ensure they are under control. Procedures, standards, and guides should be provided, which consolidates the organization's knowledge and ensures that the activities are planned, organized, and conducted against the correct design baseline. If these activities are to be carried out by several design organizations on a given development, it may be to your advantage to establish common standards for these activities so that any analyses, predictions etc. can be used as a comparison. If every designer used different techniques, you would not be able to compare the various solutions and may have to wait until you can subject the prototype to common tests.

Whilst the standard does not insert a separate heading for design activities, the supplemental requirements under "design output" clearly indicate that the activities identified above are required.

The designers should record the results of their design activities in a log book or other suitable means so that you can confirm their decisions, particularly on the selection of components for use in the design. If any research is carried out you will need confidence in its validity and the supporting evidence, particularly if important decisions are to be taken as a result of the research.

Design output

Documenting the design output

The standard requires that *the design output be documented and expressed in terms of requirements that can be verified and validated against design-input requirements.*

The standard does not state when design outputs are to be documented but it should be assumed that it is before the product is launched into production. Some organizations are eager to start producing product before the design is complete, particularly if they are marginally ahead of their competitors. In some respects it is not vital that you complete all design documentation before you commence production, providing that you have completed and approved that which is essential for production to commence. You may even start without the inspection and test specifications, providing they are available prior to commencing inspection and test. In a fast moving business you will have to take risks. The quality system should allow you to do so but only under controlled conditions. You should never operate like an unguided missile otherwise you will, in all probability, miss your target! However, the requirement for production part approval ensures that production delivery does not commence until all the necessary documentation has been produced and proven.

Expressing the requirements in terms of requirements that can be verified and validated has two meanings. You have to be able to verify that both the design input requirements and user requirements (if different) have been achieved in the product so they need to be expressed in appropriate terms. The vehicle to contain such requirements is usually a product or service specification. You also need to be able to verify that the design output meets the design input and to achieve this you will need to document your calculations and analyses.

An important requirement is missing from QS-9000, that of expressing the design output in a form suitable to manufacture, procure, inspect, test, install, operate, and maintain a product or service. In some industry sectors the design output contains all the specifications needed for these activities. In the automobile industry, prototyping and pre-production phases are an accepted and required stage through which new designs must pass. ISO 8402 contains no definition of the term *design*. In order for the design output to be expressed in terms that can be verified and validated against design input requirements, the design input requirements have to require documentation of the output necessary to manufacture, procure, inspect, test, install, operate, and maintain a product or service.

Product requirements

Expressing the design output in terms that can be verified and validated means that the requirements for the product or service have to be defined and documented. The design input requirements should have been expressed in a way that would allow a number of possible solutions. The design output requirements should therefore be expressed as all the inherent features and characteristics of the design that reflect a product which will satisfy these requirements. Hence it should fulfill the stated or implied needs, i.e. be fit for purpose.

Product specifications should specify requirements for the manufacture, assembly, and installation of the product in a manner that provides acceptance criteria for inspection and test. They may be written specifications, engineering drawings, diagrams, inspection and test specifications, and schematics. With complex products you may need a hierarchy of documents from system drawings showing the system installation to component drawings for piece-part manufacture. Where there are several documents that make up the product specification there should be an overall listing that relates documents to one another.

Service specifications should provide a clear description of the manner in which the service is to be delivered, the criteria for its acceptability, the resources required, including the numbers and skills of the personnel required, the numbers and types of facilities and equipment necessary, and the interfaces with other services and suppliers.

In addition to the documents that serve product manufacture and installation or service delivery, documents may also be required for maintenance and operation. The product descriptions, handbooks, operating manuals, user guides, and other documents which support the product or service in use are as much a part of the design as the other product requirements. Unlike the manufacturing data, the support documents may be published either generally or supplied with the product to the customer. The design of such documentation is critical to the success of the product, as poorly constructed handbooks can be detrimental to sales.

The requirements within the product specification need to be expressed in terms that can be verified. Hence you should avoid subjective terms such as "good quality components", "high reliability", "commercial standard parts" etc. as these requirements are not sufficiently definitive to be verified in a consistent manner. (See the later section on *Design acceptance criteria* and Part 2 Chapter 2 on *Clarifying standards of acceptability*.)

Design calculations

Throughout the design process, calculations will need to be made to size components and determine characteristics and tolerances. These calculations should be recorded and retained together with the other design documentation but may not be issued. In performing design calculations it is important that the status of the design on which the calculations are based is recorded. When there are changes in the design these calculations may need to be repeated. Also the validity of the calculations should be examined as part of the design verification activity. One method of recording calculations is in a designer's log book but this has the disadvantage that the log book contains all manner of things and so the calculations may not be readily retrievable when needed. Recording the calculations in separate reports or in separate files along with the computer data will improve retrieval.

Design analyses

Analyses are types of calculations but may be comparative studies, predictions, and estimations. Examples are stress analysis, reliability analysis, hazard analysis. Analyses are often performed to detect whether the design has any inherent modes of failure and to predict the probability of occurrence. The analyses assist in design improvement and the prevention of failure, hazard, deterioration, and other adverse conditions. Analyses may need to be conducted as the end use conditions may not be reproducible in the factory. Assumptions may need to be made about the interfaces, the environment, the behavior of the user etc. and analysis of such conditions assists in determining characteristics as well as verifying the inherent characteristics.

Ensuring that design output meets design input requirements

The standard requires that *the design output meets the design input requirements.*

The techniques of design verification identified in clause 4.4.7 can be used to verify that the design output meets the design input requirements. However, design verification is often an iterative process. As features are determined, their compliance with the requirements should be checked by calculation, analysis, or test on development models. Your development plan should identify the stages at which each requirement will be verified so as to warn of noncompliance as early as possible.

Defining acceptance criteria

The standard requires that *the design output contains or makes reference to acceptance criteria.*

Acceptance criteria are the requirements which, if met, will deem the product acceptable. Every requirement should be stated in such a way that it can be verified. Characteristics should be specified in measurable terms with tolerances or min/max limits. These limits should be such that will ensure that all production versions will perform to the product specification and that such limits are well within the limits to which the design has been tested (see also Part 2 Chapter 2). Where there are common standards for certain features then these may be contained in a standards manual. Where this method is used it is still necessary to reference the standards in the particular specifications to ensure that the producers are always given full instructions. Some organizations omit common standards from their specifications. This makes it difficult to specify different standards or to subcontract the manufacture of the product without handing over proprietary information.

Identifying crucial characteristics

The standard requires that the supplier *identify those characteristics of the design that are crucial to the safe and proper functioning of the product*.

Certain characteristics will be critical to the safe operation of the product and these need to be identified in the design output documentation, especially in the maintenance and operating instructions. Drawings should indicate the warning notices required, where such notices should be placed and how they should be affixed. Red lines on tachometers indicate safe limits for engines, audible warnings on computers, on smoke alarms, low oil warning lights etc. indicate improper function or potential danger. In some cases it may be necessary to mark dimensions or other characteristics on drawings to indicate that they are critical and employ special procedures for dealing with any variations. In component design, certain parts are regarded as safety-critical because they carry load. Others are not critical because they carry virtually no load, so there can be a greater tolerance on deviations from specification.

The lists of critical items that were described under *Identifying controls* in Part 2 Chapter 2, together with Failure Modes and Effects Analysis and Hazard Analysis, are techniques that aid the identification of characteristics crucial to the safe and proper functioning of the product. (See Appendix D for standards that cover these techniques.)

Reviewing design output documents

The standard requires that *the design output documents be reviewed before release*.

As stated in the section on design reviews, design documents should have been through a vetting process prior to presentation for design review. The design output may consist of many documents, each of which fulfills a certain purpose. It is important that these documents are reviewed and verified as being fit for their purpose before release, using the documentation controls developed for meeting section 4.5 of ISO 9001. In the software industry, where documentation provides the only way of inspecting the product prior to installation, document inspections called Fagan Inspections, are carried out not only to identify the errors, but to collect data on the type of error and the frequency of occurrence. By analyzing this data using statistical techniques the results assist in error removal and prevention.

Design documentation reviews can be made effective by providing data requirements for each type of document as part of the design and development planning process. The data requirement can be used both as an input to the design process and as acceptance criteria for the design output documentation review. The data requirements would specify the input documents and the content and format required for the document in terms of an outline. Contracts with procurement agencies often specify deliverable documents and by invoking formal data requirements in the contract the customer is then assured of the outputs.

Design reviews

Conducting design reviews

The standard requires that *formal documented reviews of the design results be conducted*.

A design represents a considerable investment by the organization. There is therefore a need for a formal mechanism for management and the customer (if the customer is sponsoring the design) to evaluate designs at major milestones. The purpose of the review is to determine whether the proposed design solution is compliant with the design requirement and should continue or should be changed before proceeding to the next phase. It should also determine whether the documentation for the next phase is adequate before further resources are committed. Design review is that part of the design control process which measures design performance, compares it with predefined requirements and provides feedback so that deficiencies may be corrected before the design is released to the next phase.

Although design documents may have been through a vetting process, the purpose of the design review is not to review documents but to subject the design to an independent board of experts for its judgement as to whether the most satisfactory design solution has been chosen. By using a design review methodology, flaws in the design may be revealed before it becomes too costly to correct them. Design reviews also serve to discipline designers by requiring them to document the design logic and the process by which they reached their conclusions, particularly the options chosen and the reasons for rejecting other options.

QS-9000 requires continuous improvement on price (Section II 2.1), therefore, at each design review the estimated cost of the product should be examined and the results of the value engineering activity discussed. The results of other analysis should also form part of the design review submission as identified in the APQP manual.

The standard refers only to *formal design reviews*, implying that any informal design reviews are not governed by the requirements. The formal review has to be recorded. The informal review does not need to be recorded but the act of recording alone does not make an informal review a formal review. The difference between a formal and an informal design review is a difference of purpose. The formal design review establishes compliance with requirements and authorizes release of resources for the next phase of development. The informal review may result in changes being made to the proposed design solution but occurs between formal reviews and should not result in committing resources to subsequent phases.

ISO 9004-1 contains some guidance on the elements to be considered at design reviews and so rather than reiterate perfectly suitable material I will address aspects of the design review procedures which you will need to generate. A design review is a means of controlling the design and so a design review procedure is required by virtue of the general requirements of clause 4.4.1 of the standard.

Planning design reviews

The standard requires that *formal documented reviews of the design results be planned at appropriate stages of the design*.

Design review schedules

A schedule of design reviews should be established for each product/service being developed. In some cases there will need to be only one design review, after completion of all design verification activities but depending on the complexity of the design and the risks, you may need to review the design at some or all of the following intervals:

- Design Requirement Review. To establish that the design requirements can be met and reflect the needs of the customer before commencement of design.

- Conceptual Design Review. To establish that the design concept fulfills the requirements before project definition commences.

- Preliminary Design Review. To establish that all risks have been resolved and development specifications produced for each sub-element of the product/service before detail design commences.

- Critical Design Review. To establish that the detail design for each sub-element of the product/service complies with its development specification and that product specifications have been produced before manufacture of the prototypes.

- Qualification Readiness Review. To establish the configuration of the baseline design and readiness for qualification before commencement of design proving.

- Final Design Review. To establish that the design fulfills the requirements of its development specification before preparation for its production.

Design review input data

The input data for the review should be distributed and examined by the review team well in advance of the time when a decision on the design has to be made. A design review is not a meeting. However, a meeting will often be necessary to reach a conclusion and to answer questions of the participants. Often analysis may need to be performed on the input data by the participants in order for them to determine whether the design solution is the most practical and cost effective way of meeting the requirements.

Participants at design reviews

The standard requires that *participants at each design review include representatives of all functions concerned with the design stage being reviewed, as well as other specialist personnel as required.*

The review team should have a collective competency greater than that of the designer of the design being reviewed. For a design review to be effective it has to be conducted by someone other than the designer. The APQP manual requires design reviews during the product design and development phase which ends with design verification but does not stipulate a sequence for the reviews. The requirement for participants to include representatives of all functions concerned with the design stage means that it may be difficult to meet this requirement without some members of the review panel being independent.

Design reviews are performed by management or the sponsor rather than the designers, in order to release a design to the next phase of development. A *review* is another look at something. The designer has had one look at the design and when satisfied presents the design to an impartial body of experts so as to seek approval and permission to go ahead with the next phase. Designers are often not the budget holders, or the sponsors. They often work for others. Even in situations where there is no specific customer or sponsor or third party, it is good practice to have someone else look at the design. A designer may become too close to the design to spot errors or omissions and so will be biased towards the standard of his/her own performance. The designer may welcome the opinion of someone else as it may confirm that the right solution has been found or that the requirements can't be achieved with the present state of the art. If a design is inadequate and the inadequacies are not detected before production commences the consequences may well be disastrous. A poor design can lose a customer, a market, or even a business so the advice of independent experts should be valued.

The review team should comprise, as appropriate, representatives of the purchasing, manufacturing, servicing, marketing, inspection, test, reliability, QA authorities etc. as a means of gathering sufficient practical experience to provide advance warning of potential problems with implementing the design. The number of people attending the design review is unimportant and could be as few as the designer and his/her supervisor, providing the supervisor is able to impart sufficient practical experience and there are no other personnel involved at that particular design stage. There is no advantage gained in staff attending design reviews if they can add no value in terms of their relevant experience, regardless of what positions they hold in the company. The representation at each review stage may well be different, there being just the designer and his/her supervisor at the conceptual review and representation from manufacturing, servicing etc. at the final review.

The chairman of the review team should be the authority responsible for placing the development requirement and should make the decision as to whether design should proceed to the next phase based on the evidence substantiated by the review team.

Design review records

The standard requires *records of design reviews to be maintained*.

The results of the design review should be documented in a report rather than minutes of a meeting, since it represents objective evidence that may be required later to determine product compliance with requirements, investigate design problems, and compare similar designs. The report should have the agreement of the full review team and should include:

- The criteria against which the design has been reviewed

- A list of the documentation that describes the design being reviewed and any evidence presented which purports to demonstrate that the design meets the requirements

- The decision on whether the design is to proceed to the next stage

- The basis on which confidence has been placed in the design

- A record of any outstanding corrective actions from previous reviews

- The recommendations and reasons for corrective action if any

- The members of the review team and their roles

Design review follow-up

Although not a specific requirement of the standard, the requirements in clause 4.14.2 imply that corrective actions resulting from design reviews should be tracked to ensure they are implemented as agreed and that they resolve the reported problem.

Design verification

The standard requires that *at appropriate stages of design, design verification shall be performed to ensure that the design stage output meets the design stage input requirements*.

This revision of the standard has created a distinction between design verification and design validation. There are two types of verification: those verification activities performed during design and on the component parts to verify conformance to specification and those verification activities performed on the completed design to verify performance; but more on this later.

The standard does not state when design verification is to be performed although "appropriate stages" implies that verification of the design after launch of product into production would not be appropriate.

So what are these appropriate stages? In the note which appends the requirements of 4.4.7 of the standard, the reference to design reviews implies that it is a design verification activity. The other design verification activities referred to in clause 4.4.7 are intended to precede the relevant design review and so provide input data to that review. The appropriate stages of verification will therefore mirror the design review schedule but may include additional stages. Design verification needs to be performed when there is a verifiable output. When designing a system there should be design requirements for each subsystem, each equipment, each unit, and so on down to component and raw material level. Each of these design requirements represents acceptance criteria for verifying the design output of each stage. Verification may take the form of a document review, laboratory tests, alternative calculations, similarity analyses or tests, and demonstrations on representative samples, prototypes etc. The planning and conduct of these verification activities is treated in the sections which follow.

Recording design verification measures

The standard requires *design verification measures to be recorded*.

There is no time element in this requirement, therefore it is unclear whether the design verification measures are to be recorded before verification commences or after it is complete. The fact that this requirement is part of section 4.4 implies that design verification is one of the design and development activities which should be planned as required by clause 4.4.2. It would therefore seem sensible to prepare a verification plan as a record of the design verification measures to be undertaken and then produce verification records as evidence that the design output met the design input at the appropriate stages of design.

The design verification plan should be constructed so that every design requirement is verified and the simplest way of confirming this is to produce a verification matrix of requirement against verification methods. You need to cover all the requirements, those that can be verified by test, by inspection, by analysis, by simulation or demonstration, or simply by validation of product records. For those requirements to be verified by test, a test specification will need to be produced. The test specification should specify which characteristics are to be measured in terms of parameters and limits and the conditions under which they are to be measured.

The verification plan needs to cover some or all of the following details as appropriate:

- A definition of the product design standard which is being verified.

- The objectives of the plan. You may need several plans covering different aspects of the requirements.

- Definition of the specifications and procedures to be employed for determining that each requirement has been achieved.

- Definition of the stages in the development phase at which verification can most economically be carried out.

- The identity of the various models that will be used to demonstrate achievement of design requirements. Some models may be simple space models, others laboratory standard or production standard depending on the need.

- Definition of the verification activities that are to be performed to qualify or validate the design and those which need to be performed on every product in production as a means of ensuring that the qualified design standard has been maintained.

- Definition of the test equipment, support equipment, and facilities needed to carry out the verification activities.

- Definition of the timescales for the verification activities in the sequence in which the activities are to be carried out.

- Identification of the venue for the verification activities.

- Identification of the organization responsible for conducting each of the verification activities.

- Reference to the controls to be exercised over the verification activities, in terms of the procedures, specifications, and records to be produced, the reviews to be conducted during the program, and the criteria for commencing, suspending, and completing the verification operations. Provision should also be included for dealing with failures, their remedy, investigation, and action on design modifications.

The verification plan should be approved by the designers and those performing the verification activities. Following approval the document should be brought under document control. Design verification is often a very costly activity and so any changes in the plan should be examined for their effect on cost and timescale. Changes in the specification can put back the program by months while new facilities are acquired, new jigs, cables, etc. procured. However small your design, the planning of its verification is vital to the future of the product. Lack of attention to detail can rebound months (or even years) later during production.

Alternative design calculations

Verification of some characteristics may only be possible by calculation rather than by test, inspection, or demonstration. In such cases the design calculations should be checked either by being repeated by someone else or by performing the calculations by an alternative method. When this form of verification is used the margins of error permitted should be specified in the verification plan.

Comparing similar designs

Design verification can be a costly exercise and so one way of avoiding unnecessary costs is to compare the design with a similar one that has been proven to meet the same requirements. This approach is often used in designs that use a modular construction. Modules used in previous designs need not be subject to the range of tests and examinations necessary if their performance has been verified either as part of a proven design or has been subject to such in-service use that will demonstrate achievement of the requirements. Care has to be taken when using this verification method that the requirements are the same and that evidence of compliance is available to demonstrate compliance with the requirements. Marginal differences in the environmental conditions and operating loads can cause the design to fail if it was operating at its design limit when used in the previous design.

Undertaking tests and demonstrations

Development models
ISO 9001 does not impose any requirements on the standard of development models but QS-9000 has corrected this situation. In order to be confident in the validity of the results of design verification, the design needs to be proven on models representative of those that will enter production.

If design is proven on uncontrolled models then it is likely that there will be little traceability to the production models. Production models may therefore contain features and characteristics which have not been proven. The only inspections and tests which need to be performed on production models are for those features and characteristics that are subject to change due to the variability in manufacturing, either of raw materials or of assembly processes.

It does not constrain you to use production standard models to verify the design but the characteristics being verified need to be to production standard. Other characteristics may be different providing they have no effect on the characteristics being verified.

Many different types of models may be produced to aid product development, test theories, experiment with solutions etc. However, when the design is complete, prototype models representative in all their physical and functional characteristics to the production models may need to be produced.

Prototypes are in fact required unless the requirement is waived by the customer. Although the reason may vary, prototypes will not normally be required when the design is similar to a previously proven design or standard or the design is so simple that sufficient evidence can be obtained during the production trial run.

When building prototypes, the same materials, locations, subcontractors, tooling, and processes should be used as will be used in production so as to minimize the variation.

The requirements of clause 4.11 on measuring and test equipment also apply to the design process. Development tests will not yield valid results if obtained using uncontrolled measuring equipment. Within clause 4.11 of the standard is a require-ment to identify the measurement to be made and this task is usually carried out during the design process. In fact, design is not complete until the criteria for accepting production versions have been established. Products need to be designed so as to be testable during production using the available production facilities, so the proving of production acceptance criteria is very much part of design verification.

Development tests
Where tests are needed to verify conformance with the design specification, develop-ment test specifications will be needed to specify the test parameters, limits, and operating conditions. For each development test specification there should be a corresponding development test procedure which defines how the parameters will be measured using particular test equipment and taking into account any uncertainty of measurement (see Chapter 11). Test specifications should be prepared for each testable item. While it may be possible to test whole units, equipments, or subsystems you need to consider the procurement and maintenance strategies for the product when decid-ing which items should be governed by a test specification. Two principal factors to consider are:

- Testable items sold as spare parts

- Testable items the design and/or manufacture of which are subcontracted

QS-9000 requires consideration to be given to life tests, reliability tests, and durability tests under the heading of design verification. These are treated in this book under the heading of *Design validation*. However, if you conduct trials on parts and materials to prove reliability or durability then these can be considered as verification tests. For example, you may test metals for corrosion resistance or hinges for reliability in the laboratory and then conduct validation tests under actual operating conditions when these items are installed in the final product.

Demonstrations

Tests exercise the functional properties of the product. Demonstrations, on the other hand, serve to exhibit usage characteristics such as access and maintainability, including interchangeability, repairability, and serviceability. Demonstrations can be used to prove safety features such as passenger protection. However, one of the most important characteristics that need to be demonstrated is producibility. Can you actually make the product in the quantities required economically? Does production yield a profit or do you have to produce 50 to yield 10 good ones? The demonstrations should establish whether the design is robust. Designers may be selecting components at the outer limits of their capability. A worst-case analysis should have been performed to verify that under worst-case conditions, i.e. when all the components fitted are at the extreme of their tolerance range, the product will perform to specification. Analysis may be more costly to carry out than a test and by assembling the product with components at their tolerance limits you may be able to demonstrate the robustness of the design more economically.

Reviewing design stage documents before release

As design documents are often produced at various stages in the design process they should be reviewed against the input requirements to verify that no requirements have been overlooked and that the requirements have been satisfied.

Tracking performance testing activities

The standard requires *all performance testing activities to be tracked to monitor timely completion and conformance to requirements*.

As part of the verification plan discussed previously, you should include an activity plan that lists all the planned activities in the sequence they are to be conducted and use this plan to record completion and conformance progressively. The activity plan should make provision for planned and actual dates for each activity and for recording comments such as recovery plans when the program does not proceed exactly as planned. It is also good practice to conduct test reviews before and after each series of tests so that corrective measures can be taken before continuing with abortive tests (see also under *Design validation*).

Subcontracting design verification tests

Where you do not posses the necessary facilities for conducting design verification and validation, these activities may be subcontracted. However, QS-9000 requires that you exercise technical leadership in such matters. This means that you need to enter into a formal contract with the subcontractor, apply the controls you established to meet element 4.6, and manage the test program. You should require the subcontractor to submit test plans and procedures for your approval prior to commencement of the test unless you are providing this information yourself. You need to be confident that the tests will produce valid data so the test set-up, test equipment, test environment, and monitoring methods need to be reviewed. You should have a representative present during test and retain authority for starting and stopping the test.

Design validation

The standard requires that *design validation be performed to ensure that product conforms to defined user needs and/or requirements.*

Merely requiring that the design output meets the design input would not produce a quality product or service unless the input requirements were a true reflection of the customer needs. If the input is inadequate the output will be inadequate: garbage-in-garbage-out to use a common software expression. However, the standard does not require user needs or requirements to be specified. Only contract or order requirements are required to be specified in clause 4.3 of the standard. User needs and requirements should be specified also as part of the design input requirements, but if they are, design validation becomes part of design verification!

> ■ Verification proves the design is right; validation proves it is the right design.

Design validation is a process of evaluating a design to establish that it fulfills the intended user requirements. It goes further than design verification, in that validation tests and trials may stress the product of such a design beyond operating conditions in order to establish design margins of safety and performance. Design validation can also be performed on mature designs in order to establish whether they will fulfill user requirements different to the original design input requirements. An example is where software designed for one application can be proven fit for use in a different application or where a component designed for one environment can be shown to possess a capability which would enable it to be used in a different environment. Multiple validations may therefore be performed to qualify the design for different applications.

Design validation may take the form of qualification tests which stress the product up to and beyond design limits, beta tests where products are supplied to several typical users on trial in order to gather operational performance data, performance trials, and reliability and maintainability trails where products are put on test for prolonged periods to simulate usage conditions.

In the automobile industry the road trials on test tracks are validation tests as are the customer trials conducted under actual operating conditions on pre-production models over several weeks or months. Sometimes the trials are not successful as was the case of the "Copper Cooled Engine" in General Motors in the early 1920s. Even though the engine seemed to work in the laboratory, it failed in service. Production was commenced before the design had been validated. The engine had pre-ignition problems and showed a loss of compression and power when hot. Many cars with the engine were scrapped and apart from the technical problems GM experienced with its development, it did prove to be a turning point in their development strategy, probably resulting in what is now the advanced product quality planning approach.

Again the standard does not stipulate when design validation should occur but logically, design validation of the original design should be complete before product is launched into production. Thereafter, it may be performed at any stage where the design is selected for a different application. However, for the original design the scale of the tests and trials may be such that a high degree of confidence has been achieved before the end of the trials so that pre-production can commence. Some of the trials may take years. The proving of reliability, for instance, may require many operating hours before enough failures have been observed to substantiate the reliability specification. There is no mean time between failure (MTBF) until you have a failure so you have to keep on testing to know anything about the product's reliability.

During the design process many assumptions may have been made and will require proving before commitment of resources to the replication of the design. Some of the requirements, such as reliability and maintainability, will be time-dependent. Others may not be verifiable without stressing the product beyond its design limits. With computer systems, the wide range of possible variables is so great that proving total compliance would take years. It is however necessary to subject a design to a series of tests and examinations in order to verify that all the requirements have been achieved and that features and characteristics will remain stable under actual operating conditions. With some parameters a level of confidence rather than certainty will be acceptable. Such tests are called *qualification tests*. These differ from other tests since they are designed to establish the design margins and prove the capability of the design.

Since the cost of testing vast quantities of equipment would be too great and take too long, qualification tests, particularly on hardware, are usually performed on a small sample. The test levels are varied to take account of design assumptions, variations in production processes and the operating environment.

Products may not be put to their design limits for some time after their launch into service, probably far beyond the warranty period. Customer complaints may appear years after the product launch. When investigated this may be traced back to a design fault which was not tested for during the verification program. Such things as corrosion, insulation, resistance to wear, chemicals, climatic conditions etc. need to be verified as being within the design limits.

Following qualification tests, your customer may require a demonstration of performance in order to accept the design. These tests are called *design acceptance tests*. They usually consist of a series of functional and environmental tests taken from the qualification test specification, supported with the results of the qualification tests. When it has been demonstrated that the design meets all the specified requirements, a Design Certificate can be issued. It is the design standard which is declared on this certificate against which all subsequent changes should be controlled and from which production versions should be produced.

Procedures for controlling qualification tests and demonstrations should provide for:

- Test specifications to be produced which define the features and characteristics that are to be verified for design qualification and acceptance

- Test plans to be produced which define the sequence of tests, the responsibilities for their conduct, the location of the tests, and test procedures to be used

- Test procedures to be produced which describe how the tests specified in the test specification are to be conducted together with the tools and test equipment to be used and the data to be recorded

- All measuring equipment to be within calibration during the tests

- The test sample to have successfully passed all planned in-process and assembly inspections and tests prior to commencing qualification tests

- The configuration of the product in terms of its design standard, deviations, nonconformances, and design changes to be recorded prior to and subsequent to the tests

- Test reviews to be held before tests commence to ensure that the product, facilities, tools, documentation, and personnel are in a state of operational readiness for verification

- Test activities to be conducted in accordance with the prescribed specifications, plans, and procedures

- The results of all tests and the conditions under which they were obtained to be recorded

- Deviations to be recorded, remedial action taken, and the product subject to re-verification prior to continuing with the tests

- Test reviews to be performed following qualification tests to confirm that sufficient objective evidence has been obtained to demonstrate that the product fulfills the requirements of the test specification

Design changes and modifications

The standard requires *all design changes and modifications to be identified, documented, reviewed, and approved by authorized personnel before their implementation.*

This clause covers two different requirements, requiring two quite different control processes. Design changes are simply changes to the design and can occur at any stage in the design process from the stage at which the requirement is agreed to the final certification that the design is proven. Modifications are changes made to products to incorporate design changes and occur only after the first product is built. During development, design changes that affect the prototype are usually incorporated by rework or rebuild and are not classified as modifications. Following design certification, i.e. when all design verification has been completed and the product launched into production, changes to the product to incorporate design changes are classed as "modifications".

You need to control design changes to permit desirable changes to be made and to prohibit undesirable changes from being made. Change control during the design process is a good method of controlling costs and timescales since once the design process has commenced every change will cost time and effort to address. This will cause delays while the necessary changes are implemented and provides an opportunity for additional errors to creep into the design. "If it's not broke don't fix it" is a good maxim to adopt during design. In other words, don't change the design unless it already fails to meet the requirements. Designers are creative people who love to add the latest devices and the latest technologies, to stretch performance, and to go on enhancing the design regardless of the timescales or costs. One reason for controlling design changes is to restrain the creativity of designers and keep the design within the budget and timescale.

The imposition of change control is often a difficult concept for designers to accept. They would prefer change control to commence after they have completed their design rather than before they have started. They may argue that until they have finished there is no design to control. They would be mistaken. Designs proceed through a number of stages (as described previously under *Design reviews*). Once the design requirements have been agreed, any changes in the requirements should be subject to formal procedures. When a particular design solution is complete and has been found to meet the requirements at a design review it should be brought under change control. Between the design reviews the designers should be given complete freedom to derive solutions to the requirements. Between the design reviews there should be no change control on incomplete solutions.

Design changes will result in changes to documentation but not all design documentation changes are design changes. This is why design change control should be treated separately from document control. You may need to correct errors in the design documentation and none of these may materially affect the product. The mechanisms you employ for such changes should be different from those you employ to make changes that do affect the design. By keeping the two types of change separate you avoid bottlenecks in the design change loop and only present the design authorities with changes that require their expert judgment.

The sequence of the requirements in this clause is not necessarily the sequence in which the activities will need to be carried out, so you may find a little repetition in the following sections.

Identification of design changes

At each design review a design baseline should be established which identifies the design documentation that has been approved. The baseline should be recorded and change control procedures employed to deal with any changes. These change procedures should provide a means for formally requesting or proposing changes to the design. The most effective method is by use of a Design Change Form constructed to collect all the data needed by the approval authorities. For complex designs you may prefer to separate proposals from instructions and have one form for proposing design changes and another form for promulgating design changes after approval. You will need a central registry to collect all proposed changes and provide a means for screening those that are not suitable to go before the review board (either because they duplicate proposals already made or may not satisfy certain acceptance criteria which you have prescribed).

On receipt, the change proposals should be identified with a unique number that can be used on all related documentation that is subsequently produced. The change proposal needs to:

- Identify the product of which the design is to be changed.

- State the nature of the proposed change.

- Identify the principal requirements, specifications, drawings or other design documents that are affected by the change.

- State the reasons for the change either directly or by reference to failure reports, nonconformance reports, customer requests, or other sources.

- Provide for the results of the evaluation, review, and decision to be recorded.

Identification of modifications

Since modifications are changes to products resulting from design changes, the identity of modifications needs to be visible on the product that has been modified. If the issue status of the product specification changes then you will need a means of determining whether the product should also be changed. Not all changes to design documentation are design changes which result in product changes and not all product changes are modifications. (Nonconformities may be accepted which change the product but not the design.) Changes to the drawings or specifications that do not affect the form, fit, or function of the product are usually called "alterations" and those that affect form, fit, or function are "modifications". Alterations should come under "document control" whereas design changes should come under "configuration control". You will therefore need a mechanism for relating the modification status of products to the corresponding drawings and specifications. Following commencement of production the first design change to be incorporated into the product will usually be denoted by a number, such as Mod 1, for hardware and by Version or Release number for software. The practices for software differ in that versions can be incremented by points such as 1.1, 1.2 etc., where the second digit denotes a minor change and the first digit a major change. This modification notation relates to the product, whereas issue notation relates to the documentation that describes the product. You will need a modification procedure that describes the notation to be used for hardware and software.

Within the design documentation you will need to provide for the attachment of modification plates on which to denote the modification status of the product.

Documenting design changes

The documentation for design changes should comprise the change proposal, the results of the evaluation, the instructions for change and traceability in the changed documents to the source and nature of the change. You will therefore need:

- A Change Request Form, which contains the reason for change and the results of the evaluation. This was described previously and is used to initiate the change and obtain approval before being implemented.

- A Change Notice, which provides instructions defining what has to be changed. This is issued following approval of the change as instructions to the owners of the various documents that are affected by the change.

- A Change Record, which describes what has been changed. This usually forms part of the document that has been changed and can be either in the form of a box at the side of the sheet (as with drawings) or in the form of a table on a separate sheet (as with specifications).

Where the evaluation of the change requires further design work and possibly experimentation and testing, the results for such activities should be documented to form part of the change documentation.

Documenting modifications

Prior to commencement of production, design changes do not require any modification documentation, the design changes being incorporated in prototypes by rework or rebuild. However, when product is in production, instructions will need to be provided so that the modification can be embodied in the product. These modification instructions should detail:

- Which products are affected, by part number and serial number

- The new parts that are required

- The work to be carried out to remove obsolete items and fit new items or the work to be carried out to salvage existing items and render them suitable for modification

- The markings to be applied to the product and its modification label

- The tests and inspections to be performed to verify that the product is serviceable

- The records to be produced as evidence that the modification has been embodied

Modification instructions should be produced after approval for the change has been granted and should be submitted to the change control board or design authority for approval before release.

Review and approval of design changes

Following the commencement of design you will need to set up a change control board or panel comprising those personnel responsible for funding the design, administering the contract, and accepting the product. All change proposals should be submitted to such a body for evaluation and subsequent approval or disapproval before the changes are implemented. In QS-9000, this change control board must include representatives of the customer engineering authority unless they waive this requirement. Such a mechanism will give you control of all design changes. By providing a two-tier system you can also submit all design documentation changes through such a body. They can filter the alterations from the modifications, the minor changes from the major changes. Remember that by controlling change you control cost so it is a vital organ of the business and should be run efficiently. The requirement for changes to be approved before their implementation emphasizes the importance of this control mechanism.

The change proposals need to be evaluated:

- To validate the reason for change

- To determine whether the proposed change is feasible

- To judge whether the change is desirable

- To determine the effects on performance, costs, and timescales

- To examine the documentation affected by the change and program their revision

- To determine the stage at which the change should be embodied

The evaluation may have to be carried out by a review team, by subcontractors, or by the original proposer; however, regardless of who carries out the evaluation, the results should be presented to the change control board for a decision. During development there are two decisions the board will have to make:

- Whether to accept or reject the change

- When to implement the change in the design documentation

If the board accepts the change, the changes to the design documentation can then either be submitted to the change control board or processed through your document control procedures. During development it is a common practice to accumulate design changes for incorporation into the design when design proving has been completed. If there are many of these changes a two or three stage process of incorporation may be desirable. In the event that the development model is deliverable to the customer or, as in the case of one-off systems, the changes need to be incorporated into the design before delivery. Acceptance may take place against drawings and specifications extended by change notes. However, unless the change notes accurately reflect the final design configuration, the integrity of any certification of the product against a proven design cannot be assured. There is also a temptation to cut costs by not incorporating latent design changes. This may well avert delayed delivery but will have severe consequences should modifications be necessary later or should the changes affect the integrity of the supporting handbooks and manuals. So, deciding when to incorporate the changes is a very important consideration.

Design changes can arise at any time. However, prior to production part approval, customer approval of changes is not required. Subsequent to production part approval or production implementation if the PPAP requirement is waived, QS-9000 requires all design changes to have written customer approval. Any waiver of such approval also needs to be issued by the customer in writing. Verbal approval needs to be followed by written approval from the customer and this provided before the change is implemented in production models. Whilst you may record a conversation you had with the customer, the auditors will not accept this as objective evidence of compliance.

Where the changes are to be made to proprietary designs then you need to inform your customer if you will not continue production to the old design standard. However, not all design changes need reporting to you customer, only those that affect form, fit, function, performance, and durability.

Review and approval of modifications

During production the change control board will need to make four decisions:

• Whether to accept or reject the change

• When to implement the change in the design documentation

• When to implement the modification in new product

• What to do with existing product in production, in store, and in service

The decision to implement the modification will depend on when the design documentation will be changed, when new parts and modification instructions are available. The modification instructions can either be submitted to the change control board or through your document control procedures. The primary concern of the change control board is not so much the detail of the change but its effects, its costs, and the logistics in its embodiment. If the design change has been made for safety or environmental reasons you may have to recall product in order to embody the modification. Your modification procedures need to provide for all such cases.

In some cases the need for a design change may be recognized during production tests or installation and in order to define the changes required you may wish to carry out trial modifications or experiments. Any changes to the product during production should be carried out under controlled conditions, hence the requirement that approval of modifications be given before their implementation. To allow such activities as trial modifications and experiments to proceed you will need a means of controlling these events. If the modification can be removed in a way that will render the production item in no way degraded, you can then impose simple controls for the removal of the modification. If the item will be rendered unserviceable by removing the modification then alternative means may have to be derived, otherwise you will sacrifice the product. It is for this reason that organizations provide development models on which to trial modifications.

Task list

This list is not an exhaustive task list for all design activities. It represents a sample of design control tasks that you may need to carry out. Many tasks may not be applicable for simple designs so you should be selective. They reflect one interpretation of the requirements in the standard.

1 Identify the types of products and services that the organization designs.

2 Determine the processes by which customer requirements or market needs are translated into a set of specifications for a particular product or service.

3 Analyze these processes and identify the discrete tasks that are performed.

4 Prepare procedures to control these tasks and the interfaces between them.

5 Prepare or select guides and standards which assist designers to select proven technologies, parts, materials, methods etc.

6 Qualify your design staff in the appropriate skills.

7 Prepare procedures for the conduct of design verification activities.

8 Prepare procedures for the preparation and maintenance of design and development plans.

9 Determine a methodology for identifying and specifying the documentation requirements for design activities, covering system design, hardware design, software design, service design etc.

10 Determine a methodology for design and development which integrates the major design tasks from the feasibility phase to the production phase.

11 Prepare procedures for creating speciality plans covering reliability, safety, environmental engineering etc.

12 Prepare standard requirements for subcontracted design activities which specify the documentation requirements.

13 Establish a mechanism of reviewing progress through the design and development process for in-house designs and subcontracted designs.

14 Create a procedure for controlling the allocation of work packages to various design groups and to subcontractors.

15 Produce procedures and standards governing the specification of development requirements for components of the design.

16 Produce procedures and standards governing technical interface specifications, their preparation, promulgation, and maintenance.

17 Decide on a mechanism for establishing the design baseline and for controlling changes to the baseline.

18 Set up a design change control board to review, evaluate, and approve or reject design changes.

19 Set up an interface control board to review and evaluate technical interface data.

20 Produce procedures which regulate the specification of design (input) requirements and the documentation of product specifications and drawings.

21 Produce procedures that govern the generation, proving, and publication of product/service support documents, such as handbooks, operating instructions etc.

22 Decide on a method of verifying that the design meets each of the requirements.

23 Determine how you will establish what regulatory requirements apply in the countries to which you expect your products to be exported.

24 Prepare procedures governing the construction of models for use in proving the design.

25 Establish standards for preparation of development and production test specifications and procedures.

26 Decide on the methods to be employed to make the transition from development to pre-production and from pre-production to production.

27 Establish design review procedures that operate at various levels within the design hierarchy, including subcontractors.

28 Determine the design controls you intend to impose over the design of test equipment, tools, test rigs, and other articles.

29 Produce procedures governing the preparation, review, approval, and distribution of modification instructions.

30 Decide on the conventions to be used in identifying the issue status of design documents during development and following design certification.

31 Decide on the conventions to be used to identify the modification status of products or services.

32 Create and maintain records of the implementation of customer changes in design.

33 Create and maintain records of the embodiment of modifications in production.

34 Decide on the criteria for judging when design changes should be incorporated into design documentation.

Design control questionnaire

1 How do you control and verify product design?

2 Where are your plans in which you have identified the responsibility for each design and development activity?

3 How do you ensure that the design and development plans are updated as the design evolves?

4 How do you ensure that design and verification activities are planned and assigned to qualified personnel equipped with adequate resources?

5 How do you ensure technical leadership over subcontracted design and design verification activities?

6   How do you identify, document, transmit, and regularly review the organizational and technical interfaces between different design groups?

7   How do you identify, document, and review design input requirements including applicable statutory and regulatory requirements?

8   How do you ensure that the selection of design input requirements is reviewed for adequacy?

9   How do you resolve incomplete, ambiguous, or conflicting design input requirements?

10 How do you ensure that design inputs take into consideration the results of contract reviews?

11 What evidence is there to show that design output requirements can be verified?

12 How do you ensure that the design output contains or references acceptance criteria?

13 How do you identify those characteristics of the design that are crucial to the safe and proper functioning of the product?

14 How do you ensure that design output documents are reviewed before release?

15 How are formal design reviews planned, conducted, and documented?

16 How are the results of design reviews recorded?

17 How do you ensure that design stage output meets design stage input requirements?

18 How are the design verification measures documented?

19 Under what circumstances would alternative calculations be performed?

20 Under what circumstances would design verification by similarity be valid?

21 When would tests and demonstrations be an appropriate verification method?

22 How do you ensure that design stage documents are reviewed before release?

23 How do you ensure that tests performed using prototype models are representative of the results that would be obtained using production models?

24 How is the design validated to ensure product conforms to defined user needs?

25 How do you identify, document, review, and approve design changes?

26 How do you approve modifications?

27 How do you ensure that no change is made to the design or modification made to the product without prior approval of authorized personnel?

Do's and don'ts

* Don't commence design without a written and agreed requirement.

* Do commence change control immediately after the design requirement has been agreed and issued.

* Don't allow designers to change approved designs without prior approval.

* Do determine who is to carry out which design task before you start design.

* Do give all relevant groups in the organization the opportunity to contribute to the design process.

* Do set standards for design documentation and stick to them.

* Don't use unproven material, components, or processes in new designs unless you plan to evaluate and qualify them before production commences.

* Don't assume that a proven design will necessarily be suitable for other applications.

* Do allow for designs to fail design verification in your development plans – never assume designs can be produced right first time.

* Don't start pre-production until the design has been functionally proven.

* Don't start making prototypes until the interface dimensions have been confirmed.

* Don't give designers a wish list – be specific about the purpose of the product/service.

* Don't accept changes to requirements from your customer without a change to the contract and always get them in writing.

* Do involve the specialists as soon as possible, since the later they start the more redesign will result.

* Do maintain the design requirement document even after you have produced the product specification.

* Do increase safety factors if verification by analysis is performed in lieu of test.

* Do record the design documentation status used in the performance of calculations and analyses.

* Do assess the calculations and analysis when the design changes.

* Do incorporate all design changes before any product is delivered.

Chapter 5

Document and data control

Scope of requirements

Document and data control is one of the most important aspects of the quality system. Although not the only aspect of the quality system, documentation is the foundation stone. The requirements for document and data control can be confusing since the standard doesn't specify what a document is and whether a record is a document or whether data are documents. Since data is information and documents are recorded information perhaps this clause should have been headed *Information control*. There is often confusion also between quality system documents and quality documents and between technical documents and quality documents. There is no doubt that all documents, data, and records should be controlled but the types of control will vary depending on the type of document.

In the world of documents there are two categories, those that are controlled and those that are not controlled. A controlled document is one where requirements have been specified for its development, approval, issue, revision, distribution, maintenance, use, storage, security, obsolescence, or disposal. You do not have to exercise control over each of these elements for a document to be designated a controlled document. Controlling documents may be limited to controlling their revision. On the other hand, you cannot control the revision of national standards but you can control their use, their storage, their obsolescence etc. Even memoranda can become controlled documents if you impose a security classification upon them.

There are three types of controlled documents, as illustrated in Figure 5.1:

- Policies and practices (these include control procedures, guides, operating procedures, and internal standards)

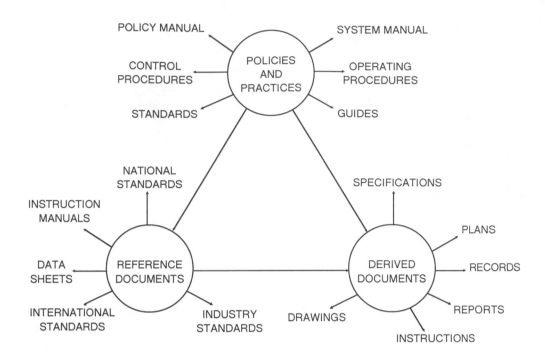

Figure 5.1 Relationship between quality documents

- Documents derived from these policies and practices, such as drawings, specifications, plans, work instructions, technical procedures, and reports

- External documents referenced in either of the above

Derived documents are those that are derived by implementing policies and procedures; for example, audit reports result from implementing the audit procedure, drawings result from implementing the design procedure, procurement specifications result from implementing the procurement procedure. There are, however, two types of derived document: prescriptive and descriptive documents. *Prescriptive documents* are those that prescribe requirements, instructions, guidance, etc., and may be subject to change. They have issue status and approval signatures, and are implemented in doing work. *Descriptive documents* result from doing work and are not implemented. They may have issue status and approval signatures. Specifications, plans, purchase orders, drawings are all prescriptive whereas audit reports, test reports, inspection records are all descriptive. This distinction is only necessary as the controls required will be different. ISO 8402 defines a record as *a document which furnishes objective evidence of activities performed or results achieved*; therefore records are documents, but what we need to know is whether the requirements of clause 4.5 apply to records.

Figure 5.2 Relationship between documents, data and records

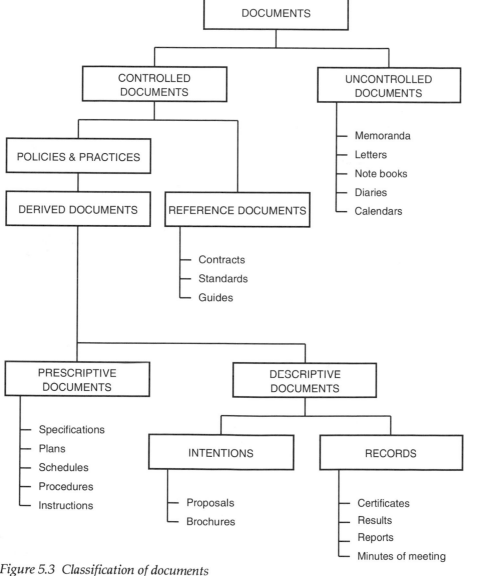

Figure 5.3 Classification of documents

Since there is no cross reference to clause 4.16 from clause 4.5 and vice versa, one can safely assume that the requirements of clause 4.5 are not intended to apply to records, even though they are documents. It would have assisted interpretation if this had been made clear in the standard.

The relationship between elements 4.5 and 4.16 is illustrated in Figure 5.2 above.

Figure 5.3 shows some examples of the different classes of documents and their relationship. All the controlled documents except records are governed by clause 4.5 of the standard. Records are governed by clause 4.16 of the standard.

The requirements of clause 4.5 therefore apply to policies and practices, derived documents, and external documents that are prescriptive but not descriptive. The descriptive documents are covered by clause 4.16 on quality records.

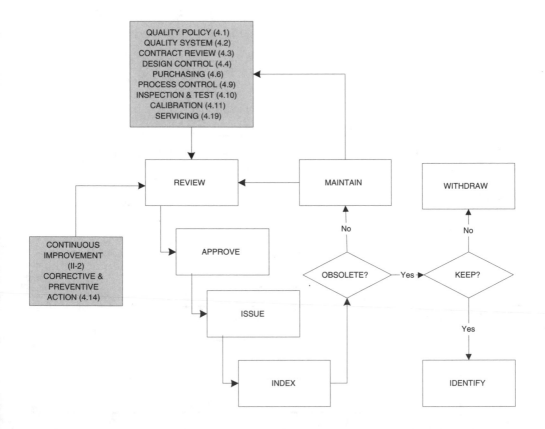

Figure 5.4 Element relationships with the document control element

The term *document* should be taken to include data or any information that is recorded and stored either on paper or magnetic media in a database or on disk. It may be both an audio and visual record although the controls that will be applied will vary depending on the media.

The requirements in element 4.5 are linked with other elements of the standard even when there is no cross reference. This relationship is illustrated in Figure 5.4.

Document control procedures

Documents which relate to the standard

The standard requires that the supplier *establish and maintain documented procedures to control all documents and data that relate to the requirements of the standard*.

Documents and data that relate to the requirements of the standard could be interpreted as including all the documents and data you produce, or be limited to those documents that are essential to the achievement and demonstration of quality. The requirement can be quite onerous since it requires that every document has an associated governing procedure. So if you include memoranda in your system, then you have to have a procedure to control them. The way out of this maze is to use the quality system to define the documents which need to be controlled.

- Ensure that your documented policies and practices specify all the documents that need to be produced and are used to produce products and service that meet the specified requirements. Any document not referred to in your published policies and procedures is therefore, by definition, not essential to the achievement of quality and not required to be under control.

- Ensure that all documents not traceable to the published policies and procedures are removed or identified as uncontrolled.

The procedures that require the use or preparation of documents should also specify or invoke the procedures for their control. If the controls are unique to the document then they should be specified in the procedure that requires the document. You can produce one or more common procedures which deal with the controls that apply to all documents. Although QS-9000 does not address all controls under clause 4.5, the provisions of clause 4.16 relating to the identification, access, filing, and storage of quality records are equally appropriate to documents in general and should be applied although it is not mandatory.

Document control process

The principal elements of document control are illustrated in Figure 5.5. This function provides for bringing existing documents under control, for controlling the preparation of new documents and for changing approved and issued documents. Each process could represent a procedure or a form. The processes may differ depending on the type of document and which organizations are involved in its preparation,

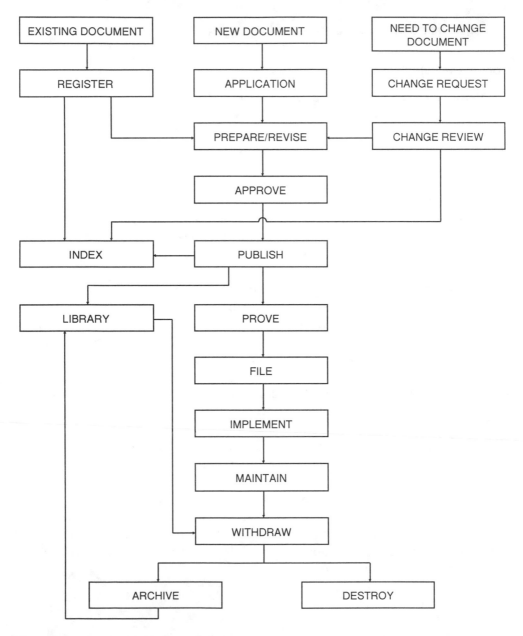

Figure 5.5 Documentation control function

approval, publication, and use. One procedure may cater for all the processes but you may need several.

The aspects you should cover in your document control procedures are as follows, some of which are addressed further in this chapter.

- Planning new documents, funding, prior authorization, establishing need etc.

- Preparation of documents, who prepares, drafting process, text, diagrams, forms etc.

- Standards for the format and content of documents, forms, and diagrams

- Document identification conventions

- Issue notation, draft issues, post approval issues

- Dating conventions, date of issue, date of approval, or date of distribution

- Document review, who reviews, and what evidence is retained

- Document approval, who approves, and how approval is denoted

- Document proving prior to use

- Printing and publication, who does it, who checks it

- Distribution of documents, who decides, who does it, who checks it

- Use of documents, limitations, unauthorized copying and marking

- Revision of issued documents, requests for revision, who approves the request, who implements the change

- Denoting changes, revision marks, reissues, sidelining, underlining

- Amending copies of issued documents, amendment instructions, amendment status

- Indexing documents, listing documents by issue status

- Document maintenance, keeping them current, periodic review

- Document accessibility inside and outside normal working hours

- Document security, unauthorized changes, copying, disposal, computer viruses, fire, theft

- Document filing, masters, copies, drafts, custom binders

- Document storage, libraries and archive, who controls, location, loan arrangements

- Document retention and obsolescence

Control of external documents

The standard requires the supplier to *establish and maintain documented procedures to control documents of external origin such as standards and customer drawings.*

The control which you exercise over external documents is somewhat limited. You cannot for instance control the revision of such documents; therefore all the requirements concerning document changes will not apply. You can, however, control the use and amendment of external documents. You can control use by specifying which versions of external documents are to be used and you can remove invalid or obsolete external documents from use or identify them in a way that users know that they are invalid or obsolete. You can control the amendment of external documents by controlled distribution of amendment instructions sent to you by the issuing agency.

There are two types of external documents, those in the public domain and those produced by specific customers. In some cases the issues of both types of documents are stated in the contract and therefore it is important to ensure that you possess the correct version before you commence work. Where the customer specifies the issue status of public domain documents that apply you need a means of preventing their withdrawal from use in the event that they are revised during the term of the contract. Where the issue status of public domain documents is not specified you may either have a free choice as to the issue you use or, as is more likely, you may have to use the latest issue in force. Where this is the case you will need a means of being informed when such documents are revised so that you can obtain the latest version. The ISO 9000 series for instance is reviewed every five years and so may be revised at five-year intervals. With national and international legislation the situation is rather different as these can change at any time. You need some means of alerting you to changes that affect you and there are several methods from which to choose:

- Subscribing to a standards updating service with the issuing agency

- Subscribing to a general publication that provides news of changes in standards and legislation

- Subscribing to a trade association that provides bulletins to its members on changes in the law and relevant standards

- Subscribing to the publications of the appropriate standards body or agency

- Subscribing to a society or professional institution that updates its members with news of changes in laws and standards

- Consulting the complementary information you receive as a registered company from government agencies, advising you of changes in legislation

- Joining a business club that keeps its members informed of such matters

- Consulting the bulletins you receive as a QS-9000 registered company from your certification body on matters affecting registration and subscribing to *ISO 9000 News* to obtain world-wide news of events and changes in the ISO 9000 arena

The method you choose will depend on the number and diversity of external documents you need to maintain and the frequency of usage.

Identifying special characteristics

The standard requires that *documents be marked with the customer's special symbols to indicate those process steps that affect special characteristics.*

This requirement, although inserted under document control, is in fact a requirement placed upon the document producers. Since the characteristics in question will be specified within documents, the required symbols should be applied where the characteristic is mentioned rather than on the face of the document. Alternatively, where a document specifies processes that affect a special characteristic, the appropriate symbol should be denoted against the particular stage in the process which affects that characteristic. They therefore need to be applied during document preparation and not to copies of the document. The instructions to apply these symbols should be included within the procedures that govern the preparation of the documents concerned.

Review and approval of customer engineering documents

The standard requires *a procedure for the timely review, distribution, and implementation of all customer engineering standards, specifications, and changes.*

Customer engineering standards and specifications are external documents; therefore your procedure for controlling external documents should also cover these documents. Where QS-9000 differs from ISO 9001 on this topic is that ISO 9001 does not require external documents to be reviewed or implemented. However, any external document received or procured for the organization should be reviewed for its applicability before it is brought under control, otherwise resources could be wasted on controlling documents that have no practical use in the organization. This requirement could be placed under "contract review" since any documents issued by customers form part of the contract and should go through contract review before acceptance and implementation.

Timely review means days not weeks or months; therefore immediately a new customer document is received it should be routed to a person authorized through procedures to carry out a review. It would be advantageous to set up an interface with your customers so that their documents are always routed to the same position in your company. The review should establish the applicability of the document and its impact on the contract. Any changed documents should be treated as an amendment to the contract and processed accordingly.

As with all controlled documents, a distribution list for customer documents should be maintained so that copies can be withdrawn, replaced, or amended when required.

Change implementation records

The standard requires a *record of the date on which each change is implemented in production to be maintained and that such implementation include updates to all appropriate documents.*

This requirement has been addressed in its general form in Part 2 Chapter 4 under *Documenting modifications* but will be amplified here. There are two types of records that need to be maintained. One deals with changes to documents and the other deals with changes to products resulting from changes to documents. The master document register or list should list all controlled internal and external documents including customer documents in terms of their title, date, and revision status. The product modification record should define the design standard of the products to be built. A simplified example is shown in Figure 5.6. What this shows are the batches produced and the revision state of the specifications to which each batch of product has been produced. It also shows the date and batch when changes were embodied. Note that ECO1001 was implemented in the design of KL7009 to raise its status from revision 2 to revision 3 when the next batch of product was built. In addition to this record you will need inspection records that denote the configuration of the build.

Another interesting aspect to this requirement of QS-9000 is that *the implementation of changes is to include updates to all appropriate documents.*

Specification /ECO	Pre-prod model Serial Numbers		Production model Serial Numbers			
	1001/1010	1011/20	2001/2100	2101/2200	2201/2300	2301/2400
KL7009	1	2	3	3	3	4
KL7500	1	1	1	2	2	2
ECO1001		12/3/95	-	-	-	-
ECO1002			21/9/95	-	-	-
ECO1003					14/11/95	-

Figure 5.6 Modification record

This means that the impact of a customer change order on your internal documents needs to be evaluated and the corresponding changes made to all affected documents. This should be performed as part of the change review process (see later in this chapter).

Document and data review and approval

The standard requires that *documents and data be reviewed and approved for adequacy by authorized personnel prior to issue.*

Reviewing documents

It is not sufficient that documents are approved prior to issue. Users particularly should participate in the preparation process so that the resultant document reflects their needs and is fit for the intended purpose. Hence the requirement that documents be *reviewed* as well as approved. You will need to be able to demonstrate that your documents have in fact been reviewed prior to issue. The presence of a signature on the front cover is not sufficient evidence. To demonstrate that documents have been reviewed you will need to show that nominated personnel have been issued with drafts for comment and that they have provided comments which have been considered by the approval authorities. A simple method is to employ a standard comment sheet on which reviewers can indicate their comments or signify that they have no comment. During the review process you may undertake several revisions. You may feel it necessary to retain these in case of dispute later, but there is no compulsion for you to do so, providing you have evidence that the review took place. You also need to show that the current issue has been reviewed so your comment sheet needs to indicate document issue status.

Reviewing and approving data

All data should be examined before use, otherwise you may inadvertently introduce errors into your work. The standard does not require that data controls be the same as document controls so you are at liberty to pitch the degree of control appropriate to the consequences of failure.

Regarding approval of data, you will need to define which data needs approval before issue, as some data may well be used as an input to a document which itself is subject to approval. It all depends on how we interpret "approved before issue". Approval before issue should be taken to mean "issue to someone else". Therefore, if you use data that you have generated then it does not need review and approval prior to use. If you issue data to someone else then it should be reviewed and approved beforehand such as in a network database. If your job is to run a computer program in order to check out a product then you might use the data resulting from the test run to adjust the computer or the program. Since you should be authorized to conduct the test your approval of the data is not required because the data has not in fact been issued to anyone else. The danger hiding in this requirement is that an eagle-eyed auditor may spot data being used without any evidence that it has been approved. As a precaution, ensure you have identified in our procedures those types of data that require formal control and that you know from where the data you are using originated.

Adequacy of documents

While the term *adequacy* is a little vague it should be taken as meaning that the document is fit for its purpose. If the objective is stated in the document, does it fulfill that objective? If it is stated that the document applies to a certain equipment, area, or activity, does it cover that equipment, area, or activity to the depth expected for such a document? One of the difficulties in soliciting comments to documents is that you will gather comment on what you have written but not on what you have omitted. So one useful method is to ensure that the procedures requiring the document specify the required content so that the reviewers can check against an agreed standard.

Authorized personnel

Authorized personnel are personnel who have been authorized to approve certain documents. In the procedure which requires the document to be produced you should identify who the approval authorities are by their role or function, preferably not their job title and certainly not their name, as both can change. The procedure need only state that the document shall be approved for example by the Chief Designer and Quality Manager prior to issue. Another method is to assign each document to an owner. The owner is a person who takes responsibility for its contents and to whom all change requests have to be submitted. A separate list of document owners can be maintained and the procedure need only state that the document be approved by the owner.

Denoting approval

The standard doesn't require that documents visibly display approval. Approval can be denoted directly on the document, on a change or issue record, in a register, or on a separate approval record. The presence of a colored header or the stamp of the issuing authority can substitute for actual signatures on documents. Providing signatures and front sheets often adds an extra sheet but no added value. The objective is to employ a reliable means of indicating to users that the document is approved. Some organizations maintain a list of authorized signatories. Where you have large numbers of people whose signatures and names may be unknown to users then this may be necessary. If you are dealing with a small group of people who are accessible and whose signatures are known, then a list of authorized signatures is probably unnecessary. The quality system will not prevent fraud only inadvertent error. All you need is a means of checking that the person who signed the document was authorized to do so. If below the signature you indicate the position of the person and require his name to be printed alongside his signature, then you have taken adequate precautions.

Issuing documents

The term *issue* in the context of documents means that copies of the document are distributed. You will of course wish to *issue* draft documents for comment but obviously they cannot be reviewed and approved beforehand. The sole purpose of issuing draft documents is to solicit comments. The requirement should be that the documents are reviewed and approved prior to *use*. Some organizations insist that even drafts are approved for issue. Others go further and insist that copies cannot be taken from unapproved documents. This is nonsense and not what is intended by the standard. Your draft documents have to look different from the approved versions either by using letter issue notation (a common convention) or by printing on colored or watermark paper. If the approved document would carry signatures, then the absence of any signature indicates that the document is not approved.

Identifying the current revision of documents

The standard requires that *a master list or equivalent document control procedure identifying the current revision status of documents be established and be readily available to preclude the use of invalid and/or obsolete documents*. It is important to note that this requirement only applies to documents and not to data.

As stated previously, staff should have a means of being able to determine the correct revision status of documents they use. You can do this through the work instructions, specification, or planning documents, or by controlling the distribution, if the practice is to work to the latest issue. However, both these means have weaknesses. Documents can get lost, errors can creep into specifications, and the cost of changing documents sometimes prohibits keeping them up to date. The issuing authority for each range of documents should maintain a register of documents showing the progression of changes that have been made since the initial issue. With configuration documents (documents which prescribe the features and characteristics of products and services) the relationship between documents of various issue state may be important. For example a design specification at issue 4 may equate with a test specification at issue 3 but not with the test specification at issue 2. This record is sometimes referred to as a Master Record Index or MRI but there is a distinct difference between a list of documents denoting issue state and a list of documents denoting issue compatibility state. The former is a Document Record Index and the latter a Configuration Record Index. You need to be careful not to imply by the title you give the index that there is a relationship between the document issues if there is no relationship.

The index may be issued or, so as to preclude use of obsolete indices, it may be prudent to keep no hard copies. With organizations that operate on several sites using common documentation it may well be sensible to issue the index so that users have a means of determining the current version of documents.

The standard does not require you only to maintain one index. You can have as many as you like. In fact if you have several ranges of documents it may be prudent to create an index for each range.

Ensuring the availability of controlled documents

The standard requires the supplier to *ensure that the pertinent issues of appropriate documents are available at all locations where operations essential to the effective functioning of the quality system are performed*. Note that the requirement does not apply to data.

This requirement contains four separate points:

a)   What are appropriate documents?

b)   What are operations essential to the effective functioning of the quality system?

c)   How do you ensure that documents are available?

d)   What are pertinent issues and how do you recognize them?

Appropriate documents are those which are needed to carry out work. The work instructions should specify the documents that are required so that any not specified are not essential. It should not be left to the individual to determine which documents are essential to perform the task.

Operations essential to the effective functioning of the system are operations that contribute to the specification, achievement, control, assurance, or management of quality. Any operation covered by the quality system is an essential operation.

Issue notation

The revision status of a document may be indicated by date, by letter, or by number, or may be a combination of issue and revision state. A pertinent issue is a document of the correct revision state. In fact the term *issue* is not an accurate description of what is required. Documents that reside on magnetic media do not have an issue state since they may not be issued. They are recognized by their revision state. Every change to a document should revise the revision index. Changes may be major, causing the document to be reissued or re-released, or they may be minor, causing only the affected pages to be revised. You will need to decide on the revision conventions to use. Software documents often use a different convention to other documents, such as Release 1.1 or Version 2.3. Non-software documents use conventions such as Issue 1, Issue 2 Revision 3, Issue 4 Amendment 2. It is safer to be consistent with your revision conventions so as to prevent mistakes and ambiguities.

Pertinent issues

The pertinent issue of documents may not be the latest issue. You may have reason to use different issues of documents such as when building or repairing different versions of the same product. In such cases you will need a means of indicating which issue of which document is to be used. One method is to specify the pertinent issues of documents in the specifications, drawings, work instructions, or planning documents. This should be avoided if at all possible since it can cause maintenance problems when documents change. It is sometimes better to declare that staff should use the latest issue unless otherwise stated and provide staff with a means of determining what the latest issue is.

A question often asked by assessors is "How do you know you have the correct issue of that document?" One way of ensuring the latest issue is to control the distribution of documents so that each time a document changes the amendments are issued to the same staff who received the original versions. If you identify authentic copies issued by the issuing authority in some way, by colored header, red stamp or other means, then it will be immediately apparent which copies are authentic and under control and which are uncontrolled. Another way is to stamp uncontrolled documents with an "Uncontrolled Document" stamp. All documents should carry some identification as to the issuing authority so that you can check the current issue if you are in doubt. The onus should always rest with the user regarding the use of documents. It is their responsibility to check that they have the correct issue of a document before commencing work. One way of signifying authenticity is to give documents copy numbers in red ink. The standard doesn't require documents to carry copy numbers but it may be a practical way of retaining control over their distribution. If documents are filed in binders by part or volume, then the binder can be given a copy number, but you will need a cross-reference list of who holds which copy.

Availability of documents

In order to make sure that documents are available you should not keep them under lock and key. You need to establish who wants which documents and when they need them. If there is a need for access out of normal working hours then access has to be provided. The more copies there are, the greater the chance that documents will not be maintained, so minimize the number of copies. A common practice is to issue documents to managers and not the users. This is particularly true of quality system documents. One finds that only the managers hold copies of the Quality Manual. In some firms all the managers reside in the same building, even along the same corridor and it is in such circumstance that one finds that these copies have not been maintained. It is therefore impractical to have all the copies of the Quality Manual in one place. Distribute the documents by location not individual. Distribute to libraries or document control centres, so that access is provided to everyone and so that someone has the job of keeping them up to date.

Reference documents

The supplemental requirement in QS-9000 covering reference documents is in fact an amplification of the document availability requirement of ISO 9001. Documents referenced within customer documents and internal documents form part of those documents to the extent specified in the documents. Sometimes the cross references are merely for guidance but often they extend the requirements of the parent document. QS-9000 requires that *the currently released editions of these documents be available at all appropriate manufacturing locations and that customer source documents be readily available*. This requirement limits availability to manufacturing locations; however, these documents may need to be available at other locations such as design and purchasing locations. The term manufacturing locations should be interpreted as a very broad location, i.e. a site rather than a department.

The standard permits customer reference documents to be consolidated i.e. brought together into one document for convenience. However, where this is done you need to ensure that the source documents are readily available so as to check the integrity of the copies you have taken. This is not meant to imply that the source documents have to be in the same location, but their location should be known to the users. One way of doing this is to define the location of customer source documents in your procedure for controlling external documents.

Obsolete and invalid documents

Ensuring removal of obsolete documents

The standard requires the supplier to *ensure that invalid and/or obsolete documents are promptly removed from all points of issue or use, or otherwise assured against unintended use.* Again you should note that this requirement does not apply to data.

It is unnecessary to remove invalid or obsolete documents if you provide staff with the means of determining the pertinent issues of documents to use. There are often valid reasons for retaining obsolete documents. What may be obsolete in one situation may not be obsolete in another. In simple terms an obsolete document is one which is no longer required for operational purposes. As stated earlier, there are cases where various issues of the same document may need to be used and in such cases none of the documents is obsolete. One may need to remove copies of previous versions of a document but retain the master for reference purposes. You cannot demonstrate to an assessor that you corrected a deficiency if you don't retain the version that contained the deficiency as well as the subsequent version.

If you do not have a means of readily distinguishing the correct version of a document, amendment instructions should require that the version being replaced is destroyed or returned to the document controller. If you allow uncontrolled copies to be taken, removal of obsolete documents becomes more difficult. However, providing you have a means of distinguishing controlled and uncontrolled documents you should have no problem. If there is no means of determining current versions, the chances of using the wrong document are significantly increased if several versions are accessible at the same location.

The standard refers to invalid documents as well as obsolete documents. Invalid documents may not be obsolete and may take several forms. They may be:

- Documents of the wrong issue status for a particular task

- Draft documents which have not been destroyed

- Documents which have not been maintained up to date with amendments

- Documents which have been altered or changed without authorization

- Copies of documents which have not been authenticated

- Unauthorized documents or documents not traceable through the quality system

- Illegal documents

Identifying invalid and obsolete documents

The standard requires that *any obsolete document retained for legal and/or knowledge preservation purposes are suitably identified*. Note that this requirement only applies to documents and not data.

One way of identifying obsolete documents is to write SUPERSEDED or OBSOLETE on the front cover, but doing this requires that the custodian is informed. When a version of a document becomes obsolete by replacement with a new version then its withdrawal can be accomplished in the amendment instructions that accompany the revision. When documents become obsolete by total replacement then this can also be accomplished with the amendment instruction. However, where a document becomes obsolete and is not replaced there needs to be a Document Withdrawal Notice which informs the custodian of the action to be taken and the reason for withdrawal.

There is no simple way of identifying invalid documents, as the reasons that they are invalid will vary. By printing authentic documents on colored paper or providing paper with a special header one can inject a degree of control. Placing the approval signatures on the front sheet will immediately identify an unapproved document. However, the onus must rest with the user who, if properly trained and motivated, will not use invalid documents.

Review and approval of changes to documents and data

The standard requires that *changes to documents and data be reviewed and approved by the same functions/organizations that performed the original review and approval unless specifically designated otherwise.*

Changes to documents

Meeting this requirement relies on what constitutes a change to a document. If you have a copy of a document and make pencil marks upon it, have you changed it? The answer is no. You have defaced it. But some assessors would argue that you have changed it, especially if you intend to work to the information you have marked on the document. In fact working to unofficial information is often the only practical solution as processing a formal change may take a considerable time. If by the time the product reaches inspection the formal change has been made then the product can be verified against the authorized document. In other cases, working to marked-up documents can be an authorized practice if you provide a legitimate means for doing so, such as a change note.

If you require an urgent change to a document a legitimate means of issuing change instructions is to generate a Document Change Note. The change note should detail the changes to be made and be authorized by the appropriate authorities. On receipt of the change note the recipients make the changes in manuscript or by page replacement, and annotate the changes with the serial number of the change note. You need to state your policy regarding changing documents. Should you allow any markings on documents, you should specify those which have to be supported by change notes and those which do not. Markings that add comment or correct typographical errors may well be acceptable providing instructions are not changed.

In order that a change be reviewed it has to be proposed and the most common method is to employ Document Change Requests. By using a formal change request it allows anyone to request a change to the appropriate authorities. By maintaining a register of such requests you can keep track of who has proposed what, when, and what progress is being made on its approval. You may of course use a memo or phone call to request a change but this form of request becomes more difficult to track and prove you have control. You will need to inform staff where to send their requests. On receipt of the request you need to provide for their review by the same bodies (not the same people necessarily) that reviewed the original document. The change request may be explicit in what should be changed or simply report a problem which a change to the document would resolve. Someone needs to be nominated to draft the new material and present it for review but, before that, the approval authorities need to determine whether they wish the document to be changed at all. There is merit in reviewing requests for change before processing in order to avoid abortive effort. Also you may receive several requests for change that conflict and before processing you will need to decide which change should proceed.

The change does not have to be reviewed and approved by the same personnel as reviewed and approved the original document. The important factor is that the same functions or organizations review and approve the change. Providing your procedures specify the review and approval authorities in terms of functions or positions and not names then the requirement is easily satisfied.

Changes to data

As with the review and approval of data you need to be careful how you control changes to data. Data that has not been issued to anyone does not require approval if changed. Only the data that has been issued to someone other than its producer need be brought under change control. If you are using data provided by someone else then in principle you can't change it without the person's permission. However, there will be many circumstances where formal change control of data is unnecessary and many where it is vital, as with scientific experiments, research, product testing, etc. One way of avoiding seeking approval to change data is to give the changed data a new identity, thereby creating new data from old data. It is perfectly legitimate as you have not changed the original data providing it can still be accessed by others. If you use a common database for any activities you will need to control changes to the input data.

Access to pertinent background information

The standard requires that *the designated organizations have access to pertinent background information upon which to base their review and approval*.

To provide these authorities with pertinent background information you will need to submit the change request to them. In fact this is another good reason to formalize the change request process. Your change requests need to specify:

* The document title, issue, and date

* The originator of the change request (who is proposing the change, his location or department)

* The reason for change (why the change is necessary)

* What needs to be changed (which paragraph, section, etc., is affected and what text should be deleted)

* The changes required (the text that is to be inserted)

The change should be processed in the same way as the original document and submitted to the appropriate authorities for approval. If approval is denoted on the front sheet of your documents then you will need to reissue the front sheet with every change. This is another good reason to use separate approval sheets. They save time and paper.

Issuing changed documents

Identifying the nature of changes

The standard requires that *where practicable, the nature of the change is to be identified in the document or the appropriate attachments*.

The nature of the change is principally the intrinsic characteristics of the change. You should therefore indicate not only what has changed but also give the reasons for change. The requirement provides a choice as to where you may place this information. To place it in the document you will need to mark the changed material either by sidelining, underlining, emboldening or some other means. You will need to reference the change authority (the change notice, amendment instruction or other notice) and provide a change record in the document on which you can denote the reason for change. Alternatively, you may provide the reasons for change on the change note or amendment instruction and it is always good practice to instruct staff to retain these instructions so as to provide a source of reference when needed.

If you operate a computerized documentation system then your problems can be eased by the versatility of the computer. Using a database you can provide users with all kinds of information regarding the nature of the change, but be careful. The more you provide the greater the chance of error and the harder and more costly it is to maintain.

Staff should be told the reason for change and you should employ some means of ensuring that where changes to documents require a change in practice, adequate instruction is provided. A system which promulgates change without concern for the consequences is out of control. The changes are not complete until everyone who is affected by them both understands them and is equipped to implement them when necessary.

An aspect not covered by the standard is the effect of one change on other documents. It is important to maintain compatibility between documents. When evaluating the change you should assess the impact of the requested change on other areas and initiate the corresponding changes in the other documents.

Reissue of changed documents

The 1987 version of the standard required that documents be reissued after a practical number of changes have been made but this provision has been removed.

The requirement stems from the days before word processing when changes were promulgated by amendment leaflet or change notes and one had to stick additional paragraphs over ones that were crossed out. In such circumstances there were only so many changes of this nature that you could make before the document became unstable and a potential source of error. If you operate in this fashion, then the number of changes may well be a limiting factor but if you use word processors, then other factors ought to be taken into account.

However, there are practical reasons even in the IT age when it may not be prudent to reissue a document after each change.

There are several types of changes you may need to consider:

- Changes affecting a whole range of documents

- Changes affecting many pages of a single document

- Changes affecting a few pages of a single document

For the change that affects a whole range of documents you will either have to reissue the complete set of documents or employ a Global Change Notice. When the cost and time required to process a change that affects many documents is prohibitive then something like a Global Change Notice (GCN) is a useful tool to have in your quality system. With a GCN you can instruct document holders to make changes to certain documents in their possession without having to identify every document. For example, if a component specification changes, a GCN can authorize the new information to be added to any documents which specify that component without having to process hundreds of documents. When the document is subsequently revised for other reasons, the GCN can be embodied, so that over a period of time all documents will eventually be brought up to date. You will need a means of alerting staff to the issue of a GCN but if you control your distribution lists this should not present a problem.

Where a change affects many pages then the document should be reissued. Even if the substantive change is minor, the knock-on effect in double-sided documents with diagrams etc. can be to change every page. With modern word-processing techniques, even adding a full stop can throw out several pages.

Where a change affects only a few pages then you can issue the changed pages with an amendment instruction informing the recipient which pages to change. Alternatively you can use the Document Change Notice (DCN) to add new pages and amend text at the same time.

If only a few words or figures are affected, then the DCN is by far the least expensive and the quickest method.

As an alternative to actually issuing changes, you may wish to process the change requests to the master and hold reissue of the document until a suitable number of changes or a significant proportion of the document, has been changed. It is not the number of changes which is significant since a single change could have far greater effect than 20 minor changes. With small documents, say 3 to 6 pages, it is often easier to reissue the whole document for each change.

Task list

1 Identify the types of document that you need to control.

2 Classify these documents so that you can apply controls appropriate to their classification.

3 Ensure your quality system procedures identify all the types of document requiring control including external documents.

4 Specify appropriate requirements for each of the controlled documents.

5 Establish numbering, dating, revision status conventions.

6 Identify the issuing authorities for the controlled documents.

7 Produce procedures for preparing, reviewing, approving, issuing, and changing controlled documents.

8 Determine where each type of document is to be stored.

9 Decide how you will indicate the approval status on documents.

10 Determine who will review and who will approve the controlled documents.

11 Decide who is to receive, distribute, and review customer documents and changes thereto.

12 Decide how you will safeguard approved documents from unauthorized change, copying, and removal.

13 Create controlled lists of documents which denote the revision status.

14 Create distribution lists for controlled documents.

15 Produce procedures for tracking embodiment of changes to customer documents.

16 Provide document custodians with stamps to mark obsolete documents upon receipt of instructions.

17 Create a formal change request mechanism for initiating changes to controlled documents.

18 Provide a fast route to change documents.

19 Provide an economic means of changing a range of documents affected by a single change.

20 Provide a means of withdrawing and disposing of documents when the product, organization, service, or process becomes obsolete.

21 Provide a means of evaluating the effects that a change in one document has on other documents.

Document control questionnaire

1 How do you control documents and data that relate to the requirements of QS-9000?

2 How do you control documents of external origin?

3 How do you ensure that documents and data are reviewed for adequacy by authorized personnel prior to issue?

4 How do you ensure that the appropriate symbols are denoted in documents that specify and affect special characteristics?

5 How do you ensure that customer engineering documents are subjected to timely review and that the documents are distributed to those concerned?

6 How do you ensure that documents and data are approved for adequacy by authorized personnel prior to issue?

7 How do you ensure that the pertinent issues of appropriate documents including customer documents are available at all locations where operations essential to the effective functioning of the quality system are performed?

8 How do you ensure that information on the current revision status of documents is readily available?

9   How do you ensure that invalid and/or obsolete documents are assured against inadvertent use?

10   What means are used to identify obsolete documents retained for legal and/or knowledge preservation purposes?

11   How do you ensure that changes to documents are reviewed by the same functions or organizations that performed the original review?

12   How do you ensure that changes to documents are approved by the same functions or organizations that performed the original approval?

13   How do you ensure that designated organizations have access to pertinent background information upon which to make their review and approval of changes to documents?

14   How do you identify the nature of changes within documents or their attachments?

15   How do you indicate the point and date at which changes in customer engineering documents are implemented in production?

Do's and don'ts

*   Don't state the issue status of reference documents in your procedures and specifications unless absolutely necessary.

*   Don't put the distribution list on controlled documents – keep it separate.

*   Don't issue documents to individuals – use titles.

*   Don't change a controlled document without an approved change notice.

*   Don't use concessions to change documents – change the document or use a change note.

*   Don't create a complex change control mechanism – it should represent the easiest way of changing a document.

* Do provide labeled binders for ranges of documents as they are more easily traced.

* Do inform staff why changes have been made.

* Don't ignore written comments to draft documents.

* Do give all change requests a unique identity.

* Don't purge every office in search of obsolete documents.

* Do provide for amending the document index before revised documents are issued.

* Don't keep all your documents in one place.

* Do keep "insurance copies" at a remote location.

* Do protect computer access from unauthorized users.

* Do use computer virus protection practices.

* Do limit distribution lists to a "need to know" basis.

* Don't impose presentation standards that are costly to meet and maintain.

* Do secure the masters of documents.

* Do review controlled documents periodically to determine whether they remain relevant.

Chapter 6

Purchasing

Scope of requirements

Most organizations need to purchase items in order to conduct their business. The purchasing requirements of the standard apply only to items needed to design, manufacture, install, maintain, or operate the products and services which it supplies to its customers. Other items are needed to sustain the business such as stationery, catering supplies, furniture etc. and may be used in design, manufacture, installation operations etc. but do not contribute to the quality of the products and services which are supplied to customers. The term *purchasing* involves the payment of money or an equivalent but the requirements still apply if items are obtained without any payment being made, at least by the organization which is to use the item. A more suitable term would be *procurement*, which does not have to involve payment. Although the principles are common sense, the detail requirements of the standard would be too onerous to apply to everything you acquire in connection with your business; so you need a means of classifying purchases so as to apply controls on the basis of their risk to the quality of the products and service supplied to customers.

In addition to products and service which are incorporated or which form part of the products and service supplied to customers, there are tools, test equipment, contract labor, facilities, calibration services, computer services, and many other items which, if not of adequate quality, may adversely affect the quality of the products and service you supply. These items should also be governed by these requirements.

Even though you may not have designed or manufactured the purchased items, you have a responsibility to ensure that such items are fit for their purpose if you sell them on to your customer either directly or as part of another product, since you selected them. If your customer selected the products then they should be governed by the requirements on purchaser supplied product (see Part 2 Chapter 7).

There are four separate clauses to this part of the standard. The first applies to all purchases, the second only to subcontractors, the third to all purchases, and the fourth when specified in the contract. Subcontractors in the context of QS-9000 are defined as providers of production materials, or production or service parts directly to a supplier to Chrysler, Ford, General Motors or other customers subscribing to QS-9000. Therefore if the parts, materials, and services are not being used in production, the subcontractors are not required to meet QS-9000. You are likely to use both production providers and non-production providers; the former are called subcontractors and the latter we could call suppliers. Although a subcontractor is normally an organization that supplies product to your specification and a supplier one who supplies product to their own specification, in the context of QS-9000 both are classed as subcontractors since both enter into a subcontract and assume some of the obligations of the primary

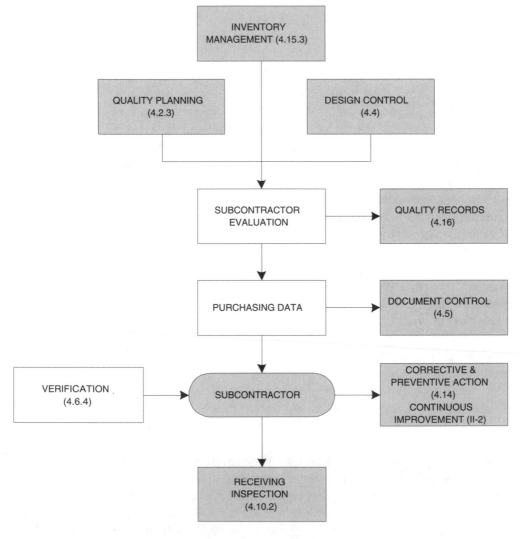

Figure 6-1 Element relationship with the purchasing element

contractor. Apart from the technical requirements, the quantity, delivery, and price requirements place the provider in such a special relationship with the Tier 1 supplier that the Tier 1 supplier has control through the supply chain.

The requirements in element 4.6 are linked with other elements of the standard even when there is no cross reference. This relationship is illustrated in Figure 6.1.

Ensuring purchased product conforms to specified requirements

The standard requires the supplier to *establish and maintain documented procedures to ensure that purchased product conforms to specified requirements*.

Once the make or buy decision has been made, control of any purchasing activity follows a common series of activities, which are illustrated in Figure 6.2. There are four key processes in the procurement cycle for which you should prepare procedures:

- The specification process, which starts once the need has been identified and ends with a request to purchase. This is covered by clause 4.6.3 of QS-9000.

- The evaluation process, which starts with the request to purchase and ends with the placement of the order or contract. This is covered by clause 4.6.2 of QS-9000.

- The surveillance process, which starts with placement of order or contract and ends upon delivery of supplies. This is covered by clause 4.6.2 & 4.6.4 of QS-9000.

- The acceptance process, which starts with delivery of supplies and ends with entry of supplies onto the inventory and/or payment of invoice. This is covered by clause 4.10.2 of QS-9000.

Although the goods inwards or goods receiving function including receipt inspection is considered part of purchasing, since it is the final stage in the purchasing process, the standard covers receipt inspection in clause 4.10. It does not address the receipt of goods activities at all, primarily because this is an accounting or inventory control function and not a function that serves the achievement of quality. Do not separate these processes just to respond to the standard if they are not separate in practice.

Whatever you purchase the processes will be very similar, although there will be variations for purchased services such as subcontract labor, computer maintenance, consultancy services etc. Where the purchasing process is relatively simple, one procedure may suffice but where the process varies you may need separate procedures so as to avoid all purchases, regardless of value and risk, going through the same process. Since it is likely that you will have one purchasing system for supplies

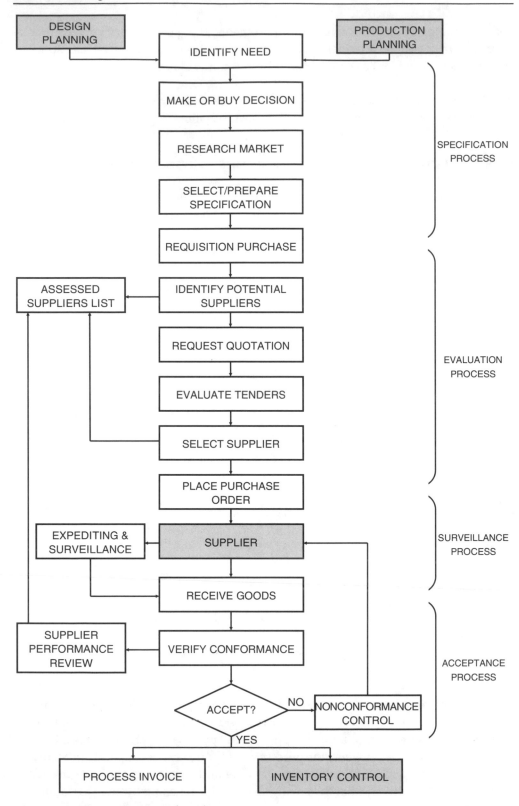

Figure 6.2 The procurement function

irrespective of whether for deliverable products or for internal consumption, it would make sense to distinguish between the procedures used for deliverable supplies and those for purely internal usage.

The standard does not define what the specified requirements are in this case. Elsewhere in the standard the term seems to relate to customer requirements but when purchasing you may well not be passing on customer requirements to your supplier. In cases other than when truly subcontracting work, you will in all probability be deriving your own requirements.

Evaluation and selection of subcontractors

The standard requires that suppliers *evaluate and select subcontractors on the basis of their ability to meet subcontract requirements, including the quality system and any specific quality assurance requirements.*

Evaluating subcontractors

Since subcontractors are to assume some of your obligations you need to make sure that they are capable of meeting your requirements before you enter into a contract. The requirements you pass to your subcontractors need to include:

• The terms and conditions of the contract.

• A specification of the product or service that you require which transmits all of the relevant requirements of the main contract.

• A specification of the means by which the requirements are to be demonstrated.

• A statement of work that you require the subcontractor to perform. It might be design, development, management or verification work. You need to be clear as to the interfaces both organizationally and technically (see Part 2 Chapter 4).

• A specification of the requirements that will give you an assurance of quality. This might be a simple reference to QS-9000 or the appropriate ISO 9000 standard, but since ISO 9000 does not give you any rights you will probably need to amplify the requirements.

QS-9000 does not require that you only purchase from QS-9000 registered subcontractors and suppliers. It does require that you use QS-9000 as the quality system requirement you impose on your subcontractors and suppliers to the extent relevant. Some of the requirements of QS-9000 may be waived if they are not applicable to the product being supplied or the processes of manufacture.

In order to select your subcontractors you will need to identify suitable candidates and request that they provide a proposal against your requirements unless you are provided with a customer approved subcontractor list. One way of doing this is to consult the national list of suppliers of assessed capability, i.e. suppliers who have gained registration to one of the ISO 9000 standards. This gives you immediate confidence that the firms have at least installed an adequate quality system. However, since the test of compliance with the standard is not particularly scientific and as each assessment is only made on a sample of the subcontractor's operations, it is by no means a guarantee that you will receive a superior service and be supplied fully compliant product on time. If you have the purchasing power then you can persuade your contractors to pursue ISO 9000 registration; however, contractors who have not gained ISO 9000 registration may be just as good. You may not have a choice if the product or service you require can only be obtained from a non-registered contractor. Using an ISO 9000 registered contractor should enable you to reduce your subcontractor controls, so by using a non ISO 9000 registered contractor you will have to compensate by performing more quality assurance activities yourself or by employing a third party.

On receipt of the proposals you can then carry out an assessment to determine if the potential subcontractors have the capability to meet your requirements. The assessment needs to look at financial stability, technical capability, management ability, resources, and quality management. Once you have the results of this assessment you can then select two or three and request them to submit a formal tender against your requirements. In the tendering phase each of the potential subcontractors are in competition so you have to observe the basic rule that what you give to one must be given to all. On receipt of the tenders you will need to conduct an evaluation to determine the winner. The evaluation phase should involve all your staff who were involved with the specification of requirements. Having selected a winner you will need to draw up the subcontract and it is most important that none of the requirements are changed without the subcontractor being informed and given the opportunity to adjust the quotation. This is the basic process although there will be differences from company to company. You will need procedures to cover each stage of the process and criteria to assess the contractors.

In making your choice you should not only look at what the contractor says they will do but what they have done in the past. Is it the sort of firm that does what it says it does or is it the sort of firm that says what you want to hear and then conducts its business differently?

Purchasing from approved subcontractors

The standard requires that *where a customer has provided an approved subcontractor list then relevant materials be purchased from subcontractors on that list.*

Customers may provide you with a list of approved subcontractors but when the customer has not provided an approved subcontractor list, you are at liberty to choose those subcontractors based on their ability to meet your requirements. This allows you to purchase from unapproved subcontractors providing you compensate for their inadequacies through subcontractor controls. However, you would not want to do this as a regular occurrence since it adds unnecessarily to your procurement costs.

The title "Approved materials for ongoing production" clearly limits the requirements to production; therefore you are permitted to use other subcontractors during the design and development phase except for materials used in prototype models (see clause 4.4.7). The note further on in the same section of the standard makes it clear that use of customer-designated subcontractors does not relieve the supplier of their quality responsibilities since the control of the subcontractor rests with the supplier. The subcontractors on the customer's list will have been approved for supply of the specified material and products and therefore you are not at liberty to choose other subcontractors. However, should other subcontractors offer services that more suit your needs then you may request they are added to the customer's list.

When selecting subcontractors of an existing product or service that satisfies your requirements with respect to quality, price, and delivery and you need assurance that continuity of supply can be assured. Sometimes you have no option but to buy from a sole subcontractor. On other occasions you are spoilt for choice. With some proprietary products you are able to select particular options so as to tailor the product or service to your requirements. It remains a proprietary product as the subcontractor has not changed anything just for you. Many of the products and services you will purchase are likely to be from catalogs. The designer may have already selected the item and quoted the part number in the specification. Quite often you are buying from a distributor rather than the manufacturer and so have to make two decisions. Will the manufacturer meet our requirements and will the distributor meet our requirements? Where you have a choice you may need to purchase some samples for evaluation purposes prior to making your final decision. So having selected a product the challenge facing the purchasing manager is to obtain it from the cheapest source. However, negotiating on price alone is damaging since the subcontractor could choose to sell their services to the highest bidder and leave you.

Should you have more than one subcontractor? Well sometimes there is only one but if there is a choice do not buy from them all as it increases complexity. The fewer the subcontractors the less work you have to do to maintain them. The standard does not impose any limits nor does it require that you have more than one. The risk is yours and if you have based the deal on mutual trust and put in place the necessary controls then the risks are minimal. You should have a force majeure clause in the contract with your customer to protect you against the unpredictable.

Constraints on purchased materials and products

The standard imposes constraints on your purchases by requiring that *all materials used in part manufacture satisfy current governmental and safety constraints on restricted, toxic, and hazardous materials as well as environmental, EMC considerations applicable to the country of manufacture* and requires *a process to assure that government and safety constraints on restricted, toxic, and hazardous substances are complied with by their subcontractors.*

In order to ensure compliance with this requirement you need to impose on your subcontractors through the purchase order, the relevant regulations and through examination of specifications, products and by on-site assessment, verify that these regulations are being met. It is not sufficient to merely impose the requirement upon your supplier through the purchase order. You can use the certified statements of authorized independent inspectors as proof of compliance instead of conducting the assessment yourself. However, such inspections may not extend to the product being supplied and therefore a thorough examination by your technical staff will be needed. Once deemed compliant, you need to impose change controls in the contract that prohibit the supplier changing the process or the product without your approval. This may not be possible when dealing with suppliers supplying product to their specification or when using off-shore suppliers where the system of law enforcement cannot be relied upon. In such cases you will need to define accurately the product required and carry out periodic inspections and tests to verify continued compliance.

Control of subcontractors

The standard requires suppliers to *define the type and extent of control exercised by the supplier over subcontractors* and goes on to require that these controls *be dependent upon the type of product, the impact of the product on the quality of the final product and, where applicable, on the quality audit reports and/or quality records of the previously demonstrated capability and performance of subcontractors.*

Defining subcontractor controls

Clause 4.6.2 requires that you define the extent of subcontractor control but neither this clause nor clause 4.6.4.1 requires you to plan, execute, and record any verification at subcontractor's premises. The standard also does not indicate where you might define your subcontractor controls since there is no mention of these controls in the clause on purchasing data.

When carrying out subcontractor surveillance you will need a plan which indicates what you intend to do and when you intend to do it and get this agreed with your subcontractor. If you intend witnessing certain tests then the subcontractor will need to give you advanced warning of their commencement so that you may attend (see also later under *Supplier verification at subcontractor's premises*.)

The quality plan would be a logical place for such controls to be defined but clause 4.2.3 does not specifically refer to subcontractor controls. Any intention that they be defined in the quality plan is hidden in 4.2.3b where it requires you to give timely consideration to the identification and acquisition of any controls etc. Some companies produce a Quality Assurance Requirement Specification which supplements ISO 9001 and also produce a Subcontractor Surveillance Plan. In most other cases the controls may be defined on the reverse side of the purchase order as standard conditions coded and selected for individual purchases.

Selecting the degree of control

The degree of control you need to exercise over your subcontractors and suppliers depends on the confidence you have in their ability to meet your requirements. In determining the degree of control to be exercised you need to establish whether:

- The quality of the product or service can be verified by you on receipt using your normal inspection and test techniques. This is the least costly of methods and usually applies where achievement of the requirements is measurable by examination of the end product.

- The quality of the product can be verified by you on receipt providing you acquire additional equipment or facilities. More costly than the previous method but may be economic if there is high utilization of the equipment.

- The quality of the product can be verified by you witnessing the final acceptance tests and inspections on the subcontractor's premises. If you don't possess the necessary equipment or skill to carry out product verification, then this method is an economic compromise and should yield as much confidence in the product as the previous methods. You do, however, have to recognize that your presence on the subcontractor's premises may affect the results. They may omit tests which are problematical or your presence may cause them to be particularly diligent, a stance which may not be maintained when you are not present.

- The verification of the product could be contracted to a third party. This can be very costly and is usually only applied with highly complex products and where safety is of paramount importance.

- The quality of the product can only be verified by the subcontractor during its design and manufacture. In such cases you have to rely on what the contractor tells you and to gain sufficient confidence you can impose quality system requirements, require certain design, manufacturing, inspection and test documents to be submitted to you for approval and carry out periodic audit and surveillance activities. This method is usually applied for one-off systems or small quantities when the stability of a long production run cannot be achieved to iron out problems.

As a minimum you need some means of verifying that the subcontractor/supplier has met the requirements of your subcontract/order and the more unusual and complex the requirements the more control will be required. If you have high confidence in a particular subcontractor/supplier you can concentrate on the areas where failure is more likely. If you have no confidence then you will need to exercise rigorous control until you gain sufficient confidence to relax the controls. The fact that a subcontractor/supplier has gained QS-9000 registration for the products and service you require should increase your confidence, but if you have no previous history of their performance it does not mean they will be any better than the subcontractor/supplier you have used for years who is not registered to QS-9000. Your subcontractor/supplier control procedures need to provide the criteria for selecting the appropriate degree of control and for selecting the activities you need to perform.

Subcontracts enable you to choose the degree of control exercised over your subcontractors. With suppliers, your choices are often limited as you have no privileges. Control over your suppliers is therefore exercised by the results of receipt inspection or subsequent inspections and tests. If your confidence in a supplier is low then you can increase the level of inspection and if high you can dispense with receipt inspection and rely on in-process controls to alert you to any deterioration in supplier performance.

Records of acceptable subcontractors

The standard requires that suppliers *establish and maintain records of acceptable subcontractors*.

This requirement does not mean that you have to maintain a list of approved suppliers. You should monitor the performance of all your subcontractors and suppliers and classify each according to prescribed guidelines. It is equally important that you list those suppliers or subcontractors that should not be used due to previously demonstrated poor performance so that you don't repeat the mistakes of the past.

Assessing subcontractors/suppliers is a costly operation. Having established that a subcontractor/supplier has or hasn't the capability of meeting your requirements you should enter their details on a list but this list is not the quality record of acceptable contractors. There needs to be evidence available that supports the decision to place and keep a subcontractor on an approved list. The quality record is the objective evidence that the subcontractor met the prescribed criteria and continues to do so. It would include the evaluation data, results of assessments, audits and the performance data that you collect following each shipment. The list should be made available to the purchasing authority, thereby avoiding the necessity of re-assessments each time you wish to subcontract work. The list of assessed subcontractors/suppliers should not only list the name and address of the company but provide details of the products and service that have been assessed. This is important since the assessment will have only covered particular products and services. Other products and services offered by the subcontractor/supplier may not have been acceptable. Some firms operate several production lines, each to different standards. A split between military products and civil products is most common. Just because the military line met your requirement doesn't mean that the civil line will also meet your requirements. Calling it a List of Assessed Subcontractors/Suppliers does not imply that it only lists approved firms and allows you to include records of all firms with which you have done business and classify them accordingly.

You will need a procedure for controlling the list of assessed subcontractors/suppliers, which covers the entry of organizations onto the list and their removal from the list.

Subcontractor/supplier performance will be evident from audit reports, surveillance visit reports, and receipt inspections carried out by you or the third party if one has been employed. You need to examine these documents for evidence that the subcontractor's quality system is controlling the quality of the products and services supplied. You can determine the effectiveness of these controls by periodic review of the subcontractor's performance: what some firms call "vendor rating". By collecting data on the performance of subcontractors/suppliers over a long period you can measure their effectiveness and rate them on a scale from excellent to poor. In such cases you should measure at least three characteristics: quality, delivery, and service. Quality would be measured by the number of defective products received; delivery would be measured by the number of days early or late; and service would be measured by the responsiveness to actions requested by you on scale of excellent to poor. The output of these reviews should be in the form of updates to the list of assessed subcontractors/suppliers.

Subcontractor quality system development

The standard requires suppliers to *perform subcontractor quality system development using QS-9000 as the fundamental quality system requirement.*

This requirement only applies to QS-9000 subcontractors and refers to all activities designed to improve the performance of the subcontractor's quality system. The term "fundamental" means the basic system rather than the tailoring carried out to meet particular customer requirements.

As noted previously, the Big Three do not demand that you require QS-9000 registration of your subcontractors but in fact many first tier suppliers are doing this. To meet the requirements of this clause you would need to invoke QS-9000 in any orders on your subcontractors. In terms of developing your subcontractors, you may at present find that none are registered to either ISO 9000 or QS-9000. You can pursue a two stage approach with your subcontractors – encouraging them to seek ISO 9000 registration first and then progress to QS-9000 registration. Alternatively, you can work with them in building their quality system and perform assessments to QS-9000 yourself. The advantage of using a third party is that it relieves you of this burden and having to maintain the resources to do it. Any doubts you may have about the efficacy of the assessment may be overcome by your subcontractor employing the same registrar as carries out your assessments.

Subcontractor delivery performance

The standard requires *100% on-time delivery performance from supplier's subcontractors and requires suppliers to provide appropriate planning information and commitments to enable their subcontractors to meet this expectation.*

A 100% on-time delivery performance means that your subcontractors must deliver supplies within the time window you specify. Unless you so specify, they do not have to operate a just-in-time system but it is obviously less costly to you if they do. It all rather depends of the quantities and volume you require and your consumption rate. With a fast consumption rate, you would need the space to store product pending use. The just-in-time system avoids this by allowing shipment directly to the production line. In order that your subcontractors can achieve 100% on-time delivery, you have to provide the same type of information and make the same commitments as your customer will to enable you to meet 100% on-time delivery to them (see Part 2 Chapter 15). You therefore need to inform your subcontractors of your production schedule and release orders to your subcontractors based on that schedule. If operating under a ship to stock system, you will need a means of notifying your subcontractor when stocks drop to the minimum level. Under such arrangements, you do not need a purchase order for every delivery as one order specifying the shipment rate will suffice.

The standard also requires you to track premium or excessive freight. Before accepting the subcontractor's quotation you need to establish what provisions have been made for shipping product and it is at that stage that the freight arrangements should be agreed. Were you to find later, not having agreed any freight provisions, that the freight costs were excessive, you may find you have agreed unwittingly to that means of shipment in the contract. However, the subcontractor may run into difficulties and attempt to compensate for delays by speedier and more costly transportation. This does need to be monitored.

Delivery advice notes will be needed to match shipments to inventory and trace problems should the need arise. A shipment notification system similar to that which you need to have with your customer will also be necessary in order to alert you to any shipment difficulties.

Purchasing data

The standard requires that *purchasing documents contain data clearly describing the product ordered.*

If you have managed for years without having to document your purchasing requirements then this clause in the standard will change all that. You need to document purchasing requirements so that you have a record of what you ordered. This can then be used when the goods and the invoice arrive to confirm that you have received what you ordered. The absence of such a record may prevent you from legitimately returning unwanted or unsatisfactory goods. As stated previously, this requirement applies to all purchases that affect the quality of the products and services you provide to your customers but there is no requirement for you to submit your purchasing documents to your vendors. In fact many purchases will be made from catalogs by telephone, quoting reference numbers and quantity required. Providing you have a record and can compare this with the goods received and the invoice then you have met the requirement (see later under *Review and approval of purchasing documents*).

Product identification

The standard requires purchasing documents to *include, where applicable, the type, class, style, grade, or other precise identification.*

The product or service identification should be sufficiently precise as to avoid confusion with other similar products or services. The vendor may produce several versions of the same product and denote the difference by suffixes to the main part number. To ensure you receive the product you require you need to consult carefully the literature provided and specify the product in the same manner as specified in the literature.

Purchasing specifications

The standard requires purchasing documents to *include, where applicable, the title or other positive identification, and applicable issue of specification, drawings, process requirements, inspection instructions, and other relevant technical data, including requirements for approval or qualification of product, procedures, process equipment, and personnel.*

If you are procuring the services of a subcontractor to design and/or manufacture a product or service then you will need specifications which detail all the features and characteristics that the product or service is to exhibit. The reference number and issue status of the specifications need to be specified in the event that it changes. This is also a safeguard against the repetition of problems with previous supplies. These specifications should also specify the means by which the requirements are to be verified so that you have confidence in any certificates of conformance that are supplied. For characteristics that are achieved using special processes (see Part 2 Chapter 9) you need to ensure that the subcontractor employs qualified personnel and equipment. Products required for particular applications need to be qualified for such applications and so your purchasing documents will need to specify what qualification tests are required.

Subcontract quality system requirements

The standard requires purchasing documents to *include, where applicable, the title, number, and issue of the quality system standard to be applied to the product.*

The inclusion of this requirement in purchasing documents requires the subcontractor/supplier to apply a quality system that meets a particular standard to the design, manufacture etc. of the product as a means of proving an assurance of compliance with your requirements. This requirement can be invoked in your purchasing documents whether or not your subcontractor/supplier is registered to a quality system standard, but doing so may cause difficulties. If the firm is not registered it may not accept the requirement or may well ignore it, in which case you will need to compensate by invoking surveillance and audit requirements in the subcontract. If your purchasing documents do not reference QS-9000 or its equivalent and you have taken alternative measures to assure the quality of the supplies then you are not noncompliant with the requirements of this clause. There is little point in imposing QS-9000 or ISO 9000 on non-registered suppliers when ordering from a catalog. It only makes sense when the supplier is prepared to make special arrangements for your particular order.

Review and approval of purchasing documents

The standard requires the supplier to *review and approve purchasing documents for adequacy of specified requirements prior to release.*

Prior to orders being placed the purchasing documents should be checked to verify that they are fit for their purpose. Again this requirement is appropriate to subcontracts but not if you do not submit your purchasing documents to your vendors. The extent to which you carry out this activity should be on the basis of risk and if you choose not to review and approve all purchasing documents then your procedures should provide the rationale for your decision. The standard does not require that the review and approval be documented. In some cases orders are produced using a computer and transmitted to the vendor directly without any evidence that the order has been reviewed or approved. The purchase order does not have to be the only purchasing document If you enter purchasing data onto a database, then a simple code used on a purchase order can provide traceability to the approved purchasing documents.

You can control the adequacy of the purchasing data in three ways:

- Provide the criteria for staff to operate under self control.

- Check everything they do.

- Select those orders which need to be checked on a sample basis.

- Classify orders depending on risk and only review and approve those which present a certain risk.

A situation where staff operate under self control is for telephone orders where there is little documentary evidence that a transaction has taken place. There may be an entry on a computer database showing that an order has been placed with a particular supplier. So how would you verify compliance with the requirements of this clause in such circumstances?

- Provide buyers with read-only access to approved purchasing data in the database.

- Provide buyers with read-only access to a list of approved suppliers in the database.

- Provide a computer file containing details of purchasing transactions with read and write access.

- Provide a procedure which defines the activities, responsibilities, and authority of all staff involved in the process.

- Train the buyers in the use of the database.

- Route purchase requisitions only to trained buyers for processing.

This method is suitable for processing routine orders; however, where there are non-standard conditions a more variable process needs to be developed. Providing you define the approach you intend to take in your procedures you should be able to demonstrate that your methods provide an adequate degree of control.

Supplier verification at subcontractor's premises

The standard requires the supplier to *specify verification arrangements and the method of product release in the purchasing documents where it is proposed that purchased product is verified at the subcontractor's premises.*

It is important that you inform the subcontractor through the contract of how the product or service will be accepted. Will it be as a result of receipt inspection at the specified destination or as a result of acceptance tests witnessed on site by your authorized representative? These details need to be specified at the tendering stage so that the subcontractor can make provision in the quotation to support any of your activities on site. If you have invoked QS-9000 in the subcontract then you are protected by clause 4.6.4.2. If you have not, then you need to specify a similar provision in your subcontract, otherwise you may lose the right to reject the product later. There is no requirement for you to document your proposal to verify product at the subcontractor's premises but such a plan would indeed be a useful section in any quality plan that you produced. (See also *Control of subcontractors* in this chapter.)

Customer verification of subcontracted product

The standard requires that *where specified in the contract the supplier's customer or his/her representative shall be afforded the right to verify at the subcontractor premises and the supplier's premises that subcontracted product conforms to specified requirements.*

The requirements pertain to your customer verifying product purchased by you either at your supplier or on your premises. Verification of purchased product is normally carried out by the supplier before or after receipt as part of the purchasing process but may also be carried out by the customer. However, due to the standard locating most of the inspection and test requirements in clause 4.10, the receipt inspection requirements are displaced.

In cases where your customer requires access to your subcontractors to verify the quality of supplies, then you will need to transmit this requirement to your subcontractor in the subcontract and obtain agreement. Where a firm's business is wholly that of contracting to customer requirements, a clause giving their customers certain rights will be written into their standard purchasing conditions. If this is an unusual occurrence, then you need to identify the need early in the contract and ensure it is passed on to those responsible for preparing subcontracts. You may also wish to impose on your customer a requirement that you are given advanced notice of any such visits so that you may arrange an escort. Unless you know your customer very well it is unwise to allow visits to your suppliers unaccompanied. You may for instance have changed, for good reasons, the requirements that were imposed on you as the main contractor when you prepared the subcontract and in ignorance your customer could inadvertently state that these altered requirements are unnecessary.

When customers visit your subcontractors or inspect product on receipt they have the right to reserve judgment on the final acceptance of the product. The product is not under their direct control and they may not be able to carry out all the tests and inspections that are required to gain sufficient confidence. Customer visits are to gain confidence and not to accept product. The same rules apply to you when you visit your subcontractors. The final decision is the one made on receipt or some time later when the product is integrated with your equipment and you can test it thoroughly in its operating environment or equivalent conditions. This is substantiated by the final clause in this section of the standard which states that *when the purchaser or his/her representative elects to carry out verification at the subcontractor's plant, such verification shall not be used by the supplier as evidence of effective control of quality by the subcontractor.*

Task list

1 Identify the broad categories of products and service which you procure.

2 Classify products and services into groups according to their potential effect on end product quality.

3 Prepare procedures for purchasing those products and services, the quality of which affects end product quality.

4 Provide forms for staff to request the procurement of goods.

5 Prepare procedures and standards that govern the specification of items to be purchased.

6 Compile a list of preferred suppliers and subcontractors that you regularly use.

7 Prepare procedures for assessing your subcontractors and suppliers.

8 Decide on the criteria for selecting subcontractors and suppliers.

9 Provide for assessment of subcontractors to be carried out before award of contract.

10 Provide standard conditions for subcontracts.

11 Provide a means for adjusting the standard conditions according to the nature of the work subcontracted.

12 Prepare procedures for producing and maintaining subcontract requirements and letting tenders.

13 Prepare procedures for evaluating tenders and selecting subcontractors.

14 Provide those responsible for the preparation of subcontracts requirements to approve them prior to issue to the subcontractor.

15 Provide resources for the control of subcontractors.

16 Prepare procedures covering the planning of subcontractor control activities.

17 Provide a means for purchasing staff to gain access to current technical data to pass on to suppliers and subcontractors.

18 Provide a means of adding and removing subcontractors and suppliers from the list of preferred suppliers and subcontractors.

19 Provide a means for changing subcontract requirements during the contract.

20 Provide a means for monitoring the subcontractor's progress in meeting the requirements.

Purchasing questionnaire

1 How do you ensure that purchased product conforms to specified requirements?

2 How do you evaluate and select your subcontractors and suppliers?

3 How do you establish the capability of your subcontractors and suppliers?

4 How do you ensure that your subcontractors comply with government safety and environmental constraints?

5 How do you determine the control to be exercised over your subcontractors/suppliers?

6 Where are your subcontractor controls defined?

7 In what documents do you record those subcontractors/suppliers that are acceptable?

8 To what extent do you cause the development of your subcontractors' quality systems towards QS-9000 compliance?

9 How do you ensure that purchasing documents clearly describe the product ordered?

10 How do you ensure that purchasing documents are reviewed and approved for adequacy of specified requirements prior to release?

11 How do you ensure your subcontractors achieve 100% on-time delivery?

12 How are your subcontractor verification requirements and methods of product release conveyed to subcontractors?

13 How do you enable customers to verify purchased product at source or upon receipt?

Do's and don'ts

* Do ensure that the requirements placed on subcontractors are compatible with those of the main contract.

* Do afford the same rights to your subcontractor on contract review as you wish afforded to you by your purchaser.

* Do provide a means of apportioning the requirements of the main contract to the subcontract.

* Do perform pre-award surveys of potential subcontractors.

* Do keep records of both supplier and subcontractor performance whether it be good or bad.

* Do maintain only one list of assessed suppliers and subcontractors.

* Don't constrain yourself to purchase only from approved suppliers – compensate for poor performers through subcontractor/supplier controls.

* Do ensure that purchasing staff and technical staff operate to the same standards and procedures.

* Do obtain proposals as to how the subcontractor proposes to control the quality of the product or service before acceptance of tender.

* Don't change the documents in the tender until after you are in a position to negotiate with the winner.

* Do obtain documentation of the subcontractor's processes so as to aid problem investigations in-house.

* Don't permit subcontractors to subcontract the work further without your approval and assessment of the proposed subcontractors.

* Do maintain a record of any articles you furnish to your subcontractors.

* Do establish a means of promptly responding to subcontractor queries and problem reports.

* Do provide feedback to subcontractors and suppliers of their performance.

* Do maintain records of all meetings and visits with suppliers and subcontractors.

Chapter 7

Customer supplied product

Scope of requirements

In many cases these requirements will not apply but in some contractual situations the customer may provide products or services for use by the supplier in connection with the contract. This clause of the standard specifies requirements that apply in such situations. The product being supplied may have been produced by a competitor, by the customer, or even by your own firm under a different contract. These requirements apply to any product supplied to you by your customer and not only to that which is to be incorporated into supplies. The customer may in fact supply facilities, equipment, software or documentation for use in conjunction with the contract, which may be provided on loan, to be returned on completion of the contract or to be retained. Customer-owned tooling and returnable packaging also constitutes customer supplied product. If you use the customer's facilities then such use should be governed by the regulations imposed in the contract rather than these requirements. If the customer supplies documentation, then unless it is required to be returned, you should assume it is yours to keep. Such documentation is not governed by these requirements although, if the customer requires the documents to be returned, then you should assume that these requirements do apply. But apply them with discretion.

The requirements in element 4.7 are linked with other elements of the standard even when there is no cross reference. This relationship is illustrated in Figure 7.1.

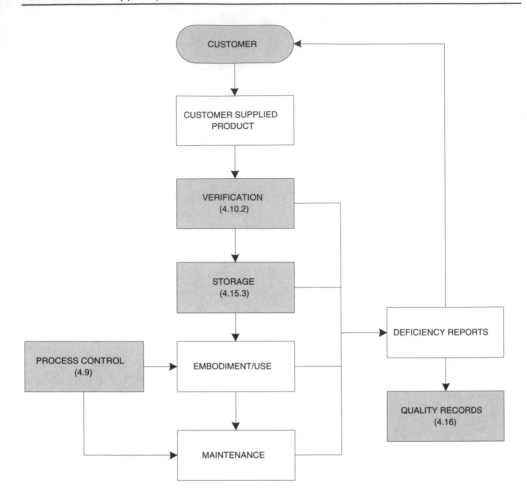

Figure 7.1 Element relationships with customer supplied product element

Verification of customer supplied product

The standard requires the supplier to *establish and maintain procedures for verification of customer supplied product provided for incorporation into the supplies or for related activities.*

When product is received from a customer it should be processed in the same way as purchased product so that it is registered and subject to receipt inspection. The inspection you carry out may be limited if you do not possess the necessary equipment or specification, but you should reach an agreement with the customer as to the extent of any receipt inspection before the product arrives. If the product does not bear an identity from which you can readily determine that it is the purchaser's property, then you should apply a label and properly identify the item. Any inspections and tests you carry out should be recorded for two reasons. Firstly to establish the condition of the item on receipt in the event that it is damaged, defective or is incomplete and secondly, to verify that it is fit for the intended purpose before use. If you fail to inspect the product on receipt you may find difficulty in convincing your customer later that the damage was not your fault. You also need to match any delivery note with the product, since the customer may have inadvertently sent you the wrong product. Unless you know what you are doing it is unwise to energize the product without proper instructions from the customer.

Storage of customer supplied product

The standard requires the supplier to *establish and maintain procedures for storage of customer supplied product provided for incorporation into the supplies or for related activities.*

Customer supplied product, if possible, should be segregated from other products to avoid mixing, inadvertent use, damage, or loss. Depending on the size and quantity of the items and the frequency with which your customer supplies such products you may require a special storage area. The storage areas should be governed by procedures which satisfy clause 4.15.3 of the standard and you may in fact be able to use the same procedures. Wherever the items are stored you should maintain a register of such items, preferably separate from the storage area in, for example, inventory control or the project office. The authorization for releasing product from storage areas may have to be different for inventory control reasons. You also need to ensure that such products are insured. You will not have a corresponding purchase order and hence they may not be registered as stock or capital assets. If you receive customer supplied product very infrequently then you will need a simple system that is only activated when necessary rather than being built into your normal system. Under such circumstances it is easy to lose these products and forget they are not your property. You need to alert staff to take extra care especially if they are high value items that cannot readily be replaced.

Maintenance of customer supplied product

The standard requires the supplier to *establish and maintain procedures for maintenance of customer supplied product provided for incorporation into the supplies or for related activities.*

Customer supplied products that are issued for incorporation into supplies don't often require maintenance; however, items for use in conjunction with the contract may be retained for such a duration that maintenance is necessary. If the products require any maintenance you should be provided with a maintenance specification and the appropriate equipment to do the job. Maintenance may include both preventive and corrective maintenance but you should clarify with your customer which it is. You may have the means for preventive maintenance, such as lubrication and calibration, but not for repairs. Always establish your obligations in the contract regarding customer supplied product, since you could take on commitments for which you are not covered contractually if something should go wrong. You need to establish who will supply the spares and re-certify the equipment following repair.

Reporting problems to the customer

The standard requires that *any such product that is lost, damaged or is otherwise unsuitable for use be recorded and reported to the customer* and again advises the supplier that *verification by the supplier does not absolve the customer of the responsibility to provide acceptable product*.

The customer is responsible for the product they supply wherever it came from in the first place. It is therefore very important that you establish the condition of the product before you store it or use it. In the event that you detect that the product is damaged, defective or is incomplete, then you should place it in a quarantine area and report the condition to the customer. Even if the product is needed urgently and can still be used, you should obtain the agreement of your customer before using inferior product, otherwise you may be held liable for the consequences.

You could use your own reject note or nonconformance report format to notify the customer of a defective product but these are not appropriate if the product is lost. You also need a customer response to the problem and so a form that combines both a statement of the problem and of the solution would be more appropriate.

You should maintain a register of customer supplied product containing the following details:

- Name of product, part numbers, serial numbers, and other identifying features

- Name of customer and source of product if different

- Delivery note reference, date of delivery

- Receipt inspection requirements

- Condition on receipt including reference to any rejection note

- Storage conditions and place of storage

- Maintenance specification if maintenance is required

- Current location and name of custodian

- Date of return to customer or embodiment into supplies

- Part number and serial number of product embodying the customer supplied product

- Dispatch note reference of assembly containing the product

These details will help you keep track of the customer supplied product whether on embodiment loan or contract loan and will be useful during customer audits or in the event of a problem with the item either before or after dispatch of the associated assembly.

Task list

1 Provide a register of all products supplied by customers and keep it under central control.

2 Make provision for customer supplied product to be processed through receipt inspection.

3 Prepare procedures for inspecting customer supplied product and notifying the customer of any problems.

4 Provide separate storage areas for customer supplied product.

5 Provide procedures for the receipt and removal of product from storage areas.

6 Make provision in your contract procedures for requiring customers to supply handling, operating, and maintenance instructions as necessary for any product they supply.

7 Provide a form for conveying to the customer the results of any defects detected during receipt inspection, maintenance, or operational use.

8 Provide a mechanism for gathering change of use and location of customer supplied product.

Customer supplied product questionnaire

1   How do you verify customer supplied product?

2   How do you store customer supplied product?

3   How do you maintain customer supplied product?

4   How do you ensure that any lost or unsuitable customer supplied product is recorded and reported to the customer?

Do's and don'ts

*   Don't lose track of customer supplied product.

*   Do make sure that users are aware that it is not company property.

*   Do give customer supplied product an identity that denotes its source.

*   Do establish the condition of customer supplied product before use.

*   Do report back to the customer any performance variation of customer supplied product following its embodiment in your product.

Chapter 8

Product identification and traceability

Scope of requirements

The requirements for product identification are intended to enable products and services with one set of characteristics to be distinguishable from products or services with another set of characteristics. Product identity is vital in many situations to prevent inadvertent mixing, to enable reordering, to match products with documents that describe them, and to do that basic of all human activities, communicate. Without codes, numbers, labels, names, and other forms of identification we cannot adequately describe the product or service to anyone else. We use terms such as "thingummybob", "widget", "you know what I mean, it's a ..." Using names, labels etc. convey meaning precisely. Traceability on the other hand is a notion of being able to trace something through a process to a point along its course either forwards through the process or backwards through the process. One needs traceability to find the root cause of problems. If records cannot be found which detail what happened to a product then naught can be done to prevent its recurrence. Traceability is key to corrective action and, although the standard only requires traceability when required by contract, assessors will seek an audit trail to determine compliance with the standard. This trail can only be laid by using the principles of traceability.

The requirements in element 4.8 are linked with other elements of the standard even when there is no cross reference. This relationship is illustrated in Figure 8.1.

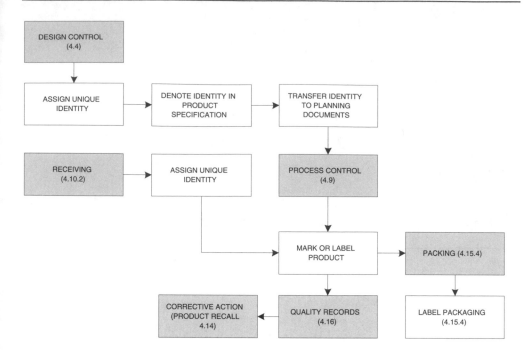

Figure 8.1 Element relationships with product identification and traceability element

Procedures for identifying product

The standard requires the supplier to *establish and maintain documented procedures where appropriate for identifying the product by suitable means from receipt and during all stages of production, delivery, and installation.*

Documented procedures are needed where the product identity is not inherently obvious. If products are so unlike that inadvertent mixing would be unlikely to occur, then a means of identifying the products is unnecessary. Inherently obvious in this context means that it would be obvious to an untrained eye. The physical differences need to be large enough to be visible to the untrained eye, therefore functional differences, no matter how significant, and slight differences in physical characteristics such as color, size, weight, appearance would constitute an appropriate situation for documented identification procedures.

Procedures for identifying product should start at the design stage when the product is conceived. The design should be given a unique identity, a name or a number, and that should be used on all related documents. When the product emerges into production, the product should carry the same number or name but in addition it should carry a serial number or other identification to enable product features to be recorded against specific products. If verification is on a "go no-go" basis, then product does not need to be serialized. If measurements are recorded then some means has to he found of identifying the measurements with the product measured. Serial numbers, batch numbers, and date codes are suitable means for achieving this. This identity should be carried on all quality records related to the product.

Apart from the name or number given a product you need to identify the version and the modification state so that you can relate the issues of the drawing and specifications to the products they represent. Products should either carry a label or markings with this type of information in an accessible position or bear a unique code number which is traceable to such information.

You may not possess any documents which describe the product purchased. The only identity may be marked on the product itself or its container. Where there are no markings then information from the supplier's invoice or other such documents should be transferred to a label and attached to the product or the container. Documents need to be traceable to the products they represent.

Traceability

The standard requires that where, and to the extent that, traceability is a specified requirement, the supplier to *establish and maintain documented procedures for unique identification of individual product or batches* and goes on to require *this identification to be recorded.*

As stated previously, traceability is fundamental to establishing and eliminating the root cause of nonconforming product and therefore it should be mandatory in view of the requirements for Corrective Action. Providing traceability can be an onerous task. Some applications require products to be traced back to the original ingot from which they were produced. In situations of safety or national security it is necessary to identify product in such a manner since if a product is used in a critical application and subsequently found defective, it may be necessary to track down all other products of the same batch and eliminate them before there is a disaster. It happens in product recall situations. It is also very important in the automobile industry: in fact, any industry where human life may be at risk due to a defective product being in circulation.

Traceability is also important to control processes. You may need to know which products have been through which processes and on what date, if a problem is found some time later. The same is true of test and measuring equipment. If on being calibrated a piece of test equipment is found to be out of calibration then it is important to track down all the equipment that has been validated using that piece of measuring equipment. This in fact is a requirement of QS-9000 clause 4.11 but no requirement for traceability is specified.

Traceability is achieved by coding items and their records such that you can trace an item back to the records at any time in its life. The chain can be easily lost if the item goes outside your control. If for example, you provide an item on loan to a development organization and they return it sometime later, without a certified record of what they did to it, you have no confidence that the item is in fact the same one, unless it has some distinguishing features; the inspection history is now invalidated since the operations conducted on the item were not certified. Traceability is only helpful when the chain remains unbroken. It can also be costly to maintain. The system of traceability you maintain should be carefully thought out so that it is economic. There is little point in maintaining an elaborate traceability system for the once in a lifetime event when you need it, unless your very survival, or society's survival, depends upon it.

It may not be practical to document separate procedures to meet this requirement. The conventions you use to identify product and batches need to be specified in the product specifications and the stage at which product is marked specified in the relevant procedures or plans. Often such markings are automatically applied during processing, as is the case with printed circuits, ceramics, castings, etc. Process setting up procedures should specify how the marking equipment or tools are to be set up.

Task list

1   Establish an identification system for products and services.

2   Provide registers or other devices for allocating identification numbers to documents that describe products or services.

3   Prepare standards or process specifications for applying identification details to products and services.

4   Decide on which types of product will be given serial numbers.

5   Provide registers for allocating serial numbers to individual products.

6   Make provision on all product records for the product identification to be recorded.

7   Decide on the convention for denoting modification status.

8   Provide specifications for producing and fixing modification plates to product.

9   Make provision in product and process records to capture source details of component parts and materials.

10 Make provision in inspection and test records to capture details of inspection, test, and measuring equipment used.

11 Provide registers for allocating batch numbers, date codes, and other identification data when appropriate.

12 Make provision on tags, labels etc. for recording product identification details.

13 Provide data storage systems which enable rapid retrieval of records by product identification.

14 Provide for remnant material to retain its identity.

15 Decide who will allocate serial numbers, batch numbers etc.

16 Provide for separated lots or batches to be identified to the original lot or batch.

17 Decide on the minimum level of traceability which is to be maintained for your products.

Product identification and traceability questionnaire

1   How do you enable products to be identified from receipt and during all stages of production, delivery, and installation?

2   How do you ensure traceability of product to original material identification, quality status, and the unit responsible for both its supply and verification?

3   How do you identify and record individual product and batches?

Do's and don'ts

* Do centralize the identification system so as to prevent duplication of codes.

* Do specify the product identification details in the product specification and denote where and with what materials identification is to be applied.

* Don't claim a higher level of traceability than is necessary for the type of business.

* Do make it a routine that identification data is checked at each inspection and test stage.

* Don't use product that has lost its identity.

* Don't mix product as a safeguard against loss of identity.

* Do place identification labels where the product user can see them.

* Do provide a means of tracing the results of verification activities to the characteristics specified in the product specification.

Chapter 9

Process control

Scope of requirements

The process referred to in this section of the standard is the result producing process, the process of implementing or replicating the design. It is the process which is cycled repeatedly to generate product or to deliver service. It differs from the design process in that it is arranged to reproduce product or service to the same standard each and every time. The design process is a journey into the unknown, whereas the production process is a journey along a proven path with a predictable outcome. The design process requires control to keep it on course towards an objective, the production process requires control to maintain a prescribed standard. The title used in ISO 9004 is Production rather than Process and since all work can be described by a series of processes, the requirements can be applied to all result producing processes. Although the subject of the requirements is production and installation, these are not terms used in the service industries. One delivers or provides a service; however, the measures described are equally applicable to services if you alter the terminology to that of the service industries. In the software industry, for instance, process control applies to the process of replication, delivery, and installation rather than to the coding of software, which is considered part of design and development within the context of QS-9000.

There are two ways in which product quality can be controlled. By controlling the product which emerges from the producing processes or by controlling the processes through which the product passes. Process control relies upon control of the elements that drive the process, whereas product control relies upon verification of the product as it emerges from the process. In practice it is a combination of these which yields products of consistent quality. Figure 9.1 serves to illustrate this concept. If you concentrate on the process output to the exclusion of all else, you will find there is a high level of rework of the end product. If you concentrate on the process using the results of the product verification, you will gradually reduce rework until all output product is of consistent quality.

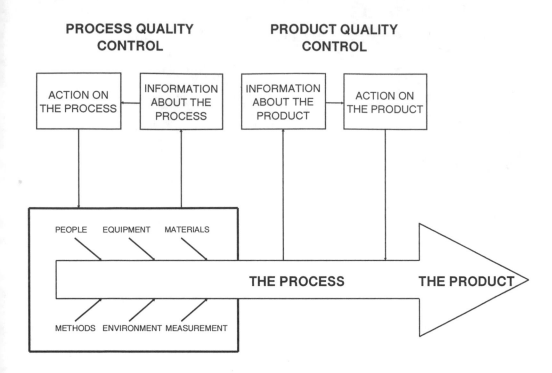

Figure 9.1 Process control model

The requirements in element 4.9 are linked with other elements of the standard even when there is no cross reference. This relationship is illustrated in Figure 9.2.

Planning production, installation, and servicing processes

The standard requires that the supplier *identifies and plans the production, installation, and servicing processes which directly affect quality*.

In order to identify the production processes required to produce a particular product you must first have a production requirement in the form of product specifications which define the features and characteristics of the product that are to be achieved. By studying these specifications you will be able to identify the processes required to turn raw materials and bought-out components into a finished product. With manufactured products the processes may include machining, welding, fabrication, assembly, forming, plating, painting, heat treatment etc. Having identified the processes, you need to plan their implementation. These plans, often called *route cards*, route an item through the various processes from raw material to finished product. You may need separate plans for each process and each part, with an overall plan that ensures the product goes through the right processes in the right sequence. The number of plans

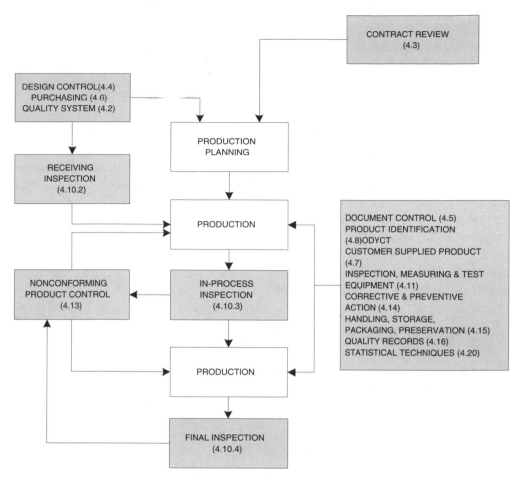

Figure 9.2 Element relationships with the process control element

is usually determined by the manner in which the specifications are drawn up. You may have drawings for each part to be made or one drawing covering several parts.

The APQP manual provides a means for implementation of the requirement for the production processes to be planned. The APQP requires production control plans, process flow charts, process instructions, and the control plan. The control plan may need to be supplemented by a routing card or shop traveler and in such cases there should be complete compatibility between the two documents. Care must be taken to ensure that no changes are made to the manufacturing processes that were used to gain production part approval.

For installation operations you will need an installation requirement and an installation plan. Similarly for any other process which represents the core for your business, you will need a requirement and a plan to achieve the requirement. The plan should detail the processes you need to implement in order to achieve the requirement.

Pre-production

Design verification is often only performed on one or two prototypes which are representative of production models but this small sample is unlikely to contain all the variables that may arise during full-scale production. With complex equipment, production does not normally follow development. A period of pre-production is often needed in order to eradicate bugs in the design and prove the production equipment, materials, documentation, tooling, and facilities. ISO 9001 does not require production proving before launching into full-scale production; however, QS-9000 does require a production trial run using production tooling, equipment, facilities, and cycle time. The specific pre-production activities are covered in section 4 of the APQP manual. It may reveal unsuitable materials, uneconomic techniques, unworkable procedures or unreliable equipment. The requirements for approval of processes and equipment (see later) relate to the processes and equipment itself rather than to the product. Any new production procedures and techniques should also be proven prior to being used in full-scale production. What seemed satisfactory during development may be unfit for the task during production.

Ensuring that work is carried out under controlled conditions

The standard requires that the supplier *ensures that the production, installation, and servicing processes are carried out under controlled conditions*.

To ensure that the processes are carried out under controlled conditions the production plans need to:

* Identify the product in terms of the specification reference and its issue status.

* Define the quantity required.

* Define which section is to perform the work.

* Define each stage of manufacture and assembly.

* Provide for progress through the various processes to be recorded so that you know what stage the product has reached at any one time.

* Define the special tools, processing equipment, jigs, fixtures, and other equipment required to produce the product. General-purpose tools and equipment need not be specified since your staff should be trained to select the right tool for the job.

* Define the methods to be used to produce the product either directly or by reference to separate instructions.

- Define the environment to be maintained during production of the product in anything other than ambient conditions.

- Define the process specifications and workmanship standards to be achieved.

- Define the stages at which inspections and tests are to be performed.

- Define any special handling, packaging, and marking requirements to be met.

- Define any precautions to be observed to protect health and safety.

These plans create a basis for ensuring that work is carried out under controlled conditions, but the staff, equipment, materials, processes, and documentation must be up to the task before work commences. The control plans required in clause 4.2.3 will in fact fulfill this need. A simple production process is illustrated in Figure 9.3. The shaded boxes indicate interfaces external to the production process. The variables are too numerous to illustrate the intermediate steps.

Installation plans need to cover similar material but in addition may include:

- Site surveys

- Site preparation

- Transport and delivery of materials and equipment

- Inspection of equipment entering the site

- Storage of equipment awaiting installation

- Storage of spares and consumables

- Installation of equipment

- Commissioning tests

- Acceptance tests

- On-site maintenance before handover

- Handover to customer

- Return of surplus and defective goods

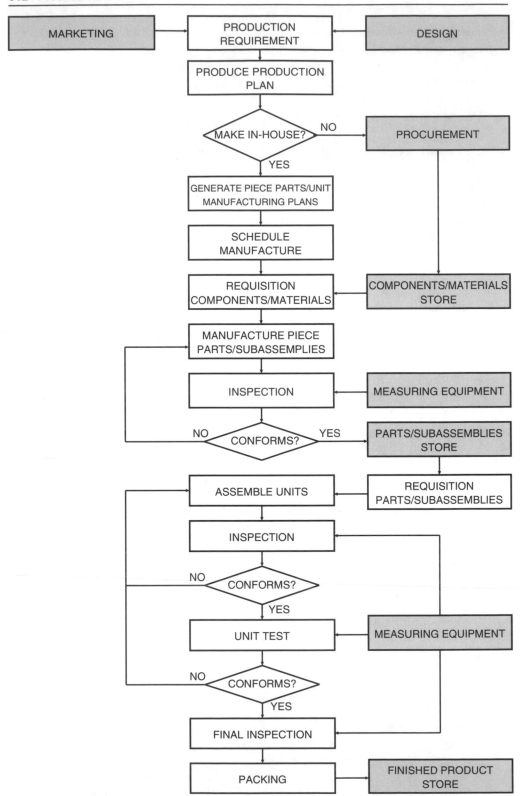

Figure 9.3 The production process: simplified version

For servicing the plans need to define as appropriate:

* The item to be serviced

* The service to be performed

* The responsibility for performing the work including the inspections and tests

* The activities to be carried out

* The process specifications and workmanship standards to be achieved

* The procedures for disposing of any waste or defective product

* The tools, equipment, and other aids to carry out the service and any inspections and tests

* The manuals and other literature which specify how the tasks have to be performed

* The consumable materials and spares required

* The environment to be maintained if anything other than ambient

* The handling and cleanliness requirements

* The precautions to be observed to protect health and safety

* The checks, inspections, tests, and adjustments to be made

Documented procedures

The standard requires controlled conditions to *include documented procedures defining the manner of production, installation, and servicing where the absence of such instructions would adversely affect quality.*

The documented procedures referred to are level 3 documents since the only change from the 1987 edition of ISO 9001 was to change the term *documented work instructions* to *documented procedures*. However, one can take the alternate view that the procedures referred to are level 2 documents since there is no general requirement for the supplier to establish and maintain documented procedures for controlling production, installation, and servicing processes as there would be if ISO 9000 had been consistent in itself. Whichever view you take, you still need to document those elements of the quality system that relate to production, installation, and servicing processes (clause 4.2.1) and take steps to deal with problems requiring preventive action (clause 4.14.3). Therefore if level 2 control procedures are needed to prevent problems then they should be produced.

There need to be instructions to cause work to happen as procedures do not by themselves cause work to commence, they define how work is to be carried out. The production plan referred to previously is a work instruction, since it instructs those to whom it applies to carry out certain tasks. Control procedures may include assembly procedures, plating procedures, painting procedures, maintenance procedures etc. and differ from process specifications (see later) in that the process specification defines the results to be achieved in operating a process rather than how to run the process. These procedures should define:

- The qualifications required for the person carrying out the procedure, if any special qualifications are required

- The preparatory steps to be taken to prepare the product for processing

- The preparatory steps to be taken to set up any equipment

- The steps to be taken to process the product

- The precautions to observe

- The settings to record

The standard only requires procedures where their absence would adversely affect quality. (Strangely enough their presence doesn't ensure quality unless they are followed.) So what can you get away with? Any operation that relies on skills doesn't need a procedure. However, the operator will not be clairvoyant and so you may need to provide procedures for simple tasks simply to convey special safety, handling, packaging, and recording requirements. You need to ensure that you don't make your processes so complex that bottlenecks arise when the slightest variation to plan occurs. The setting up of equipment, other than equipment typical of the industry, may also need to be specified to ensure consistent results. In fact any operation that requires tasks to be carried out in a certain sequence to obtain consistent results should be specified in a procedure.

By imposing formal controls you safeguard against informality which prevents you from operating consistent, reliable, and predictable processes. The operators and their supervisors may know the tricks and tips for getting the equipment or the process to operate smoothly. You should discourage informal instructions as you cannot rely on them being used when those who know them are absent. If the tip or trick is important then encourage those who know them to bring them to the process owner's attention so that permanent changes can be made to make the process run smoothly all the time.

> ■ **Procedures are needed where consistency in results is vital.**

Suitable production, installation, and servicing equipment

The standard requires controlled conditions to *include the use of suitable production, installation, and servicing equipment.*

The production, installation, and servicing equipment should be selected during the planning process. In selecting such equipment you should determine whether it is capable of producing, maintaining, or handling conforming product consistently. You need to ensure that the equipment is capable of achieving the specified dimensions within the stated tolerances. Process capability studies can reveal deficiencies with equipment which are not immediately apparent from inspection of the first off.

Suitable working environments

The standard requires controlled conditions to *include suitable working environment.*

The working environment may need to be controlled, not for the benefit of the staff but to achieve the required characteristics. To achieve high performance from electronic components, particle and chemical contamination has to be minimized during fabrication and assembly. To produce appearance items to the regulatory standards, high levels of cleanliness need to be maintained during production. For these and many other reasons, the production environment may need to be controlled. If these conditions apply then you should:

- Document the standards that are to be maintained.

- Prohibit unauthorized personnel from entering the areas.

- Provide training for staff who are to work in such areas.

- Provide alarm systems to warn of malfunctions in the environment.

- Provide procedures for maintaining the equipment to these standards.

- Maintain records of the conditions as a means of demonstrating that the standards are being achieved.

ISO 9001 is not specific on what is meant by "working environment". Since ISO 9001 only applies to product and factors that affect the product then "working environment" means the environment in which work on product is carried out. If temperature, cleanliness, humidity, electromagnetic, and other environmental factors need to be controlled to ensure conforming product then their control provides a suitable working environment.

Should an organization not provide safeguards for its people then it may still be able to meet its customer requirements and deliver conforming product as is the case with builders not wearing hard hats on a building site. The only product issue involved is if the blood from a head wound stains the building material and renders it nonconforming with the governing appearance standards! QS-9000 has overcome this dilemma by imposing requirements that do apply to both product and people and these are addressed in the next section.

Compliance with government safety and environmental regulations

The standard requires *a process to ensure compliance with all applicable government safety and environmental regulations.*

This requirement signals a significant departure from ISO 9000 by addressing matters outside product quality. The commitments made by the Big Three to their customers cannot be met without an assurance of supplies of parts and materials from their suppliers. Integrity through the supply chain is vital. Customers cannot switch suppliers if one fails to deliver since it would be too disruptive to production. Although it may be possible to order competing parts if both parts can be supplied to different models of vehicles, the pressure to drive down costs and hence prices makes this almost out of the question except for high risk parts. Assurance of supply depends not only on product quality but on the supplier remaining in business and acting in a manner that does not compromise the customer. There are several factors in this context that could disrupt continuity of supply or hazard the reputation of customers:

* A failure to observe government health and safety regulations could close a factory for a period.

* Health and safety hazards could result in injury or illness and place key personnel out of action for a period.

* Environmental claims made by the Big Three to customers regarding conservation of natural resources, recycling etc. may be compromised if environmental inspections of suppliers shows a disregard for such regulations.

* The unregulated discharge of waste gases, effluent, and solids may result in public concern in the local community and enforced closure of the plant by the authorities.

* A failure to take adequate personnel safety precautions may put product at risk.

- A failure to dispose of hazardous materials safely and observe fire precautions could put plant at risk.

- A failure to provide safe working conditions for personnel may result in public concern and local and national inquiries that may harm the reputation of the supplier.

The standard requires you to have a process to ensure compliance. In fact you need a system (a series of interconnected processes) since the means to ensure compliance need to be planned, organized, and controlled in a manner that is compatible with, or integrated with other management systems. To ensure compliance means to make certain of compliance and this is no easy task. It needs to be managed.

Safety and environmental policies need to be established and approved by executive management. A system for implementing the policy that will ensure compliance with government safety and environmental regulations needs to be established, documented, implemented, and evaluated for continued suitability and effectiveness. The system has to be planned, organized, and controlled so that it achieves its purpose. A person or persons should therefore be appointed with responsibility for the safety and environmental management system and responsibilities of those who work the system should be defined and documented. The person could be the same person who is responsible for the quality system as a whole or a dedicated professional with expert knowledge of the regulations.

Some of the topics your safety and environmental management system should address are as follows:

- Methods for capturing the relevant safety and environmental regulations and ensuring you are kept up to date with revisions

- Methods for assessing the health and safety hazards and environmental effects present in your organization and its operations relative to the regulations

- Safety and environmental objectives and targets based on the results of the safety and environmental assessment

- A program for achieving the safety and environmental objectives

- Methods for making staff aware of their safety and environmental responsibilities, the benefits of compliance, and consequences of a failure to comply

- Methods for conveying the regulations through policies and practices to the point of implementation

- Methods for alerting staff to hazardous situations

- Methods for creating controlled conditions in which safety hazards and adverse environmental effects are a minimum

- Methods for dealing with accidents, incidents, and emergency situations, investigating their cause and preventing recurrence

- Methods for monitoring conformance with the policies and practices and for assessing the extent of compliance with the regulations

- Methods of measuring the achievement of safety and environmental objectives and targets

- Maintenance of records to demonstrate compliance with the prescribed regulations and effective operation of the management system

The safety and environmental management system is a subsystem of the quality system and therefore the provisions established for documentation control, corrective and preventive action, auditing, and management review should also be applied to this system. Instructions concerning safety and environmental issues should be integrated into the control and operating procedures such that the instructions are given at the stage in the process when they apply. In this way staff do not have to consult several documents and the chance of error is reduced.

Compliance with reference documents

The standard requires controlled conditions to *include compliance with reference standards/codes, quality plans, and/or documented procedures*.

The product specification should provide all necessary processing requirements that need to be implemented when carrying out particular processes; however, some of the requirements may need to be defined in separate process specifications which are invoked by reference. You may need to develop your own process specifications, but there are many national standards that may suit your needs and they come with the added benefit that they have been proven to work. The quality plan or procedures should not contain any further product requirements but may provide the verification methods to be employed, the precautions to be observed, and the recording requirements to be met. You need to identify in your production plans each of these documents at the stage at which they should be applied, otherwise there is the possibility that they may be overlooked.

Controlling process and product characteristics

The standard requires controlled conditions to *include the monitoring and control of suitable process parameters and product characteristics during production, installation, and servicing.*

Controlled conditions include in-process monitoring and in-process inspection and test. All controls have to have a verification stage and a feedback loop. You cannot control production processes without performing some kind of verification.

The production of some products can be controlled simply by inspection after the product has been produced. In other cases, you may have to monitor certain process parameters to be sure of producing conforming product. By observing the variability of certain parameters using control charts, you can determine whether the process is under control within the specified limits.

Process monitoring can be achieved by observing sensors installed in the production process which measure key process parameters or by taking samples at discrete intervals and taking prescribed measurements. In both cases the measurements should be recorded for subsequent analysis and any decision made to allow the process to continue or to stop should also be recorded together with the reasons for the decision. The data to be recorded should be specified in advance on the forms or computer screens provided at the workstation. This will give personnel a clear indication of what to record, when, and where to record it. It also simplifies auditing if data is required in all boxes on a form or computer screen. A blank box indicates an unusual occurrence that should be checked. The forms should also indicate the accept/reject limits so that the operator can easily judge when the process is out of control. The standard does not require inspection to be carried out by full-time inspectors. The term *inspector* is not used but it can apply to anyone performing an inspection.

Operators should be trained to both operate the plant and control the process. As added assurance you should take samples periodically and subject them to a thorough examination. The sampling plan should be defined and documented and operators trained to determine what causes the results they observe. Process control comes about by operators knowing what results to achieve, by knowing what results are being achieved and by being able to correct performance should the results not be as required. They need to understand what is happening during processing to cause any change in the results as they are being monitored. You will need to define in the process specification the parameters to be observed and recorded and the limits within which the process is to be controlled (see also Part 2 Chapter 20).

> ■ **Understand what causes the dots on the chart to vary.**

Designated special characteristics

The standard requires *compliance with all customer requirements for designation, documentation and control of special characteristics and to provide documentation showing compliance as requested.*

The requirements governing special characteristics are also covered in clause 4.2.3 and 4.5.1. In this clause, it requires the designation of special characteristics which should have been accomplished during advanced product quality planning (as required by clause 4.2.3) so no further designation should be necessary. As for the documentation of special characteristics, the symbols should have been applied both when establishing the process controls and preparing the control plan (clause 4.2.3) and associated documentation during the planning phase (clause 4.5.1). Therefore the requirements not previously addressed are for the control of special characteristics and evidence of compliance, i.e. quality records.

As is stated in the standard, all characteristics are important and need to be controlled, however, some need special attention as excessive variation may affect product safety, compliance with government regulations, fit, form function, appearance, or the quality of subsequent operations. Designating such characteristics with special symbols alerts planners and operators to take particular care. It also alerts those responsible for dispositioning nonconforming product to exercise due care when reaching their decisions.

The control plans should make provision for the customer specific controls required in Section III of QS-9000 and these must be implemented. Evidence is required to show that all the controls specified in the control plan have been implemented and a way of doing this is to make provision for recording verification of conformity against the relevant requirement in the control plan.

Approval of processes and equipment

The standard requires controlled conditions to *include the approval of processes and equipment as appropriate.*

The term *approval* can be taken to mean certification or qualification, the difference being that *certification* is performed each time the equipment is repaired and *qualification* only when the equipment is introduced into service. The standard only refers to the term qualification in connection with special processes, but this clause does not distinguish between special and ordinary processes and equipment. However, there are two levels of approval that apply to processes and equipment: initial qualification approval and periodic setting-up approval.

The product and process validation phase in the APQP manual covers these points and together with the PPAP, fulfills the requirements of this particular clause. However, there may be cases where the APQP and PPAP do not apply so some general guidance is warranted.

All processes and equipment should be proven capable of performing the task for which they were designed and so should either be subject to qualification tests or process capability tests. There may be documentation available from the supplier of the equipment which adequately demonstrates its capability, otherwise you may need to carry out qualification and capability tests to your own satisfaction. In the process industries the plant is specially designed and so needs to be commissioned and qualified by the user. Your procedures need to provide for such activities and for records of the tests to be maintained.

When equipment or plant is taken out of service, either for maintenance or for repair, it should not be re-introduced into service without being subject to formal acceptance tests that are designed to verify that it meets your declared standard operating conditions. Your procedures need to provide for such activities and for records of the tests to be maintained.

Workmanship criteria

The standard requires controlled conditions to *include criteria for workmanship which is stipulated in the clearest practical manner*.

The output from many processes depends upon the skill of the producer in manipulating materials, interpreting the requirements, applying knowledge, and the proper use of equipment. The results of some processes cannot be directly measured using gages, tools, test and measuring equipment and so an alternative means has to be found of determining what is conforming product. The term given to such means is Workmanship Criteria, criteria that will enable producers and inspectors to gain a common understanding of what is acceptable and unacceptable. Situations where this may apply in manufacturing are soldering, welding, brazing, riveting, deburring etc. It may also include criteria for finishes, photographs, printing, blemishes, and many others.

QS-9000 identifies a class of parts called "appearance items". Appearance is a subjective characteristic so means need to be provided to reduce the subjectivity and make judgment more objective. Appearance items are those with surface finish characteristics that are visible to the end user. These items will be designated by your customer so you don't need to guess which items they are.

The standard requires the supplier *to make special provisions for items designated as "appearance items"*.

Samples indicating the acceptable range of color, grain, and texture may be needed and if not provided by your customer, those that you provide will need customer approval.

The criteria need to be defined by documented standards or by samples and models which clearly and precisely define the distinguishing features that represent both conforming and nonconforming product. In order to provide adequate understanding it may be necessary to show various examples of workmanship from acceptable to unacceptable so that the producer or inspector doesn't strive for perfection or rework product unnecessarily. These standards, like any others, need to be controlled. Documented standards should be governed by the document control provisions. Samples and models need to be governed by the inspection, measuring, and test equipment provisions and be subject to periodic examination to detect deterioration and damage. They should be certified as authentic workmanship samples and measures taken to preserve their integrity. Ideally they should be under the control of the inspection authority or someone other than the person responsible for using them so that there is no opportunity for them to be altered without authorization. The samples represent your company's standards, they do not belong to any individual and, if used by more than one person, you need to ensure consistent interpretation by training the users.

It is also important when selecting personnel for making appearance decisions, to ensure that they have the requisite physical attributes. Eyesight and color blindness tests should be conducted when appropriate. Lighting conditions should be appropriate for the evaluations performed, avoiding shadows, glare, and other adverse factors. The tests need to be conducted periodically as a safeguard against deterioration in the relevant physical attributes.

Maintenance of equipment

The standard requires *suitable maintenance of equipment to ensure continuing process capability*.

In a manufacturing environment, this requirement applies to the process plant, machinery and any other equipment upon which process capability depends. The requirement for documented procedures in 4.9a implies that you will need procedures for maintaining this equipment and this means that you will need:

- A list of the equipment upon which process capability depends

- Defined maintenance requirements specifying maintenance tasks and their frequency

- A maintenance program that schedules each of the maintenance tasks on a calendar

- Procedures defining how specific maintenance tasks are to be conducted

- Procedures governing the decommissioning of plant prior to planned maintenance

- Procedures governing the commissioning of plant following planned maintenance

- Procedures dealing with the actions required in the event of equipment malfunction

- Maintenance logs which record both the preventive and corrective maintenance work carried out

In a service environment if there is any equipment upon which the capability of your service depends then this equipment should be maintained. Maintenance may often be subcontracted to specialists but nevertheless needs to be under your control. If you are able to maintain process capability by bringing in spare equipment or using other available equipment then your maintenance procedures can be simple. You merely have to ensure you have an operational spare at all times. Where this is not possible you can still rely on the call-out service if you can be assured that the anticipated downtime will not reduce your capability below that which you have contracted to maintain.

The requirement does not mean that you have to validate all your word-processing software or any other special aids you use. Maintenance means retaining in an operational condition and you can do this by following some simple rules.

Preventive maintenance

The standard requires *the supplier to provide appropriate resources for machine/equipment maintenance and to develop an effective planned total preventive maintenance system for key process equipment*.

The essential elements of equipment maintenance are addressed above under the general heading and in detail in Part 2 Chapter 19 under *Servicing* and, although written for deliverable equipment, are applicable to process equipment.

In this additional clause, there are several new requirements that will be addressed here. Key process equipment is that equipment which has a direct relationship with production of the product and on which production deliveries depend. Section II 3.4 also covers tool maintenance but it would appear that it addresses corrective maintenance and not preventive maintenance.

The phrase "effective planned total preventive maintenance system" needs some explanation. *Planned maintenance* is maintenance carried out with forethought as to what is to be checked, adjusted, replaced etc. *Preventive maintenance* is maintenance carried out at predetermined intervals to reduce the probability of failure or performance degradation. Inserting the word "total" implies that the maintenance should cover all tools and equipment. An effective maintenance system should be one that achieves its objectives in minimizing downtime, i.e. the period of time in which the equipment is not in a condition to perform its function. *Corrective maintenance* is maintenance carried out after a failure has occurred and is intended to restore an item to a state in which it can perform its required function. So in this clause we are concerned with retaining equipment in a state in which it can perform its required function.

Predictive maintenance is part of planned preventive maintenance. In order to determine the frequency of checks you have to predict when failure may occur. Will failure occur at some future time, after a certain number of operating hours, when being operated under certain conditions, or some other time? An example of predictive maintenance is vibration analysis. Sensors can be installed to monitor vibration and thus give a signal when normal vibration levels have been exceeded. This can signal tool wear and wear in other parts of the machine in advance of the stage where nonconforming product will be generated.

The equipment manufacturer's manuals should indicate the recommended preventive maintenance tasks and the frequency they should be performed covering such aspects as cleaning, adjustments, lubrication, replacement of filters and seals, inspections for wear, corrosion, leakage, damage etc.

Another source of data is from your own operations. Monitoring tool wear, corrective maintenance, analyzing cutting fluids and incident reports from operators you can obtain a better picture of a machine's performance and predict more accurately the frequency of checks, adjustments, and replacements. For this to be effective you need a reporting mechanism that causes operators to alert maintenance staff to situations where suspect malfunctions are observed. In performing such monitoring you cannot wait until the end of the production run to verify whether the tools are still producing conforming product. If you do you will have no data to show when the tool started producing nonconforming product and will have to inspect the whole batch.

An effective maintenance system depends upon it being adequately resourced. Maintenance resources include people with appropriate skills, replacement parts and materials, access to support from OEMs when needed, and the funds to purchase this material. If the equipment is no longer supported by the OEM, then you may have to cannibalize old machines or manufacture the parts yourself. This can be a problem since you may not have a new part from which to take measurements. At some point you need to decide whether it is more economical to maintain the old equipment than to buy new. Your inventory control system needs to account for equipment spares and to adjust spares holding based on usage.

For the system to be effective there also has to be control of documentation, maintenance operations, equipment, and spare parts. Manuals for the equipment should be brought under document control. Tools and equipment used to maintain the operational equipment should be brought under calibration and verification control. Spare parts should be brought under identity control and the locations for the items brought under storage control. The maintenance operations should be controlled to the extent that maintenance staff should know what to do, know what they are doing and be able to change their performance should the objectives and requirements be not met. Whilst the focus should be on preventive maintenance, one must not forget corrective maintenance. The maintenance crew should be able to respond to equipment failures promptly and restore equipment to full operational condition in minimum time. The function needs resourcing to meet both preventive and corrective demands since it is downtime that will have most impact on production schedules.

The exact nature of the controls should be as appropriate to the item concerned, the emphasis being placed upon that which is necessary to minimize operational equipment downtime. It would be far better to produce separate procedures for these tasks rather than force fit the operational procedures to maintenance applications.

Special processes

The standard defines special processes as *processes, the results of which cannot be fully verified by subsequent inspection and testing of the product and where, for example, processing deficiencies may become apparent only after the product is in use.*

Many processes do not present any difficulty in the verification of the output against the input requirements regardless of the tools, personnel, facilities, or other means used to carry out the process. The resultant features and characteristics are relatively easily determined. However, there are some processes where conforming product is totally dependent upon the capability of personnel, equipment and facilities used, and where conformance cannot be fully verified by examination of the end product at any stage of assembly. If any of these factors is less than adequate, deficiencies may not become apparent until long after the product enters service. Among such processes are welding, soldering, adhesive bonding, casting, forging, forming, heat treatment, protective treatments, and inspection and test techniques such as X-ray examination, ultrasonics, environmental tests, and mechanical stress tests.

Within your quality system you should produce and maintain a list of special processes that have been qualified and a list of the personnel who are qualified to operate them. In this way you can easily identify an unqualified process or an unauthorized person, or an obsolete list if you have neglected to maintain it.

Ensuring compliance with unverifiable characteristics

The standard requires *special processes to be carried out by qualified operators and/or continuous monitoring and control of process parameters to ensure that the specified requirements are met.*

Where process capability relies upon the competence of personnel, personnel operating such processes need to be appropriately educated and trained and undergo examination of their competency. Where there is less reliance on personnel but more on the consistency of materials, environment, and processing equipment, operations should be monitored continuously by inspection, observation, or other techniques.

Qualification of processes

The standard requires that *the requirements for any qualification of process operations including associated equipment and personnel be specified.*

To limit the potential for deficiencies to escape detection before the product is released, special processes should be documented in the form of procedures and specifications that will ensure the suitability of all equipment, personnel, and facilities and prevent varying conditions, activities, or operations. Qualification in the context of special processes means that you need to conduct a thorough assessment of the processes to determine their capability to maintain or detect the conditions needed to produce conforming product consistently. The limits of capability need to be determined and the processes only applied within these limits. In qualifying the processes you need to qualify the personnel using them by training and examination as well as the materials, equipment, and facilities employed. It is the combination of personnel, materials, equipment, and facilities which ensure qualified processes.

In production you need to ensure that only those personnel, equipments, materials, and facilities that were qualified are employed in the process, otherwise you will invalidate the qualification and inject uncertainty into the results. If subcontracting special processes you need to ensure that the subcontractor only employs qualified personnel and has qualified process equipment and facilities (see Part 2 Chapters 6 and 18).

Records of qualified processes

The standard requires that *records be maintained for qualified processes, equipment, and personnel, as appropriate.*

The records of qualified personnel using special processes should be governed by the training requirements covered in Part 2 Chapter 18. Regarding the equipment, you will need to identify the equipment and facilities required within the process specifications and maintain records of the equipment in terms of:

- Type designation and serial number

- Manufacturer's name and address

- Date of purchase

- Date of installation

- Date of qualification

- Date of any re-qualification

- Process in which used

- Process specification applicable

- Maintenance schedule

- Record of planned and corrective maintenance

- List of problem reports

This data may be needed to trace the source of any problems with product which was produced using this equipment. To take corrective action you will also need to know the configuration of the process plant at the time of processing the product. If only one piece of equipment is involved then the above records will give you this information but if the process plant consists of many items of equipment which are periodically changed during maintenance, then you will need to know which equipment was in use when the fault is likely to have been generated.

Process monitoring and operator instructions

The standard requires *documented process monitoring and operating instructions for all employees having responsibility for operation of processes* and requires *the instructions to be accessible at the work station.*

There is somewhat of a conflict between the requirements of this clause and that of clause 4.9a. Clause 4.9.1 requires procedures regardless of need and clause 4.9a permits the absence of procedures where quality will not be adversely affected. Procedures which define the manner of production and instructions that define how to operate processes are one and the same. You should also take account of clause 4.2.2 which addresses the level of documentation needed. If you have a manufacturing process that relies on skill and training then instructions at the work station are unnecessary. For example, if fixing a tool in a tool holder on a lathe is a skill, learnt during basic training, then you don't have to provide instructions at each work station where normal tool changes take place. However, if the alignment of the tool is critical and requires knowledge of a setting up procedure, then obviously documented instructions are necessary. Even for basic skills you can still provide standard machinery data books accessible near to the work station, but a failure to do so should not be regarded as a noncompliance. There is merit in not providing basic text books to operators since the information is soon outdated and operators relying on such data instead of consulting the authorized data may inadvertently induce variation into the process.

The standard requires these instructions to be accessible at the work station. This is often prone to misinterpretation. For a start you need to define what constitutes a "work station". Is it a manufacturing cell where operations of the same type are performed or an individual machine? Next you need to define the meaning of *accessible*. Does it mean visible by the operator of the machine, in a cupboard near the machine or on a shelf in the area? If a group of people work in an area equipped with several small machines of the same type, set up to the same specification, then one set of instructions would probably suffice. If an area has several machines some of which are of a different type and those that are the same have a different set-up configuration, then instructions for each machine may be necessary. If the machines are huge and to access each requires one to walk some distance from your work station, regardless of set-up configuration, instructions may be needed at each machine. Use your common sense. Too many copies of the same document creates the chance that one may get missed when revisions occur. Single page instructions, encapsulated in plastic to prolong their life, can be posted on or close to the machine as a source of reference.

The standard also requires that the instructions be derived from the sources listed in the APQP manual which means that all instructions should be traceable to one or more of the listed documents. They should form a set so that there are no instructions used outside those that have been approved by the planning team. This is to make sure that no unauthorized practices are employed.

Another important aspect to consider is the use of informal practices, practices known only to the particular operator. Process capability should be based on formal routines otherwise repeatability cannot be assured when operators change.

The standard specifies a number of aspects that should be included in these instructions. Not all need to be included in each instruction provided there are adequate cross references which enable the operator to locate the necessary instructions and prevent any from being overlooked.

Preliminary process capability studies

The standard requires *process capability studies for each supplier-designated or customer-designated special characteristic for new processes and that the data meets customer requirements*.

The object of a process control system is to make economic and sound decisions about the actions affecting the process. Data concerning the variations in process performance are collected and analyzed and decisions taken as to whether action on the process is or is not necessary to maintain production of conforming product (see Figure 9.3). However, process control and process capability are not one and the same.

A process is in control when the average spread of variation coincides with the nominal specification for a parameter. The range of variation may extend outside the upper and lower limits but the proportion of parts within the limits can be predicted. This situation will remain as long as the process remains in statistical control. A process is in statistical control when the source of inherent variation is from common causes only, i.e. a source of variation which affects all the individual values of the process output and appears random. Common cause variation results in a stable and repeatable distribution of results over time. When the sources of variation cause the location, spread, and shape of the distribution to change, the process is not in statistical control. These sources of variation are due to special or assignable causes and must be eliminated before commencing with process capability studies. It is only when the performance of a process is predictable that its capability to meet customer expectations can be assessed.

Process capability studies are studies conducted to obtain information about the inherent variation present in processes that are under statistical control in order to reduce the spread of variation to less than the tolerances specified in the product specification.

> ■ **A capable process will produce all parts within the specified limits.**

During the process design and development phase (section 3 of APQP manual) a preliminary process capability plan is required to be developed and then during the product and process validation phase, the preliminary process capability analysis is required to be performed. Preliminary process capability studies are those based on measurements collected from one operating run to establish that the process is in statistical control and hence no special causes are present. Studies of unpredictable processes and the determination of associated capability indices has little value. The standard requires these preliminary studies to show acceptable results for special characteristics before production part approval can be given. These studies and associated indices only apply to the measurement of variables and not attributes (see below).

Several measures of process capability have evolved and are presented as indices: C_p, C_{pk}, and P_{pk}. These are defined in Appendix A.

Acceptable processes are those with a P_{pk} value ≥ 1.67. Those with P_{pk} between 1.33 and 1.67 may not meet customer requirements but approval may be granted. If $P_{pk} < 1.33$ the process is not acceptable.

A full treatment of the subject is given in the Fundamental SPC manual; however, the object of the studies is to compute the indices and then take action to reduce common cause variation by preventive maintenance, mistake proofing, operator training, revision to procedures and instructions etc.

The standard advises that the inherent limitations of attribute data prevent their use for preliminary statistical studies since specification values are not measured. Attribute data have only two values (conforming/nonconforming, pass/fail, go/no-go, present/absent) but they can be counted, analyzed, and the results plotted to show variation. Measurement can be based on the fraction defective such as parts per million (PPM). Whilst variables data follows a distribution curve, attribute data varies in steps since you can't count a fraction. There will either be zero errors or a finite number of errors.

Ongoing process performance requirements

The standard requires *the supplier to meet the ongoing performance requirements of the customer or meet specified default values*.

Following production launch, process capability and performance should be measured continually in order to demonstrate that your processes remain capable and the capability index continues to rise. The standard requires appropriate action to be taken on characteristics that are either unstable or non-capable. This relates to those characteristics that have not been designated as special characteristics since the processes which produce these have to be capable to obtain production part approval. You are required to institute reaction plans to contain process output and continually improve performance. Improvement may also be required on characteristics with a $C_{pk} < 1.33$ as the customer may require higher values whether or not the characteristics have been designated as special.

Modified preliminary or ongoing capability requirements

Where the customer requires either higher or lower capability requirements than the default values then the standard requires *the Control Plan to be annotated accordingly*.

The capability requirement will normally be defined by the customer and these may be changed in light of experience, either relaxing or tightening the values. The standard does not require the control plan to be changed but annotated, meaning the new values should be placed alongside the original values. This will require a revision of the plan as marked up copies are not permitted without approved change order.

Verification of job set-ups

The standard requires *job set-ups to be verified as producing parts that meet all requirements and that documentation be available for set-up personnel.*

In setting up a job prior to commencing a production run, you need to verify that all the requirements for the part are being met. You will therefore need job set-up instructions so as to ensure each time the production of a particular part commences that the process is set up against the same criteria. However, you will need to produce more than one part to verify that the process is stable. You need to form a sample large enough to take statistical measurement. If the measurements taken on the product fall within the central third of the control limits then the set-up can be approved; if not, then adjustments should be made and further samples produced until this condition is achieved.

Documentation verifying job set-ups should include documentation to perform the set-up and records that demonstrate that the set-up has been performed as required. This requires that you record the parameters set, the sample size and retain the control charts used which indicate performance to be within the central third of the control limits. These records should be retained as indicated in clause 4.16 of the standard.

Prior approval of process changes

The standard requires *the prior approval from customers of any changes in part numbers, product characteristics, manufacturing location, material sources, and production process environment and that a record of process change effective dates be maintained.*

Prior approval of changes to processes is addressed in 4.4.9 and 4.13.4 of Section I and clause 1.1 of Section II; however, there are some subtle differences. Clause 4.4.9 deals with design changes, clause 4.13.4 deals with inadvertent or unintended changes. In this clause of the standard, you are reminded that you need to seek customer approval even if making processes changes in order to bring about improvement.

Task list

1 Identify the result-producing processes.

2 Provide for the production requirement to be documented and made available to the production planners.

3 Prepare procedures for planning production of product lines, batched and single products.

4 Prepare procedures for providing instructions governing production activities where necessary.

5 Prepare procedures for provisioning tools, equipment, and facilities needed for production.

6 Establish standards of workmanship where appropriate and provide means for their control.

7 Provide suitable environments for the conduct of production operations.

8 Provide libraries or other areas where staff can gain access to the documentation needed to produce the product.

9 Install controls to enable operators to monitor production processes.

10 Provide travelers or route cards to route product through the production process into storage areas.

11 Carry out pre-production runs on new designs to prove the production set-up and debug the design.

12 Qualify all new process plant and equipment prior to use in production.

13 Train and qualify operators working with special processes.

14 Prepare and maintain a list of special processes and records of these processes.

15 Provide designated work-in-progress areas for holding product waiting further processing.

16 Provide designated areas or bins for product waiting inspection.

17 Provide equipment and containers for the safe transportation of product between operations.

18 Provide separate areas for reworking, repairing, or modifying product.

19 Provide a means of distributing parts from storage areas to assembly stations.

20 Provide security and protection for workmanship standards.

21 Identify any equipment that is vital to your operation and make provision for its maintenance or replacement in the event of failure.

Process control questionnaire

1 How do you ensure that production processes that directly affect quality are identified, planned, and carried out under controlled conditions?

2 How do you ensure that installation processes that directly affect quality are identified, planned, and carried out under controlled conditions?

3 How do you ensure that servicing processes that directly affect quality are identified, planned, and carried out under controlled conditions?

4 In which documents do you define the manner of production?

5 In which documents do you define the manner of installation?

6 In which documents do you define the manner of servicing?

7 In which documents do you define the production equipment?

8 In which documents do you define the installation equipment?

9 In which documents do you define the servicing equipment?

10 In which documents do you define the production working environments?

11 In which documents do you define the installation working environments?

12 In which documents do you define the servicing working environments?

13 In which documents do you define the reference standards, codes of practice, quality plans, and procedures to be complied with during production?

14 In which documents do you define the reference standards, codes of practice, quality plans, and procedures to be complied with during installation?

15 In which documents do you define the reference standards, codes of practice, quality plans, and procedures to be complied with during servicing?

16 How do you monitor and control process and product characteristics during production?

17 How do you monitor and control process and product characteristics during installation?

18 How do you monitor and control process and product characteristics during servicing?

19 How do you approve processes and equipment?

20 How do you define criteria for workmanship?

21 How do you ensure continued process capability?

22 In which documents do you define how process equipment is maintained?

23 In which documents do you identify the processes which produce results that cannot be fully verified by subsequent inspection and testing of product?

24 How do you ensure that the results of these processes comply with specified requirements?

25 How are the requirements for process qualification specified?

26 In what documents do you record those processes, personnel, and equipment that have been qualified?

Do's and don'ts

* Do record the issue status of documents used to fabricate product.

* Don't destroy labels attached to product when removed for assembly or installation – transfer data to assembly records before destroying the labels.

* Don't permit product to exit from the production process without having a plan for the operations to be carried out until its return.

* Don't inspect product until it reaches the planned inspection stage.

* Don't work to instructions unless provided in the quality system procedures, product specification, production plan or in approved change notices or remedial action instructions.

* Don't countenance informalities, work-around plans or unwritten tips as they create problems when those who know them are absent.

* Don't work to marked-up specifications unless covered by an approved change note.

* Don't use parts which have lost their identity.

* Don't skip operations without considering the effects and obtaining planning approval.

* Do gain set-up approval before commencing long production runs.

* Do delegate as much control to the operator as possible but provide the means for enabling self control.

* Don't put dots on charts without knowing what causes the results.

* Do monitor the effects of adjusting the process.

* Don't conduct experiments on the production line.

* Don't give control of the process to inspection.

* Do display process flowcharts in strategic areas to remind staff of the relationships.

Chapter 10

Inspection and testing

Scope of requirements

Inspection and test are methods of verifying that product complies with the specified requirements. A more suitable term for this section of the standard would be "Product/service verification", as used in ISO 9004, since inspection and test are only two methods of verification. Others are demonstration, analysis, and validation of records or a combination of such methods. Product verification is not limited to production, installation, and servicing. The inspections, tests, demonstrations, and other forms of verification that are used in product and service development should also be governed by these requirements as a means of ensuring that the product upon which design verification is carried out conforms with the prescribed requirements. If the product is noncompliant it may invalidate the results of design verification. Inspection and test also applies to any inspection, measuring, and test equipment that you design and manufacture to ensure that it is capable of verifying the acceptability of product, as required by clause 4.11 of the standard. Product verification is part of process control and not something separate from it, although the way the requirements are structured may imply otherwise.

It should also not be assumed that these requirements are only intended for implementation by a department with the title Inspection or Test. Whenever a product is supplied, produced or repaired, rebuilt, modified or otherwise changed, it should be subject to verification that it conforms with the prescribed requirements and any deficiencies corrected before being released for use. That is what control means. Control is not just the inspection part of the process and hence quality control, which for years was the name given to inspection departments, was misunderstood. Inspection and test don't control quality. Inspection and test merely measure achieved quality and pass the results to the producer for remedial action.

The requirements in element 4.10 are linked with other elements of the standard even when there is no cross reference. This relationship is illustrated in Figure 10.1.

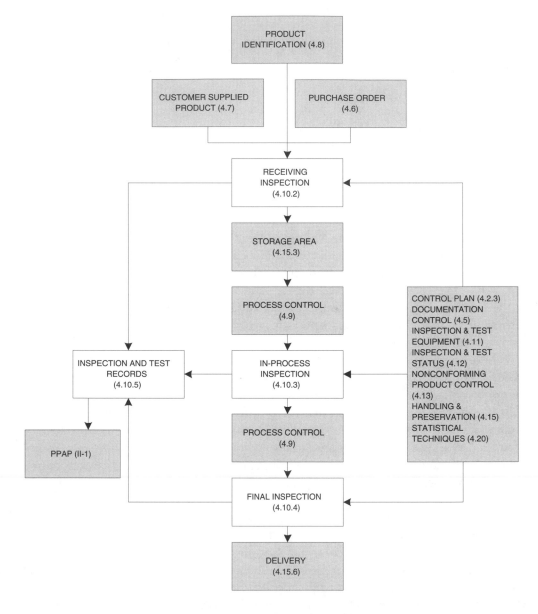

Figure 10.1 Element relationships with the inspection and testing element

Inspection and test planning

Documenting inspection and test procedures

The standard requires suppliers to *establish and maintain documented procedures for inspection and testing activities in order to verify that the specified requirements for product are met*.

The way the requirement is worded implies that the purpose of the procedures is to verify that specified requirements are met rather than this be the purpose of carrying out the inspection and test. Whether the procedures verify that specified requirements have been met or whether the inspections and tests achieve this purpose is immaterial, as you have to verify that you have met the specified requirement and have records which demonstrate this.

To meet this requirement for documented procedures you will need two types of procedure: procedures which provide for the necessary inspections and tests to be planned and carried out at the appropriate stage of the process and procedures for carrying out the specific inspections and tests. However, this is not to say that you need to document how you conduct every type of inspection or test. You only need procedures which define how inspections and test are to be performed when the lack of them will adversely affect the result. Where the inspection and test methods are no more than using the tools of the trade then no procedures will be necessary providing the acceptance criteria are specified in a specification, drawing, or other such document.

The requirement only relates to the specified requirements (i.e. the requirements specified by the customer) but clearly you will need to verify that the product meets the requirements which you have prescribed in the product or process specification.

Use of accredited laboratories for inspection and testing

The standard requires *use of accredited laboratory facilities when required by customers*.

QS-9000 recognizes that some organizations may not possess all the inspection and test resources to carry out receiving, in-process, and final inspection. Where use of external inspection laboratories is necessary General Motors require compliance with their standard on the evaluation and accreditation of supplier test facilities, however, QS-9000 registration is an acceptable alternative.

Documenting inspections and tests

The standard requires that *the required inspecting and testing and the records to be established be detailed in the quality plan or documented procedures.*

The standard provides a choice as to whether you define the inspections and tests required in a quality plan or in documented procedures. You may of course need to do both. As the quality system is often designed to accommodate all products and services you supply, it may not specify inspections and tests which are needed for particular products. This is one of the roles of the quality plan. Within such a plan you should identify the verification stages during product development, production, installation, and servicing as applicable. These stages will vary depending on the product, so your quality plan will be product, contract or project specific (see Part 2 Chapter 2). There may well be many routine inspections and tests that are needed which are carried out by type of product regardless of contract or project and these can be specified in your documented procedures, which need to be invoked within the quality plan. If the degree of special planning needed for the product, contract or project is limited to these inspections and tests then the plan is the Control Plan. These plans may of course be integrated with your production, installation, or servicing plans as covered in Part 2 Chapter 9. This clause could have been made more consistent with those in sections 4.2 and 4.9 if the term "inspection and test planning" had been used to describe the requirements. A reference to "control plans" under this heading would also have been appropriate.

In defining your inspection and test requirements it is necessary not only to specify what inspections and test are required and when, but to define the acceptance criteria and the frequency of inspection and test. Is the acceptance criteria that defined in the product specification or are the limits to be closed to gain better control over the process? Is every product to be inspected or are the quantities so large that it would be economically unviable? If sampling is to be performed what is the acceptance criteria? Answers to these and other questions need to be provided by your documented inspection and testing requirements.

QS-9000 requires *the acceptance criteria for attribute data sampling plans to be zero defects and that the criteria for all other situations to be documented and approved by the customer.*

With attribute data the product either has or has not the ascribed attribute, it can therefore either pass or fail the test. There are no gray areas. Attributes are measured on a go or no-go basis. With variables, the product can be evaluated on a scale of measurement. However, with inspection by attributes we sometimes use an acceptable quality level (AQL) that allowed us to ship a certain percent defective in a large batch of product – probably no more than 10 in 1000, but to the automobile industry that is not good enough. QS-9000 standard imposes a strict requirement on characteristics that are measured by attributes. There shall be no AQL, there shall be zero percent defective in the sample selected for inspection otherwise the batch shall be rejected. This is what it implies as your customer does not want to be supplied any defective products.

For inspection by variables the acceptance criteria has to be specified and the place to specify it is the Control Plan which is submitted to your customer for approval.

The second part of the requirement deals with inspection and test records, which are also covered in clause 4.10.5. The difference between these requirements is that clause 4.10.1 requires you to document the records to be established (in other words "define") in the quality plan or procedures and clause 4.10.5 requires you to produce the records defined in the quality plan or procedures. Your inspection and test procedures therefore need to specify or contain the forms on which you intend to record the results of the inspections and tests performed. The details are covered later in this chapter, but there are two types of record to be considered: the record that shows which inspections and tests have been performed and the record that shows the results of these inspections and tests. One may be a route card, shop traveler or document which acts as both a plan of what to do and a record of the progress made and the other may be a table of results with specified parameters and accept/reject criteria.

Receiving inspection and testing

The standard requires that the supplier *ensures that incoming product is not used or processed (except in the circumstances described in 4.10.1.2) until it has been inspected or otherwise verified as conforming to specified requirements* and requires that *verification be in accordance with the quality plan or documented procedures.*

When we purchase items as individuals it is a natural act to inspect what has been purchased before using it. To neglect to do this may result in us forfeiting our rights to return it later if found defective or nonconforming. When we purchase items on behalf of our employers we may not be as tenacious. We don't get the same pleasure out of it and are not necessarily eager to see what the product can do for us. So the company has to enforce its own receipt inspection policy as a way of protecting itself from the mistakes of its suppliers. Another reason for inspecting product on receipt is that it is often the case that characteristics are not accessible for inspection or test after subsequent processing. Characteristics that have not been verified on receipt may never be verified. This is the main purpose behind the requirement rather than of forfeiting your rights.

The key phrase in this clause is "or otherwise verified" as it allows you to receive product into your company and straight onto the production line if you have verified that it conforms to the specified requirements before it arrives. An example of this is where you have performed or witnessed acceptance tests on the supplier's premises. You may also have obtained sufficient confidence in your supplier that you can operate a "Just-in-time" arrangement but you must be able to show that you have a continuous monitoring programme which informs you of the supplier's performance.

Regarding purchases made by the supplier, there are three parties: the ultimate customer, the supplier, and the supplier's supplier (the subcontractor). The standard has overlooked the fact that items are often inspected on receipt for conformance with the supplier's purchase order and not against requirements placed by the supplier's customer. Product may be nonconforming with the supplier's requirements but not the supplier's customer's requirements, since QS-9000 only requires positive recall if nonconforming with the customer's requirements.

The standard requires that you ensure that incoming product is not used or processed until verified as conforming, but how do you do this? The only way to make certain of this is to install a "gate" through which only conforming items may pass. You need to register the receipt of items and then pass them to an inspection station equipped to determine conformance with your purchasing requirements. If items would normally pass into storage areas following inspection then as a safeguard you should also make provision for the storeperson to check that all items received have been through inspection, rejecting any that have not. By use of labels attached to items you can make this a painless routine (see Part 2 Chapter 12). If some items are routed direct to the user then you need a means of obtaining written confirmation that the items conform to the prescribed requirements so that at receipt inspection you can provide evidence that:

- Nothing comes into the company without being passed through inspection.

- Nothing can come out of inspection without it being verified as conforming.

If the user is unable to verify that requirements have been met, you will need to provide evidence either that it has passed your receipt inspection or that it has been certified by the vendor.

This requirement poses something of a dilemma when purchasing subcontract labor since clearly it cannot be treated the same as product. You still need to ensure, however, that the labor conforms with your requirements before use. Such checks will include verification that the personnel provided have the requisite qualifications, skills, and knowledge and they are who they say they are. These checks can be made on the documentary evidence provided, such as certificates, but you will probably wish to monitor their performance since it is the effort you have purchased, not the people. You will not be able to verify whether they are entirely suitable until you have evaluated their performance. Subcontract labor could be classified as product released prior to verification being performed and so you need to keep records of the personnel and their performance during the tenure of the contract.

Receipt inspection doesn't have to be a department, a section, a separate room, a full time job for someone or a particular person. It is a process through which all product must pass, even those received on a "Just-in-time" basis. Someone should verify that they can pass uninspected. At a customs post some people are stopped others are waved through; all are inspected to some degree, it all depends on the confidence gained by observation.

The verification carried out, however, has to be in accordance with some plan. The standard requires firstly that you verify conformance and then that you should do it in accordance with some plan or other. Your plans, therefore have to prescribe the acceptance criteria for carrying out such verification. If the standard required that you verify conformance in accordance with the quality plan, as it does in clause 4.10.3, then it would give you the option of not specifying any measures at all in your quality plan for verifying conformance, but this has been covered by the requirements of 4.10.1 as already explained.

So what should you put into your quality plan or documented procedures on receipt inspection? The main aspects to cover are as follows:

- Define how the receipt inspection personnel obtain current purchasing requirements.

- Categorize all items that you purchase so that you can assign levels of receipt inspection based on given criteria (see later).

- For each level of inspection, define the checks that are to be carried out and the acceptance criteria to be applied.

- Where dimensional and functional checks are necessary, define how the receipt inspection personnel obtain the acceptance criteria and how they are to conduct the inspections and tests.

- Define the action to be taken when the product, the packaging, or the documentation is found acceptable.

- Define the action to be taken when the product, the packaging, or the documentation is found unacceptable.

- Define the records to be maintained.

As stated previously everything should be passed through a receipt inspection. However, in order to relate the degree of inspection to the importance of the item, you should categorize purchases, an example of which is as follows:

- If the subsequent discovery of a nonconformance will not cause design, production, installation, or operational problems of any nature then a simple identity, carton quantity, and damage check may suffice. An example of this would be stationery.

- If the subsequent discovery of a nonconformance will cause minor design, production, installation, or operational problems then you should examine the features and characteristics of the item on a sampling basis. An example of this would be electrical, electronic, or mechanical components.

- If the subsequent discovery of a nonconformance will cause major design, production, installation, or operational problems then you should subject the item to a complete test to verify compliance with all prescribed requirements. An example of this would be an electronic unit.

These criteria would need to be varied depending on whether the items being supplied were in batches or separate. But these are the kind of decisions you need to make in order to apply practical receipt inspection procedures.

Determining the amount and nature of receiving inspection

The standard requires that *in determining the amount and nature of receiving inspection, consideration should be given to the control exercised at the subcontractor's premises and recorded evidence of conformance provided.*

Within your procedures you need to provide a means of identifying which items have been subject to inspection at the subcontractor's premises and the receipt inspection action to be taken depending on the level of that inspection. In some cases, the product may have been accepted by your representative on the subcontractor's premises. In another case, a product from the same batch may have been accepted by your representative but not the one that has been delivered. Alternatively your representative may have only performed a quality audit to gain a level of confidence. You need to specify the inspection to be carried out in all such cases. The standard emphasizes that consideration should also be given to the recorded evidence provided. Even if someone has performed inspection at the subcontractor's premises, if there is no evidence of conformance the inspections are of little value. The fact that an inspection was carried out is insufficient. There has to be a statement of what was checked and what results were obtained and a decision as to whether conformance has been achieved. Without such evidence you may have to repeat some of the inspections carried out on the subcontractor's premises.

Receiving inspection methods

The standard requires *use of one or more specified methods for determining incoming product quality.*

In QS-9000 you are limited to choosing one or more receiving inspection methods from a list of five methods, some of which have been addressed previously.

If the subcontractor supplies statistical data from the manufacturing process that indicates that quality is being controlled, then an analysis of this data based on assurances you have obtained through site evaluation can provide sufficient confidence in part quality to permit release into the organization.

Sampling inspection should be used when statistical data is unavailable to you or you don't have the confidence for permitting ship to line.

Assessments by second or third parties can be an acceptable alternative but it depends on the standards used for the assessments. A QS-9000 assessment alone would not give sufficient confidence to remove all receiving inspection for deliveries from that particular supplier. You have to examine product as well as the system until you have gained the confidence to reduce inspection and eventually remove it. Subsequently continual assessment of the subcontractor should be carried out.

Part evaluation by accredited contractors or test laboratory provides independent verification which can substitute for your own receiving inspection, providing you maintain control over the contractor.

Where you have required your subcontractors to send a warrant or certificate of conformity testifying the consignments conformity with the order, then you cannot omit all receiving checks. The warrant allows you to reduce your incoming checks and this is recognized by QS-9000 as it only permits warrants to be used in combination with one of the other methods. The standard also requires that warrants be supported with test results and this means you have to impose this requirement in your purchasing documents. However, be careful to specify exactly what test results you require and in what format you require them presented as you could be provided with attribute data when you want variables data.

Premature release of product

The standard requires that *where incoming product is released for urgent production purposes, prior to verification, it shall be positively identified and recorded in order to permit immediate recall and replacement in the event of nonconformance to specified requirements.*

If you do release a batch of product prior to verification being performed and one out of the batch is subsequently found to be nonconforming, you will need to retrieve all others from the same batch. This may not be as simple as it seems. In order to retrieve a component that has subsequently been assembled into a printed circuit board, which has itself been fitted into a unit along with several other assemblies, you have to have a good traceability system. Not only that, but the traceability system has to be in operation constantly. You never can tell when product is going to be needed for urgent production purposes.

It would be considered prudent to prohibit the premature release of product if you did not have an adequate traceability system in place. If in fact any nonconformances in a component will be detected by the end product tests then it may be worth allowing production to commence without the receipt tests being available, in which case the tests are only confidence checks and not verification checks. Since the requirement applies prior to verification then if only one product is received and released prior to verification one would think that there is no need to positively identify it to permit recall, as you would know where it was if you found it to be nonconforming. However, the nonconformance may have been reported to you by the supplier after delivery. The standard does not stipulate when and by whom the nonconformance may have been detected. If you lose the means of determining conformance by premature release, then don't release the product until you have verified it is acceptable.

In-process inspection and testing

The standard requires the supplier to *inspect, test, and identify product as required by the quality plan or documented procedures*.

In-process inspection is carried out in order to verify those features and characteristics that would not be accessible to verification by further processing or assembly. When producing a product that consists of several parts, sub-assemblies, assemblies, units, equipments, and subsystems, each part, sub-assembly etc. needs to be subject to final inspection but may also require in-process inspection for the reasons given above. Your quality plan, or better still the production plan (see Part 2 Chapter 9), should define all the in-process inspection and test stages that are required for each part, sub-assembly, assembly etc. In establishing where to carry out the inspections, a flow diagram may help. The inspections and tests need to occur after a specified feature has been produced and before it becomes inaccessible to measurement. This doesn't mean that you should check features as soon as they are achieved. There may be natural breaks in the process where the product passes from one stage to another or stages at which several features can be verified at once. If product passes from the responsibility of one person to another then there should be a stage inspection at the interface to protect the producer even if the features achieved are accessible later. Your inspection and test plans should:

• Identify the product to be inspected and tested.

- Define the specification and acceptance criteria to be used and the issue status which applies.

- Define what is to be inspected at each stage. Is it all work between stages or only certain operations? The parameters to be verified should include those which are known to be varied by the manufacturing processes. Those which remain constant from product to product need verifying only once, usually during design proving.

- Define the inspection aids and test equipment to be used. There may be jigs, fixtures, gages, and other aids to inspection that are needed. Standard measuring equipment would not need to be specified as your inspectors and testers should be trained to select the right tools for the job. Any special test equipment should be identified.

- Define the environment for the measurements to be made if critical to measurement accuracy (see Part 2 Chapter 11).

- Identify the organization which is to perform the inspections and tests.

- Make provision for the results of the inspections and test to be recorded.

Held product

The standard requires the supplier to *hold product until the required inspection and tests have been completed or necessary reports have been received and verified except when product is released under positive recall procedures. Release under positive recall procedures shall not preclude the activities outlined in 4.10.3a.*

In continuous production, product is inspected by taking samples from the line which are then examined while the line continues producing product. In such cases you will need a means of holding product produced between sampling points until the results of the tests and inspections are available. You will also need a means of releasing product when the results indicate that the product is acceptable. So a Product Release Procedure or Held Product Procedure may be necessary. The standard implies, however, that if you have released product under positive recall procedures you do not need to hold product while in-process inspection and tests are performed. The reference to clause 4.10.3a is also ambiguous since the inspections and tests carried out in accordance with the quality plan or documented procedures may not cover those necessary to verify product on receipt into the plant. It would be wise to hold any product until you have completed your inspections and tests regardless of positive recall procedures being in force.

Defect prevention methods

The standard recommends *inspection activities be directed towards defect prevention rather than defect detection*.

By recommending a defect prevention approach, the standard is suggesting that you seek ways of reducing reliance on inspection as a means of controlling product quality. By doing so you will gain greater control over the processes that produce products by improving the capability of the manufacturing processes of both your subcontractors and your own operations. Whilst some inspection will always be necessary it should be used as a verification that the process controls are working properly and therefore should be conducted when product has completed processing rather than when product is in-process. Defect prevention is driven by Simultaneous Engineering performed by the cross-functional teams working together and using the techniques given for quality and productivity improvement in Section II 2.2 and the provisions made to meet the requirements of Section II 3.1 and 3.2 as well as the process controls of element 4.9.

It is interesting to note that in ISO 9001, the word *defect* does not appear for the simple reason that a defect is nonfulfillment of intended usage requirements and has legal connotations in the context of product liability (see also Part 2 Chapter 13). The authors of QS-9000 have not taken the same precautions but no significance should be attributed to the word *defect* in the context in which it is used in this clause of QS-9000. Perhaps a more appropriate phrase would have been *error detection* since the term *error proofing* is used in the text.

Final inspection and testing

Final inspection is in fact the last inspection of the product that you will perform before dispatch but it may not be the last inspection before delivery if your contract includes installation. The term *final inspection* has three meanings:

- The inspection carried out on completion of the product. Afterwards the product may be routed to storage areas rather than to a customer.

- The last inspection carried out before dispatch. Afterwards you may install the product and carry out further work.

- The last inspection that you as a supplier carry out on the product before ownership passes to your customer. This is the final inspection of all inspections.

In place of the term *final inspection*, the term *product acceptance* is more appropriate and tends to convey the purpose of the inspection rather than the stage of the inspection.

Completing the evidence of conformance

The standard requires that the supplier *carries out final inspection and testing in accordance with the quality plan and/or documented procedures to complete the evidence of conformance of the finished product to the specified requirements.*

To accomplish this, you need to specify either in the quality plan or the documented procedures, the inspections and tests you intend to carry out to verify that the product meets specified requirements. In Part 2 Chapter 4 there is a description of a Design Verification Plan and this includes a specification of the tests and inspections to be performed on each production item as a means of ensuring that the qualified design standard is being maintained. This requires that you produce something like an Acceptance Test Plan which contains, as appropriate, some or all of the following:

- Identity of the product to be inspected and tested

- Definition of the specification and acceptance criteria to be used and the issue status which applies

- Definition of the inspection aids and test equipment to be used (see above)

- Definition of the environment for the measurements to be made (see Part 2 Chapter 11)

- Provision for the results of the inspections and test to be recorded (these need to be presented in a form that correlates with the specified requirements)

Having carried out these inspections and tests it should be possible for you to declare that the product has been inspected and tested and objective evidence produced that will demonstrate that it meets the specified requirements. Any concessions given against requirements should also be identified. If you can't make such a declaration then you haven't done enough verification. Whether or not your customer requires a certificate from you testifying that you have met the requirements you should be in a position to produce one. The requirement for a certificate of conformance should not alter your processes, your quality controls, or your procedures. One advantage of QS-9000 is that it will enable you to build a quality system that will give you the kind of evidence you need to assure your customers that your product meets their requirements without having to do anything special.

Ensuring all inspections and test have been carried out

The standard requires *the quality plan or documented procedures for final inspection and testing to require that all the specified inspections and tests, including those specified either on receipt of product or in-process, have been carried out and that the data meets specified requirements.*

There are two aspects to final inspection. One is checking what has gone before and the other is accepting the product.

Final inspection and test checks should detect whether:

- All previous inspections and checks have been performed.

- The product bears the correct identification, part numbers, serial numbers, modification status etc.

- The as-built configuration is the same as the issue status of all the parts, sub-assemblies, assemblies etc. specified by the design standard.

- All recorded nonconformances have been resolved and remedial action taken and verified.

- All concession applications have been approved.

- All inspection and test results have been collected.

- Any result outside the stated limits is either subject to an approved concession, an approved specification change, or a retest which shows conformance with the requirements.

- All documentation to be delivered with the product has been produced and conforms to the prescribed standards.

Where the standard requires data to meet specified requirements this could be interpreted in two ways. If the specified requirements included data requirements then clearly you would have to satisfy them. But if the specified requirements did not define what you had to record then whatever you record you will have met the specified requirements. Alternatively, the standard could be interpreted, and this is more likely, as implying that the results you achieve are within the limits defined by the specified requirements. The next clause requires you to complete the evidence. You may have some difficulty with this as the specified requirements may not define the same parameters as you are measuring and some analysis may be necessary to correlate the results. This analysis is all part of inspection even though it may be performed by another group of people.

Ensuring no incomplete product is dispatched

The standard requires that *no product be dispatched until all the activities specified in the quality plan or documented procedures have been satisfactorily completed and the associated data and documentation are available and authorized*.

This requirement can impose unnecessary constraints if you take it literally. Many activities in quality plans and procedures are performed to give early warning of nonconformances. This is in order to avoid the losses that can be incurred if failure occurs in later tests and inspections. The earlier you confirm conformance the less costly any rework will be.

> ■ **The later the inspection the more costly the rework.**

Therefore you should not hold shipment if later activities will verify the same parameters whether or not earlier activities have been performed. It is uneconomic for you to omit the earlier activities, but if you do, and the later activities confirm that the end product meets the requirements, and that this can be demonstrated, then it is also uneconomic to go back and perform those activities that have not been completed. Your quality plan could cover installation and maintenance activities which are carried out after dispatch and so it would be unreasonable to insist that these activities were completed before dispatch or to insist on separate quality plans just to sanitize a point. A less ambiguous way of saying the same thing is to require no product to be dispatched until objective evidence has been produced to demonstrate that it meets the specified or contracted requirements and authorization for its release has been given.

You need four things before you can release product whether it be to a storage area, to the customer, to the site for installation or anywhere else:

- Sight of the product

- Sight of the requirement with which the product is to conform

- Sight of the objective evidence which purports to demonstrate that the particular product meets the requirement

- Sight of an authorized signatory or the stamp of an approved stamp holder who has checked that the particular product, the evidence, and the requirement are in complete accord

Layout inspection and functional testing

The standard requires *layout inspection and functional verification for all products at frequencies determined by the customer*.

When a product undergoes design verification and validation, the tests are conducted on a small sample of product that is representative of the production standard. The variation in materials, environment, and characteristics that is possible over long production runs cannot be fully predicted and therefore, periodic tests are necessary to verify that the product in current production is of the same standard as the product that gained production approval. In some industries these checks are called verification of qualification (VOQ); in the automobile industry they are called layout inspection and functional verification.

A layout inspection is the complete measurement of all part dimensions shown on the design record and a functional verification is testing to ensure that the part conforms to all customer and supplier engineering performance and material requirements.

The frequency of such checks and the sample size will be specified by the customer and could be annually or more or less often depending on quantities produced and other considerations.

The tests and inspections carried out need to be to the same specifications and procedures as those used for the original production part approval and as amended by subsequent approved engineering changes. The results of the tests should be recorded in the same format as the original tests unless otherwise required by the customer.

Inspection and test records

The standard requires that the supplier *establishes and maintains records which provide evidence that the product has been inspected and/or tested*.

Types of inspection and test records

Your inspection and test records or verification records should be of two forms: one which indicates what inspections and tests have been carried out and the other which indicates the results of such inspections and test. They may be merged into one record but when parameters need to be recorded it is often cleaner to separate the progress record from the technical record. Your procedures, quality plan, or product specifications should also indicate what measurements have to be recorded.

Content of inspection and test records

The standard requires that *the inspection and test records show clearly whether the product has passed or failed the inspections and/or tests according to defined acceptance criteria.*

Don't assume that because a parameter is shown in a specification that an inspector or tester will record the result. A result can be a figure, a pass/fail, or just a tick. Be specific in what you want recorded as you may get a surprise when gathering the data for analysis. If you use computers then you won't have the same problems but beware, too much data is probably worse than too little. In choosing the method of recording measurements, you also need to consider whether you will have sufficient data to minimize recovery action in the event of the measuring device subsequently being found out of calibration. As a general rule, only gather that data you need to determine whether the product meets the requirements or whether the process is capable of producing a product that meets the requirements. You need to be selective so that you can spot the out-of-tolerance condition. All inspection and test records should define the acceptance criteria, the limits between which the product is acceptable and beyond which the product is unacceptable and therefore nonconforming.

Action required on failed product

The standard requires the *procedures for control of nonconforming product to apply to any product which fails to pass any inspection and/or test.*

The standard emphasizes that a nonconforming product is one which has failed a planned inspection and/or test. Up to that stage the product is neither conforming nor nonconforming, it is merely in-process. Hence the requirements of section 4.13 only apply after product or service has been inspected or tested and are clearly not intended to be applied at any other stage.

Identifying the inspection authority

The standard requires that *records identify the inspection authority responsible for the release of conforming product.*

The inspection authority is the organization that decided whether the product was conforming or nonconforming.

It may be an individual or an organization. Within an organization you may wish to identify the individual responsible so that you can go back to him and ask questions. This is more likely in the case of a reject decision as opposed to an acceptance decision. As products emerge from the organization there is less need to identify individuals, and more of a need to identify which organization made the decision but it can be either. It is also important to protect your staff from prying users or customers or those with a grudge against the person who released the defective product, by avoiding putting the name of an individual on a product. The use of numbered inspection stamps avoids this possibility.

The inspection authority for a document is the person who approved it. There may be other personnel in the chain such as the issuing authority or the publishing authority, but the person who verified the content is normally the approval authority. With documents that carry signatures you have less protection from prying users and so here is a good reason for excluding the name of the author or approver from the finished document if it is to be used externally.

Some organizations maintain a list of authorized signatures as a means of being able to trace signatures to names of people who carry certain authority. If you have a large number of people signing documents and records and there is a possibility that the wrong person may sign a document, then the list is a good tool for checking that there has been no abuse of authority. Otherwise, the name of the individual and his or her position below or alongside the signature should be adequate. The quality system is a tool for achieving quality not for detecting criminals. If people want to commit fraud they will and the only system that comes close to preventing such incidents is a real-time computerized quality system. But even that is not immune to the determined hackers.

Task list

1   Establish a receipt inspection area for processing incoming goods.

2   Prepare procedures for inspecting and testing incoming goods.

3   Classify goods so as to apply inspection and test according to the need.

4   Define the criteria for acceptance of goods into the organization.

5   Appoint an authority for releasing incoming product to storage areas or for use.

6   Establish means of dealing with nonconforming product.

7   Provide measuring facilities and equipment for use in the receipt inspection area and measures for their control.

8   Provide a quarantine area to place nonconforming product pending disposition.

9   Establish a means of tracing product back to its inspection on receipt.

10 Produce procedures for in-process and final inspection and test.

11 Provide for inspection and test plans to be produced for verifying product through the various stages of production.

12 Provide a means for progressing the inspections and tests and for identifying those responsible for carrying them out.

13 Provide inspection stations in-process to which product is passed for inspection.

14 Provide inspection aids, tools, and measuring equipment appropriate for the task.

15 Provide environmental controls for inspection and test areas where measurement accuracy requires them.

16 Provide facilities for inspectors to obtain current versions of all relevant product specifications, drawings, and process specifications.

17 Provide a means of recording inspection and test results so that any omissions can be checked at subsequent inspections.

18 Provide secure areas for storing inspection and test records.

19 Provide areas for held product pending results of final inspection.

20 Provide for products to re-enter the inspection flow following rework, repair, or modification.

Inspection and testing questionnaire

1   How do you establish the inspections and tests required to verify that the specified requirements for product are met?

2   In which procedures are the inspection and test activities documented?

3   In which documents are the inspecting and testing requirements defined?

4   In which document do you specify the inspection and test records to be established?

5   How do you ensure that product is not used until verified as conforming with specified requirements?

6   How do you ensure that product is not processed until verified as conforming with specified requirements?

7   How do you ensure that product is not dispatched until verified as conforming with specified requirements?

8   How is the amount and nature of receipt inspection determined?

9   When you need to release incoming product for urgent processing, how do you enable immediate recall and replacement in the event of nonconformances being revealed?

10 How do you ensure that incoming product released for urgent production purposes is identified and recorded?

11 How do you ensure that product is inspected, tested, and identified as required by the quality plan or documented procedures?

12 How do you ensure product is held until the required inspections and tests or necessary reports have been received and verified?

13 What measures are being taken to reduce reliance on in-process inspection as a means of error detection?

14 In which documents do you define the inspections and tests required to complete the evidence of conformance with specified requirements?

15 How do you ensure that no product is dispatched until all the inspections and tests specified have been satisfactorily completed?

16 Which documents record the evidence that product has been inspected and tested, and passed or failed defined acceptance criteria?

17 How do you ensure that records identify the inspection authority responsible for the release of product?

Do's and don'ts

* Do attach labels to products on receipt to indicate their inspection status.

* Don't mix inspected product with uninspected product.

* Don't permit the release of incoming product until it has either passed inspection or a sample has been taken for inspection.

* Do ensure current purchasing data is available at the place of receipt inspection.

* Don't place product back in the receipt inspection area once it has been released.

* Do keep a register of the articles placed in quarantine.

* Don't permit articles to be removed from quarantine without authorization, a record of why they have been removed and who has removed them.

* Don't permit product to skip planned inspections and tests without the prior authorization of the planners.

* Do re-plan inspection and test in the event of rework, repair, or modification action.

* Don't accept product back into the inspection flow without verification that previous inspection stages have not been invalidated.

* Don't delegate inspection and test operations to others without confirming that they meet the criteria for trained inspectors and testers.

* Don't permit designers to tinker with deliverable product.

* Do re-validate processes that have been stopped for remedial action before running product.

* Don't use gages or other tools for inspection and test purposes unless verified accurate.

* Don't release nonconforming product until remedial action has been authorized and taken.

* Don't permit inspectors to rework product unless they produced it.

* Do train operators to inspect and test their own work.

* Do monitor inspection errors, classify them, and act on those which are under your control.

* Do protect product after inspection operations.

* Do keep a check on the criteria your inspectors are using to accept product.

Chapter 11

Inspection, measuring, and test equipment

Scope of requirements

The integrity of products depend upon the quality of the devices used to create and measure their characteristics. This part of the standard specifies requirements for ensuring the quality of such devices. If the devices you use to create and measure characteristics are inaccurate, unstable, damaged, or in any way defective then the product will not possess the required characteristics and further more you will not know it. You know nothing about an object until you can measure it, but you must measure it accurately and precisely. Hence the devices you use need to be controlled.

However, these requirements go further than merely controlling the devices used for measurement. They address the measurements themselves, the selection of the devices for measurement and also apply to devices which create product features, if they are used for product verification purposes. If you rely on jigs, tools, fixtures, templates, patterns etc. to form shapes or other characteristics and have no other means of verifying the shape achieved, then these devices become a means of verification. If you use software to control equipment, simulate the environment or operational conditions, or carry out tests and you rely on that software doing what it is supposed to do, without any separate means of checking the result, then the quality of such software becomes critical to product verification. In fact the requirements apply to metrology as a whole rather than being limited to the equipment that is used to obtain the measurement and therefore a more appropriate title of the section would be "Control of measurements".

Devices that you use for product verification at all stages in the quality loop need to be controlled and this includes devices used for inspection and test on receipt of product, in-process, and final acceptance before release to the customer. It also includes devices used during design and development for determining product characteristics and for design verification. Some characteristics cannot be determined by calculation and have to be derived by experiment. In such cases the accuracy of devices you use must be controlled, otherwise the parameters stated in the resultant product specification may not be achievable when the product reaches production.

Should you not use measuring devices in your organization then these requirements will not apply. If your means of verification are limited to visual inspection or professional judgment, as is the case with organizations that deal only with documentation, then you have no devices to control. However, you may use tools or computer

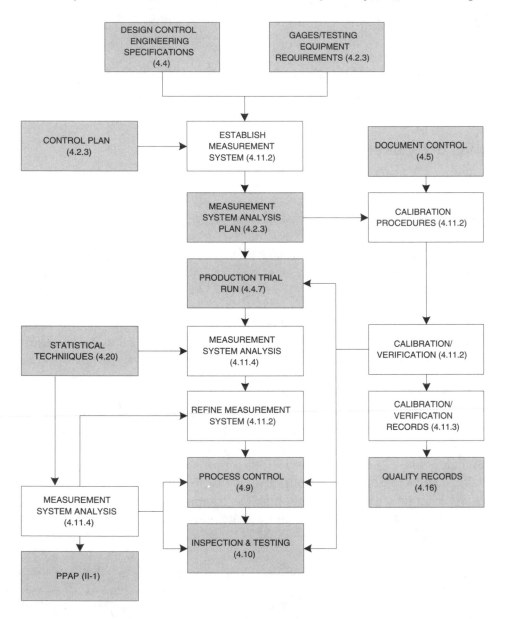

Figure 11.1 Element relationships with the inspection, measuring, and test equipment element

software to assist you determine conformance and these will need to be proven capable of producing a reliable result.

The standard refers you to ISO 10012 for guidance in meeting these requirements and there are other standards referenced in Appendix D that cover this subject in far more detail.

The requirements in element 4.11 are linked with other elements of the standard even when there is no cross reference. This relationship is illustrated in Figure 11.1.

Inspection, measuring, and test equipment procedures

The standard requires the supplier to *establish and maintain documented procedures to control, calibrate, and maintain inspection, measuring, and test equipment including test software.*

Procedures are required for the control and maintenance of inspection, measuring, and test equipment and to cover test software, not only for calibration. This section of the standard is often referred to as the calibration requirement but it goes far beyond mere calibration. In assessing compliance with section 4.11, there are at least 30 requirements to check (see the questionnaire at the end of this chapter) and calibration is only one of them. Figure 11.2 shows the processes needed to control, calibrate, and maintain inspection, measuring, and test equipment. The shaded boxes indicate interfaces with other processes.

The requirement for procedures does not stipulate that they have to address all 30 requirements of this section of the standard. Procedures are required only for the control, calibration, and maintenance of these devices. The requirements in clause 4.11a, for instance, requiring you to determine the measurements to be made and the accuracy required are not requirements concerning the control, calibration, and maintenance of these devices. They are requirements concerning measurement. The procedure requirement only addresses the devices used for measurement and therefore does not apply to software other than software used for measurement.

Whether you have one procedure or twenty to address this requirement you need to cover all types of equipment as well as test software if you use it. Some of the requirements of this section may need to be addressed in procedures developed for other purposes, such as the requirement for determination of measurements.

Procedures for the control, calibration, and maintenance of measuring devices will need to cover the various types of devices you employ for measurement purposes, such as:

- Electronic measuring equipment

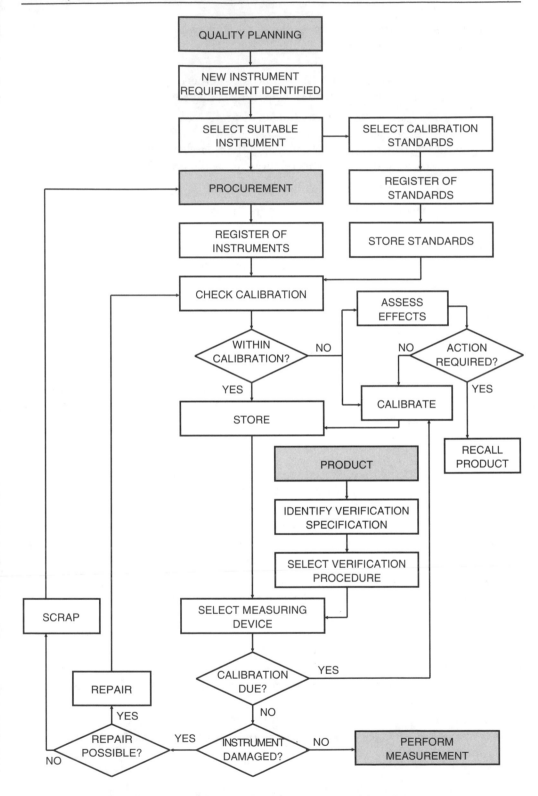

Figure 11.2 Inspection, measuring and test equipment control function

- Mechanical measuring devices

- Test software

- Forming tools and equipment

The procedures needed to specifically calibrate and maintain these devices will vary but the procedures you employ to control the use of these devices may be common.

Control of inspection, measuring, and test equipment

The standard requires the supplier to *control inspection, measuring, and test equipment used to demonstrate the conformance of product to the specified requirements.*

Control in this instance can mean several things:

- Knowing what devices are used for product verification purposes so that you can distinguish between controlled and uncontrolled devices. You will need to maintain a list of devices for this purpose.

- Knowing where the equipment is located so that you can recall it for calibration and maintenance. You will need a Recall Notice for this purpose.

- Knowing who the current custodian is so that you have a name to contact.

- Knowing what condition the equipment is in so that you can prohibit its use if the condition is unsatisfactory. You will need a Defect Report for this purpose.

- Knowing when the instrument's accuracy was last checked so that you can have confidence in its results. Calibration records and labels fulfill this need.

- Knowing what checks have been made using the instrument since it was last checked, so that you can repeat them should the instrument be subsequently found out of calibration. This is only necessary for instruments whose accuracy drifts over time, i.e. electronic equipment. It is not normally necessary for mechanical devices. You will need a traceability system for this purpose.

- Knowing that the measurements made using the instrument are accurate so that you can rely on the results. A valid calibration status label will fulfill this purpose.

- Knowing that the instrument is only being used for measuring the parameters for which it was designed, so that results are reliable and equipment is not abused. The abuse of measuring devices needs to be regulated primarily to protect the device but also, if high pressures and voltages are involved, to protect the person. Specifying the devices to be used for making measurements in your work instructions will serve this purpose.

You may not need to know all these things about every device used for product verification but you should know most of them. This knowledge can be gained by three means:

- By controlling the selection of measuring devices

- By controlling the use of measuring devices

- By controlling the calibration of measuring devices

You may know where each device is supposed to be, but what do you do if a device is not returned for calibration when due? Your procedures should track returns and make provision for tracking down any maverick devices, since they could be being used on product acceptance.

Calibration of inspection, measuring, and test equipment

The standard requires the supplier to *calibrate inspection, measuring, and test equipment used to demonstrate the conformance of product to the specified requirements*.

Calibration is concerned with determining the values of the errors of a measuring instrument and often involves its adjustment or scale graduation to the required accuracy. You should not assume that just because a device was once accurate it will remain so forever. Some devices, if well treated and retained in a controlled environment, will retain their accuracy for very long periods. Others, if poorly treated and subjected to environmental extremes, will lose their accuracy very quickly. Ideally you should calibrate measuring devices before use so as to prevent an inaccurate device being used in the first place and afterwards to confirm that no changes have occurred during use. However, this is often not practical and so intervals of calibration are established which are set at such periods as will detect any adverse deterioration. These intervals should be varied with the nature of the device, the conditions of use and the seriousness of the consequences should it produce incorrect results.

It is not necessary to calibrate all test and measuring equipment. Some equipment may be used solely as an indicator, such as a thermometer, a clock, or a tachometer. Other equipment may be used for diagnostic purposes, to indicate if a fault exists. If such devices are not used for determining the acceptability of products and services or process parameters then their calibration is not essential. However, you should identify such devices as for "Indication Purposes Only" if their use for measurement is possible. You don't need to identify all clocks and thermometers fixed to walls unless they are used for measurement. Having observed that you record the time when observations were made, a zealous assessor may suggest that the clock be calibrated. If the time is not critical to product or process acceptability, then calibration is unnecessary.

There are two systems used for maintaining the accuracy and integrity of measuring devices: a calibration system and a verification system. The calibration system determines the accuracy of measurement and the verification system determines the integrity of the device. If accuracy is important then the device should be included in the calibration system. If accuracy is not an issue but the device's form, properties or function is important then it should be included in the verification system. You need to decide the system in which your devices are to be placed under control and identify them accordingly.

There are two types of devices subject to calibration. There are those that are adjustable and those that are not. An adjustable device is one where the scale or the mechanism is capable of adjustment (e.g. micrometer, voltmeter, load cell). For non-adjustable devices a record of the errors observed against a known standard can be produced which can be taken into account when using the device (e.g. slip gage, plug gage, surface table, thermometer).

Comparative references are not subject to calibration. They are, however, subject to verification. Such devices are those which have form or function where the criteria is either pass or fail (i.e. there is no room for error) or where the magnitude of the errors does not need to be taken into account during usage. Such devices include software, steel rules/tapes, templates, forming, and molding tools. Devices in this category need carry no indication of calibration due date. The devices should carry a reference number and verification records should be maintained showing when the device was last checked. Verification of such devices include checks for damage, loss of components, function etc. (See later in this chapter.)

Some electronic equipment has self calibration routines built in to the start-up sequence. This should be taken as an indication of serviceability and not of absolute calibration. The device should still be subject to independent calibration at a defined frequency.

> ■ **Use not function determines need for calibration.**

Maintenance of inspection, measuring, and test equipment

The standard requires the supplier to *maintain inspection, measuring, and test equipment used to demonstrate the conformance of product to the specified requirements*.

In addition to calibrating the devices you will need to carry out preventive and corrective maintenance in order to keep them in good condition. Preventive maintenance is maintenance to reduce the probability of failure, such as cleaning, testing, inspecting, replenishment of consumables etc. Corrective maintenance is concerned with restoring a device after a failure has occurred to a condition in which it can perform its required function. These activities may cover a wide range of skills and disciplines depending on the nature of the measuring devices you use. The skills will include software development skills if you use test software, for instance, or electronic engineering if you use electronic equipment. You can of course subcontract the complete task to a specialist who will not only maintain the equipment but, on request, carry out calibration. Be careful to confirm that the subcontractor is qualified to perform the calibrations to national standards and provides a valid certificate of calibration.

Control, calibration, and maintenance of test software

The standard requires the supplier to *control, calibrate, and maintain test software used to demonstrate the conformance of product to the specified requirements*.

This requirement is similar to that stated in clause 4.11.2 of the standard and addressed later in this chapter. The checks and rechecks required to prove that the software is capable of verifying the acceptability of product are a means of calibrating test software. However, test software does not wear or drift with age or use and so cannot be calibrated against a standard traceable to national standards. To control test software you need to consider what it is that you need to control. As a minimum you should control its use, modification, location (in terms of where it is installed), replication, and disposal. Requirements for other controls are covered in clause 4.11.2 of the standard, where they can be applied to test software.

Use is controlled by specifying the software by type designation and version in the development and production test procedures or a register which relates products to the test software which has to be used to verify its acceptability. You should also provide procedures for running the software on the host computer or automatic test equipment. They may of course be menu driven from a display screen and keyboard rather than paper procedures.

Modifications should be controlled in a manner which complies with the requirements of clauses 4.4.9 and 4.5 of the standard (see Part 2 Chapter 4).

The location could be controlled by index, register, inventory, or other such means which enables you to identify on what machines particular versions of the software are installed, where copies and the master tapes or disks are stored.

Replication and disposal could be controlled by secure storage and prior authorization routines where replication and disposal is carried out only by authorized personnel or organizations.

Ensuring measurement uncertainty is known

The standard requires the supplier to *use equipment in a manner which ensures that measurement uncertainty is known and is consistent with the required measurement capability*.

There is uncertainty in all measurement processes. There are uncertainties attributable to the measuring device being used, the person carrying out the measurements and the environment in which the measurements are carried out. When repeated measurements are taken with the same device on the same dimension of the same product and the results vary, this is measurement uncertainty (see also under *Precision and accuracy*). When you make a measurement with a calibrated instrument you need to know the specified limits of permissible error (how close to the true value the measurement is). If you are operating under stable conditions, then you can assume that any calibrated device will not exceed the limit of permissible error. Stable conditions exist when all variation is under statistical control. This means that all variation is due to common causes only and none due to special causes. In other cases you will need to estimate the amount of error and take this into account when making your measurements. Test specifications and drawings etc. should specify characteristics in true values, i.e. values that do not take into account any inherent errors. Your test and inspection procedures, however, should specify the characteristics to be measured, taking into account all the errors and uncertainties that are attributable to the equipment, the personnel, and the environment when the measurement system is in statistical control (see later under *Measurement system analysis*). This can be achieved by tightening the tolerances in order to be confident that the actual dimensions are within the specified limits (see also under *Measurement system analysis*).

Proving test hardware, comparative references, and test software

Where test software or comparative references such as test hardware are used as suitable forms of inspection, the standard requires that *they be checked to prove that they are capable of verifying the acceptability of product prior to release for use during production, installation, and servicing and shall be rechecked at prescribed intervals*. The standard also requires the supplier to *establish the extent and frequency of such checks and to maintain records as evidence of control*.

Test hardware and software

The requirements for control of test software and hardware and other verification devices should apply not only to production, installation, and servicing but to design, development, and operations. The integrity of these devices is critical to the resultant product, whether it be a deliverable product to a customer or a product being developed or in use. The design of test software and test hardware should be governed by the requirements of clause 4.4 although this is not mandated by the standard; indeed, if these requirements are applied, the design verification requirements should adequately prove that the devices are capable of verifying the acceptability of product. However, the design control requirements may be impractical for many minor verification devices. The hardware which provides the environment for the test software should also be controlled, and while it may not measure any parameters its malfunction could result in nonconforming product being accepted. Complex hardware of this nature should be governed by the design controls of clause 4.4 if designed in-house as it ensures product quality. If bought out, you should obtain all the necessary manuals for its operation and maintenance and it should be periodically checked to verify it is fully operational.

Jigs, tools, and fixtures

Drawings should be provided for jigs, fixtures, templates, and other hardware devices and they should be verified as conforming with these drawings prior to use. They should also be proven to control the dimensions required by checking the first off to be produced from such devices. Once these devices have been proven they need checking periodically to detect signs of wear or deterioration. The frequency of such checks should be dependent on usage and the environment in which they are used. Tools that form characteristics, such as crimping tools, punches, press tools etc., should be checked prior to first use to confirm they produce the correct characteristics and then periodically to detect wear and deterioration. Tools that need to maintain certain temperatures, pressures, loads etc. in order to produce the correct characteristics in materials should be checked to verify that they will operate within the required limits.

Steel rules, tapes, and other indicators of length should be checked periodically for wear and damage and although accuracy of greater than 1mm is not normally expected, the loss of material from the end of a rule may result in inaccuracies that affect product quality.

While you may not rely entirely on these tools to accept product, the periodic calibration or verification of these tools may help prevent unnecessary costs and production delays. While usage and environment may assist in determining the frequency of verification hardware checks, these factors do not affect software. Any bugs in software have always been there or were introduced when it was last modified. Software therefore needs to be checked prior to use and after any modifications have been carried out, so you cannot predetermine the interval of such checks.

Reference materials

Comparative references are devices which are used to verify that an item has the same properties as the reference. They may take the form of materials such as chemicals which are used in spectrographic analyzers or those used in tests for the presence of certain compounds in a mixture or they could be materials with certain finishes, textures etc. Certificates should be produced and retained for such reference materials so that their validity is known to those who will use them. Materials which degrade over time should be dated and given a use by date. Care should be taken to avoid cross contamination and any degradation due to sunlight. A specification for each reference material should be prepared so that its properties can be verified.

Measurement design data

Where and to the extent that the availability of technical data pertaining to the measurement devices is a specified requirement, the standard requires *such data to be made available, when required by the customer or customer's representative, for verification that it is functionally adequate.*

Where you devise original solutions to the measurement of characteristics the theory and development of the method should be documented and retained as evidence of the validity of the measurement method. Any new measurement methods should be proven by rigorous experiment to detect the measurement uncertainty and cumulative effect of the errors in each measurement process. The samples used for proving the method should also be retained so as to provide a means of repeating the measurements should it prove necessary.

Identifying measurements to be made and accuracy required

The standard requires the supplier to *determine the measurements to be made and the accuracy required.*

These are the measurements required to carry out product verification rather than the measurements to calibrate a measuring device. The measurements to be made should be identified in test specifications, process specifications and drawings etc., but often these documents will not define how to take the measurements. The method of measurement should be defined in test and inspection procedures which, as stated previously, take into account the measurement uncertainty, the devices used to perform the measurements, and the environment. The reason for requiring measurements to be identified is so that you have a means of relating the parameter to be measured to the device employed to make the measurement and hence determine whether the device is capable of the required accuracy. There should be a tolerance on all dimensions so as to determine the accuracy required. You may use general tolerances to cover most dimensions and only apply specific tolerances where this is warranted by the application. Although this requirement appears in the standard under *Inspection, measuring, and test equipment*, it is a design process requirement or a quality planning requirement and should be addressed as part of product and process design and preparation for production.

■ Specifications define which characteristics to measure, procedures define how the characteristics should be measured.

Selecting appropriate inspection, measuring, and test equipment

The standard requires the supplier to *select the appropriate inspection, measuring, and test equipment that is capable of the accuracy and precision necessary.*

There are two categories of equipment which determine the selection of equipment. There are general-purpose and special-to-type equipment. It should not be necessary to specify all the general-purpose equipment needed to perform basic measurements, which would be expected to be known by appropriately trained personnel. You should not need to tell an inspector or tester which micrometer, vernier calliper, voltmeter or oscilloscope to use. These are the tools of the trade and they should select the tool which is capable of measuring the particular parameters with the accuracy and precision required. However, you will need to tell them which device to use if the measurement requires unusual equipment or the environmental conditions prevailing require that only equipment be selected that will operate in such an environment. In such cases the particular devices to be used should be specified in the test or inspection procedures. In order to demonstrate that you selected the appropriate device at some later date, you should consider recording the actual device used in the record of results. With mechanical devices this is not normally necessary since wear should be detected well in advance of there being a problem by periodic calibration.

With electronic devices subject to drift with time or handling, a record of the device used will enable you to identify suspect results in the event of the device being found to be outside the limits at the next calibration. A way of reducing the effect is to select devices that are several orders of magnitude more accurate than needed. (See later under *Action on equipment found out of calibration.*)

Accuracy and precision

Turning now to the requirement for accuracy and precision. Accuracy and precision are often perceived as synonyms but they are quite different concepts. *Accuracy* is the difference between the average of a series of measurements and the true value. *Precision* is the amount of variation around the average. So you can have a measuring device which gives a large variation around the true value with repeated measure-

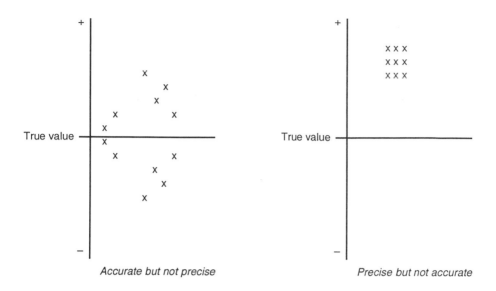

Figure 11.3 Dispersion of measurements relative to the true value

ments but whose average is the true value (see Figure 11.3). Alternatively you could have a device which gives small variation with repeated measurements around a value which is wide of the true value. The aim is to obtain both accuracy and precision. The difference in accuracy and precision can cause expensive errors. You should not assume that the result you have obtained is both accurate and precise unless the device has been calibrated immediately prior to use and the results of its accuracy and precision provided. In many cases you can rely on the calibration certificate informing you that the device has been calibrated but sometimes you will need the results of the calibration in order to compensate for the inherent errors. (See also under *Measurement system analysis* later in this chapter.)

On occasions you may require a measurement capability that exceeds the known state of the art, such accuracy and precision that no available device can achieve. If under contract to a customer you should inform your customer of this situation so that you can negotiate the measures needed to develop the technology required. (See Part 2 Chapter 2 on *Identifying new measurement capabilities*.)

Identifying devices that can affect product quality

The standard requires the supplier to *identify all inspection, measuring, and test equipment including measurement devices that can affect product quality*.

Devices that can affect product quality are those which are used:

- To measure product characteristics, such as devices which measure mass, length of time or derivatives of these parameters

- To form product characteristics, such as jigs, tools, and fixtures

- To control processes that create product characteristics, such as sensors which indicate temperature, pressure, volume etc.

In order to meet this requirement you will either need a register or listing of all devices that can effect product quality or label each device so that those that affect product quality are distinguishable from those that do not. This is not the same as a calibration label, as some devices that affect quality may not require calibration. It should be possible for anyone to determine whether or not the characteristics of the device should be controlled.

The register or listing should include the following details as appropriate:

- Name of device, type designation, and serial number in order to distinguish it from others

- Specification or drawing defining the device together with its date and issue status as a record of the acceptance criteria

- Date of manufacture or purchase to determine its age and origin

- Name of custodian and the location of the device in order to trace and resolve problems

- Date when proven against specification and first off in order to determine when it was first deemed serviceable

- Date when re-verification is required

- Details of any modifications and repairs

- Details of any limitations of use

- Details of application if restricted to particular processes, products, ranges etc.

Calibration operations

Calibrating and adjusting devices against certified equipment

The standard requires the supplier to *calibrate and adjust all inspection, measuring, and test equipment including measurement devices at prescribed intervals, or prior to use, against certified equipment having a known valid relationship to nationally recognized standards.*

Calibration against certified equipment

Calibration has been addressed previously; however, all calibrations should be traceable through an unbroken chain to a national or international measurement standard. If you calibrate your own devices you will need in addition to the "working standards" that you use for measurement, calibration standards for checking the calibration of the working standards. The calibration standards should also be calibrated periodically against national standards held by your national measurement laboratory. This unbroken chain ensures that there is compatibility between measurements made in different locations using different measuring devices. By maintaining traceability you can rely on obtaining the same result (within the stated limits of accuracy) wherever and whenever you perform the measurement, providing the product you are measuring remains stable. If you calibrate your own standards you should comply with ISO 10012.

The relationship between the various standards is illustrated in Figure 11.4.

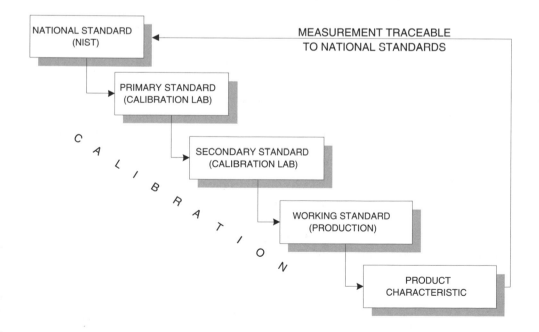

Figure 11.4 Traceability of standards

Adjustment of devices

Regarding the adjustment of measuring devices, adjustment is only possible with devices that have been designed to be adjustable. Mechanical devices are normally adjusted to the null position on calibration. Electronic devices should only be adjusted if found to be outside the limits. If you adjust the device at each calibration you are not able to observe drift. Adjustments may also degrade the instrument if made very frequently. It is best to observe the adage:

> ■ **If it is well within specification leave well alone.**

If the observed drift is such that the device may well be outside the specified limits by the next calibration then adjustment will be necessary.

Documenting the basis for calibration

The standard requires the supplier to *document the basis used for calibration where no nationally recognized standards exist*.

In some situations there may be no national standard against which to calibrate your devices. Colors and textures are two examples. If you face this situation, then you should gather together a group of experts within your company or trade association and establish by investigation, experimentation, and debate what constitutes the standard. Having done this you should document the basis of your decisions and produce a device or number of devices which can be used to compare the product with the standard using visual, quantitative, or other means.

Defining the calibration process

The standard requires the supplier to *define the process employed for the calibration of inspection, measuring, and test equipment, including details of equipment type, unique identification, location, frequency of checks, check method, acceptance criteria, and the action to be taken when results are unsatisfactory*.

The standard requires you to define the calibration process rather than the calibration procedures. Calibration procedures will define how you control all calibration activities. The calibration process required only applies to the process of calibrating a particular device. This does not mean that you have to define the process of calibrating every device. The process of calibration may be:

- Detailed in the device manufacturer's manuals and handbooks

- Detailed in published standards or reference books

- So simple that one would expect it to be known by calibration personnel

Whichever method applies you should define it within your quality system. You should maintain lists of all the devices which require calibration and indicate in these lists:

- The device type, identification number, and serial number

- The calibration method to be used, cross referring to the manuals or individual procedures as appropriate

- The frequency of calibration

- The location of the device

A calibration process may consist of no more than a single data sheet but may also consist of several pages for very complex equipment. Even if you possess all the manufacturer's manuals and these cover calibration, it is still good practice to generate your own data sheet as a means of tailoring the method to your own needs. You may wish to limit adjustments, add checks, provide clearer instructions, or generate your own records and as part of the process the proforma should be included.

The documents that define the calibration process themselves are "derived" documents and therefore will be governed by your control procedure. They do not need to be listed along with all your other control and operating procedures in the index of quality system documents. A separate index of calibration methods should be maintained. Calibration methods are like test and inspection procedures, they are product specific.

Indicating calibration status

The standard requires the supplier to *identify inspection, measuring, and test equipment with a suitable indicator or approved identification record to show the calibration status.*

All devices subject to calibration should display an identification label which, either directly or through traceable records, indicates the authority responsible for calibrating the device and the date when the calibration is due. Don't state the actual calibration date since this relies on users having knowledge of the calibration frequency. The standard requires that measuring equipment show its calibration status to any potential user. Measuring instruments too small for calibration status labels showing the due date may be given other types of approved identification. It is not mandatory that users identify the due date solely from the instrument itself but they must be able to determine that the instrument has been calibrated. Serial numbers alone do not do this unless placed within a specially designed label that indicates that the item has been calibrated or you can fix special labels that show a circular calendar marked to show the due date. If you do use serial numbers on special labels then they need to be traceable to calibration records that indicate the calibration due date.

Devices used for indication purposes only or for diagnostic purposes should also display an identity which clearly distinguishes them as not being subject to calibration. If devices are taken out of use for prolonged periods, it may be more practical to cease calibration and provide a means of preventing inadvertent use with labels indicating that the calibration is not being maintained. You may wish to use devices that do not fulfill their specification either because part of the device is unserviceable or because you were unable to perform a full calibration. In such cases, you should provide clear indication to the user of the limitation of such devices.

Maintaining calibration records

The standard requires the supplier to *maintain calibration records for inspection, measuring, and test equipment*.

Calibration records are records of the calibration activities that have taken place. These records should include where appropriate:

- The precise identity of the device being calibrated (type, name, serial number, configuration if it provides for various optional features)

- The name and location of the owner or custodian

- The date calibration was performed

- Reference to the calibration procedure, its number, and issue status

- The condition of the device on receipt

- The results of the calibration in terms of readings before adjustment and readings after adjustment for each designated parameter

- The date fixed for the next calibration

- The permissible limits of error

- The serial numbers of the standards used to calibrate the device

- The environmental conditions prevailing at the time of calibration

- A statement of measurement uncertainty (accuracy and precision)

- Details of any adjustments, servicing, repairs, and modifications carried out

- The name of the person performing the calibration

- Details of any limitation on its use

It is important to record the as received condition in order to determine whether the device was outside the prescribed limits when last used. It also permits trends to be monitored and the degree of drift to be predicted.

QS-9000 imposes additional requirements for calibration records which require *calibration and verification records for all gages, measuring and test equipment, including employee-owned gages to include certain specified data*.

The records required are only for formal calibrations and verification and not for instances of self calibration or zeroing using null adjustment mechanisms. Reference to employee owned gages should not be taken as being limited to gages. It applies to any employee owned devices used for measurement. The clause also makes reference to the terms calibration/verification. Whilst calibration usually involves some adjustment to the device, non-adjustable devices are often verified rather than calibrated. However, as was discussed previously, it is not strictly correct to regard all calibration as involving some adjustment. Slip gages and surface tables are calibrated but not adjusted. An error record is produced to enable users to determine the uncertainty of measurement in a particular range or location and compensate for the inaccuracies when recording the results.

Action on equipment found out of calibration

The standard requires the supplier to *assess and document the validity of previous inspection and test results when inspection, measuring, and test equipment is found to be out of calibration*.

This is perhaps the most difficult of requirements to meet for some organizations. The standard does not allow any relaxations but clearly it is not always possible or practical to be able to trace product to the particular devices used to determine its acceptability. The requirements apply not only to your working standards but also to your calibration standards. When you send these away for calibration, you will need a method of tracing the devices they were used to calibrate if they are found to be out of calibration themselves. If you have a small number of measuring devices and only one or two of each type, then it may not be too difficult to determine which products were accepted using a particular device. In large organizations that own many pieces of equipment that are constantly being used in a variety of situations, meeting the requirements can be very difficult. One way is to record the type and serial number of the devices used to conduct a series of inspections and tests but you will also have to record the actual measurement made. Some results may be made in the form of ticks or pass/fail and not by recording actual readings. In these cases you have a problem in determining whether the amount out of calibration would be sufficient to reject the product. If the product is no longer in the factory then in extreme circumstances this situation could result in you having to recall the product from your customer or distributor.

The additional requirement on calibration records covers this aspect and requires a record of notification to the customer if suspect product has been shipped.

In order to reduce the effect, you can select measuring devices that are several orders of magnitude more accurate than your needs so that when the devices drift outside the tolerances, they are still well within the accuracy you require. There still remains a risk that the device is wildly inaccurate due to being damaged or a malfunction. In such cases you need to adopt the discipline of re-calibrating devices that have been dropped or are otherwise suspect before further use.

You need to determine your policy in this area and be very careful as to what you claim to achieve. You will need a procedure for informing the custodians of unserviceable measuring devices and one for enabling the custodians to track down the products verified using the unserviceable device and assess the magnitude of the problem. You will need a means of ranking problems in order of severity so that you can resolve the minor problems at the working level and ensure that significant problems are brought to the attention of the management for resolution. It would be irresponsible for a junior technician to recall six months' production from customers and distributors based on a report from the calibration laboratory. You need to assess what would have happened if you had used serviceable equipment to carry out the measurements. Would the product have been reworked, repaired, scrapped or the requirement relaxed. Remember the product specification is but an interpretation of what constitutes fitness for use. Out of "spec" doesn't mean unsafe, unusable, unsalable etc.

Protection of measuring equipment

Ensuring that environmental conditions are suitable

The standard requires the supplier to *ensure that the environmental conditions are suitable for the calibration, inspections, measurements, and tests being carried out.*

This requirement hides an important provision. It not only applies to inspection, measuring, and test equipment but to the measurements that are performed with that equipment. Anywhere you intend performing product verification or monitoring processes you need to ensure that the environmental conditions are suitable. By *environmental conditions* is meant the temperature, pressure, humidity, vibration, lighting, cleanliness, dust, acoustic noise etc. of the area in which such measurements are carried out. To avoid having to specify the conditions each time, you need to establish the ambient conditions and write this into your procedures. If anything other than ambient conditions prevail, you may need to assess whether the measuring devices will perform adequately in these conditions. If you need to discriminate between types of equipment then the ones most suitable should be specified in the verification procedures.

If you cannot select suitable equipment for your current environment, you may then have to control the environment in order to carry out the measurements. In such areas the environmental factors important to maintaining stable measurement should be monitored and the monitoring equipment calibrated. Chart recorders enable you to monitor conditions without having to be in constant attendance. The environment should be controlled in areas where calibration is carried out in order to provide stable conditions in which accurate and precise measurement can be taken. However, some modern equipment is so stable that environmental controls are unnecessary except in special circumstances.

Ensuring that accuracy and fitness for use is maintained

The standard requires the supplier to *ensure that the handling, preservation, and storage of inspection, measuring, and test equipment is such that the accuracy and fitness for use is maintained*.

When not in use, measuring devices should always be stored in the special containers provided by the manufacturer. Handling instructions should be provided with the storage case where instruments may be fragile or prone to inadvertent damage by careless handling. Instruments prone to surface deterioration during use and exposure to the atmosphere should be protected and moisture absorbent or resistant materials used. When transporting measuring equipment you should provide adequate protection. Should you employ itinerant service engineers, ensure that the instruments that they carry with them are adequately protected as well as being calibrated (see Part 2 Chapter 15 for further details on handling, storage, and preservation).

Safeguarding inspection, measuring, and test equipment

The standard requires the supplier to *safeguard inspection, measuring, and test facilities including both test hardware and test software from adjustments which would invalidate the calibration setting*.

The purpose of this requirement is to ensure that the integrity of the measurements is maintained by precluding errors that can occur if measuring equipment is tampered with.

Unlike the other requirements, which only referred to inspection, test, and measuring equipment, this clause adds test facilities. Facilities include the equipment and the area or room in which it is kept or used. Test facilities are any room, area or complex in which tests are carried out. Inspection, measuring and test facilities include functional and environmental test laboratories, test and inspection chambers, calibration rooms, clean rooms, computer rooms, and any area where tests are being conducted either with staff in attendance, remotely or with staff paying monitoring visits. To safeguard against deliberate or inadvertent adjustments, these areas should be restricted to authorized personnel. They should be locked when no one is in attendance and the key in the custody of an authorized person or in a secure safe. You will also need some form of security to prevent calibration standards being inadvertently used as working standards.

To safeguard against any deliberate or inadvertent adjustment to measuring devices, seals should be applied to the adjustable parts or to the fixings securing the container if appropriate. The seals should be designed so that tampering will destroy them. Such safeguards may not be necessary for all devices. Certain devices are designed to be adjusted by the user without needing external reference standards, for example zero adjustments on micrometers. If the container can be sealed then you don't need to protect all the adjustable parts inside.

Your procedures need to specify:

- Which verification areas have restricted access and how you control access

- The methods used for applying integrity seals to equipment

- Who is authorized to apply and break the seals

- The action to be taken if the seals are found to be broken either during use or when being calibrated

Measurement systems analysis

The standard requires *evidence that appropriate statistical studies have been conducted to analyze the variation present in the results of each type of measuring and test equipment system.*

In ISO 9001 the terms accuracy and precision are used and these were explained previously. QS-9000 takes the study of measurement further and divides variation into five classes. Although QS-9000 has not deleted the requirement on measurement uncertainty, compliance with the measurement system analysis requirement achieves the same purpose.

A measurement system consists of the operations (the measurement tasks and the environment in which they are carried out), procedures (how the tasks are performed), devices (gages, instruments, software etc. used to make the measurements), and the personnel used to assign a quantity to the characteristics being measured.

Measurement systems must be in statistical control so that all variation is due to common cause and not special cause. QS-9000 therefore requires that you devise a measurement system for all measurements specified in the Control Plan in which all variation is in statistical control.

It is often assumed that the measurements taken with a calibrated device are accurate and indeed they are if we take account of the variation which is present in every measuring system and bring the system under statistical control. Variation in measurement systems arise due to bias, repeatability, reproducibility, stability, and linearity.

Bias is the difference between the observed average of the measurements and the reference value.

Repeatability is the variation in measurements obtained by one appraiser using one measuring device to measure an identical characteristic on the same part.

Reproducibility is the variation in the average of the measurements made by different appraisers using the same measuring instrument when measuring an identical characteristic on the same part.

Stability is the total variation in the measurements obtained with a measurement system on the same part when measuring a single characteristic over a period of time.

Linearity is the difference in the bias values through the expected operating range of the measuring device.

It is only possible to supply parts with identical characteristics if the measurement system as well as the production processes are under statistical control. In an environment in which daily production quantities are in the range of 1000 to 10 000 units, inaccuracies in the measurement system that go undetected can have a disastrous impact upon customer satisfaction and hence profits.

Gage and test equipment requirements are required to be formulated during product design and development (see APQP manual section 2) and this forms the input data to the process design and development phase. During this phase a measurement system analysis plan is required to accomplish the required analysis. During the product and process validation phase, measurement system evaluation is required to be carried out during or prior to the production trial run and then during full production continuous improvement is required to reduce measurement system variation.

The *Measurement Systems Analysis Manual* provides excellent guidelines for selecting procedures to assess the quality of a measurement system. It includes an introduction to measurement systems, explains the factors that cause variation in a measurement system, has guidance for preparing for a measurement system study, and includes step by step procedures for determining the degree of each type of variation present in a measurement system.

Task list

1 Produce and maintain a list of the devices that will be used for measuring product and process characteristics.

2 Produce and maintain a list of all tools, jigs, fixtures etc. that will be used as a means of inspection.

3 Produce a list of the software that will be used to verify product or process characteristics and to control equipment that is used to verify product and process characteristics.

4 Provide recall notices to recall devices requiring calibration.

5 Provide defect reports for reporting details of unserviceable equipment.

6 Provide labels for fixing to devices in order to denote their calibration status.

7 Provide facilities for the storage of calibration records.

8 Prepare procedures for controlling the use of measuring devices.

9 Prepare procedures for controlling the calibration of measuring devices.

10 Prepare procedures controlling the development and maintenance of software used in measurement systems.

11 Provide a calibration laboratory or select an approved laboratory to calibrate your measurement devices.

12 Arrange for the calibration of your calibration standards.

13 Prepare calibration procedures or data sheets for each measuring device.

14 Process all measuring devices through your established calibration system.

15 Ensure your test and inspection procedures identify the measurements to be made and the accuracies required.

16 Provide containers for transportation of measuring devices.

17 Provide procedures for tracing product verified with equipment and standards found out of calibration.

18 Validate software used for measurement purposes or which drives measuring equipment.

19 Make provision for recording the identity of devices used in product/process verification.

20 Provide specification and drawings for all jigs, tools, gages etc. used for measurement purposes.

21 Establish a register of all reference materials used to judge characteristics of samples.

22 Provide specifications and validation certificates for reference materials.

23 Provide secure storage for reference materials and avoid cross contamination and degradation.

24 Perform measurement system studies on each measurement system and bring the system under statistical control.

Inspection, measuring, and test equipment questionnaire

1   How do you control devices used to demonstrate conformance of product with specified requirements?

2   How do you calibrate devices used to demonstrate conformance of product with specified requirements?

3   How do you maintain devices used to demonstrate conformance of product with specified requirements?

4   What documented procedures have you established to control, calibrate, and maintain inspection, measuring, and test equipment?

5   What documented procedures have you established to control and maintain comparative references?

6   What documented procedures have you established to control, validate, and maintain test software?

7   How do you ensure that measurement uncertainty is known and consistent with the required measurement capability?

8   How do you ensure that devices used as suitable forms of inspection are proven capable of verifying the acceptability of product prior to their use for production, installation, or servicing?

9   How do you ensure that such devices remain capable of verifying the acceptability of product?

10   What records are kept to demonstrate you have control over test software?

11   What records are kept to demonstrate you have control over comparative references?

12   In which documents do you define your measurement design data?

13   How do you determine the measurements to be made and the accuracy required to demonstrate conformance of product to specified requirements?

14   How do you ensure that appropriate inspection, measuring, and test equipment is selected?

15   How do you ensure that inspection, measuring, and test equipment is capable of the accuracy and precision necessary?

16 How do you ensure all calibrated inspection, measuring, and test equipment has a known valid relationship to nationally recognized standards?

17 How do you identify whether an item of inspection, measuring, and test equipment can affect product quality?

18 How do you ensure that all inspection, measuring, and test equipment that can affect product quality is calibrated at prescribed intervals or prior to use?

19 How do you ensure that devices are adjusted when they have drifted outside the specified limits?

20 In what documents is the process employed for the calibration of inspection, measuring, and test equipment defined?

21 In what documents do you record the basis used for calibration where no nationally recognized standards exist?

22 What action is taken with previous verification results when devices are found to be out of calibration?

23 What means do you use to identify the calibration status of inspection, measuring, and test equipment?

24 What documents record the calibration of inspection, measuring, and test equipment?

25 How do you ensure that environmental conditions are suitable for the calibrations being carried out?

26 How do you ensure that environmental conditions are suitable for the inspections, measurements, and tests being carried out?

27 How do you maintain the accuracy and fitness for use of inspection, measuring, and test equipment during handling and storage?

28 How do you safeguard inspection, measuring, and test equipment from adjustments that would invalidate the calibration setting?

29 How do you safeguard test facilities from adjustments that would invalidate the calibration setting?

30 How do you safeguard test software from adjustments that would invalidate the calibration setting?

Do's and don'ts

* Don't bring devices under control of the measurement system if they are not used in performing measurements.

* Do fix labels to all devices that have been designed for inspection purposes and indicate their calibration status.

* Do calibrate personal tools if they are to be used for making acceptance decisions.

* Do take account of measurement uncertainty in determining the acceptability of product.

* Do vary the intervals of calibration with the proven stability of the device.

* Do require external calibration laboratories to provide calibration certificates and results.

* Don't use calibration labels that will not retain their markings in the equipment's operating environment.

* Do provide set-up instructions and diagrams for making special measurements.

* Do calibrate working standards against calibration standards having at least an order of accuracy greater than the working standards.

* Don't continue using measuring equipment that has sustained damage even if it appears to have had no effect.

* Do verify that your subcontractors have an adequate calibration system.

* Don't calibrate test devices in the same environment as they will be used unless you compensate for the environmental effects on measurement accuracy.

* Do retain calibration records for periods that match the period from manufacture to end of warranty or longer.

* Do keep calibration records in secure areas.

* Do display notices in calibration rooms and test laboratories etc. to warn of prohibited access to unauthorized persons.

* Don't leave the doors of calibration and test rooms open when vacated.

* Don't purchase any second-hand measuring equipment without the original manual.

* Don't permit measuring equipment to collect on the floor while waiting calibration.

Chapter 12

Inspection and test status

Scope of requirements

The requirements for inspection and test status are identification requirements that enable conforming product to be distinguishable from nonconforming product. Another term would be Verification Status since means other than inspection and test may be used to determine whether an item conforms with a requirement. The requirements mainly apply to manufactured product but can equally apply to software and to deliverable documentation. They also apply to services which involve a product such as maintenance, transport, computing etc., but it is difficult to apply the requirements to services such as teaching, consultancy, accounting etc. Conforming services can only be mixed with nonconforming services if they remain accessible to the user. If services are found nonconforming they are usually stopped and measures put in place to prevent their use until corrected.

The requirements in element 4.12 are linked with other elements of the standard even when there is no cross reference. This relationship is illustrated in Figure 12.1.

Identifying inspection and test status

The standard requires the supplier to *identify the inspection and test status of product by suitable means, which indicate the conformance or nonconformance of product with regard to inspection and tests performed.*

Inspection and test status is either reject or accept. There are no gray areas. If not fully conforming the product should be rejected and identified as such. If conforming the product should be accepted and identified as such. If a nonconforming product is later deemed acceptable, the identification should be changed but this leads to problems. If the rejection was for cosmetic reasons, providing it is not an "appearance item", then

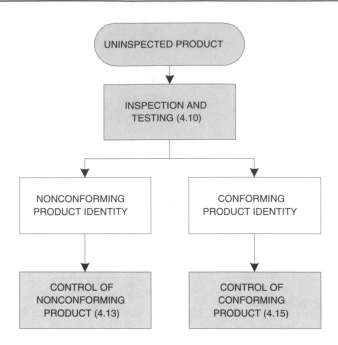

Figure 12-1 Element relationships with the inspection and test status element

there is no problem but if the rejection was an out of tolerance condition the product should either be reworked, repaired or regraded since the original decision may not be acceptable to all customers. If you do not do these things then the internal concessions should be carried through to the final inspection label, so that if a customer requires products to a particular specification you can check whether the out of tolerance condition will be acceptable.

You are only required to indicate whether product conformed to the inspections and tests performed. This is not the same as indicating whether the product conformed to the customer requirements. It may well have passed the prescribed inspections and tests but these inspections and tests may not have been sufficiently comprehensive to verify conformance to all the customer's requirements. However, the only indication you can give is the product's conformance or nonconformance with some verification requirement. It follows therefore that you should not go around putting reject labels on products, or acceptance labels for that matter, if you have not performed a specific inspection to determine conformance. There are only three conditions: "uninspected", "inspected and found conforming", and "inspected and found nonconforming". If you have a policy of applying labels only after inspection then anything without a label is therefore deemed uninspected, unless it has been installed and the label removed.

Identifying inspection and test status is not just a matter of tying a label on a product. The status should be denoted by an authorized signature, stamp, mark, or other identity which is applied by the person making the accept/reject decision and which is secure from misuse. Signatures are acceptable means of denoting verification status on paper records but are not suitable for computerized records. Secure passwords and write-only protection has to be provided to specific individuals. Signatures in a workshop environment are susceptible to deterioration and illegibility, which is why numbered inspection stamps with unique markings have evolved. The ink used has to survive the environment and if the labels are attached to the product for life, it is more usual to apply an imprint stamp on soft metal or a bar code.

Customers sometimes stipulate additional identification requirements and QS-9000 requires that these requirements be met. The method of identification depends upon the type, size, quantity, or fragility of the product. You can mark the product directly, or tie a label to it or the container in which it is placed. You can also use records remote from the product providing they bear a unique identity which is traceable to the product.

Marking products has its limitations as it may damage the product, be removed, or deteriorate during subsequent processing. If applied to the product directly, the location and nature of identification should be specified in the product drawings or referenced process specifications. If applied to labels which themselves are permanently secured to the product, the identification has to be visible when the product is installed so as to facilitate checks without its removal.

Small and fragile products should be held in containers and the container sealed and marked with the inspection status. Large products should either carry a label or have a related inspection record.

In some situations the location of a product can constitute adequate identification of inspection status. However these locations need to be designated as "Awaiting Inspection", "Accepted Product", or "Reject Product" or other such labels as appropriate to avoid the inadvertent placement of items in the wrong location. The location of product in the normal production flow is not a suitable designation unless an automated transfer route is provided.

When a service is out of service then tell your customers. Services which rely on products should carry a label or a notice when accessed. A bank cash machine is one example where a notice is displayed when the machine is out of service. In some cases customers may have to be informed by letter or telephone.

With software the verification status can be denoted in the software as a comment or on records testifying its conformance with requirements.

With documentation you can either denote verification status by an approval signature on the document or by a reference number, date, and issue status which is traceable to records containing the approval signatures.

Maintaining inspection and test status

The standard requires the supplier to *maintain the identification of inspection and test status of the product, as defined in the quality plan and/or documented procedures throughout production, installation, and servicing to ensure that only product that has passed the required inspections and tests (or released under an authorized concession) is dispatched, used or installed.*

Maintaining inspection and test status means retaining the status markings once they have been affixed or recorded until your responsibility for the product ceases. Labels should be attached in a way that prevent their detachment during handling. If labels have to be removed during further processing, then the details should be transferred to inspection records so that at a later date the status of the components in an assembly can be checked through the records. At dispatch, the inspection status of product should be visible. Any product without inspection status identification should be quarantined until reinspected and found conforming.

It should be possible when walking through a machine shop, for example, to identify which products are awaiting inspection, which have been inspected and found conforming and which have been rejected. If, by chance, some product were to become separated from their parent batch, it should still be possible to return the product to the location from whence it came. A machine shop is where this type of identification is essential, it is where mix-ups can occur. In other places, there may not be the same possibility of a mix-up and if it is simply not possible then inspection and test identification does not need to be so explicit.

Not all product intended for delivery may in fact have passed the required inspections and tests as the customer may have waived some of the requirements for that particular delivery. Hence the reference to release under an authorized concession. Identifying product correctly will help preclude any unidentified or nonconforming product from being delivered, used, or installed. However, the only way to make certain is to remove them from areas where they may be dispatched, used, or installed.

Inspection and test status procedures

The standard doesn't require a procedure covering inspection and test status; however, as clause 4.2 requires a documented quality system, you will need to document the methods employed to denote inspection and test status. If you use stamps then you will need a register to allocate stamps to particular individuals and to indicate which stamps have been withdrawn. When a person hands in a stamp it is good practice to avoid using the same number for 12 months or so to prevent mistaken identity in any subsequent investigations.

Task list

1 Document the methods you employ to denote inspection and test status for hardware, software, documents, and services.

2 Specify the status identification methods to be used in product drawings and specifications.

3 Provide separate designated areas for holding product awaiting inspection, passed inspection, and failed inspection.

4 Label these areas to prevent inadvertent misplacement of product.

5 Maintain registers of inspection stamp holders.

Inspection and test status questionnaire

1 How do you identify product in a way that indicates its conformance or nonconformance with regard to inspections and tests performed?

2 How do you ensure the identification of inspection and test status is maintained throughout production and installation?

Do's and don'ts

* Don't re-assign inspection stamps to another individual until a reasonable period of time has elapsed.

* Do secure stamps from unauthorized use.

* Don't leave stamps unattended.

* Don't lend your stamp to another person.

* Don't stamp anything unless you have personally inspected the item.

* Don't stamp any document unless there is a proper location to place the stamp because it could mean anything – a stamp has to indicate that the specified requirements have been met.

Chapter 13

Control of nonconforming product

Scope of requirements

The definition of nonconformity in ISO 8402 states that it is the nonfulfillment of specified requirements; therefore a nonconforming product is one that does not conform to the specified requirements. Why it has to be "specified requirements" and not plain requirements is unclear. Specified requirements are either requirements prescribed by the customer and agreed by the supplier in a contract for products or services, or are requirements prescribed by the supplier which are perceived as satisfying a market need. This limits the term *nonconformance* to situations where you have failed to meet customer requirements; however, ISO 8402 1987 suggests that nonconformity also applies to the absence of one or more quality system elements, but clearly the requirements of clause 4.13 cannot be applied to nonconformance with quality system requirements. It would be unusual to segregate a nonconforming person (although the prisons are full of them) or a nonconforming activity, or scrap, rework, or return to a supplier a nonconforming policy, procedure, or activity (although these are more likely, except we don't usually use this terminology in such cases). Both QS-9000 and ISO 9004 only address nonconformity in the context of products, processes, and services and when addressing quality system elements use the term *deficiencies*. Some assessors use the term *nonconformance* to describe a departure from the requirements of the standard but it would be preferable if they chose the term noncompliance to avoid any confusion. The requirements of clause 4.13 therefore only apply to products, processes, and services and not to activities, quality system elements, or procedures.

The standard does not make it clear whether these requirements apply to nonconformities detected while the supplier is responsible for the product or after the supplier's responsibility ceases, as is the case with nonconformity reports received from customers. Reports of nonconformities are also addressed under Corrective

Action in clause 4.14 but it is assumed that in this case the standard is concerned with extrernal reports of nonconformities.

The limitation of the term to specified requirements causes problems when you have failed to meet your own requirements but still meet the specified requirements. What does one call such an error? There will be cases also where you fully satisfy the specified requirements but the product is unfit for use because of omissions in the specified requirements. ISO 8402 states that the nonfulfillment of intended usage requirement is a defect. QS-9000 does not address the subject of defects since it assumes that a product which meets the specified requirements must meet intended usage requirements. However, a product may fail to meet the specified requirements and still be fit for use. The definition of quality complicates the issue even more. ISO 9000 requires that you meet specified requirements, it does not require that you produce products which satisfy stated or implied needs, or satisfy intended usage requirements. In practice, however, you should produce products and services which:

- Satisfy the specified requirements

- Satisfy intended usage requirements

- Satisfy stated or implied needs

- Satisfy your own requirements

All these may be in harmony but there may be occasions when there is conflict. To avoid any confusion you should classify all failures to meet these four requirements as nonconformances and then assign classification so as to treat each according to its merits.

The requirements in element 4.13 are linked with other elements of the standard even when there is no cross reference. This relationship is illustrated in Figure 13.1.

Suspect nonconforming product controls

The standard requires *the requirements of element 4.13 to be applied to product suspected of being nonconforming* as well as product that is known to be nonconforming.

This addition in QS-9000 is intended to cause you to look further than the product that has been found to be nonconforming and to seek out other products which may possess the same characteristics as those found to be nonconforming. These other products may be in the same batch awaiting release or have already been released to customers. This later situation can arise if you discover the measuring or processing equipment to be inaccurate or malfunctioning. Any product that has passed through that process since it was last confirmed serviceable is now suspect. This aspect is also covered in clause 4.11.2f. Seeking suspect product should also be a factor to be considered when determining corrective action (see Part 2 Chapter 14).

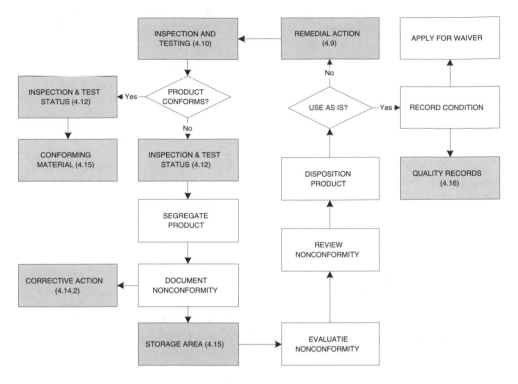

Figure 13.1 Element relationships with the control of nonconforming product element

Another example of suspect product is when product is mishandled but shows no obvious signs of damage. This may arise when product is dropped or not handled in the stipulated clean conditions or in accordance with electrostatic safe handling procedures.

Suspect product should be treated in the same manner as nonconforming product and quarantined until dispositioned. However, until a nonconformity can be proven, the documentation of the nonconformity merely reveals the reason for the product being suspect.

Classifying nonconformances

Although the standard does not recognize any classification of nonconformances the practical application of nonconformance controls require controls to be balanced with the severity of the nonconformance. It is not necessary to seek concessions from a customer against requirements that have not been specified, or seek design authority approval for workmanship imperfections. The definition of the term *defect* in ISO 8402, and the fact that there are many requirements other than those specified in a contract or needed to satisfy market needs, demands that it is sensible to classify noncon-formances into three categories:

- Critical Nonconformance: a departure from the specified requirements which renders the product or service unfit for use

- Major Nonconformance: a departure from the specified requirements in-cluded in the contract or market specification

- Minor Nonconformance: a departure from the supplier's requirements not included in the contract or market specification

Note that these are not the same as the nonconformity classifications used in assessing quality systems; see Part 1 Chapter 5.

Ensuring that nonconforming product is not used

The standard requires the supplier to *establish and maintain documented procedures to ensure that product that does not conform to specified requirements is prevented from inadver-tent use or installation.*

A nonconformance exists only when product has been inspected against an acceptance standard and found not to comply. Prior to this the product is either serviceable or unserviceable. Unserviceable products are not necessarily nonconforming, they may simply lack lubrication or calibration. A piece of test equipment, the calibration date of which has expired, is not nonconforming, it is merely unserviceable. When checked against a standard it may be found to be out of calibration and then it is noncon-forming, but it could be found to be within the specified calibration limits.

The only sure way of preventing inadvertent use of nonconforming product is to destroy it, but that may be a little drastic in some cases. It may be possible to eliminate the nonconformance by repair, completion of processing, or rework. A more practical way of preventing the inadvertent use or installation of nonconforming or unservice-able products is to identify the product as nonconforming or unserviceable and then place it in an area where access to it is controlled. These two aspects are covered further below.

Identifying nonconforming product

The standard requires the supplier to *provide for the identification of nonconforming product.*

The most common method is to apply labels to the product that are distinguishable from other labels. It is preferable to use red labels for nonconforming and unserviceable items and green labels for conforming and serviceable items. In this way you can determine product status at a distance and reduce the chance of confusion. You can use segregation as a means of identifying nonconforming product but if there is the possibility of mixing or confusion then this means alone should not be used.

On the labels themselves you should identify the product by name and reference number, specification, and issue status if necessary and either a statement of the nonconformance or a reference to the service or nonconformance report containing full details of its condition. Finally the person or organization testifying the nonconformance should be identified either by name or inspection stamp.

Unlike products, nonconforming services are usually rendered unavailable for use by notices such as "Out of Order" or by announcements such as "Normal service will be resumed as soon as possible". Products are often capable of operation with nonconformances whereas services tend to be withdrawn once the nonconformance has been detected, however trivial the fault.

Documenting nonconforming product

The standard requires the supplier to *provide for the documentation of nonconforming product*.

There are several ways in which you can document the presence of a nonconformance. You can record the condition:

- On a label attached to the item

- On a form unique to the item, such as a nonconformance report

- Of functional failures on a failure report and physical errors on a defect report

- In a log book for the item, such as an inspection history record or snag sheet

- In a log book for the workshop or area, such as a process log

The detail you record depends upon the severity of the nonconformance and to whom it needs to be communicated. In some cases a patrol inspector or quality engineer can concess minor snags on a daily basis, as can an itinerant designer. Where the problem is severe and remedial action complicated, a panel of experts may need to meet and rather than gather around the nonconforming item, a form or report may be more practical on which to document the remedial action. In some cases the details may need to be conveyed to the customer off-site and in such cases a log book or label would be inappropriate. It is important when documenting the nonconformance that you record as many details as you can since they may be valuable to any subsequent investigation to prevent its recurrence. In addition to the product name, reference number, serial number, and specification issue, you may need to record the operating conditions, temperature, humidity, time of day, identification of inspection and test equipment used and any other details that may help diagnose the cause.

Evaluation of nonconforming product

The standard requires the supplier to *provide for the evaluation of nonconforming product*.

Evaluating nonconforming product is a process of determining the effects of the nonconformance, classifying it as to its severity and providing information of use to those who will decide what to do about it. Establishing the cause of the noncon-formance so as to avoid making further nonconforming product is dealt with under *Corrective action*; however, with new products the remedial action may well take the form of a redesign which will not only eliminate the nonconformance but prevent it from recurring with that particular product. Of course, it may not prevent it from recurring with other designs; that is the purpose of preventive action (see Part 2 Chapter 14).

Segregation of nonconforming product

The standard requires the supplier to *provide for the segregation (when practical) of nonconforming product*.

Segregation of nonconforming product (or separating good from bad) places it in an area with restricted access. Such areas are called *quarantine areas*. Products should remain in quarantine until disposal instructions have been issued. The area should be clearly marked and a register maintained of all items that enter and exit the area. Without a register you won't be able to account for the items in the area, check whether any are missing, or track their movements. The quarantine store may be contained within another area, providing there is adequate separation that prevents mixing of conforming and nonconforming articles. Where items are too large to be moved into a quarantine area, measures should be taken to signal to others that the item is not available for use and this can be achieved by cordons or floor markings. With services the simplest method is to render the service unavailable or inaccessible.

Disposition of nonconforming product

The standard requires the supplier to *provide for the disposition of nonconforming product and for notification to the functions concerned*.

Disposition means to dispose of or decide what to do with the nonconforming item: whether to use it, repair it, scrap it etc. The options available are discussed later. By providing for the disposition of product you have to determine the action to take and notify those who are to carry it out. You cannot merely accumulate nonconforming items in a quarantine area. Apart from anything else they occupy valuable space and could present a hazard as they deteriorate. To implement this requirement you will need a form or other such document in which to record the decision and to assign the responsibility for the remedial action.

Defining disposition responsibility

The standard requires the supplier to *define the responsibility for review and authority for the disposition of nonconforming product*.

The decision on product acceptance is a relatively simple one because there is a specification against which to judge conformance. When product is found to be nonconforming there are three decisions you have to make:

- Can the product be made to conform?

- If not, is it fit for use?

- If not, can it be made fit for use?

The authority for making these decisions will vary depending on the answer to the first question. If the product can be made to conform regardless of the severity of the nonconformance simply by rework or completing operations, then these decisions can be taken by operators or inspectors, providing rework is economical. Decisions on scrap, rework, and completion would be made by the authority providing the funds rather than the design authority. If the product cannot be made to conform by using existing specifications then decisions requiring a change or a waiver to a specification should be made by the authority responsible for drawing up or selecting the specification.

It may be sensible to use investigators or quality engineers to review the options to be considered and propose remedial actions for the authorities to consider. In your procedures or the quality plan you should identify the various bodies that need to be consulted for each type of specification. Departures from customer requirements will require customer approval, departures from design requirements will require design approval, departures from process requirements will require process engineering approval etc. The key is in identifying who devised or selected the requirement in the first place. All specifications are but a substitute for knowledge of fitness for use so any departure from such specification must be referred back to the specification authors for a judgment.

Review of nonconforming product

The standard requires the supplier to *review nonconforming product in accordance with documented procedures* and advises that *it may be:*

a) *Reworked to meet the specified requirements, or*

b) *Accepted with or without repair by concession, or*

c) *Regraded for alternative applications, or*

d) *Rejected or scrapped.*

Several terms here may need explanation as they are unusual outside manufacturing industry.

Rework means the continuation of processing that will make an item conform to specification. Rework requires only normal operations to complete the item and does not require any additional instructions. Rework when applied to documents means correcting errors without changing the original requirement.

If you choose to accept a nonconforming item as is without rework, repair etc., then you are in effect granting a *concession* or waiving the requirement for that particular item only. If the requirements cannot be achieved at all then this is not a situation for a concession but a case for a change in requirement. If you know in advance of producing the product or service that it will not conform with the requirements, then you can request a deviation from the requirements, also called a *production permit*. Concessions apply after the product has been produced, production permits apply before it has been produced and both are requests that should be made to the acceptance authority for the product.

In some cases products and services are offered in several models, types, or other designations but are basically of the same design. Those which meet the higher specification are graded as such and those which fail may meet a lower specification and can be *regraded*. The grading should be reflected in the product identity so that there is no confusion.

The inclusion of the term *rejected* is not a disposition since all nonconforming items are initially rejected. Items may be rejected and then returned to their supplier for action but all other rejections should be subject to one of the other dispositions.

Scrapping an item should not be taken lightly since it could be a high value item. Scrap may be an economical decision with low cost items, whereas scrapping high value items may require prior authorization as salvage action may be possible to yield spares or alternative applications.

The list in the standard omits two other possibilities, those of modification and completion. A product that is nonconforming may be so due to errors in the specification and can be eliminated by a modification to the design. The product may meet the specified requirement but be unfit for use, in which case this is a major modification. This would be unlikely for a product that has been through PPAP.

Alternatively, the product may meet the supplier's specifications but not meet the customer or market specified requirements; this calls for a minor modification. Some modifications may be necessary only for certain batches due to variations in material or component tolerances. Modifications may be necessary to overcome component obsolescence or changes in bought parts that were not covered by the procurement specification, in which case a re-submission of the PPAP will be necessary.

Completion of product is different to rework as rework implies something was carried out incorrectly whereas returning product for completion implies that something was not done at all. This is a minor distinction but can be a useful classification in subsequent analysis.

The documented procedures that you require to meet this requirement should specify the authorities who make the decision, where it is to be recorded and what information should be provided so that it can be implemented and verified as being implemented.

To implement these requirements your nonconformance control procedures need to cover the following:

- Specify how product should be scrapped or recycled, the forms to be used, the authorizations to be obtained.

- Specify the various repair procedures, how they should be produced, selected, and implemented.

- Specify how modifications should be defined, identified, and implemented.

- Specify how production permits (deviations) and concessions (waivers) should be requested, evaluated, and approved or rejected.

- Specify how product should be returned to its supplier, the forms to be used and any identification requirements so that you can detect it on its return.

- Specify how regrading product is to be carried out, the product markings, prior authorization, and acceptance criteria.

Control of reworked product

The standard requires *rework instructions to be accessible and utilized by the appropriate personnel in their work areas.*

This requirement is no different to that of clause 4.5.2a with one minor exception. It contains a requirement for the instructions to be utilized. An auditor would therefore expect to find staff consulting the rework instructions when carrying out rework. In the other case, the documents need to be available but not necessarily utilized, i.e. being used. Information in the documents can be memorized or become habit through familiarity with the process. Rework instructions are often unique to the nonconformity and so personnel cannot rely on prior knowledge.

Rework on service parts

The standard permits *visible rework on the exterior of products supplied for service applications only with prior customer approval*

In order to meet this requirement you will need to:

a) Identify in the drawings, plans etc. those products which are supplied for service applications; i.e. for vehicle servicing, maintenance, and repair.

b) Provide the means for making rework invisible where there are cost savings over scrapping the item.

c) Stipulate on the drawings etc. the approved rework techniques.

Deviating from approved processes

The standard requires *prior written customer authorization whenever the product or process is different from that currently approved.*

This may seem a very onerous requirement since it stops you changing almost anything without customer approval. In the context of nonconforming product, it applies to any action you take to eliminate the nonconformity other than scrapping and regrading the item, if permitted. Any rework and repair procedure has to be approved in the PPAP submission. Obviously to improve performance continuously you must change something, but not the product's physical and functional characteristics, the key process parameters, or the dimensions and tolerances of the tools and gages used. It also applies to your subcontractors so you will need a PPAP submission from each of your subcontractors and to put in place procedures to regulate deviations from the approved standard.

However, this does not imply that you must not deviate. QS-9000 allows for such a situation but you must seek prior authorization. It means that before you perform the rework on production items you must obtain authorization to apply the procedure. You will need a procedure for conveying the information to the customer, obtaining approval, and keeping records of the expiration date or quantity authorized. Concessions or waivers are issued only on specific quantities or for a specific duration so cannot be open-ended.

You also have to have a system of identifying the concessed product up to shipment so that the shipping staff can apply the same identity to the shipping containers. One way of doing this is to tag the parts with a special label, neither Red nor Green (signifying reject or pass) so that the identity of concessed product will not be overlooked.

Use of nonconforming product

The standard requires that *where required by the contract, the proposed use or repair of product which does not conform to specified requirements shall be reported for concession to the customer or customer's representative.*

The only cases where you need to request concession from your customer are when you have deviated from one of the customer requirements and cannot make the product conform. Even when you repair a product, providing it meets all of the customer requirements, there is generally no need to seek a concession from your customer. While it is generally believed that nonconformances indicate an out-of-control situation, providing you detect and rectify them before release of the product then you have quality under control and have no need to report nonconformances to your customer. A special application of this requirement is the subject of an additional clause in QS-9000.

Recording the actual condition of nonconforming product

The standard requires the supplier to *record the description of nonconformity that has been accepted, and of repairs, to denote the actual condition.*

The original nonconformance report should indicate the nature of the nonconformance but after rework, or completion of operations, the nonconformance will have been eliminated. Where the nonconformance was accepted as is without rework, repair, or changing the specification then the actual condition is the original condition and this can be specified by the original nonconformance report. If the product has to be repaired or modified then the actual condition can be specified by the repair, salvage, or modification scheme, which is usually a separate document and can either be detailed on the nonconformance report or cross referenced to it. A lot of time can be saved if this information is readily accessible when problems arise later.

Reinspection of repaired and reworked product

The standard requires the supplier to *reinspect repaired and reworked product in accordance with the quality plan and/or documented procedures.*

Any product that has had work done to it should be reinspected prior to it being released. The work may not have been carried out as planned and could have affected features that were previously found conforming. There may be cases where the amount of reinspection is limited and this should be stated as part of the remedial action plan. However, after rework or repair the reinspection should verify that the product meets the original requirement, otherwise it is not the same product and must be identified differently.

The inspection and test records should indicate the original rejection, the disposition, and the results of the reinspection so that there is traceability of the decisions that were made.

Nonconformity reduction plan

The standard requires *nonconforming product to be quantified and analyzed and a prioritized reduction plan established.*

Element 4.13 of ISO 9001 deals with specific nonconformities and element 4.14 the action to eliminate their cause and prevent their recurrence. This additional QS-9000 requirement does seem to duplicate what is covered in clause 4.14.2. However, it does add a significant aspect: a reduction plan. One could be complying with element 4.13 and 4.14 of ISO 9001 but have no reduction plan since element 4.14 does not impose any time constraints on corrective action or require the incidence of nonconformity be reduced. It is quite possible to take corrective action continuously and still not reduce the number of nonconformities. The requirement may be in the wrong place (i.e. in 4.13 rather than 4.14) but it is a useful addition nonetheless.

The nonconformance data should be collected and quantified using one of the seven quality tools (see Part 2 Chapter 14), preferably the Pareto analysis. You can then devise a plan to reduce the 20% of causes that account for 80% of the nonconformities. However, be careful not to degrade other processes by your actions (see *Theory of constraints* in Part 2 Chapter 2). The plan should detail the action to be taken to eliminate the cause and the date by which a specified reduction is to be achieved. You should also monitor the reduction therefore the appropriate data collection measures need to be in place to gather the data at a rate commensurate with the production schedule. Monthly analysis may be too infrequent. Analysis by shift may be more appropriate.

Task list

1 Decide on what products and processes will be governed by the nonconformance control procedures.

2 Develop a means of classifying nonconformances.

3 Decide on who the acceptance authority is to be for each product, project, or contract for each class of nonconformance.

4 Provide forms or logs for recording details of nonconformances.

5 Provide reject labels for identifying nonconforming articles.

6 Provide serviceable and unserviceable labels for identifying operational equipment.

7 Provide a register of nonconformance reports.

8 Decide on who is to evaluate nonconformances.

9 Prepare procedures for processing nonconforming articles.

10 Provide quarantine areas in which to place articles pending disposition action.

11 Prepare procedures for controlling these quarantine areas.

12 Set up a review board to disposition nonconformances and allocate responsibilities.

13 Set up a file for storing records of nonconformance dispositions.

14 Provide for product to re-enter the process for rework, repair, or modification action.

15 Provide a means of controlling the return of reject articles to suppliers.

16 Provide a means for scrapping unusable articles under controlled conditions.

17 Provide forms for requesting deviations and waivers from your customer when appropriate.

18 Provide a means for tracking remedial actions on nonconforming articles.

Control of nonconforming product questionnaire

1   How do you ensure that product which does not conform to specified requirements is prevented from inadvertent use or installation?

2   How do you ensure nonconforming product is identified?

3   How do you ensure nonconforming product is documented?

4   How do you ensure nonconforming product is evaluated?

5   How do you ensure nonconforming product is segregated?

6   How do you ensure nonconforming product is dispositioned and concerned functions notified?

7   In which documents do you define the responsibility for the review and the authority for the disposition of nonconforming product?

8   How do you ensure that dispositions on nonconforming product are implemented as specified?

9   How do you seek permission for the purchaser to use or repair product that does not conform to specified requirements?

10   In which document do you record the description of nonconformity or repairs that has been accepted?

11   How do you ensure that repairs and reworked product is reinspected in accordance with documented procedures?

Do's and don'ts

* Don't apply the nonconformance controls of the standard to anything other than products and services.

* Do specify the requirement as well as the actual condition on nonconformance reports.

* Do schedule verification activities so as to detect nonconformances as early as possible.

* Do consider the cost of replacement against the cost of rework or repair.

* Do check other articles if the nonconformance appears to be symptomatic of the producing process.

* Don't change the design by means of a nonconformance report or concession.

* Do make nonconformance data available at final inspection.

* Do confirm the nonconformance before advocating remedial action.

* Don't identify nonconformances in a manner that will leave a permanent mark on the article.

* Do remove nonconforming articles from the process as soon as the nonconformance has been confirmed.

* Do provide limited access to quarantine areas.

* Do investigate the history of the nonconformance before specifying remedial action – the previous remedial action may not have been successful.

* Do record the remedial action required and the nature of re-verification.

* Do obtain agreement to any repair instructions prior to being implemented.

* Do file nonconformance data where operators and inspectors can review it.

* Don't limit the nonconformance review board to members of the quality department.

* Do subject reported subcontractor nonconformances to equal treatment.

* Do achieve unanimous agreement on the disposition of all nonconformances.

* Do keep the records of the nature of nonconformance, the disposition, and the result of post remedial action verification together.

Chapter 14

Corrective and preventive action

Scope of requirements

Corrective action is the pattern of activities which traces the symptoms of a problem to its cause, produces solutions for preventing the recurrence of the problem, implements the changes, and monitors that the changes have been successful. Corrective action provides a feedback loop in the control cycle. Inspection detects nonconformance, nonconformance control identifies, segregates, and rectifies the nonconforming item, and corrective action serves to prevent the nonconformance from recurring. While the notion of correction implies that it could be as concerned with the nonconforming item as with the cause of nonconformance, correcting the nonconforming item is a remedial action. It doesn't stop it recurring. Preventing the recurrence of a nonconformance is a corrective action. A problem has to exist for you to take corrective action. When actual problems don't exist but there is a possibility of failure, then action of preventing the occurrence of a nonconformance, or any problem for that matter, is a preventive action. So we have Remedial Action, Corrective Action, and Preventive Action, all with different meanings. Remedial Action is covered by clause 4.13 and Corrective and Preventive Action by clause 4.14 of the standard. Further details of preventive action can be found in ISO 9004-4.

Let us take a medical analogy. You have a head cold so you go to the doctor for advice. The doctor prescribes a remedy – "take two pills three times a day and the cold symptoms should subside". You do as the doctor advises and indeed the cold symptoms subside. This is *remedial action*. You then return to the doctor year after year with the same problem and ask the doctor to prescribe a means of preventing the cold symptoms from recurring each year. The doctor prescribes a course of injections which will prevent the symptoms occurring. You take the course of injections and behold, you do not feel cold symptoms ever again. This is *corrective action*. You observe over the years that the course of injections work providing you continue with the regime. You have a daughter who has never had a head cold and, mindful of the treatment you are given, wish to preserve your daughter from the suffering you have had over the years. You seek the doctor's advice which is that you enter your daughter onto a course of injections to safeguard against the risk of attracting the cold virus. Your daughter undertakes the prescribed course of treatment and never experiences a head cold. This is *preventive action*.

Whilst compliance with the requirements of element 4.14 will lead to improvement in performance, this is brought about due to actual and potential nonconformities. The section of QS-9000 on Continuous Improvement is somewhat different. It presupposes you are already meeting the customer's product requirements and that processes are capable. It indirectly asks the question "Can you do it better?" In other words can you meet customer requirements more efficiently and effectively by using less resources, having less corrective measures etc.

Returning to the standard, this clause also only addresses the correction and prevention of nonconformances, i.e. departures from the specified requirements. It does not address the correction of defects, of inconsistencies, of errors or in fact any deviations from your internal specifications or requirements. As explained in Part 2 Chapter 13, a departure from a requirement that is not included in the "Specified Requirements" is not a nonconformance, so the standard does not require corrective action for such deviations. This is a short-sighted view since preventing the recurrence of any problem is a sensible course of action to take, providing it is economical. Economics is, however, the crux of the matter. If you include every requirement in the "Specified Requirements", then you not only overcomplicate the nonconformance controls but the corrective and preventive action controls as well.

The corrective action requirements fail to stipulate when corrective action should be taken except to say that they shall be to a degree appropriate to the risks encountered. There is no compulsion for the supplier to correct nonconformances before repeat production or shipment of subsequent product. However, immediate correction is not always practical. You should base the timing of your corrective action on the severity of the nonconformances. All nonconformances are costly to the business, but correction is also costly and should be matched to the benefits it will accrue (see later under *Risks*). Any action taken to eliminate a nonconformance before the customer receives the product or service could be considered a preventive action. By this definition, final inspection is a preventive action since it should prevent the supply of nonconforming product to the customer. However, an error becomes a nonconformance when detected at any acceptance stage in the process, as indicated in clause 4.12 of the standard. Therefore an action taken to eliminate a potential nonconformance prior to an acceptance stage is a preventive action. This rules out any inspection stages as being preventive action measures. They are detection measures only.

The requirements in element 4.14 are linked with other elements of the standard even when there is no cross reference. This relationship is illustrated in Figure 14.1.

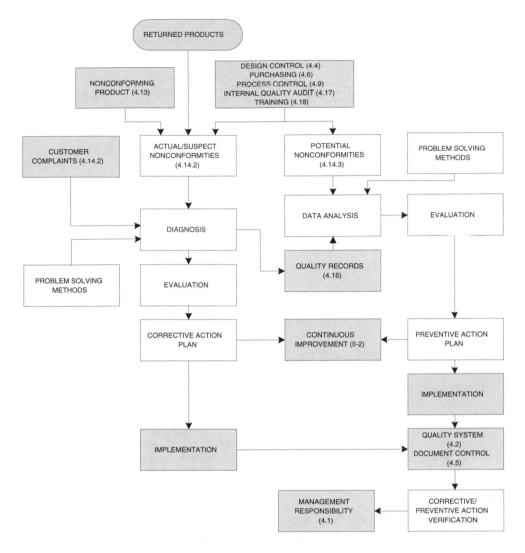

Figure 14.1 Element relationships with the corrective and preventive action element

Corrective and preventive action procedures

The standard requires the supplier to *establish, document, and maintain documented procedures for implementing corrective and preventive action.*

Since the source of nonconformances is so variable it may not be practical to have a single corrective or preventive action procedure. It may be more practical to embody corrective action provisions in the following procedures:

- Failure investigation procedure

- Nonconforming material review procedure

- Customer complaints procedure

- Quality system document change procedure

- Specification change procedure

- Maintenance procedures

Preventive action provisions on the other hand may be embodied in the following procedures:

- Performance analysis procedure

- Design review procedure

- Design analysis procedures (reliability, safety, maintainability etc.)

- Supplier/subcontractor performance review procedure

- Management review procedure

- Continuous improvement procedure

The standard only requires a procedure for implementing corrective and preventive action and not for determining it, although the requirements of clauses 4.14.2 and 4.14.3 do require the actions to be determined, presumably before being implemented!

Assessing the degree of corrective and preventive action necessary

The standard requires *that any corrective or preventive action taken to eliminate the causes of actual or potential nonconformities is to a degree appropriate to the magnitude of problems and commensurate with the risks encountered.*

The standard does not require you to take corrective action on every nonconformance or prevent every potential nonconformance. Here it is suggested that the decision to act should be based on the magnitude of the problem and the risks encountered. It is therefore implying that you only need act on the vital few. In fact this is good practice anyway, but to find that vital few you have to collect and analyze *most* of the data in the first place. Having made your proposals you should then conduct a risk analysis as part of the solution. Before managers will take action, they need to know:

- What is the problem or potential problem?

- Has the problem been confirmed?

- What are the consequences of doing nothing, i.e. what effect is it having?

- What is the preferred solution?

- How much will the solution cost?

- How much will the solution save?

- What are the alternatives and their relative costs?

- If I have to act, how long have I got before the effects damage the business?

Whatever you do, don't act on suspicion, always confirm that a problem exists or that there is a certain chance that a problem will exist if the current trend continues.

> ■ **Validate causes before proclaiming action.**

Implementing and recording changes in procedures

The standard requires the supplier to *implement and record changes in the documented procedures resulting from corrective and preventive action*.

To do this you need a link between your corrective and preventive action procedures and your change control procedures. If your Corrective Action Report (e.g. CAR023) indicated that procedure XYZ requires a change, then a reference to the Document Change Request (e.g. DCR134) initiating a change to procedure XYZ will provide the necessary link. The Change Request can then indicate as the reason for change the Corrective Action Report. If you don't use formal change requests then the Amendment Instructions can cross reference the Corrective Action Report. Alternatively, if your procedures carry a change record, the reason for change can be added. There are several methods to choose from, but whatever the method you will need some means of tracking the implementation of corrective actions. This use of forms illustrates one of the many advantages of form serial numbers.

There is only a requirement for a record of changes in procedures and not changes in plans, specifications, and drawings, which are clearly not procedures, but whether it be procedures, work instructions, or other types of instructions, you will need to be able to demonstrate that you have a system for preventing the recurrence of nonconformances.

Corrective action

Effective handling of customer complaints

The standard requires *the corrective action procedures to include the effective handling of customer complaints.*

You can only handle effectively those customer complaints that you receive and record. Customers may complain about your products and services but not go the extent of writing a formal complaint. Complaints may arise in conversation between the customer and your sales and service staff and this is where you have to instil discipline and ensure the complaints are recorded. Your customer complaints procedure should cover the following aspects to be effective:

- A definition of when a message from a customer can be classified as a complaint

- The method of capturing the customer complaints from all interface channels with the customer

- The registration of complaints so that you can account for them and monitor progress

- A form on which to record details of the complaint, the date, customer name etc.

- A process for acknowledging the complaint so that the customer knows you care

- A process for investigating the nature of the complaint

- A process for replacing product, repeating the service or for compensating the customer

Although under the heading of corrective action, there is merit in preparing a customer feedback procedure rather than limiting the procedure to complaints. Your staff should be informed of the compliments made by customers as well as the complaints, since it improves morale.

Customer complaints are addressed under the heading of corrective action; however, you should not limit your action to eliminating the cause and preventing recurrence. You also need to take remedial action to deal with the particular complaint.

Effective handling of reports of nonconformities

The standard requires *the corrective action procedures to include the effective handling of reports of product nonconformities*.

The reports of nonconformities could be internal or external reports of nonconformities although the standard does not make this clear. Internal reports of nonconformities should be covered by the requirements of clause 4.13. The next requirement concerning the investigation of nonconformities does relate to both internal and external reports. An external nonconformity report is not necessarily a customer complaint. The customer may have merely returned the product claiming it to be defective. When the customer has done this several times a complaint may well follow.

Another area where there may be some overlap is with the servicing requirements of section 4.19. The servicing arrangements may include provision for responding to requests from the customer for assistance. On investigation it may be found that the problem is caused by a nonconforming product that you have supplied, so in effect the customer is reporting a nonconformance. Should you address the arrangement for dealing with service calls under Servicing or under Corrective Action? The simple answer is under Servicing, since that is where your staff will expect to find the policies and practices defined. If you have written your quality manual around the standard then obviously you should address this situation under Corrective Action.

The standard does not address product recall other than in the context of releasing product for urgent production purposes in clause 4.10.2.3. The reported nonconformities from your customers may be so severe that you have to recall product, not just one or two but the whole batch or several batches between two dates or serial numbers. Product recall can be considered to fall within the scope of handling reported nonconformities, so your corrective action procedures need to address product recall. In fact it would probably make sense to institute a separate product recall procedure.

Assuming that the standard is only referring to external reports of nonconformities, your procedures should cover very similar processes to those for handling customer complaints:

- The method of receiving and identifying returned product

- The method of logging reports of nonconformities from customers

- The process of responding to customer requests for assistance

- The process of dispatching service personnel to the customer's premises

- A form on which to record details of the nonconformance, the date, customer name etc.

- A process for acknowledging the report so that the customer knows you care

- A process for investigating the nature of the nonconformance

- A process for replacing, or repairing nonconforming product and restoring customer equipment into service

- A process for assessing all product in service that is nonconforming, determining and implementing recall action if necessary

Returned product analysis

The standard requires *a recorded analysis of parts returned from customers to initiate corrective action to prevent recurrence.*

ISO 9001 covers this requirement in clause 4.14.2b and this is addressed in the next section in this chapter. However, the parts returned from dealers, customer manufacturing plants etc. may not be nonconforming. They may be obsolete, surplus to requirements, or have been used in trials etc. Whatever the reason for return, you are required to log each return and perform an analysis to reveal opportunities for corrective action when appropriate. You should process these items as indicated previously but prior to expending effort on investigations, you should establish your liability and then investigate the cause of any nonconformities for which you are liable.

Investigating the cause of nonconformities

The standard requires the supplier to *investigate the cause of nonconformities relating to product, process, and quality system and record the results of the investigation.*

All nonconformances are caused and all causes within your control can be avoided. All it needs is concerted action to prevent their recurrence. There are three types of corrective action: product related, process related, and system related. Product-related nonconformities can be either internal or external, as addressed previously, and you will have nonconformance reports to analyze. Process-related nonconformities may arise out of a product nonconformity but if you expect something less than 100% yield from the process then the reject items may not be considered nonconformities. They may be regarded as scrap. By analysing the process you can find the cause of low yield and improve performance of the process. Product and process nonconformities may be detected at planned inspection and test stages and may also be detected during product and process audits. System-related nonconformities can arise out of system audits and clause 4.17 on internal audits requires timely corrective actions for all types of audits. Clause 4.17 does not cover external audits but this is covered by the above requirement. So how would you respond to these requirements?

Your corrective action procedures need to cover the collection and analysis of product nonconformity reports and the collection and analysis of process data to reveal process nonconformities. The corrective action provisions of your internal audit procedure need to address the causes of the nonconformities and you will need an additional procedure to deal with external audits, investigating the cause of any nonconformities and recording the results. The procedure also needs to cover the investigation of customer complaints as the previous requirement only dealt with the handling of complaints.

You have to record the results of the investigations but not the corrective action you need to take. Even in clause 4.17 on internal quality audits, the requirement for the agreed corrective action to be recorded has been omitted. The results of the audit, the action taken and its effectiveness have to be recorded but not the agreed corrective action. ISO 10011-1 does not require agreed corrective actions to be recorded either.

Some nonconformances appear random but often have a common cause. In order to detect these causes, statistical analysis may need to be carried out. The causes of such nonconformances are generally due to noncompliance with or inadequate working methods and standards. Other nonconformances have a clearly defined special or unique cause which has to be corrected before the process can continue. Special cause problems generally require the changing of unsatisfactory designs or working methods. They may well be significant or even catastrophic. These rapidly result in unsatisfied customers and loss of profits. In order to investigate the cause of nonconformances you will need to:

• Identify the requirements which have not been achieved.

• Collect data on nonconforming items, the quantity, frequency, and distribution.

• Identify when, where, and under what conditions the nonconformances occurred.

• Identify what operations were being carried out at the time and by whom.

The best way of collecting this information is by using a Nonconformance Report Form which is completed at the time the occurrence is detected so as to prevent the loss of such data.

Having collected the data you will need to sort it and manipulate it so as to reveal the significance of the nonconformances and theorize about the possible causes. There may be several causes, in which case there will be some that dominate the others. Your job is to discover the dominant cause of the nonconformance and test the theories to find the actual cause, using disciplined problem solving methods (see below).

The source of causes is not unlimited. Nonconformities are caused by one or more of the following:

- Deficiencies in communication

- Deficiencies in documentation

- Deficiencies in personnel training and motivation

- Deficiencies in materials

- Deficiencies in tools and equipment

- Deficiencies in the operating environment

Each of these is probably caused by deficiencies in management, their planning, organization, or control.

Once you have identified the true cause of the nonconformity you can propose corrective action to prevent its recurrence. Eliminating the cause of nonconformity and preventing the recurrence of nonconformity are essentially the same thing. The key to successful diagnosis of causes is to keep asking the question: why? When you encounter a "don't know" then continue the investigation to find an answer.

Use of problem solving methods

The standard requires *the use of disciplined problem solving methods when an internal or external nonconformance occurs*.

This requirement is partially addressed in the previous section; however, the subject of disciplined problem solving methods will be addressed here. Disciplined methods are those proven methods that employ fundamental principles to reveal information. There are two different approaches to problem solving. The first is used when data are available as is the case when dealing with nonconformities. The second approach is when not all the data needed are available.

The seven quality tools in common use are as follows:

1   Pareto diagrams used to classify problems according to cause and phenomenon

2   Cause and effect diagrams used to analyze the characteristics of a process or situation

3   Histograms used to reveal the variation of characteristics or frequency distribution obtained from measurement

4   Control charts used to detect abnormal trends around control limits

5   Scatter diagrams used to illustrate the association between two pieces of corresponding data

6   Graphs used to display data for comparative purposes

7   Check-sheets used to tabulate results through routine checks of a situation

The further seven quality tools for use when not all data is available are:

1   Relations diagram used to clarify interrelations in a complex situation

2   Affinity diagram used to pull ideas from a group of people and group them into natural relationships

3   Tree diagram used to show the interrelations among goals and measures

4   Matrix diagram used to clarify the relations between two different factors (e.g. QFD)

5   Matrix data-analysis diagram used when the matrix chart does not provide sufficiently detailed information

6   Process decision program chart used in operations research

7   Arrow diagram used to show steps necessary to implement a plan (e.g. PERT)

There are other techniques such as force field analysis and the simple why? why? technique which often reveals the root cause of a problem very quickly.

Determining corrective actions

The standard requires *corrective action procedures to include determining the corrective action needed to eliminate the cause of nonconformities.*

You will need a means of recording both the cause and the proposed solutions. You can either incorporate the information within the Nonconformance Report or provide a separate Corrective Action Report.

The report should also make provision for the proposed solution to be approved or rejected. Remember that anyone may investigate nonconformances and propose corrective actions but the responsibility for taking the corrective action rests with those responsible for the process (see Part 2 Chapter 1).

To prevent a nonconformity from recurring you may need to take action on product which is in service. Some products may not have failed simply because they may not have been used in the manner needed to cause failure. Nevertheless there is a nonconformance if some product has failed and it is discovered that it is a common-cause nonconformance and all product is affected. You then need to decide whether to recall all product that has the defect and devise a recall plan and put it into effect.

Your corrective action plan should therefore address as appropriate:

* Action on the nonconforming item to remove the nonconformity

* A search for other similar items which may be nonconforming (i.e. suspect product)

* Action to recall product containing suspect nonconforming product

* Immediate action to prevent recurrence such as warning notices, alerts etc.

* Longer term action to prevent recurrence such as changes to plans, procedures, specifications, training etc.

You could classify the first three actions as nonconformity control actions and the other two as corrective actions, but the important factor is that they are linked and therefore procedural boundaries should not cause one or the other to be neglected.

Ensuring that corrective actions are effective

The standard requires the supplier to *apply controls to ensure that corrective actions are taken and that they are effective*.

This contains two separate requirements: one for verifying that the prescribed action has been taken and the other for verifying that the action has been effective in eliminating the original nonconformance. The Corrective Action report should define the corrective action to be taken, the actionee, and the date by which it is to be completed. The actionee should report when the action has been completed so that it may be verified. The effectiveness of some actions can be verified at the same time but quite often the effectiveness can only be checked after a considerable lapse of time. Remember it took an analysis to detect the nonconformance so it may take further analysis to detect that the nonconformance has been eliminated. In such cases the report should indicate when the checks for effectiveness are to be carried out and provision made for indicating that the corrective action has or has not been effective.

Some corrective actions may be multidimensional in that they may require training, changes to procedures, changes to specifications, changes in the organization, changes to equipment and processes, in fact so many changes that the corrective action becomes more like an improvement program. When corrective actions require interdepartmental action, it may be necessary to set up a corrective action team to introduce the changes. Each target area should be assigned to a person with responsibility in that area reporting to a team leader. In this way the task becomes a project with a project manager equipped with the authority to make the changes through the department representatives. Checking the effectiveness becomes a test of the system carried out over many months. Removing the old controls and committing yourselves to an untested solution may be disastrous, so it is often prudent to leave the existing controls in place until your solution has been proven to be effective.

Your quality system therefore needs to accommodate various corrective action strategies, from simple intradepartmental analysis with solutions that affect only one area, procedure, process, or product to projects that involve many departments, including suppliers and customers on occasion. Your corrective action procedures need to address these situations so that when the time comes you are adequately equipped to respond promptly.

Preventive action

Detecting and eliminating potential causes of nonconforming product

The standard requires the supplier to *use appropriate sources of information to detect and eliminate potential causes of nonconforming product*.

The purpose behind such a requirements is to provide a means of detecting any deterioration in standards. What may appear trivial on a case by case basis may well be significant when taken over a longer period or a larger population. This detective work is another form of inspection, although this time it focuses on processes and not on specific products. Managers have a habit of reacting to events particularly if they are serious nonconformances such as a customer complaint. What we are all poor at is perceiving the underlying trends that occur daily and gradually eat away at our profits. We therefore need a means of alerting management to these trends so that they may consider the corrective action to take.

To analyze anything you have to have data. If you have no data on processes, work operations, concessions, service reports, and customer complaints then this clause requires that you create some. Without data you cannot know if your processes are under control, if your customers are satisfied, if your service personnel carried out the planned service etc. It is not sufficient to claim that you have had no concessions or customer complaints. You have to have a system for capturing such matters should they occur. Introducing ISO 9000 does generate a lot of paper but it should all serve a specific purpose. Plan the data requirements carefully so that you:

- Only collect data on events that you intend to analyze

- Only analyze data with the intention of discovering problems

- Only provide solutions to real problems

- Only implement solutions that will improve performance

You also have to take care and avoid the "garbage in garbage out" syndrome. Your analysis will only be as good as the data you are provided with. If you want to determine certain facts then you have to ensure that the means exist for the necessary information to be obtained. To do this you may have to change the input forms or provide new forms on which to collect the data. The data needed for corrective action is rarely of use to those providing it so design your forms with care. Reject any incomplete forms as a sign that you are serious about needing the data. A sure sign that forms have become obsolete is the number of blank boxes. Also it is better to devise unique forms for specific uses rather than rely on general multipurpose forms, since they degrade the reliability of the data.

The requirement contains some terms that need explaining.

- *Processes* in this context means those series of related activities that turn inputs into outputs of added value. They include design, procurement, manufacture, packing, delivery, installation, maintenance, operations, and disposal as well as the processes which serve these primary processes, such as calibration, training, inspection, test, document control etc.

- *Work operations* are operations that form part of the above processes but include manual work, knowledge work, and management work associated with these processes.

- *Concessions* are any relaxations granted by the customer, design authority, inspection authority or other body authorized to accept nonconforming product.

- *Quality records* are those records identified in Part 2 Chapter 16. This is a bit of a catch-all as concessions, service reports, customer complaints, and data from processes and work operations are all quality records. However, the standard does not cross refer to clause 4.16 at every mention of records or similar documents and therefore the requirements of 4.16 only apply in those cases where it is referenced. Service reports, for instance, do not have to comply with the requirements of clause 4.16.

- *Service reports* are reports from service or maintenance personnel identifying the nature of faults, the components replaced, and time taken. They are required in clause 4.19.

- *Customer complaints* are any reports of dissatisfaction from the customer whether written by the customer or recorded from a telephone conversation.

A potential cause of nonconforming product is a situation where either a deterioration exists which will result in nonconformance if allowed to continue or the conditions are such that a failure is possible even though there is no evidence that it will shortly occur.

Regarding processes and work operations, you will need to establish performance indicators as a means of determining whether the potential for generating nonconformances is present. Establish standards for each of the processes and collect data on how well the standards are being achieved. Such factors as quantity processed, process yield, time through process, quantity of waste, and process downtime are useful measures of performance and indicators of quality.

Regarding concessions, you will need to register all requests for concessions to product requirements and carry out a periodic analysis to detect trends. Is it always the same product, the same requirement, the same person or are there other variables that indicate that the requirements are unachievable and in need of change? Under ideal conditions there should be no need for requesting concessions. The process should be fully capable of producing the goods. But if it happens frequently, there may be some underlying cause that has been overlooked.

Regarding quality records, you will need to be selective and choose for analysis those which will yield some useful data. Don't embark upon a progressive analysis without good reason as it can be a fruitless exercise.

Regarding service reports, these should be collected from the servicing or maintenance personnel and analyzed for repetitive problems. The data can also be used to compute the actual reliability, maintainability, and many other characteristics of the products.

Dealing with problems requiring preventive action

The standard requires that *the preventive action procedures include the determination of steps needed to deal with any problems requiring preventive action.*

This is probably one of the most powerful requirements in the standard, much under used in ISO 9000 quality systems. If you examine the words closely you will find that it can be applied to any situation where measures can be taken to prevent problems. A common weakness in many organizations is the absence of planning. Planning is a preventive action. We plan to achieve an objective which we would fail to meet if we didn't make adequate provision for the resources and activities needed to meet our objective. Therefore although the standard does not require plans for every activity, if preparation is necessary before an activity can take place and such preparation has not been accomplished then you have not determined the steps needed to deal with any problems requiring preventive action and are therefore noncompliant with QS-9000.

The action taken during process monitoring (see Part 2 Chapter 9) can be considered preventive action when corrections are made to the process ahead of nonconformities being produced. Hence Statistical Process Control is a technique which serves non-conformity prevention as well as detection.

The steps you need to take to deal with specific problems will vary depending on the nature of the problem. The part that can be proceduralized is the planning process for determining the preventive action needed. A typical process may be as follows:

- Establish a means of collecting relevant data and transmitting it to personnel for analysis.

- Analyze the data and search for trends and conditions which signal a deterioration in standards.

- Establish the concentration of the variance.

- Establish if the variance is significant both statistically and economically.

- Determine the effects if the trends continue.

- Gain agreement on the problem. (Expending further effort may be uneconomic if no one agrees with your prognosis.)

- Investigate the cause of the deterioration.

- Isolate the dominant cause.

- Devise a strategy for eliminating the cause together with alternative strategies, their limitations and consequences.

- Gain agreement on the strategy.

- Prepare an improvement plan which, if implemented, would eliminate the potential problem and not cause any others.

- Prepare a timetable and estimate resources for implementing the plan.

- Gain agreement of the improvement plan, timetable, and resources before going ahead.

The procedure would need to define the authority and responsibilities of those involved, the methods used to analyze the data and the recommended format of any improvement plan, so that any plans submitted to management gain their agreement. Some plans may be very simple and require no more than an instruction to implement an existing procedure. Others may be more involved and require additional resources. The improvement plan should be seen as defining a quality objective and hence, if a major change in performance is necessary, should be part of your Improvement Program, which was addressed in Part 2 Chapter 1. In this way you are seen to operate a coherent and coordinated improvement strategy rather than a random and unguided strategy. While those on the firing line are best equipped to notice the trends, any preventive action should be coordinated so that the company's resources are targeted at the problems that are most significant.

Initiating preventive action

The standard requires that *the preventive action procedures include the initiation of preventive action and application of controls to ensure that it is effective.*

This requirement addresses the implementation of the improvement plan prepared to deal with problems requiring preventive action. The improvement plan should have defined who is to take the preventive action and also the extent of the action to be taken: that is, only in the area where the trend was detected or over a much wider area. In initiating the action (see also Part 2 Chapter 1 under *Personnel with organizational freedom*) you need to carry it out in an organized manner, as follows:

- Notify those who will be affected by the change.

- Take the action in accordance with the prescribed control procedures.

- Monitor the effects of the action and collect the data.

- Analyze the data to determine whether the potential problem has been averted.

- Audit the implementation of the preventive action to verify that the agreed plans have been followed and conditions stabilized.

Ensuring that information is submitted for management review

The standard requires that *the preventive action procedures confirm that the relevant information on actions taken including changes to procedures is submitted for management review.*

To ensure that information on your preventive actions is considered by the management review of the quality system, you should document the problem, the plan to solve it, the action actually taken, and the result. However, this section of the standard does not require you to produce any records of preventive action since no cross reference is made to clause 4.16. You could therefore meet the requirement by ensuring that those with intimate knowledge of the preventive actions taken attend a management review meeting and give a verbal report. The changes to procedures, if any, will have been documented because it is required by clause 4.14.1 and since you have to maintain records of management reviews, you will capture the information on preventive actions, and thus meet the requirement. If you operate a more complex quality system, verbal reports may not be reliable and so you will need to maintain records of preventive actions, as stated previously. Your management review procedure, if you have one (see Part 2 Chapter 1), should therefore make provision for collecting preventive action data.

Task list

1 Provide a means of collecting data from all verification operations.

2 Set up a procedure for recording customer complaints.

3 Provide a means for collecting design change and document change requests.

4 Provide in the relevant procedures requirements for recording and transmitting data pertinent to any subsequent corrective action analysis.

5 Provide, where relevant, a means of recording continuous processes to detect deviation from the agreed standard.

6 Establish performance indicators for each significant process.

7 Establish a method of recording the baseline performance for each of these processes.

8 Decide on who is to collect and analyze the data for determination of both corrective and preventive actions.

9 Decide on who is to investigate and propose corrective actions and preventive actions.

10 Prepare procedures for the analysis, investigation, and determination of the causes of potential and actual deviation including the formation of diagnostic teams where necessary.

11 Provide tools and techniques to help investigators discover the causes of potential and actual deviation and determine their significance.

12 Provide for solutions to prevent the occurrence and recurrence of deviations to be proposed and agreed.

13 Provide forms for recording the agreed corrective and preventive action and target dates for completion.

14 Prepare procedures for reporting the results of the analyses to management.

15 Provide links between the corrective and preventive action reports and document, product, process, and organization changes.

16 Provide procedures for product recall.

17 Provide an escalation procedure for use when corrective and preventive action target dates have been exceeded or where detected problems require management action.

18 Provide procedures for managing corrective and preventive action programs where collective action is required.

19 Provide visual evidence of required performance against actual performance at work locations.

20 Provide procedures for verifying that corrective and preventive actions achieve their objectives.

Corrective and preventive action questionnaire

1   In what documents have you defined your corrective action and preventive action procedures?

2   How do you ensure that the corrective or preventive action taken is to a degree appropriate to the magnitude of the problem and commensurate to the risks encountered?

3   How do you implement and record changes resulting from corrective and preventive action?

4   How do you handle customer complaints?

5   How do you handle reports of product nonconformities?

6   How do you ensure that the cause of nonconforming product is investigated?

7   How do you eliminate the cause of nonconformities?

8   How do you ensure that corrective actions are taken and are effective?

9   What sources of information are used to detect, analyze, and eliminate potential causes of nonconformity?

10   How are problems requiring preventive action dealt with?

11   How is preventive action initiated?

12   What controls ensure the effectiveness of preventive actions?

13   How do you ensure that information on preventive action is submitted for management review?

Do's and don'ts

* Don't take action before you have confirmed the presence of a problem.

* Don't announce you have confirmed that a problem exists before you have assessed its significance.

* Do check that the agreed corrective actions are being taken.

* Don't wait until the due date for the completion of the action to check if work has started.

* Do accept legitimate reasons for inaction and agree on new target dates.

* Don't display performance data unless those affected agree to it being displayed.

* Do look for potential causes of deviation; don't wait until the alarm bells ring.

* Do concentrate on the vital few problems.

* Do monitor the trivial problems to detect a systematic deterioration in standards.

* Do enlist the support of the organization responsible for the problem to investigate the cause.

* Don't impose corrective actions on other organizations.

* Don't collect data for the sake of it – always have a purpose.

* Do classify the problems into groups that have a common cause and special cause.

* Do attract management's attention to special cause problems and obtain commitment to action.

* Do train your investigators in diagnostic techniques.

* Don't persist with proposals for corrective action if management tells you they are not economic – find more economic solutions.

* Do capture your organization's recovery plans into the corrective action system.

* Do impress on management that corrective action procedures exist to save resources.

* Do tell your complaining customers the action you have taken to resolve their problem.

* Don't limit your corrective action system to products – apply it to all operations including management decision making.

Chapter 15

Handling, storage, packaging, preservation, and delivery

Scope of requirements

These requirements are concerned with conformance control, that is ensuring that products remain conforming once they have been certified as conforming. A more apt heading would have been *Control of conforming product*. While they appear in the quality loop (see ISO 9004) after inspection and test, they are by no means only applicable at this stage. They should appear in the quality loop at several stages since handling, storage, preservation, and packing can be carried out following receipt of items from suppliers up to dispatch of end product to customers.

They mainly apply to products as most of them are concerned with protecting the product from damage and deterioration. They apply to the end product and any items that either form part of the product or are used to produce the product, including any tools, test equipment, and processing materials. Although it is possible for some types of services to deteriorate, this use of the term is covered by the process control and auditing requirements. The only requirements that do apply to services are those for identification, unless product is used in the delivery of a service. If the servicing is done to a product, whether or not owned by the supplier, then protection of that product is important.

The requirements in element 4.15 are linked with other elements of the standard even when there is no cross reference. This relationship is illustrated in Figure 15.1.

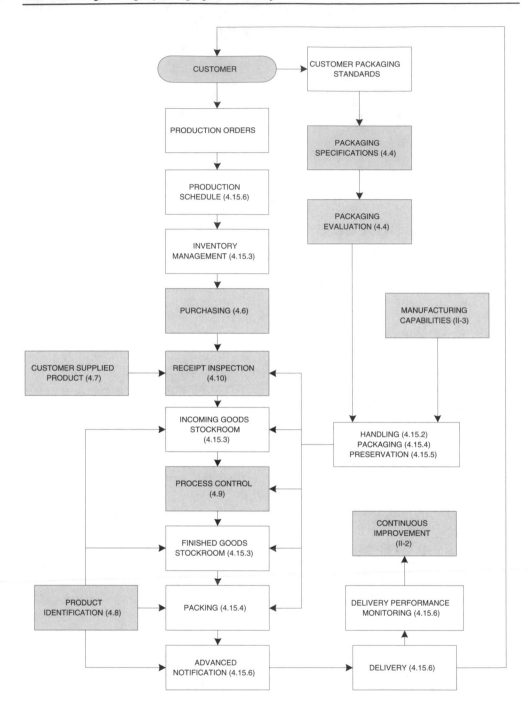

Figure 15.1 Element relationships with the handling, storage, packaging, preservation, and delivery element

Handling, storage, packaging, preservation, and delivery procedures

The standard requires the supplier to *establish and maintain documented procedures for handling, storage, packaging, preservation, and delivery of product.*

It is likely that you will need two types of procedure to cover these requirements, one general and the other specific.

You will need a means of identifying when handling, storage, packing, preservation, and delivery procedures will be required and a method of preparing, identifying, publishing, selecting, and controlling specific procedures covering these subjects. These aspects should be covered by a general procedure.

The identification of special handling, storage, packing, preservation, and delivery provisions usually occurs in the design stage or the manufacturing or service planning phase, by assessing the risks to product quality during its manufacture, storage, movement, transportation, and installation. Having identified that there is a risk to product quality you may need to prepare instructions for the handling, storage, packing, preservation, and delivery of particular items.

In addition to issuing the procedures you will need to reference them in the appropriate work instructions so that they are implemented when necessary. In some cases it may be more appropriate to include these provisions as an integral part of other procedures rather than have separate procedures. Whatever the method, you will need to have traceability from the identification of need to implementation of the provisions and from there to the records of achievement.

Handling

The standard requires the supplier to *provide methods and means of handling that prevent damage or deterioration.*

The standard does not specify the subject which is to be prevented from damage and deterioration. It could be the product, the person, or both. Handling provisions serve two purposes both related to safety. Protection of the product from the individual and protection of the individual handling the product. By referring back to clause 4.15.1 it would appear that element 4.15 of the standard is only concerned with safety of the product and not the individual; however, the two cannot and should not be separated and handling procedures should address both aspects. Personnel safety is covered by element 4.9.

Handling product can take various forms, depending on the hazard you are trying to prevent from happening. In some cases notices on the product will suffice, such as

"LIFT HERE" or the notices on batteries warning of acid. In other cases you will have to provide special containers or equipment. There follows a short list of handling provisions which your procedures may need to address:

- Lifting equipment

- Pallets and containers

- Conveyors and stackers

- Design features for enabling handling of product

- Handling of electrostatic sensitive devices

- Handling hazardous materials

- Handling fragile materials

Storage

The standard requires the supplier to *use designated storage areas or stock rooms to prevent damage or deterioration of product, pending use or delivery.*

In order to preserve the quality of items that have passed receipt inspection they should be transferred to a storage area in which they are secure from damage and deterioration. You need secure storage areas for several reasons:

- For preventing personnel from entering a storage area and removing items without authorization.

- For preventing items from losing their identity. Once the identity is lost it is often difficult, if not impossible, to restore complete identification without testing material or other properties.

- For preventing vermin damaging the stock.

- For preventing climatic elements causing stock to deteriorate.

While loss of product may not be considered a quality matter, it is if the product is customer property or if it prevents you from meeting your customer requirements. Delivery on time is a quality characteristic of the service you provide to your customer and so secure storage is essential.

To address these requirements you will need to identify and specify the storage areas that have been established to protect product pending use or delivery. Although it need be only a brief specification, the requirements to be maintained by each storage area should be specified, based on the type of product, the conditions required to preserve its quality, its location, and environment. Products that require storage at certain temperatures should be stored in areas that maintain such temperatures. If the environment in the area in which the room is located is either uncontrolled or at a significantly higher or lower temperature, then an environmentally controlled storage area will be required.

All items have a limit beyond which deterioration may occur and so temperature, humidity, pressure, air quality, radiation, vibration etc. may need to be controlled. At some stage, usually during design or manufacturing or service planning, the storage conditions need to be defined and displayed. In many cases dry conditions at room temperature is all that is necessary but problems may occur when items requiring non-standard conditions are acquired. You will need a means of ensuring that such items are afforded the necessary protection and your storage procedures need to address this aspect. It is for this reason that it is wiser to store items in their original packaging until required for use. If packets have to be opened, then they should be sealed again before return into storage.

The requirement is for you to designate storage areas. This means that any area where product is stored should have been designated for that purpose so that the necessary controls can be employed. If you store product in undesignated areas then there is a chance that the necessary controls will not be applied.

> ■ **The quality system should make the right things happen by design and not by chance.**

You can identify the areas you have designated for storage of different types of product in your quality manual or in a general storage control procedure. You can then place notices and markers around the area, if necessary, to indicate the boundaries where the controls are applied.

Receipt and dispatch from storage areas

The standard requires the supplier to *stipulate appropriate methods for authorizing receipt and the dispatch to and from storage areas*.

The content of storage areas should be known at all times so that you can be confident that only that which is in the area is of a known condition. Storage areas containing conforming items should be separate from those containing nonconforming items (see later). It follows therefore that when an item is taken from storage areas the person taking it should be able to rely on it conforming unless otherwise stated on the label. If free access is given to add and remove items in such areas, then this confidence is lost. If at any time the controls are relaxed, then the whole stock becomes suspect.

There is often a need to supply items as free issue, as the loss of small value items is less than the cost of the controls to prevent such loss. This practice can be used only if the quality of the items can be determined wholly by visual inspection by the person using them.

There are, however, issues other than quality which will govern the control of items in store. Inventory control is a vital part of any business. Stock ties up capital, so the less stock that is held the more capital the firm has available to apply to producing output.

A common solution, which satisfies both the inventory control and quality control, is to institute a stock requisition system. Authorization of requisitions may be given by a person's superior or can be provided via a work order. If someone has been authorized to carry out a particular job then this should authorize the person to requisition the items needed. Again for inventory control reasons, you may wish to impose a limit on such authority requiring the person to seek higher authority for items above a certain value.

The standard does not require stock records or inventory lists; however, without such a system you can't demonstrate you have control over the receipt and dispatch of items from stock. The standard also does not require you to identify the location of items in stock, although without some reliable method of retrieving and accounting for items you can't demonstrate that unauthorized items have not entered the stock.

Stock condition assessments

The standard requires the supplier to *assess the condition of product in stock at appropriate intervals in order to detect deterioration.*

Each time the store controller retrieves an item for issue, there is an opportunity to check the condition of stock and this requirement should be written in to the storage procedures. However, some items may have a slow turnover in stock, particularly maintenance stores where spares are held pending use. There is also a need to check the overall condition of the stock periodically for damage to the fabric of the building or room. Rain water may be leaking onto packaging and go undetected until that item is removed for use.

Some items may deteriorate when dormant, such as electrolytic capacitors or two part adhesives. Others deteriorate with the passage of time regardless of use, such as rubbers, adhesive tape, chemicals. These are often referred to as "Shelf Life Items" or

"Limited Life Items". Dormant electronic assemblies can deteriorate in storage and provision should be made to retest equipment periodically or prior to release if in storage for more than one year.

The assessment interval should depend on the type of building, the stock turnover, the environment in which the storage area is located and the number of people allowed access, and a period fixed and stated in your procedures. The interval may vary from area to area and should be reviewed and adjusted as appropriate following the results of the assessment.

Inventory management system

The standard requires *an inventory management system to be established and documented*.

To enable you to achieve 100% on-time delivery (clause 4.15.6) you need to ensure you have adequate stocks of parts and materials to make the products ordered in the quantities required. In typical commercial situations predicting the demand for your products is not easy and so organizations tend to carry more inventory than needed to cope with unexpected demand. The possibility of an unexpected increase in demand leads to larger inventories since an out-of-stock situation may result in lost customer orders. Most companies have to rely on forecasts and estimates. The Big Three protect you to some extent from fluctuations in demand by giving you advanced notification of their production and service requirements so that your production schedule can be "order driven". Should an increase in demand be necessary you should be given adequate warning so that you can increase your inventory. If this is not the case then you need suitable clauses in your contract with the Big Three to protect you against unexpected fluctuations in demand that may cause you to fail to meet the 100% on-time delivery requirement.

Inventory management is concerned with maintaining economic order quantities so that you neither order too much stock nor too little to meet your commitments. The stock level is dependent upon what it costs both in capital and in space needed to maintain such levels. Even if you employ a ship to line principle, you still need to determine the economic order quantities. Some items have a higher value than others thereby requiring a higher degree of control. Using the Pareto principle you will probably find that 20% of inventory requires a high degree of control to enable you to control 80% of the inventory costs.

It is not my purpose here to elaborate on inventory management as this is a management function in its own right. From the quality management viewpoint, however, there are some factors that need to be considered.

An inventory management system is required to be established, meaning set up on a permanent basis to meet defined inventory policies and objectives approved by executive management. It has to be documented, meaning that there should be a description of the system, how it works, the assignment of responsibilities, the codification of best practice, procedures, and instructions. The system has to be planned, organized, and controlled so that it achieves its purpose. A person should therefore be appointed with responsibility for the inventory management system and responsibilities of those who work the system should be defined and documented. Records should be created and maintained that show how order quantities have been calculated so that the calculations can be verified and repeated if necessary with new data. The records should also provide data adequate for continual improvement initiatives to be effective.

The inventory management system is a subsystem of your QS-9000 quality system although it may not be considered part of an ISO 9000 quality system since it is not a requirement of ISO 9001. However, whether or not 100% on-time delivery is a requirement of your customers, you won't retain customers for long if you continually fail to meet their delivery requirements regardless of the quality of the products you supply. It is only in a niche market that you can retain customers with a long waiting list for your products. In competitive markets you need to exceed delivery expectations as well as product quality expectations to retain your market position.

In addition to establishing a documented inventory management system, the standard requires the system to optimize turnover time, meaning that the time a part goes through the system from receipt to use should be an optimum. To achieve this you will need to have metrics for receiving and storage times.

The system is also required to assure stock rotation, meaning that parts and materials are used on a first-in-first-out (FIFO) basis. This requires the picking system to be date sensitive.

Finally the system is required to minimize inventory levels based on known demand and risk. It is usually obvious when the levels are too high but difficult to verify that minimum levels have been achieved. The minimum levels need to take account of failures, waste, damage etc. as well as test samples for production and development and other uses that can eat into the inventory.

Even if QS-9000 did not require you to have an inventory management system, you would need to have one to meet the customer delivery requirements.

Controlling packing, packaging, and marking processes

The standard requires the supplier to *control packing, packaging, and marking processes (including materials used) to the extent necessary to ensure conformance to specified requirements.*

Packing is an activity and packaging a material in this context. A Packing specification defines how an item should be packed, whereas a Packaging specification details the nature of the package.

Control means setting standards, verifying conformance, and taking action on the difference. So the control of packaging and marking processes means that you have to set packaging and marking standards or requirements, verify that these requirements are being met by inspection, test, or analysis and then remedy any deficiencies found.

Packing, packaging, and marking processes need to be controlled so that product remains in its original condition until required for use. Packing processes should be designed to protect the product from damage and deterioration under the conditions that can be expected during storage and transportation.

Control of packing and marking processes commences during the design phase or the manufacturing or service planning phase. Packaging design should be governed by the requirements of clause 4.4, although if you only select existing designs of packaging these requirements would not be applicable.

Several packaging activities are required during product development and are addressed in the APQP manual. In process design and development, the packaging standards need to be determined. These are general and not product specific. They are often specified by the customer but if not they will need to be selected or developed. Packaging specifications, which are product specific, also need to be developed during the process design and development phase. Consideration needs to be given to material handling equipment and environmental constraints during storage and transit. During the product and process validation phase, packaging provisions are required to be evaluated to prove that the packaging affords the necessary protection during handling, storage, and transportation.

You will need a means of identifying the packaging and marking requirements for particular products and then procedures for the design of suitable packaging including the preservation and marking requirements. Depending on your business you may need to devise packages for various storage and transportation conditions, preservation methods for various types of product and marking requirements for types of product associated with their destination. Packages for export may require different markings than those for the home market. Those for certain countries may have to comply with particular laws.

Markings should be applied both to primary and secondary packaging as well as to the product itself. Markings should also be made with materials that will survive the conditions of storage and transportation. Protection can be given to the markings while in store and in transit but in use they have no protection. Markings applied to the product therefore need to be resistant to cleaning processes both in the factory and in use.

Where applicable, preservation processes should require that the product be cleaned before being packed and preservative applied. In other cases the product may need to the stored in sealed containers in order to retard decay, corrosion, or contamination.

There are several national standards which can be used to select the appropriate packaging, marking, and preservation requirements for your products. Your procedures should make provision for the selection to be made by qualified personnel at the planning stage and for the requirements thus selected to be specified in the packing instructions to ensure their implementation.

Each of the customers subscribing to QS-9000 have special packaging and marking requirements so you will need to ensure that these requirements are met and do not conflict with any other packaging and marking provisions you need to make. Where the requirements of customers differ, you need a means of ensuring the relevant requirements are implemented for particular consignments. Customer requirements, or your translation of these into operating procedures and standards, need to be available where packing operations are performed.

Packing can be classed as a special process since once the units are placed in the containers and the containers sealed, the only way to subsequently verify the right units are in the right containers is to break the seal and inspect the contents. Your packing controls should therefore give you sufficient confidence concerning the contents of containers without having to break the seals.

Packing instructions should provide not only for protecting the product but for including any documentation that should accompany the product, such as:

- Assembly and installation instructions

- License and copyright notices

- Certificates of conformity

- Packing lists identifying the contents of the container

- Export documents

- Warranty cards

The packing instructions are one of the last instructions you provide and probably the last operation you perform so present the last opportunity for you to make mistakes. They may be your last mistakes but they are the first the customer sees. The error you made on component assembly probably won't be found, but the slightest error in the packaging, the marking, or the enclosures will almost certainly be found so this process needs careful control. It may not be a skilled process but all the same it is vital to your image.

Preserving and segregating product

The standard requires the supplier to *apply appropriate methods for preservation and segregation of product when such product is under the supplier's control.*

Preserving product while the product is under your control may be addressed by your handling and packaging provisions, but in-process preservation may also be necessary to protect finishes from deterioration during further processing. Such measures need to be specified in the work instructions for particular products. For products that start to deteriorate when the packaging seal is broken, the supplier's responsibility extends beyond delivery to the point of use and so markings have to be applied to the containers to warn the consumers of the risks.

The preservation processes should be designed to prolong the life of the product by inhibiting the effect of natural elements. While the conditions in the factory can be measured, those outside the factory can only be predicted, which is why the markings on packaging are so important to warn handlers of any dangers or precautions they must observe.

Limited Life Items should be identified so as to indicate their useful life. The expiry date should be visible on the container and provisions should be made for such items to be removed from stock when their indicated life has expired.

Segregation is another important requirement and not only for nonconforming product as specified in clause 4.13. Segregation is vital in many industries where products can only be positively identified by their containers. It is also important to prevent possible mixing or exposure to adverse conditions or cross-contamination. Examples where segregation makes sense are:

- Toxic and nontoxic materials

- Flammable and non-flammable materials

- Limited life items

- Explosives

- Dry and wet ingredients

Segregation is also not limited to the product but also to the containers and tools used with the product. Particles left in containers and on tools, no matter how small, can cause blemishes in paint and other finishes. If these are risk areas in your manufacturing process then procedures have to be put in place that will prevent product mixing.

Segregation may also be necessary in the packaging of products not only to prevent visible damage but electrical damage, as with electrostatic sensitive devices. Segregation may be the only way of providing adequate product identity, as with fasteners. While a well-equipped laboratory can determine the difference between products and materials the consumer needs a simple means and labeled packets are often a reliable and economic alternative.

Delivery

Protection of product after final inspection

The standard requires the supplier to *arrange for the protection of the quality of product after final inspection and test and, where contractually specified, this protection shall extend to include delivery to destination.*

The ISO 9001 requirements do not add anything that isn't covered in clause 4.15.4 although the heading signals a quite different requirement and this has been addressed by the additional clauses in QS-9000. The requirement that the supplier arrange for protection of the product is different from the requirement in clause 4.15.4 for the supplier to preserve the product but the main purpose of the packaging requirements is to afford protection to the product. Packaging does have another purpose, that of easing handling and distribution. These are economic and marketing considerations rather than quality considerations.

It is quite common for companies to document their delivery practices covering preparation for delivery, packaging, preservation, documentation checks, delivery documentation including, where applicable, export documents, transportation practices etc. However the standard only requires that you address the product protection aspects. How you ensure the correct product of the correct quantity with correct documentation gets to the required destination is not required. The final inspection requirements require you to complete the evidence of compliance with the specified requirements, but only with respect to the finished product. These requirements also require you to complete all activities stated in the procedures or quality plan before product is dispatched. The standard does not, but it should, require no product to be dispatched until all the relevant specified requirements have been complied with. This ambiguity in clause 4.10.4 and the omission of adequate requirements in clause 4.15.6 do not provide what is needed to ensure that only consignments that comply with the specified requirements are released. Maybe the next revision of the standard will rectify this anomaly.

After implementing all the requirements of QS-9000 you should be able to certify with each delivery that the products supplied have been designed and produced under conditions that meet QS-9000 and tests and inspections carried out to confirm their conformance with the contractual requirements. The standard does not require such a certificate of conformance and while not essential it is a good way of giving your customers confidence. You may have many product lines, some may not be registered to QS-9000, your customers may know this and so a certificate provides the appropriate objective evidence. Although many certificates are indeed worthless, by suitable regulation their quality can be assured.

Supplier delivery performance monitoring

The standard requires *systems to be established to support 100% on-time shipments to meet customer production and service requirements and to monitor adherence to established lead time requirements.*

To guarantee shipment on time, you either need to maintain an adequate inventory of finished goods, for shipment on demand, or utilize only predictable processes and obtain sufficient advanced order information from your customer. When you examine some of the requirements in QS-9000, you may be tempted to question how you can continually improve performance, reduce prices, minimize space, material travel, equipment downtime, process variation etc. and meet 100% on-time shipments. You can't unless you have a partnership with your customer in which there is mutual assistance to meet common objectives. Without sufficient lead time on orders you will be unlikely to meet the target. However, the standard does acknowledge that you may not always be successful. There will be matters outside your control and matters over which you have complete control. It is the latter that you can do something about and take corrective action should the target not be achieved.

Firstly, you need to estimate the production cycle time during the production trial runs in the product and process validation phase as defined in the APQP manual. An assessment of the PFMEA should enable you to identify the risk areas and build in appropriate contingencies. An assessment of your subcontractor's previous delivery performance will also enable you to predict their future performance. There are, however, many factors that will not feature in the technical assessment that may jeopardize shipment and this is where the quality system is most beneficial. Internal audits and management reviews will highlight activities that present unacceptable risk to achieving shipment targets. However, the primary source of information will arise in the regular meetings of the cross-functional teams. The problem here is that you will be dealing mostly with actual problems rather than suspect problems so preventive action may be too late.

One of the factors requiring improvement in Section II is timing and this can relate not only to delivery timing but reduction in lead-time. When new processes become stabilized over long periods and the frequency of improvement reduces as more and more problems are resolved, you will be able to reduce lead time.

Your planning and delivery procedures need to record estimated and actual delivery dates and the data collected and analyzed through a delivery performance monitoring procedure. When targets are not met you should investigate the cause under the corrective action procedures and formulate corrective action plans. Where the cause is found to be a failure by the customer to supply some vital information or equipment, then it would be prudent not to wait for the periodic analysis but react promptly.

Advanced shipment notification system

The standard requires *a computerized system for online transmittal of advanced shipment notification and a method of backup in the event of failure.*

The customer will advise on the format of the advanced shipment notification (ASN). A computerized system will give you flexibility such that you are able to transmit the information immediately the shipment is loaded. You could use a fax machine as your backup since transmission is nearly as fast but this is likely to present the customer with data handling problems. A computerized transmission feeds the data directly onto the customer database without additional data entry. Your backup system should do the same so that your customer perceives no noticeable change in the quality of information.

Documentation checks are vital at this stage since you are being judged on your on-time shipment performance. A delay caused by an error in the ASN will jeopardize all your hard work to meet the shipment date. The system that prints the container labels should therefore use the same data that is entered onto the ASN in order to avoid error. Eliminate human transcription errors and you are halfway there. The only other problem is making sure that what's in the box is what it says on the label.

Task list

1 Produce procedures for developing storage, handling, and packing instructions.

2 Identify handling requirements for bulky, fragile, sensitive, and hazardous items.

3 Identify storage conditions for hazardous and environmentally sensitive items.

4 Identify packaging and preservation requirements for all types of items.

5 Identify marking requirements for items, secondary and primary packaging.

6 Provide storage areas or rooms for items pending use.

7 Provide separate storage areas or rooms for items awaiting disposal, remedial action, or further processing.

8 Assess conditions of stock and storage areas, rooms, and buildings periodically.

9 Specify segregation rules for keeping items and materials apart.

10 Provide procedures for controlling limited life items.

11 Establish retest conditions for items which may deteriorate when dormant.

12 Provide packing instructions for packing certain types of product.

13 Establish delivery performance monitoring systems.

14 Schedule production to match customer orders.

Handling, storage, packaging, and delivery questionnaire

1 How are procedures for handling, storage, packaging, preservation, and delivery established, documented, and maintained?

2 How do you prevent damage or deterioration of product in handling?

3 How do you prevent damage or deterioration of product in storage?

4 How do you prevent damage or deterioration of product during delivery?

5 Which areas have you designated for the storage of product pending use or delivery?

6 How do you authorize receipt into storage areas or stock rooms?

7 How do you authorize dispatch from storage areas or stock rooms?

8 How do you detect deterioration in the condition of product in stock?

9 How do you control packing and packaging processes including the materials used?

10 How do you control preservation processes including the materials used?

11 How do you control marking processes including the materials used?

12 How do you preserve product when such product is under your control?

13 How do you segregate product when such product is under your control?

14 How do you ensure that the quality of product after final inspection and test is protected up to its destination?

15 How do you ensure 100% on-time delivery and monitor adherance to lead time requirements?

16 What systems are employed to provide advance notification of shipment?

Do's and don'ts

* Don't allow items into storage areas without being subject to satisfactory inspection.

* Don't allow unauthorized access to storage areas.

* Don't store items that have lost their identity with items that haven't.

* Do segregate serviceable items from unserviceable items.

* Do segregate limited life items.

* Do identify items with special handling, storage, or packaging requirements.

* Do identify remnant material.

* Don't allow packaging seals to be broken other than by authorized personnel.

* Do identify contents of containers on the outside.

* Do remove life expired items from the serviceable items store.

* Do instruct storekeepers on the effects of lost identity, mixing product, handling and packaging methods.

* Do maintain good housekeeping practices in storage and packaging areas.

* Do provide check lists for packaging operations.

* Do issue articles on a first in first out basis.

* Don't permit unauthorized disposal of items suspected as being damaged.

* Do inspect items for identity, damage, and deterioration prior to issue.

* Don't replenish stock other than with articles of the same specification.

Chapter 16

Control of quality records

Scope of requirements

Throughout the standard, various clauses reference the clause on quality records and, so as to avoid repetition, the common requirements for quality records are assembled under one heading. The requirements, however, are not limited to those clauses in which this requirement is referenced since many other clauses refer to records. However, as all clauses will generate some documentary evidence it should not be assumed that all such documents are quality records. The requirements, however, apply only to original records and not to any copies other than copies taken for security reasons or subcontractor records. There are several types of document used in a quality system and only some are classified as quality records. As quality records are documents it might be assumed that the requirements of clause 4.5 on document and data control apply to quality records. Since 4.16 is not cross referenced in clause 4.5, there is clearly no requirement for you to apply the requirements for document control to quality records. (See also Part 2 Chapter 5.) Figure 5.2 illustrates the difference between quality records and documents.

The requirements in element 4.16 are linked with other elements of the standard even when there is no cross reference. This relationship is illustrated in Figure 16.1.

Types of quality records

The standard requires that *quality records be maintained to demonstrate conformance to specified requirements and the effective operation of the quality system.*

But what are quality records, you may ask? If we put all the references to clause 4.16 together we get a list of 21 quality records:

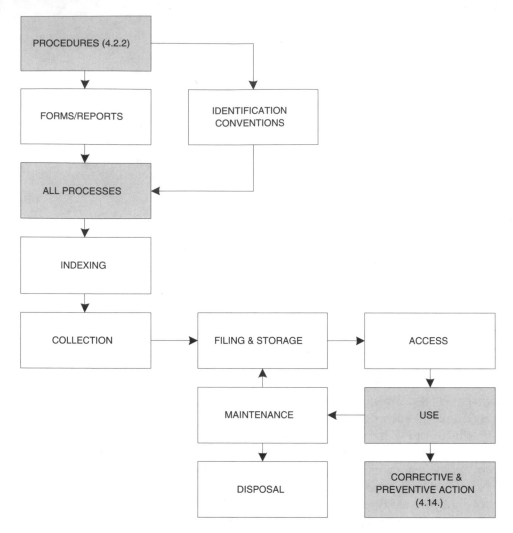

Figure 16.1 Element relationships with the quality records element

- Management review records (clause 4.1.3)
- Contract review records (clause 4.3)
- Design review records (clause 4.4.5)
- Design verification measures (clause 4.4.7)
- Process/product change implementation records (clause 4.5.2)
- Records of acceptable subcontractors (clause 4.6.2)
- Records of unsuitable customer supplied products (clause 4.7)
- Product identification records (clause 4.8)
- Qualified process records (clause 4.9)
- Qualified equipment records (clause 4.9)

- Qualified personnel records (clause 4.9)
- Positive recall records (clause 4.10.2.3)
- Inspection and test records (clause 4.10.5)
- Verification records for test hardware and test software (clause 4.11.1)
- Calibration records (clause 4.4.11.2)
- Nonconformance records (clause 4.13.2)
- Nonconformance investigation records (clause 4.14.2)
- Subcontract quality records (clause 4.16)
- Audit result records (clause 4.17)
- Follow-up audit records (clause 4.17)
- Training records (clause 4.18)

These are the minimum number of records to be created and maintained. There are a further seven quality records which a scan of the standard will reveal, although there is no cross reference to clause 4.16.

- Calibration status identification record (clause 4.11.2)
- Procedure change records (clause 4.14.1)
- Subcontractor surveillance records (clause 4.6.2)
- PPAP waiver records (clauses 4.4.9 and 4.13.4)
- Tooling record (clause 4.16)
- Returned part analysis records (clause 4.14.2)
- Production part approval records (Section II 1.1)

Although records are mentioned in clause 4.1.2.1 this clause deals with responsibilities and authority and contains no requirements to generate any records.

These lists tell us something about the nature of quality records, especially by what is not included. Absent from the lists are policies, procedures, instructions, plans, specifications, and any other prescriptive documents. The records all have one thing in common: they describe the results of some activity, the results of inspections, tests, reviews, audits, assessments, calculations etc. and hence are descriptive documents. However, these lists are dominated by records relating to product quality rather than to the operations of the quality system. In addition to audit records, the following records may need to be maintained to demonstrate the effectiveness of the quality system:

- Customer complaints
- Warranty claims
- Failure analysis reports
- Process capability studies

- Service reports

- Concessions

- Change requests

- Subcontractor assessments

- Performance analysis

- Deviations and waivers

- Modification records

- Contract change records

- Quality cost data

It is advisable to identify all your quality records within your procedures. This will then avoid arguments on what is or is not a quality record, because once you have chosen to identify a record as a quality record you have invoked all the requirements that are addressed in this chapter. Any document which describes the achieved features and characteristics of a product or service are quality records. Also those records which will demonstrate that work has been planned, organized, resourced, monitored, verified, and corrected when found deficient are quality records. The note following the requirement acknowledges that quality records can be in hard copy or held on a computer disk or magnetic tape. Should both forms be held, you will need to declare which are the masters and then provide the appropriate security to prevent inadvertent loss or damage (see below).

Identification of quality records

The standard requires the supplier to *establish and maintain documented procedures for the identification of quality records*.

Whatever the records they should carry some identification so that you can determine what they are, what kind of information they record and what they relate to. A simple way of doing this is to give each record a reference number and a name or title.

Records can take various forms: reports containing narrative, computer data, forms containing data in boxes, graphs, tables, lists, and many others. Where forms are used to collect data, they should carry a form number and name as their identification. When completed they should carry a serial number to give each a separate identity. Records should also be traceable to the product or service they represent and this can be achieved either within the reference number or separately, providing the chance of mistaken identity is eliminated. The standard does not require records to be identifiable to the product involved but unless you do make such provision you will not be able to access the pertinent records or demonstrate conformance to specified requirements.

Collection of quality records

The standard requires the supplier to *establish and maintain documented procedures for the collection of quality records*.

In order to demonstrate the achievement of quality and the effectiveness of the quality system, records will need to be gathered in from the locations where they were produced. This is more than a convenience since you will be unable to analyze all the data efficiently unless you have it in front of you. If you are lucky enough to operate a computer network and all the data is available on the network, then data collection is a simple affair. However, many organizations still rely on paper records and so you will need a means of enabling such records to be either submitted to the analysis points or collected from source. To facilitate the collection of records you will need to insert submission or collection instructions in the relevant procedures which specify the records.

Indexing of quality records

The standard requires the supplier to *establish and maintain procedures for the indexing of quality records*.

This is a similar requirement to that concerned with the identification of quality records but it serves a different purpose. You will need a means of ensuring that you have all the records that have been produced and that none are missing or, if they are, you know the reason. A simple means of indexing quality records is to create and maintain registers listing the records in numerical order as reference or serial numbers are allocated. The records could be filed in sequence so that you can easily detect if any are missing, or you can file the records elsewhere, providing your registers or your procedures identify the location.

Access to quality records

The standard requires the supplier to *establish and maintain procedures for the access of quality records*.

This new requirement supplements that for records to be readily retrievable but in addition implies a further requirement for security of records. After addressing the filing and storage requirements, you need to ensure that the records are accessible to those who will need to use them. This applies not only to current records but to those in the archive and any "insurance copies" you may have stored away. A balance has to be attained between security of the records and their accessibility. You may need to consider those who work outside normal working hours and those rare occasions when the trouble shooters are working late, perhaps away from base with their only contact via a computer link. As implied above, access has two meanings, one allowing access and the other prohibiting access. If your records are held on a computer database, then password protection may be necessary. If they are held in a locked room or filing cabinet then you need to nominate certain persons as key holders and ensure that these people can be contacted in an emergency. Your procedures should define how you provide and prohibit access to the records.

Filing quality records

The standard requires the supplier to *establish and maintain documented procedures for the filing of quality records.*

The requirement for filing quality records is linked to the indexing requirement. You should know where to find your quality records so that you can retrieve them when needed. They will be needed to demonstrate compliance with the standard to an assessor or to a customer and they will be needed to carry out the corrective action and management review requirements. One method is to create a filing system that allocates file locations to certain types of documents. Remember, these records are not personal property or the property of a particular department; they belong to the organization and are a record of the organization's performance. Such records should not be stored in personal files. The filing system you create should therefore be integrated with the organization's main filing system and the file location should either be specified in the procedure which defines the record or in a general filing procedure. However, don't state the room number, otherwise your procedures will become difficult to maintain if you move offices often.

If you operate a computerized records system, then filing will be somewhat different although the principles are the same as for paper records. Computerized records need to be located in named directories for ease of retrieval and the locations identified in the procedures.

Storage of quality records

The standard requires the supplier to *establish and maintain documented procedures for the storage of quality records* and in addition requires *quality records to be stored in facilities that provide a suitable environment to prevent damage or deterioration and to prevent loss.*

Linked to the filing and indexing requirement, this requirement addresses the conditions of storage and also provides the reasons: i.e. to prevent loss. On the subject of loss, you will need to consider loss by fire, theft, and unauthorized removal. If using computers you will also need to consider loss through computer viruses and unauthorized access, deletion, or the corruption of files. A booking in/out system should be used for completed records when they are in storage, in order to prevent unauthorized removal.

Records soon grow into a mass of paper and occupy valuable floor space. To overcome this problem you may choose to microfilm the records but keep them in the same location or archive them in some remote location. In both cases you need to control the process and the conditions of storage. With paper archives you will need to maintain records of what is where, and if the archive is under the control of another group inside or outside the organization, you will need adequate controls to prevent loss of identity and inadvertent destruction.

It is always risky to keep only one copy of a document. If computer generated, you can easily make another copy provided you always save it, but if manually generated, its loss can be very costly. It is therefore prudent to produce additional copies of critical records as an insurance against their inadvertent loss. These "insurance copies" should be stored in a remote location under the control of the same authority that controls the original records. Insurance copies of computer disks should also be kept in case of problems with the hard disk or file server, if you use one.

Maintenance of quality records

The standard requires the supplier to *establish and maintain procedures for the maintenance of quality records*. In addition it requires *records to be retained in such a way that they are readily retrievable and legible*.

There are three types of maintenance regarding quality records:

- Keeping records up to date

- Keeping the information in the records up to date

- Keeping the records in good condition

Some records are designed to collect data as they pass through the process and need to be promptly updated with current information. Remember:

> ■ **The job isn't done until the paperwork is complete.**

The filing provisions you have made should enable your records to be readily retrievable; however, you need to maintain your files if the stored information is to be of any use. In practice, records will collect at the place they are created and unless promptly removed to secure files may be mislaid, lost, or inadvertently destroyed. Once complete, quality records should not be changed. If they are subsequently found inaccurate, new records should be created. Alterations to records should be prohibited as they bring into doubt the validity of any certification or authentication as no one will know whether the alteration was made before or after the records were authenticated.

In the event that alterations are unavoidable due to time or economic reasons, then errors should be struck through so that the original wording can still be read, and the new data added and endorsed by the certifying authority.

Records, especially those used in workshop environments, can become soiled and so provisions should be made to protect them against attack by lubricants, dust, oil, and other materials which may render them unusable. Plastic wallets can provide adequate protection while records remain in use.

Disposition of quality records

The standard requires the supplier to *establish and maintain documented procedures for the disposition of quality records*.

Disposition in this context means the disposal of records once their useful life has ended. The requirement is therefore a little ambiguous particularly as there is also a requirement on the retention of records; however, retention times are one thing and disposal procedures quite another.

As said previously, records are the property of the organization and not personal property so their destruction should be controlled. The controls should ensure that records are not destroyed without prior authorization and, depending on the medium on which data is recorded and the security classification of the data, you may also have to specify the method of disposal. The management would not be pleased to read details in the national press of the organization's performance, collected from a waste disposal site by a zealous newspaper reporter.

Demonstrating conformance to specified requirements

The standard requires that *quality records be maintained to demonstrate conformance to specified requirements*.

The impact of this requirement depends upon what constitutes the specified requirements. The standard does not require you to demonstrate conformance with every requirement of QS-9000. However, if your customer has invoked QS-9000 in the contract then this clause requires that you maintain sufficient records to demonstrate compliance. As stated elsewhere in this book, there is no definition clarifying what specified requirements are. Therefore, if they are all the requirements that you have specified in your quality system, your plans, specifications etc., then this requirement is the most onerous in the standard. A pragmatic approach to take is to declare in your quality manual that the "specified requirements" are "specified customer requirements".

Demonstrating the effective operation of the quality system

The standard requires that *quality records be maintained to demonstrate the effective operation of the quality system.*

One can demonstrate the effective operation of the quality system in several ways:

* By examination of customer feedback

* By examination of quality system audit results

* By examination of the management review records

* By examination of quality cost data

Showing records that every requirement of the standard has been met will not, however, demonstrate that the system is effective. You may have met the requirement but not carried out the right tasks or made the right decisions. The effectiveness of the quality system should be judged by how well it fulfills its purpose (see Part 1 Chapters 1 & 4 and Part 2 Chapters 2 & 17). There is in fact no requirement for you to do this and while it may seem that this is the purpose of the requirement, if this was the case it would be clearly stated as such. Some assessors may quote this requirement when finding that you have not recorded a particular activity that is addressed in the standard. They are not only mistaken but attempting to impose an unnecessary burden on companies, which will be perceived as bureaucratic nonsense. One can demonstrate the effectiveness of the system simply by producing and examining one or more of the above records.

Pertinent subcontractor quality records

The standard requires that *pertinent subcontractor quality records be an element of these data.*

The subcontractor records that are delivered to you should form part of your records. However, the controls you can exercise over your subcontractor's quality records are somewhat limited. You have a right to the records you have paid for but no more unless you invoke the requirements of this clause of the standard in your subcontract. Your rights will probably only extend to your subcontractor's records being made available for your inspection on their premises so you will not be able to take away copies. It is also likely that any subcontractor records you do receive are copies and not originals. Before placing the contract you will need to assess what records you will require to be delivered and what records the contractor should produce and retain.

Retention of quality records

The standard requires *the retention times of quality records to be established and recorded* and QS-9000 adds retention times for the following specific records:

- Production part approval records

- Tooling records

- Purchase orders and amendments

- Control charts

- Inspection and test results

- Internal quality audit records

- Management review records

- Superseded parts documents

It is important that records are not destroyed before their useful life is over. There are several factors to consider when determining the retention time for quality records:

- *The duration of the contract.* Some records are only of value while the contract is in force.

- *The life of the product.* Access to the records will probably not be needed for some considerable time, possibly long after the contract has closed. On defence contracts the contractor has to keep records for up to 20 years and for product liability purposes, in the worst case situation (taking account of appeals), you could be asked to produce records up to 17 years after you made the product.

- *The period between quality system assessments.* Assessors may wish to see evidence that corrective actions from the last assessment were taken. If the period of assessment is three years and you dispose of the evidence after two years, you will have some difficulty in convincing the assessor that you corrected the deficiency.

You will also need to take account of the subcontractor records and ensure adequate retention times are invoked in the contract.

The way the record retention requirements are phrased implies that records must not be retained after the specified time; however, the additional requirement that the retention periods are to be considered "minimums" does allow suppliers to dispose of the records any time after the end of the specified period. Whilst the IASG argue that records have to be disposed of eventually to comply, the timescale is open ended.

The purchase orders referred to can be both customer and supplier purchase orders. However it would have been more clear had the requirement stipulated contracts and purchase orders since the term purchase order is not used in clause 4.3.2 on contract review. Although the requirement for retention of purchase orders is placed in element 4.16, they are not in fact "quality records" but "specifications". The same applies to the copies of documents from superseded parts.

The retention times for production records depends upon when supply of the part ceases. The definition in QS-9000 states that a part remains active until tooling scrap authorization is given or when written authorization to deactivate the part is given from the customer.

Where you actually specify the retention times can present a problem. If you specify it in a general procedure you are likely to want to prescribe a single figure, say five years for all records. However, this may cause storage problems and so it may be more appropriate to specify the retention times in the procedures that describe the records. In this way you can be selective.

Superseded parts data

The standard requires *copies of documents from superseded parts required for new parts qualification to be retained in the new part file*.

Where a new part supersedes an existing part, evidence from the qualification tests on the old part may be used to qualify the new part and justify not repeating the tests. If all that has changed is the part number or some other cosmetic feature, then use of the old data would be justified. However there has to be a new part file and this would be incomplete without the qualification test data so copies of the superseded part documents need to be retained in the new part file. The only ambiguity is where the new part is subject to full qualification tests making the old part test data invalid. In such cases a reference to the old part file would suffice.

You will also need a means of determining when the retention time has expired so that if necessary you can dispose of the records. The retention time doesn't mean that you must dispose of the records when the time expires, only that you must retain the records for at least that period. Records will need to be dated, the files which contain the records dated and, if stored in an archive, the shelves or drawers dated. It is for this reason that all documents should carry a date of origin and this requirement needs to be specified in the procedures that describe the records. A simple method is to store the records in bins which carry the date of disposal, if you can rely on the selection process.

While the requirement applies only to quality records, retention times are also necessary for many other documents since one cannot demonstrate you have or had operations under control without specifications, plans, procedures etc. You may also need to retain tools, jigs, fixtures, test software, in fact anything that is needed to repair or reproduce equipment in order to honor your long-term commitments.

Availability of quality records

The standard requires *quality records to be made available for evaluation by the customer or his representative for an agreed period, where agreed contractually*.

Providing you adopt the methods described previously, any records required by your customer will be available, easily retrievable and in good condition. Should the customer specify a retention period greater than what you prescribe in your procedures, then special provisions will need to be made and this is a potential area of risk. Customers may choose not to specify a particular time and require you to seek approval before destruction. Any contract which requires you to do something different creates a problem in conveying the requirements to those who are to carry them out. The simple solution is to persuade your customer to accept your policy. You may not want to change your procedures for one contract and so if you can't change the contract, the only alternative is to issue special instructions. You may be better off storing the records in a special contract store away from the normal storage area or alternatively attach special labels to the files to alert the people looking after the archives.

Quality records procedures

The standard requires that the supplier *establish and maintain procedures covering quality records* and from the foregoing, it should be clear what they need to address.

You may only need one procedure which covers all the requirements but it is often not practical. The provisions you make for specific quality records should be included in the procedures for controlling the activity being recorded. For example, provisions for inspection records should be included in the inspection procedures, provisions for design review records should be included in the design review procedure. Within such procedures you should provide the forms, or content requirements for the records, the identification, collection/submission provisions, the indexing and filing provisions. It may be more practical to cover the storage, disposal, and retention provisions in separate procedures since they may not be type-dependent. Where each department retains its own records, these provisions may vary and so warrant separate procedures.

Authentication of records

Apart from inspection and test records (clause 4.10.5), the standard does not require records to be authenticated, certified, or validated. A set of results without being endorsed with the signature of the person who captured them lacks credibility. Facts that have been obtained by whatever means should be certified for four reasons:

- It provides a means of tracing the result to the originator in the event of problems.

- It indicates that the provider believes them to be correct.

- It enables you to verify whether the originator was appropriately qualified.

- It gives the results credibility.

If the records are generated by computer and retained in computerized form, a means needs to be provided for the results to be authenticated.

Task list

1 Identify all the records that demonstrate the achievement of quality.

2 Identify all the records that demonstrate the effectiveness of the quality system.

3 Give each record a name and a reference number, and completed forms a serial number.

4 Create and maintain registers for allocation of reference numbers and serial numbers.

5 Quote the product/service identification number on all related records.

6 Include record collection or submission provisions in your procedures.

7 Introduce file references for containing records.

8 Take "insurance copies" of all important records.

9 Introduce computer virus controls.

10 Provide means by which authorized staff can access records outside normal working hours.

11 Restrict access to records held on computer disk or tape.

12 Introduce booking in and out systems for files and records in storage.

13 Control storage conditions of paper, microfilm, and computerized records.

14 Introduce filing disciplines, clean desk policies etc.

15 Provide plastic wallets for records that may become soiled in use.

16 Introduce a disposal procedure for documentation.

17 Introduce standard clauses for insertion into subcontracts on quality records.

18 Specify retention times for quality records in the related procedures.

19 Store records by disposal date.

20 Provide a means of varying the retention times for specific customers.

Quality records questionnaire

1 In which document do you identify the records which demonstrate conformance to specified requirements?

2 In which documents do you identify the records which demonstrate the effective operation of the quality system?

3 How do you identify your quality records?

4 How do you collect your quality records?

5 How do you index your quality records?

6 How do you provide and prevent access to quality records?

7 How do you file your quality records?

8 How do you store your quality records?

9 How do you maintain your quality records?

10 How do you dispose of your quality records?

11 How do you ensure that pertinent subcontractor quality records are maintained?

12 How do you ensure that all quality records remain legible?

13 How do you ensure that quality records are readily retrievable?

14 How do you ensure that quality records are stored in facilities that provide a suitable environment that minimizes deterioration, damage and prevents loss?

15 In which documents do you record the retention times of quality records?

Do's and don'ts

*   Don't retain boxes of forms that serve no purpose.

*   Don't permit unauthorized deletions on certified records.

*   Don't permit the unauthorized design of record blanks.

*   Don't change record blanks without authorized changes to the related procedure.

*   Don't leave records lying about.

*   Don't archive uncompleted records.

*   Don't lose track of where records are stored.

*   Don't forget to transfer records to their new owners.

*   Do ensure someone is made responsible for maintaining each type of record.

*   Do record all product and process acceptance decisions.

*   Do record all changes to the quality system.

*   Do record all changes to design, products, processes, and measuring devices.

*   Do ensure all records are dated.

*   Do record the date on which new documents and changes become effective.

*   Do test new records for their fitness for use before general release.

*   Do denote the issue status on record blanks.

Chapter 17

Internal quality audits

Scope of requirements

The requirements for internal audits apply to audits of the quality system, including the policies, practices, products, and services to which the quality system relates. They are not limited to audits of procedures. In order to determine whether the quality system is effective in maintaining control, you have to check that the resultant products and services meet the specified requirements and that prescribed quality objectives are being achieved. If the products and services are not meeting the specified requirements, or the prescribed objectives are not being achieved, then something is clearly amiss with the quality system. The requirements do not apply to audits of suppliers or subcontractors since they are covered in clause 4.6 of the standard.

The purpose of quality audits is to establish, by an unbiased means, factual information on quality performance. Quality audits are the measurement component of the quality system. Having established a quality system it is necessary to install measures that will inform management whether the system is being effective. Installing any system without some means of verifying whether it is doing the job it is intended to do is a waste of time and effort. This is why the internal audit requirement is so important. Audits gather facts, they should not change the performance of what is being measured and should always be performed by someone who has no responsibility for what is being measured. Audits should not be performed to find faults, to apportion blame or to investigate problems, other techniques should be used for this purpose. Far more detailed guidance appears in ISO 10011 Parts 1, 2 & 3; all that is addressed in this chapter are the specific requirements of QS-9000.

The requirements in element 4.17 are linked with other elements of the standard even when there is no cross reference. This relationship is illustrated in Figure 17.1.

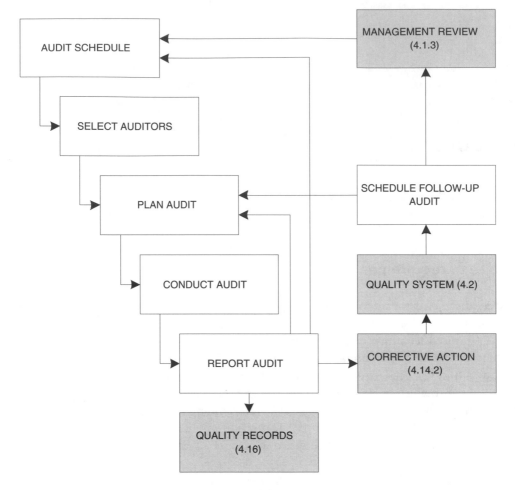

Figure 17.1 Element relationships with the internal quality audits element

Audit procedures

The standard requires the supplier to *establish and maintain documented procedures for planning and implementing internal quality audits.*

The standard requires procedures for both planning and implementing audits and these should cover the following:

*   Preparing the annual audit program

*   The selection of auditors and team leader if necessary

*   Planning audits of each type

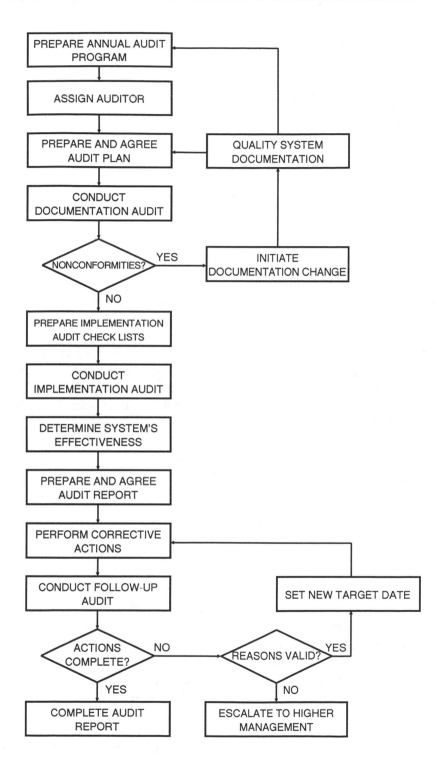

Figure 17.2 The quality system audit process

- Conducting the audit

- Recording observations

- Determining corrective actions

- Reporting audit findings

- Implementing corrective actions

- Confirming the effectiveness of corrective actions

- The forms on which you plan the audit

- The forms on which you record the observations and corrective actions

- Any warning notices you send out of impending audits, overdue corrective actions, escalation actions

The system audit process is shown in Figure 17.2. Certain activities such as the opening and closing meeting have been omitted for clarity since they are not always needed for internal audits. The product audit process would be somewhat different but the principles would be the same. Further guidance on the conduct of audits can be found in Appendix C.

The audit program

The standard requires audits to be planned but does not specify whether it is the system which should be planned or whether it is individual audits that should be planned. The overall plan is in fact a program since this should have dates on which the audits are to be conducted. There is no requirement for audits to be comprehensive; however, planned audits may not be comprehensive and comprehensive audits may not be planned, so there is a need to ensure that the audit program covers all aspects of the quality system in all areas in which it is employed. The coverage of the audit program should be designed so that it obtains sufficient confidence in operations to be able to declare that the system is effective. There may be a need for different types of audit programs depending on whether the audits are of the quality system, processes, products or services. The audit program should be presented as a calendar chart showing where and when the audits will take place.

All audits should be conducted against a standard for the performance being measured. Examinations without such a standard are surveys and not audits. Audits can also be conducted against contracts, project plans, specifications, in fact any document with which the organization has declared it will comply.

An audit of one procedure or requirement in the standard in one area will not be conclusive evidence of compliance if the same procedures and requirements are also applicable to other areas. Where operations are under different managers but performing similar functions you cannot rely on the evidence from one area, as management style, commitment, and priorities will differ. In order to ensure that your audit program is comprehensive you will need to draw up a matrix showing what policies, procedures, standards etc. apply to which areas of the organization. One audit per year covering 10% of the quality system in 10% of the organization is hardly comprehensive. However, there are cases where such an approach is valid. If sufficient confidence has been acquired after conducting a comprehensive series of audits over some time, the audit program can be adjusted so that it targets only those areas where change is most likely, auditing other areas less frequently.

Procedures will contain many provisions, not all of which may be susceptible to verification at the time of the audit, either due to time constraints or because work for which the provisions do apply has not been scheduled. It is therefore necessary to record which aspects have or have not been audited and engineer the program so that over a one to three year cycle all procedures and all requirements are audited in all areas at least once.

Planning quality audits

The detail plan for each audit may have dates if it is to cover several days but the main substance of the plan will be what is to be audited, against what requirements and by whom. At the detail level, the specific requirements to be checked should be identified based upon risks, past performance, and when it was last checked. Overall plans are best presented as program charts and detail plans as check lists. Audit planning should not be taken lightly. Audits require effort from auditees as well as the auditor so a well-planned audit designed to discover pertinent facts quickly is far better than a rambling audit which jumps from area to area looking at this or that without any direction.

Check lists, while being a plan, should only be an aid so as to allow the auditor to follow trails that may lead to the discovery of pertinent facts. However, there is little point in drawing up a check list then putting it aside. The check list should represent the minimum aspects to be checked so that following the audit you have evidence that indicates:

- Which activities were compliant

- Which activities did not comply

- Which activities were not checked

Verifying compliance with planned arrangements

The standard requires the supplier to *carry out audits to verify whether quality activities and related results comply with planned arrangements*.

The term *quality activities* is not defined in ISO 8402 and while it may seem obvious it can create confusion. If we list all the activities which can affect quality then we could say that these are all quality activities. But many of these are also design, purchasing, manufacturing, and installing activities. Can they also be quality activities? Quality activities are not restricted to the activities of the quality department or other similar departments. The only clue in the standard as to what quality activities are is in clause 4.1.2.1 where it requires the responsibility of all personnel who manage, perform, and verify work affecting quality to be defined. So a quality activity is any activity that affects the ability of a product or service to satisfy stated or implied needs.

The related results are the results produced by implementing the policies and procedures. They include documents, decisions, products, and services. It is not enough for internal audits to verify that procedures are being followed. They have to verify whether the outputs of these procedures comply with the prescribed requirements.

Planned arrangements is another unusual term, especially when throughout the standard the terms *documented quality system* and *documented procedures* have been used. However, so that audits are not restricted to documented procedures and policies, the term planned arrangement has been used. It encompasses contracts, specifications, plans, objectives, strategies, in fact any arrangement made by the organization to satisfy customer needs. You therefore need to define what constitutes your planned arrangements.

QS-9000 requires that *the working environment be considered in the audit process*. The environment is defined in QS-9000 as all of the process conditions surrounding or affecting the manufacture and quality of a part or product. On the face of it, this limits the environment to that affecting the product. However, there are aspects which directly affect the product such as handling, cleanliness, temperature etc. and those that indirectly affect the product such as lighting, housekeeping, ventilation etc. If the personnel cannot see, or become dizzy through fumes, then the product may be damaged or nonconforming product may be released. If personnel could be injured and blood drip onto the product then obviously this needs to be prevented. The methods used to provide a safe and suitable working environment should be a part of your planned arrangements and be included in your audit check lists.

The requirement tends to limit the working environment to manufacturing areas but the working environment in the marketing, design, purchasing, quality assurance departments may have an indirect affect on product quality if we take into account noise, housekeeping, staff attitude, and management style. It is difficult to concentrate and make sound decisions when the working area is noisy and other colleagues cause distraction.

Audits can take several forms:

- The System Audit: to verify that the quality system complies with the appropriate part of QS-9000. The system audit is a composite of a documentation audit and implementation audit (see below).

- The Strategic Quality Audit: to verify that the strategic plans of the organization address specified legal, environmental, safety, and market quality requirements.

- The Policy Audit: to verify that the documented policies promulgate the requirements of the standard and the objectives of the business.

- The Organization Audit: to verify that the organization is equipped and resourced to implement the policies and achieve the stated objectives.

- The Documentation Audit: to verify that the documented practices implement the approved policies and the relevant requirements of the standard.

- The Implementation Audit: to verify that the documented practices are being followed and that there are no undocumented practices employed that affect quality. This can be divided into two parts, one addressing upper management and their implementation of the strategic plans and one addressing staff and their implementation of the procedures.

- The Process Audit: to verify that the result-producing processes control products and service within the defined limits.

- The Product or Service Audit: to verify that the resultant products and services meet the prescribed requirements.

Determining the effectiveness of the system

The standard requires the supplier to *carry out audits to determine the effectiveness of the system.*

Even when you have verified that policies are being met, procedures are implementing policies and procedures being implemented etc., you need a means of determining whether the system is being effective. You could be doing everything you say you will do but still not be satisfying customers.

The requirement is also somewhat duplicated in clause 4.1.3 on management reviews. You are required to conduct management reviews to ensure quality system effectiveness and conduct internal quality audits to determine the effectiveness of the system. It would appear that the audit collects the evidence and the review ensures that it is collected.

There are two dimensions to effectiveness: the results gained by measuring effectiveness and the effectiveness of the method used to determine the results. There are several methods which can be used to determine the effectiveness of the quality system:

- Quality audit
- Performance monitoring
- Quality costing
- Customer surveys

Management should not be surprised by what customers are saying about them. They should know how good their products and services are and how well they satisfy customer needs. Part of this confidence should come from the quality audit. Audits should be providing management with knowledge they don't possess, not telling them what they already know as a fact. The audit and not the customer should be the first to reveal problems. If audits only report historical facts they are ineffective. If having conducted an audit, problems are later revealed which were clearly present when the audit was conducted, then the audit has not been effective or if subsequent audits reveal facts that should have been detected during previous audits then measures should be taken to adjust the auditing method or the audit plan.

Effectiveness is concerned with doing the right things rather than with doing things right. So if the system enabled management to stop the development of products for which there was no requirement, discover a potential safety problem, anticipate customer needs ahead of the competition, cut waste by 50%, successfully defend a product liability claim, meet all the delivery targets agreed with the customer, then you would probably say that the system was pretty effective. If on the other hand the system allowed the shipment of defective products every day, lost one in three customers, allowed the development of unsafe products to reach the market, or the failure of a revolutionary power plant, you would probably say that the system was pretty ineffective. So the first thing you have to do is establish what you want the quality system to do. Because without a yardstick as a measure, you can't determine whether the system is effective or not. Many systems are only designed to meet the standard with the result that you can deliver defective product providing you also deliver some which are not defective. The standard cannot and should not tell you what targets to meet; that is why you need to define your quality objectives (see Part 2 Chapter 1) and use performance monitoring as a means of determining whether these objectives are being achieved. One measure of quality is the cost of nonconformance.

In order to discover whether you are doing the right things a measure of the distribution of effort would help. If you were spending 50% of the effort on appraisal and corrective activities then clearly your operations are not effective or efficient. Quality costs can help reveal this data and while it should not be used as a measure of absolute costs, it does help in determining whether there have been improvements if you take measurements before and after the introduction of change. So while not a requirement, it can be argued that quality costs should be used as one of the methods of determining the effectiveness of the quality system.

Scheduling quality audits

The standard requires the supplier to *schedule audits on the basis of the status and importance of the activity*.

Status of the activity

Status has three meanings in this context: the first to do with the relative position of the activity in the scheme of things, the second to do with the maturity of the activities and the third to do with the performance of activities. There is little point in conducting in-depth audits on activities that add least value. There is also little point auditing activities that have only just commenced. You need objective evidence of compliance and that may take some time to be collected. Where the results of previous audits have revealed a higher than average performance in any area (such as zero nonconformities on more than two occasions), the frequency of audits may be reduced. However, where the results indicate a lower than average performance (such as a much higher than average number of nonconformities), the frequency of audits should be increased.

Importance of the activity

On the importance of the activity, you have to establish to whom is it important: to the customer, the managing director, the public, your immediate superior? You also need to establish the importance of the activity upon the effect of noncompliance with the planned arrangements. For example, not ordering the correct grade of steel may only delay fabrication if you are lucky but if not detected in time may result in the component failing in service. Getting the purchase specification correct is important so this activity should be audited.

Importance also applies to what may appear minor decisions in the planning or design phase. If such decisions are incorrect they could result in major problems downstream. Getting the decimal place wrong or the units of measure wrong can have severe consequences if not detected. Audits should verify that the appropriate controls are in place to detect such errors before it is too late.

Previously on the subject of the comprehensiveness of audits it was suggested that you ensure all procedures and policies are verified in all areas at least once every one to three years. The status and importance of the activities will determine whether the audit is once a month, once a year or left for three years.

The independence of auditors

The standard requires that *internal quality audits be carried out by personnel independent of those having direct responsibility for the activity being audited.*

By being independent of the audited activities, the auditor is unaware of the pressures, the excuses, the informal instructions handed down and can examine operations objectively without bias and without fear of reprisals. It is for this reason that the auditor should have no direct responsibility for the work being audited.

To ensure their independence, auditors need not be placed in separate organizations. Although it is quite common for quality auditors to reside in a quality department it is by no means essential. There are several solutions:

* Auditors can be from the same department as the activities being audited, provided they are not responsible for the activities being audited.

* Separate independent quality audit departments could be set up, staffed with trained auditors.

* Implementation audits could be carried out by trained line personnel supervised by an experienced quality auditor.

You can show compliance with this requirement by defining where the auditors fit into the organization by means of an organization chart and by giving position titles in the reports of the audit.

As internal audits can comprise documentation audits, implementation audits, product audits, process audits etc., it is not necessary to train everyone assigned to carry out audits in the auditing techniques defined in ISO 10011. This is one of the ambiguities in the series of standards. The term quality audit is defined in such a way that it encompasses all types of audit and yet ISO 10011 only applies to quality system audits where the objective evidence is obtained through interviewing personnel. When conducting product audits knowledge and skill in reading specifications, planning tests, setting up and operating test and measuring equipment is more relevant. In fact the audits may well be carried out by an accredited test laboratory.

Reporting the results of audits

The standard requires the *results of the audits to be recorded and brought to the attention of the personnel having responsibility in the area audited*.

The results of audits of practice against procedure or policy should be recorded as they are observed and you can either do this in note form to be written up later or directly onto observation forms especially designed for the purpose. Some auditors prefer to fill in the forms after the audit and others during the audit. The weakness with the former approach is that there may be some dispute as to the facts if presented some time later. It is therefore safer to get the auditee's endorsement to the facts at the time they are observed. In other types of audits there may not be an auditee present. Audits of procedure against policy can be carried out at a desk. You can check whether the documents of the quality system satisfy all the clauses of the standard at a desk without walking around the site, but you can't check whether the system is documented unless you examine the operations in practice. There may be many activities which make the system work that are not documented.

The audit report should state the results of the audit, what was found compliant as well as what was found noncompliant.

As the use of computer networks become more widespread, auditing the practice against procedure will be possible without leaving your desk and can be carried out without the auditee knowing.

Whichever the approach, the report should be presented to the manager of the area audited; if several managers are affected, then it should also be presented to the manager above them. Audit reports should not be issued to a person's manager without their knowledge and agreement.

Taking timely corrective action

The standard requires *the management personnel responsible for the area to take timely corrective action on the deficiencies found by the audit*.

Unless the auditee is someone with responsibility for taking the corrective action, the auditee's manager should determine the corrective actions required. If the action required is outside that manager's responsibility, the manager and not the auditor should seek out the appropriate authority and secure a corrective action proposal. Your policy manual should stipulate management's responsibility for taking timely corrective action and define what timely means. Timely to one person may be untimely to another. The standard should require timely and effective corrective action and that is more likely to yield the right result. The standard does not actually require that corrective actions be proposed and target dates set for their completion. Even clause

4.14 does not require corrective action proposals to be recorded. In reality there are three actions which the manager responsible should take:

- Remedial action to correct the particular nonconformity

- Research for other examples of nonconformity and to establish how widespread the problem is

- Establish the root cause of the nonconformity and prevent its recurrence

A proposed corrective action may not remove the noncompliance, it may be a palliative leaving the problem to recur again at some future time. Target dates should be agreed for all corrective actions and the dates should be met as evidence of commitment. Assessors will search your records for this evidence so impress on your managers the importance of honoring their commitments. The target dates also have to match the magnitude of the deficiencies. Small deficiencies which can be corrected in minutes should be dealt with at the time of the audit otherwise they will linger on as sores and show a lack of discipline. Others which may take 10-15 minutes should be dealt with within a day or so. Big problems may need months to resolve and an orchestrated program to implement. The corrective action in all cases if implemented should remove the problem, i.e. restore compliance. A corrective action should not be limited to generating another form as it can be rejected by another manager, thereby leaving the deficiency unresolved.

Follow-up audits

The standard requires that *follow-up audit activities record the implementation and effectiveness of the corrective action taken*.

The standard does not in fact require follow-up audits but clearly if follow-up action is necessary to verify any corrective actions that have been taken, it should do two things: verify that the agreed action has been taken and verify that the original nonconformity has been eliminated. Follow-up audits may be carried out immediately after the planned completion date of the corrective action or at some other agreed time. However, unless the audit is carried out relatively close to the agreed completion date, it will not be possible to ascertain if the action was timely.

The auditor who carries out the follow-up audit need not be the same as carried out the initial audit. In fact there is some merit in using different auditors in order to calibrate the auditors.

When all the agreed nonconformities have been eliminated the audit report can be closed. The audit remains incomplete until all actions have been verified as being completed. Should any corrective action not be carried out by the agreed date then the auditor needs to make a judgment as to whether it is reasonable to set a new date or to escalate the slippage to higher management. For minor problems, when there are more urgent priorities facing the managers, setting a new date may be prudent. However, you should not do this more than once. Not meeting the agreed completion date is indicative either of a lack of commitment or incompetent estimating and both indicate that there is a more deep-rooted problem to be resolved.

Task list

1   Decide on the scope of the audit program.

2   Produce an annual audit program.

3   Devise a method of determining when parts of the system were last audited.

4   Decide on the types of audits to be conducted and the level of staff to conduct them.

5   Determine the standards against which the organization is to be audited.

6   Train your quality auditors to a defined standard and train sufficient auditors to enable your program to be met.

7   Use auditing as a means of familiarizing staff with the operations of the organization.

8   Allocate trained auditors to the program.

9   Plan individual audits.

10   Produce audit procedures that cover products, processes, and organizations.

11   Provide forms for recording observations, recommendations, and corrective actions.

12   Conduct the audits to the defined plan and procedure with a clear objective.

13   Record the results of audits, both noncompliances and compliances.

14   Devise a means of tracking the status of corrective actions.

15   Provide a means for linking the corrective actions arising from audits to documentation changes, organization changes, process changes, design changes etc.

16 Assess audit data periodically and determine the effectiveness of auditing.

17 Provide for changing audit methods and training should auditing be not as effective as expected.

18 Create check-lists for assisting in following an audit trail through a department or process.

19 Audit your procedures immediately following their issue as a means of testing their auditability.

20 Conduct a system audit at least once a year to verify that the system is still intact and compliant with the standard.

Internal quality audits questionnaire

1 In which documents have you defined your procedures for planning and implementing internal quality audits?

2 How do you verify whether quality activities and related results comply with planned arrangements?

3 How do you determine the effectiveness of the quality system?

4 Which documents constitute the internal quality audit plans?

5 How do you ensure that audits are scheduled on the basis of the status and importance of the activity to be audited?

6 How do you ensure that all audits are carried out by personnel independent of those having responsibility for the activities audited?

7 In which documents are the results of quality audits recorded?

8 How do you ensure that the results of audits are brought to the attention of the personnel having responsibility in the area being audited?

9 How do you ensure that management personnel responsible for the area audited take timely corrective action on deficiencies found by the audit?

10 How do you verify the effectiveness of any corrective actions taken?

Do's and don'ts

* Don't limit the scope of your audit program to the procedures.

* Do select your auditors carefully.

* Don't use aggressive staff for auditing.

* Don't persist in enforcing compliance with trivia.

* Do adjust the audit program to cover aspects that have attracted management attention.

* Don't audit for the sake of it – define your objective and make it important enough for management to take notice of the results.

* Do keep a log of audits and a log of corrective action reports.

* Don't go into an area unannounced – always give advanced warning.

* Do explain the purpose and objectives of the audit to the manager before you commence.

* Do review the relevant documents before you audit operations.

* Do follow audit trails to discover facts and don't break the trail until you have uncovered the facts.

* Do check downstream of the operation being audited to gather facts on its effectiveness.

* Do be helpful to the auditee, don't argue but don't accept everything at face value.

* Don't be critical of anyone's work or how they operate.

* Do listen to what the auditee and his or her manager say.

* Don't leave the scene of the audit without obtaining agreement to corrective actions and either setting a target date for their completion or agreeing on a date by which the target date will be set.

* Do act professionally, be courteous, tactful, and diplomatic, and avoid nit picking.

* Do establish whether your audit objective has been achieved before completing the audit.

* Do reduce the frequency of audits if you have confidence in a particular area.

* Don't copy the audit report to anyone other than the auditee's manager without the manager's consent.

Chapter 18

Training

Scope of requirements

The specification, achievement, control, and assurance of quality requires personnel who are competent to carry out these tasks and although this clause of the standard only addresses training, it is adequate training rather than qualifications that will give personnel the skills they need. ISO 9004 identifies qualifications and motivation as well as training as key factors in achieving quality. Qualifications are often prerequisites for certain jobs but without training in the particular jobs in which they are engaged, personnel will not yield their full potential. Qualifications impart knowledge, whereas training imparts skills. However, without the right motivation any amount of qualifications and training will be wasted. Motivation is not something one can make mandatory. It is a function of the working environment, the management style and behavior. However, one can motivate staff by enabling them to have control over their performance. These requirements apply to all personnel performing activities that can affect the quality of the products or services supplied. They include personnel in management, design, purchasing, producing operations, installation, verification, servicing, auditing, and packing, in fact any activity that requires skill to perform well. They do not apply to the training of customers or users in the operation of equipment or services provided by the supplier. This is the customer's/user's responsibility.

The requirements in element 4.18 are linked with other elements of the standard even when there is no cross reference. This relationship is illustrated in Figure 18.1.

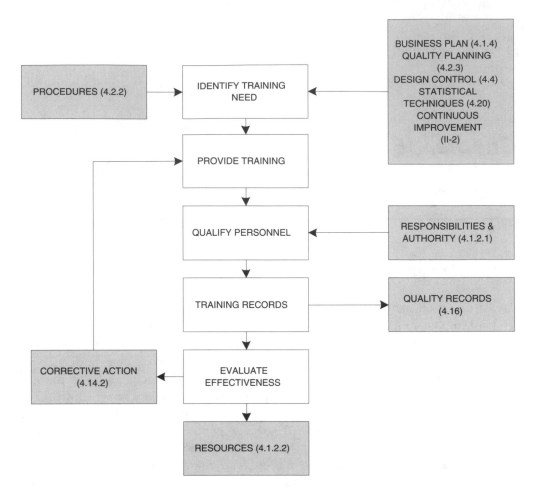

Figure 18.1 Element relationships with the training element

Training as a strategic issue

The standard requires *training to be viewed as a strategic issue affecting all of the supplier's personnel*.

It is not uncommon to find organizations only training operational staff and not managers. Also, training as a formal activity is often only executed when the need is obvious such as when new technology is introduced. Training is therefore sometimes viewed as a tactical issue and not a strategic issue. As a strategic issue, training would feature in the business plan as a means to move the company forward towards new goals. However, there is a gray area between training and education. Training imparts skills and education imparts knowledge but one cannot practically undergo training without prior knowledge so the two are often delivered together. If you treat training and education as one and the same, then it will become apparent that all employees will require training at sometime or other.

No improvement comes about without change in some parameters of the business. It is futile to set goals tougher than last year without considering what has to be changed to meet them. Sometimes the changes will be in technology, in product design, in procedures, in attitudes and behavior but all will require people to do differently tomorrow what they did yesterday. To demonstrate you are in fact viewing training as a strategic issue, the CEO and executive managers will need to show how they have prepared their resources to meet the identified goals. One such item of preparation is the training and education of the people concerned. Company wide initiatives require company wide training programs with the necessary budgets approved by the executive managers. The CEO will need to show that the training has not been limited to operators but extends to all managers including the CEO.

Identifying training needs

The standard requires the supplier to *establish and maintain documented procedures for identifying training needs*.

Training should not be carried out just because a training course is available. Training is expensive and should be directed at meeting specific needs. Training needs can be identified in two ways: as requirements for training and as a plan for providing the required training. Requirements for training arise in several ways:

- In job specifications

- In process specifications, maintenance specifications, operating instructions etc.

- In development plans for introducing new technologies

- In project plans for introducing new equipment, services, operations etc.

- In marketing plans for launching into new markets, new countries, new products and services

- In contracts where the customer will only permit trained personnel to operate customer owned equipment

- In corporate plans covering new legislation, sales, marketing, quality management etc.

- From an analysis of nonconformances, customer complaints, and other problems

- In developing design skills (4.4.2), problem solving skills (4.14.1), statistical skills (4.20.2)

The procedures that govern these activities should include provisions for training. As a minimum they should specify the skills and knowledge required of a person carrying

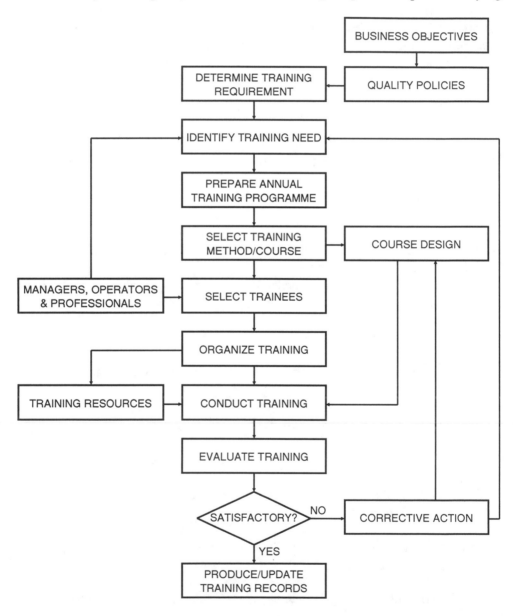

Figure 18.2 The training function

out the activities and where necessary the examination criteria for judging that the person has acquired an adequate level of proficiency. The training process is outlined in Figure 18.2 and shows that training needs arise out of business objectives and quality policy.

While not specified in the standard, the requirement for identifying training needs has two dimensions: new training needs and retraining needs. Retraining should be identified by assessing the effectiveness of training and on the recency of training, and then scheduling the appropriate courses.

Once the training requirements have been specified, managers should plan the training needed by their staff. This requires a training plan. Although the standard doesn't specifically require a training plan, without one you may have difficulty demonstrating that you have identified the training needs. All plans must serve an objective. You train people for a purpose: to give them skills which you want them to have. The skills required must be specified in the first place. You could have several training plans each covering a different subject. Technical training could be separate from managerial training and professional training separate from manual skill training. Each manager should plan for the training of his or her own staff so there may be department training plans, divisional training plans, company training plans etc.

The training plans should identify the person responsible for coordinating the training, the type of training, the organization that will deliver the training, the course material to be provided, examination and certification arrangements, the venue, the dates of the courses, and the attendees.

It is interesting to note that the only procedures required are for identifying training needs and not for designing training courses, conducting training or maintaining records.

This clause does not require suppliers to establish procedures for identifying personnel certification requirements. While unnecessary in most situations, personnel certification is necessary for special processes (see Part 2 Chapter 9). Certification would also be necessary for teachers, lecturers, and other personnel upon whose judgment the determination of quality depends.

Providing for training

The standard requires the supplier to *provide for the training of all personnel performing activities affecting quality*.

This requirement can be rather onerous especially if your staff have not had any training that can be demonstrated. Much training is carried out "on the job". A person learns a trade or profession by practice and experience as well as by formal training.

It can be assumed that the supplier need only provide that training which has been identified and not all training a person needs to do the job, since it is likely that the individual will have received training of some form before starting with the organization. You will need evidence of such previous training either by copies of training certificates or signed application forms declaring the training the individual claims to have received. Periodic staff appraisal should thereafter be used to assess the adequacy of a person's skills and knowledge and identify the need for retraining or re-assignment of tasks as appropriate.

Training often requires tools, equipment or other aids on which the student may develop skills: skills needed to operate or maintain the equipment. Where such equipment is provided you need to ensure that:

- It is representative of the equipment that is in operational service.

- It adequately simulates the range of operations of the service equipment.

- It is designated as training equipment and only used for that purpose.

- Records are maintained indicating the serviceability of the equipment and its design standard, including records of repairs and modifications.

Students undertaking training may inadvertently damage the equipment. It may also be necessary to simulate or inject fault conditions so as to teach diagnostic skills. Training activities may degrade the performance, reliability, and safety of the training equipment and so it should be subject to inspection before and after training exercises. The degree of inspection required will depend on whether the equipment has been designated for use only as training equipment or whether it will be used either as test equipment or to provide operational spares. If it is to be used as test or operational equipment then it will need to be re-certified after each training session. During the training sessions records will need to be maintained of any fault conditions injected, parts removed and any other act that may invalidate the verification status of the equipment. In some cases it may be necessary to refurbish the equipment and subject it to the full range of acceptance tests and inspections before its serviceability can be assured. Certification can only be maintained while the equipment remains under controlled conditions. As soon as it passes into a state where uncontrolled activities are being carried out, its certification is immediately invalidated. It is for such reasons that it is often more economical to allocate equipment solely for training purposes.

Qualification of personnel

The standard requires that *personnel performing specific assigned tasks be qualified on the basis of appropriate education, training and/or experience, as required.*

This requirement is somewhat vague as it does not define what a specific assigned task is. Any task assigned to an individual could be a specific assigned task: window cleaning, typing, fitting, managing, designing etc. Within organizations some staff are appointed to particular positions that are unique in the organization and others perform jobs that are common within a particular group. So the window cleaning, typing, and fitting jobs are not specifically assigned whereas the manager, and sometimes the designer, is assigned a specific task unique to themselves. Such personnel make judgments upon which the determination of quality depends and so they should be qualified to make such judgments. You will need to maintain documentary evidence that these personnel have the necessary education, training, and experience to carry out the tasks assigned to them. This is where job specification can help. For each of these positions, not the individuals but the position they occupy, you should produce a job specification which specifies the requirements an individual must meet to occupy this position. It should include academic qualifications, training, and experience requirements, as well as personal characteristics, so that in recruiting for the position, you have a specification with which to compare candidates.

Evaluation of training effectiveness

The standard requires *the effectiveness of training to be periodically evaluated.*

The flow chart in Figure 18.1 clearly shows that an evaluation of the effectiveness of training is necessary for control of the training function, but how do you do it?

There are three parts to the evaluation:

* An evaluation of the training course or training activity immediately on completion

* An evaluation of the training received weeks after the training

* An evaluation of the skills developed months after the training

Training course evaluation (the initial stage)

The evaluation of the course by the students is not very effective since it is not evaluating what they have learnt. However, it can produce opportunities for improvement in the training courses. If running in-house training courses this can be most beneficial but with external courses it only helps you decide whether to use that course again. If the course has an examination then this is a measure of the effectiveness of training but it depends on the type of examination. A written examination for a practical course does not test skill. It tests knowledge and more often it is a test of memory and so is ineffective as a training metric. The most common cause of failure in any examination is a failure to read the question asked but there could be many reasons why someone failed that are not indicative of the quality of the training course or the instructor.

Training effectiveness – short term (the intermediate stage)

Once the student returns to work, it is important that the skills and knowledge learnt are put to good effect. A lapse of weeks or months before the skills are used will certainly reduce effectiveness, in fact little or no knowledge or skill may have been retained. Training is not about doing it once and once only. Training is about doing it several times and frequently. One never forgets how to ride a bicycle or drive a car regardless of the period between doing it, because the skill was embedded through prolonged training and use immediately afterwards. Therefore to ensure effectiveness of training you have to put the person into work that requires the skills. Management should ensure that all staff undergoing training are given the opportunity to practice their skills following training The person's supervisor should then examine his/her performance through sampling work pieces, reading documents he/she produces, and observing the person doing the job. The method you use depends upon the skills being used. If you have experts in the particular skills then in addition to appraisals by the supervisor, the expert should also appraise the person's performance.

Training effectiveness – long term (the final stage)

After several months doing a job and applying the new skills, the trainee will acquire techniques and habits. The techniques may show not only that the skills have been learnt but they are now being developed through self training. The habits may indicate that some essential aspects of the training had not been understood and that some reorientation is necessary. It is also likely that the person may have regressed to the old way of doing things and this may be due to matters outside of his/her control. The environment in which people work and the attitudes of the people they work with can have both a motivating and demotivating effect on an individual. Again the supervisor should observe the trainee's performance and engage the expert to calibrate his judgment. If the regression is significant some retraining may be necessary as well as looking at the cause and dealing with this.

Periodic evaluation

Once the skills have been acquired through evidence of a person's performance, the supervisor can revert to the annual appraisal of performance and identify retraining needs through that process.

Maintaining training records

The standard requires the supplier to *maintain appropriate records of training*.

Whenever any training is carried out you should record on the individual's personal file details of the course taken, the dates, duration, and exam results if one was taken. Copies of the certificate should be retained on file as evidence of training. You may find it useful to issue each individual with a personal training log, but do not rely on this being maintained or retained by the person. Often training records are held at some distance away from an individual's place of work and in certain cases, especially for certificated personnel performing special processes, individuals should carry some identification of their proficiency so as to avoid conflict if challenged.

Records of training should include records of formal training where the individual attends a training course and on-the-job training where the individual is given instruction while performing the job. The records should indicate whether the prescribed level of competence has been attained. This is often not indicated for formal training unless there is an examination at the end of the course. In such cases, such formal training needs to be followed by on-the-job examination. The records should also indicate who has conducted the training and there should be evidence that this person or organization has been assessed as competent to deliver the training.

Training records should contain evidence that the effectiveness of training given has been evaluated and this may be accomplished by a signature and date from the supervisor against the three stages of evaluation – initial, intermediate, final.

Periodically, training records should be reviewed to identify gaps and the recency of training so as to give retraining if the time lapse is too great to be a reliable indication of competence.

You will need two types of training records: those records relating to a particular individual and those relating to particular activities. The former is used to identify an individual's competence and the latter to select trained competent people or to check the competence of those who have performed particular activities. Those trained in particular skills should be entered on a list so as to provide a means for managers to select staff for given assignments. In some cases, selection of the right person for the job may have to be performed as jobs arise, such as in maintenance.

Task list

1 Identify jobs that require particular skills.

2 Document the training requirements for specific jobs.

3 Produce and maintain training plans to implement the training requirements.

4 Implement only that training defined in the training plans.

5 Monitor the effectiveness of training.

6 Maintain personal records of training.

7 Maintain skill or activity based records of training.

8 Review training records periodically to identify retraining.

9 Make skill records available to managers on site.

10 Identify equipment used for training purposes.

11 Provide procedures for controlling the standard of training equipment.

12 Prepare procedure for evaluating the effectiveness of training and recording the results.

Training questionnaire

1 How do you identify training needs?

2 How do you ensure that personnel performing specific assigned tasks are qualified on the basis of appropriate education, training, and/or experience?

3 How do you ensure that training is provided for all personnel performing work affecting quality?

4 How do you evaluate the effectiveness of training and how often is the evaluation performed?

5 In what documents do you record the training provided?

Do's and don'ts

* Don't specify that training is required if it cannot be provided.

* Don't assign personnel to tasks for which you have specified training requirements unless the personnel are appropriately trained.

* Don't rely on a person's own training records.

* Do keep central records of staff training.

* Do provide managers with ready access to staff training records.

* Do provide a certificate to every person who has received specific training.

* Do ensure that any training equipment is of a representative standard before training commences.

* Don't use training equipment for operational purposes unless it is certified to current design standards before operational use.

* Do assign people to jobs in which they can exercise the skills they have acquired from recent training.

* Don't base your evaluation of training effectiveness on the course evaluation – nothing could be further from the truth.

Chapter 19

Servicing

Scope of requirements

Servicing is an activity that primarily applies to manufactured products. One services a motor car, a washing machine, or a photocopier. However, servicing is a post-delivery activity and can also include after-sales service, product support, help lines, customer service and enquiry desks etc. The term is not defined in ISO 8042; however, traditionally the term to *service* means to replenish consumables needed to keep an item in operating condition. Servicing is also not a term that is used in the quality loop of ISO 9004. The only activity which comes between installation and operation and disposal is "technical assistance and maintenance". If you carry out the type of servicing defined above then compliance with this clause of QS-9000 is a relatively simple affair. If on the other hand you provide technical assistance or carry out maintenance, repair, product support, logistics support, or any other post-delivery activity the interpretation of these requirements presents a problem. Apart from the word "servicing" this clause conveys nothing which is not covered elsewhere in the standard. Note that your servicing operations also have to comply with the requirements of clause 4.9. You will also note that this requirement only applies when servicing is a specified requirement. The standard does not state which party may have specified it or where it may be specified. If technical assistance or maintenance is specified rather than servicing, it would appear that you do not strictly have to document your technical assistance and maintenance activities.

Servicing is a specified requirement when the contract requires you to service the products provided. If the contract does not require you to service your products or support the servicing of your products by others, then element 4.19 does not apply. On the other hand, if your core process is servicing and your contract is for servicing only then you cannot ignore the other elements of the standard, you have to apply all of them that are relevant, but the core of your business is covered by 4.9 on process control.

You may provide services to your customer such as an installation service, a technical support service, a laboratory service, diagnostic service, or customer training etc. These are services and not servicing and should be addressed as activities governed by elements 4.1 through 4.18 and 4.20.

If servicing in its broader sense is concerned with keeping an item in operating condition, it follows that to do so must also include restoring an item to an operating condition should malfunction or failure be found. As with the motor car undergoing a 10 000 mile service, if the timing is out, the mechanic corrects it so that the vehicle is restored to an operating condition.

Servicing then becomes much more than the replenishment of consumables and involves design of the service, design and use of the tools, design and use of measuring, handling, and test equipment, purchasing of spares and consumables, preventive and corrective maintenance.

The requirements in element 4.19 are linked with other elements of the standard even when there is no cross reference. This relationship is illustrated in Figure 19.1.

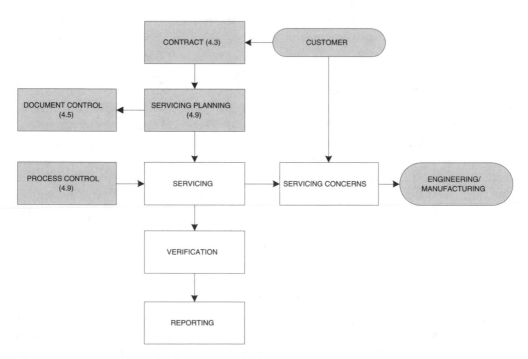

Figure 19.1 Element relationships with the servicing element

Performing servicing

Where servicing is a specified requirement the standard requires the supplier to *establish and maintain documented procedures for performing these services.*

Applying the definition to servicing as in ISO 9004, servicing procedures would need to cover the following:

- Design and validation of special purpose tools and equipment

- Control of measuring and test equipment

- Supply and verification of installation instructions

- Supply and verification of assembly instructions

- Supply and verification of commissioning instructions

- Supply and verification of operating instructions

- Supply and verification of spare parts lists

- Supply and verification of servicing instructions

- Logistics support service covering technical assistance, supply of spares, servicing

ISO 9001 covers the design, purchasing, handling, and measuring equipment activities in the appropriate clauses and QS-9000 covers preventive and corrective maintenance in 4.9. To provide adequate procedures for maintenance you will need to:

- Define maintenance requirements covering what is to be maintained, by whom, and to what depth.

- Define service restoration instructions covering the actions required to restore equipment or facilities into service, including restoration and response times. This is usually first line maintenance and may not require any repair action.

- Define maintenance instructions stating the performance parameters to be maintained, the frequency of maintenance, how it is to be conducted, the action to be taken in the event of failure, the procedures to be followed in carrying out repairs and the training required of those performing the maintenance tasks.

- Define spares schedules listing the spares by identification number, manufacturer, and quantity required on site to maintain the specified service availability.

- Produce or acquire handbooks that detail the equipment to be maintained and procedures on fault finding, repair, and verification after repair.

A typical maintenance function in an organization that services operational units is illustrated in Figure 19.2.

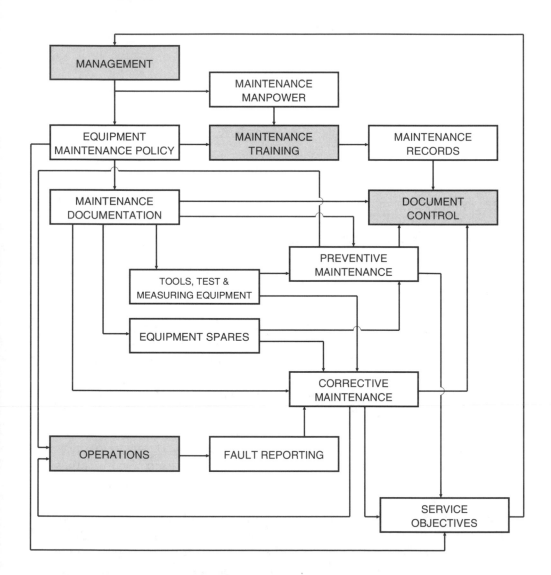

Figure 19.2 The maintenance function

If your operation is such that your after-sales service consists of technical assistance, then to provide adequate procedures for technical assistance you will need to:

- Specify the service in terms of its scope, what is included, what is excluded, response times, the action in the event of a complaint etc.

- Define operating procedures covering the receipt and recording of calls or letters, their acknowledgment and who to route them to for action.

- Provide technical support covering problem logs, actions taken, advice given, promises made, and details of follow-up on the product or service.

- Establish a complaints procedure covering the recording, investigation, and resolution of complaints.

Reporting that services meet specified requirements

The standard requires that the supplier *establish and maintain documented procedures for reporting that services meet specified requirements*.

It is of interest to note that no reference is made to clause 4.16 of the standard regarding quality records. The servicing reports therefore are not classed as quality records but are included in the list of documents to be used to detect, analyze, and eliminate potential causes of nonconformities (see clause 4.14.3).

Servicing reports should specify the following as applicable:

- The identity of the product to the service activity

- The date on which the service took place

- The organization responsible for performing the service

- The condition of the product prior to servicing and any running time, mileage, or other indication of life expired

- The specification defining the service or maintenance carried out, quoting the relevant part if not all requirements were verified

- The items exchanged, consumables used, item repaired, adjusted etc.

- The duration of the activity and the name of who performed it

- Details of any inspections and tests carried out to verify serviceability of the item

This information is likely to be recorded at the time the service is carried out and may well be remote from the parent plant, so allowance for this should be made in the procedures. Provision needs to be made for this information to be collected, stored, and any corrective actions taken as a result of unusual trends being detected (see Part 2 Chapter 14).

Verifying that servicing meets specified requirements

Where servicing is specified in the contract, the standard requires the supplier to *establish and maintain documented procedures for verifying that servicing meets specified requirements*.

Whatever your definition of servicing, you will need to verify that you provide the service you say you provide. This can be achieved in several ways.

If your service is maintenance, then you need to monitor the restoration and response times and determine your performance. You will also need to verify that the maintenance performed was effective by monitoring the incidence of recall to fix.

If your service is simply technical assistance then you need to monitor enquiries, complaints, tributes, and problems, their distribution frequency and significance, and the action to be taken to improve performance.

Communication of service concerns

The standard *requires information on service concerns to be communicated to manufacturing, engineering, and design activities*.

Whilst you may not service your products, others may well do so and the standard requires that you collect information generated by the servicing organizations and convey it to those who can use it to improve the product and the manufacturing processes. This means that you will need to establish liaison links with servicing organizations and enlist their support in reporting to you any concerns they have about the serviceability or maintainability of the product, the availability of spare parts, and the usability of the manuals and other information you have provided.

You should set up a common entry point for such data and put in place an evaluation function to convey appropriate data to the manufacturing, engineering, and design activities. A corrective action form or improvement form could be used to convey the data and obtain a written response of the action to be taken. A log of servicing reports would assist in tracking servicing concerns and demonstrate you were making effective use of the data.

Task list

1 Define the service levels that you intend to provide up to and after warranty expires.

2 Define the measures you need to take to honor your obligations to service products supplied to your customers.

3 Provide servicing staff with current instruction manuals for the equipment they are servicing.

4 Create forms for reporting servicing calls, time spent, components changed etc.

5 Set up a mechanism for analysing service reports so as to determine response times, time to repair, and total downtime.

6 Provide a means whereby servicing staff can use the in-house calibration service for their equipment.

7 Train servicing staff in the operation and maintenance of the equipment.

8 Prepare procedures for the receipt, repair, and return into service (or disposal) of components removed by servicing staff.

9 Prepare procedures for collecting, analyzing, and diagnosing servicing concerns.

Servicing questionnaire

This questionnaire is somewhat limited as there are only three specific servicing requirements in the standard. As other parts of the standard apply to servicing you should consult the relevant questionnaires to help establish your policies in this area.

1 How do you ensure that servicing is performed in a way that meets the specified requirements?

2 How do you report servicing activities?

3 How do you ensure that servicing is verified in a way that meets the specified requirements?

4 How do you ensure that information from servicing organizations is collected and used to effect improvement?

Do's and don'ts

* Don't specify levels of service beyond your capability.

* Do allocate adequate resources to provide the specified services.

* Do provide staff with adequate instructions on how to carry out the servicing.

* Do collect data on your servicing performance.

* Do create a means whereby servicing staff can keep abreast of changes in the quality system.

* Do institute a means of controlling servicing documentation and equipment.

Chapter 20

Statistical techniques

Scope of requirements

Statistical techniques can be used for a variety of reasons, from sampling product on receipt to market analysis. Any technique that uses statistical theory to reveal information is a statistical technique, but not all applications of statistics are governed by the requirements of this part of the standard. The only statistical techniques which need control are those used to determine the acceptability of a product or service or the capability of a process that produces the product or service. Any activity where you rely on statistical evidence rather than physical measurement is an activity which should be governed by these requirements. The use of recognized techniques is important to the confidence one has in the result. It is similar to the use of measuring equipment that has been calibrated against known standards of accuracy. Unless you actually check every product, measure every attribute or variable you cannot be 100% certain. But that is costly and you can be 99.99% certain by using statistical techniques; 99.99% may be sufficiently accurate for your needs.

The requirement may not apply to all product acceptance decisions. If your acceptance of the end product does not depend upon acceptance decisions being made on its component parts, then any sampling carried out on receipt inspection or in-process is not important to the product acceptance decision and can therefore be ignored in your documented quality system. This is a wise course of action if you can be sure this will always be the case but if you can't, and more often than not you won't know, it is prudent to encompass all sampling activities in your quality system.

The requirements in element 4.20 are linked with other elements of the standard even when there is no cross reference. This relationship is illustrated in Figure 20.1.

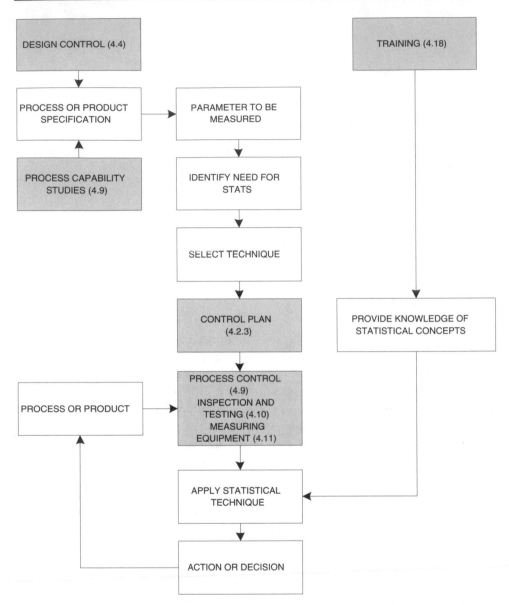

Figure 20.1 Element relationships with the statistical techniques element

Identifying the need for statistical techniques

The standard requires the supplier to *identify the need for statistical techniques required for establishing, controlling and verifying process capability and product characteristics.*

The standard does not require you to use statistical techniques but identify the need for them. Within your procedures you will therefore need a means of determining when statistical techniques will be needed to determine product characteristics and process capability. One way of doing this is to use check lists when preparing customer specifications, design specifications, and verification specifications and procedures. These check lists need to prompt the user to state whether the product characteristics or process capability will be determined using statistical techniques and if so which techniques are to be used.

Techniques for establishing and controlling process capability are essentially the same – the difference lies in what you do with the results. Firstly you need to know if you can make the product or deliver the service in compliance with the agreed specification. For this you need to know if the process is capable of yielding conforming product. Statistical Process Control techniques (SPC) will give you this information. Secondly you need to know if the product or service produced by the process actually meets the requirements. SPC will also provide this information. However, having obtained the results you need the ability to change the process so that all product or service remains within specified limits and this requires either real-time or off-line process monitoring to detect and correct variance. To verify process capability you rerun the analysis periodically using sampling techniques by measuring output product characteristics and establishing that the results demonstrate that the process remains capable.

There are many uses for statistical techniques in establishing and controlling product characteristics.

- A technique for verifying product characteristics is *receipt inspection*, where sampling can be used on large quantities to reduce inspection costs and improve throughput.

- *SPC* is a technique for controlling product characteristics as well as controlling processes.

- A technique for establishing product characteristics is *reliability prediction*, where the reliability targets cannot be measured without testing many hundreds of product over many thousands of hours. (On long production runs of low value items, reliability testing is possible but with one-off systems of high value it is not cost effective and so reliability has to be predicted using statistical techniques.)

- Another technique for establishing product characteristics is *market analysis* where the customer requirements are revealed by market survey and determined by statistical techniques for inclusion in specifications.

- *Design by experiment* is where product characteristics are established by conducting experiments on samples or by mathematical modeling to simulate the effects of certain characteristics and hence determine suitable parameters and limits.

QS-9000 requires these tools *to be determined during the advanced quality planning process and the results included in the Control Plan*. When carrying out the quality planning you will be examining intended product characteristics and it is at this stage that you will need to consider how their achievement is to be measured and what tool or technique is to be used to perform the measurement. A range of statistical techniques is described in the Fundamental Statistical Process Control reference manual so no further discussion is given here. However, this manual only covers SPC. References to other techniques can be found in Appendix C.

Implementing and controlling the application of statistical techniques

The standard requires that the supplier *establish and maintain documented procedures to implement and control the application of statistical techniques*.

Where statistical techniques are used for establishing, controlling, and verifying process capability and product characteristics, procedures need to be produced for each application such that you would have a Process Control Procedure, Process Capability Analysis Procedure, Receipt Inspection Procedure, Reliability Prediction Procedure, Market Analysis Procedure etc. The procedures need to specify when and under what circumstances the techniques should be used and provide detailed instruction on the sample size, collection, sorting, and validation of input data, the plotting of results and application of limits. Guidance will also need to be provided to enable staff to analyze and interpret data, convert data, and plot the relevant charts as well as make the correct decisions from the evidence they have acquired. Where computer programs are employed, they will need to be validated to demonstrate that the results being plotted are accurate, since you may be relying on what the computer tells you rather than on any direct measurement of the product.

Knowledge of basic statistical concepts

The standard requires *basic statistical concepts to be understood throughout the supplier's organization as appropriate*.

The standard does not require that all staff understand statistical concepts, only those appropriate, which means those staff who determine, apply, verify, and audit the techniques. It is not sufficient to train staff only in the techniques they need to use as they need a wider appreciation of the concepts for them to apply them properly. The staff assigned to quality planning need an even wider appreciation of statistical concepts and it is probably useful to have an expert in your company who staff can call upon from time to time. If the primary technique is SPC then you should appoint an SPC Coordinator who can act as mentor and coach to the other operators of SPC techniques.

All managers need a basic appreciation but those in production ought to be able to apply the techniques their staff use so that they can detect when they are not being applied correctly. Auditors need to be able to determine whether the right techniques are being applied and whether the techniques are being applied as directed. Remember that the auditor's task is to determine whether the system is effective, so the ability to detect the use of inappropriate techniques is essential.

Task list

1   Identify product and process acceptance decisions that are based on statistical techniques.

2   Determine and document the statistical theory or national standards used.

3   Provide instructions, charts, and other data to enable staff to use the techniques properly.

4   Review the techniques periodically and revise them if necessary to take advantage of new development in the field.

5   Monitor the effectiveness of the decisions and adjust your rules accordingly.

6   Perform studies in the pre-production period to determine the capability of the manufacturing processes.

7   Perform studies to show that the combination of measurement equipment tolerances or variations and the design tolerances cannot result in non-conforming product.

8   Perform studies to prove the soundness of acceptable quality levels.

Statistical techniques questionnaire

1   How do you identify the need for statistical techniques required for establishing process capability?

2   How do you identify the need for statistical techniques required for controlling and verifying process capability?

3   How do you identify the need for statistical techniques required for establishing product characteristics?

4   How do you identify the need for statistical techniques required for controlling and verifying product characteristics?

5   How do you control the application of identified statistical techniques and ensure training of personnel using them?

6   What documented procedures exist for implementing the identified statistical techniques?

Do's and don'ts

*   Don't rely on statistical techniques unless you have evidence they are valid.

*   Don't claim emphatically that all products meet the specification if conformance is determined by statistical techniques.

*   Do record the basis on which decisions are made if using statistical techniques.

*   Don't flinch results on the borderline, take more samples.

*   Don't derive your sampling plans from unproven statistical methods.

*   Do locate control charts where they will provide use as a nonconformance prevention tool.

Chapter 21

Production part approval

Scope of requirements

The production part approval process (PPAP) is intended to validate that products made from production materials, tools, and processes meet the customer's engineering requirements and that the production process has the potential to produce product meeting these requirements during an actual production run at the quoted production rate.

The process commences following design and process validation during which a production trial run using production standard tooling, subcontractors, materials etc. produces the information needed to make a submission for production part approval. Until approval is granted, shipment of production product will not be authorized. If any of the processes change then a new submission is required and shipment of parts produced to the modified specifications or from modified processes is not authorized until approval is granted.

When one considers the potential risk involved in assembling unapproved products into production vehicles, it is hardly surprising that the Big Three impose such stringent requirements. The process is similar in other industries but more refined and regulated in mass production where the risks are greater.

The requirements for PPAP are defined in Section II of QS-9000. They could just as easily have been defined in clause 4.4 or clause 4.9 of Section I since there is nothing particularly significant about the requirements when viewed against some of the other additional requirements to ISO 9001.

The applicability of PPAP procedures is affected by several factors so definitive solutions cannot be offered. The fundamental requirement is that if you supply product to the Big Three you have to have PPAP procedures in place to gain QS-9000

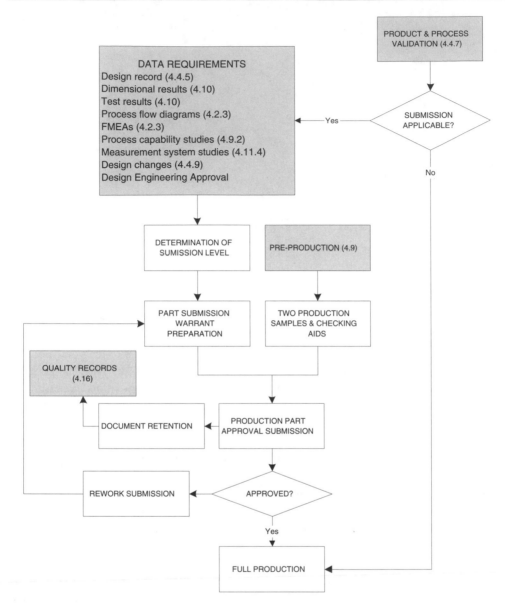

Figure 21.1 Element relationships with the production part approval process element

registration. If you have been supplying parts for some time without PPAP approval then you should confirm with your customer that you may continue to do so.

You may not have to prepare PPAP submissions for all the parts you supply and neither may your subcontractors but there are situations where subcontractor PPAP submissions are required; e.g. GM require PPAP of all commodities supplied by subcontractors to first tier suppliers. The standard does point out that suppliers are responsible for subcontracted material and services so if your submission relies on your subcontractors operating capable processes, then you should be requesting a PPAP submission from them.

The requirements in Section II-1 are linked with other elements of the standard even when there is no cross reference. This relationship is illustrated in Figure 21.1.

Submission requirements

Production part approval submissions are required in several situations: for new parts or products, modified parts and following the correction of a discrepancy on a previously submitted part. Submissions are also required in a number of situations involving changes to the production process, materials, tooling, subcontractors etc. A new submission will be required if production has been inactive for 12 months or more or if shipment has been suspended due to quality problems.

A number of documents are required to be completed for each part according to particular submission levels. The customer will choose the submission level. This will depend upon QS-9000 compliance, quality recognition status, part criticality, previous part submissions, and supplier expertise. There are data retention and data submission requirements but of the 14 documents required all have to be produced for each level. The only difference is that depending on the level, some have to be submitted and others retained and be readily available to customer representatives on request. The documentation required is as follows, none of which would not have been produced by implementing the APQP manual:

- A production part submission warrant – a form that captures essential information about the part and contains a declaration about the samples represented by the warrant

- Appearance approval report – a form that captures essential information about the appearance characteristics of the part

- Design records including specifications, drawings, and CAD/CAM math data

- Engineering change orders not yet incorporated into the design data but embodied in the part

- Dimensional results using a proforma or a marked up print

- Test results

- Process flow diagrams

- Process FMEA

- Design FMEA where applicable

- Control plans

- Process capability study report

- Measurement system analysis report

Whilst the process specifications are to be referenced in the Control Plan and the plan submitted to the customer, there is no requirement for process specifications, re-work/repair procedures to be submitted. In addition the submission does not solely consist of paperwork. Suppliers are required to submit two sample parts and the inspection and test aids specific to the part being submitted (fixtures, models, templates, etc.)

The process

The data on which the PPAP submission is based should be generated during the production trials on a sample size which is usually set by the customer. At this stage the design standard will be relatively stable although some ECOs may not have been incorporated into the drawings. If the results of the preliminary process capability analysis show that further refinement is required to bring the process under statistical control then further samples should be produced until the process capability index meets the requirement. Coupled with the process capability studies is measurement system analysis which has to demonstrate that the measurement system is under statistical control with only common cause variation present.

The objective during the data generation phase is to detect special causes of variation and eliminate them. Once eliminated, the focus needs to be on common cause variation to bring the capability within the specification limits. When this state is achieved, the PPAP submission can be made with confidence.

Chapter 22

Continuous improvement

Scope of requirements

Improvement in business performance is essential for growth and profit, but the QS-9000 requirements are not concerned with your growth and profits, they are concerned with product quality, and one definition of product quality that signals improvement potential is "freedom from defects". Achieving quality becomes a quest to eliminate defects and in so doing reduce variation in the operational processes. However, even when there are no defectives, there will still be variation. One might well question the need to reduce variation when there are no defectives but by reducing variation you will have fewer breakdowns, fewer errors, less space allocated to inventory, less waste etc., in fact fewer problems and increased profit as a result.

This section of QS-9000 deals with improvements in quality that will cause improvements in delivery, lead time, and price. The requirements deal with incremental improvements rather than breakthrough; with improvements by better control rather than improvement by raising standards, although some of the changes made will result in new internal standards being established. These requirements complement those of element 4.14. on corrective and preventive action but differ in fundamental concepts. The improvements are targeted at processes which are already capable and acceptable. These improvements will result in doing better what we already do rather than doing things differently – this is innovation. The standard does not require innovation but continuous improvements are not classed as innovative improvements. Innovations cause a step rise in performance rather than a gradual rise. QS-9000 deals mainly with a gradual rise in performance. Sloan provides an example from the 1920s that, from a product viewpoint, is crucial to survival. "Two factors influence growth. One is the process of continuous product improvement which stimulates consumer demand by providing increasing values for the customer's dollar. The other is growth in the economy and the effect of general economic conditions on the sales

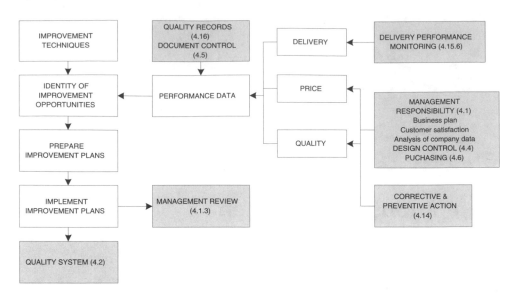

Figure 22.1 Element relationships with the continuous improvement element

of the industry." You can increase value by driving down price as well as introducing innovations in product design.

The requirements in Section II-2 are linked with other elements of the standard even when there is no cross reference. This relationship is illustrated in Figure 22.1.

Deploying a comprehensive continuous improvement philosophy

The standard requires *a comprehensive continuous improvement philosophy to be deployed throughout the organization.*

A philosophy in this context means the system of values by which the organization functions. A continuous improvement philosophy is therefore a system of values which drives the organization to improve its performance continually. (*Continuous* means without breaks or interruption – such as continuous stationery; *continual* means repeated regularly and frequently – a term that fits this concept rather better.)

Improvements in quality

The starting point in building this system of values is self analysis. It is of little use to declare a policy of continual improvement if the will to implement it does not exist. Many organizations are content to meet the specification every time and once achieved believe they have made all the improvement to which resources should be committed There are four questions that each manager should be able to answer:

- Can we make it OK?

- Are we making it OK?

- Have we made it OK?

- Could we make it better?

Meeting the specification every time means that you have obtained satisfactory answers to the first three questions – but why stop there? Could you make it better? Often the answer is "yes" but it will cost a lot of money and after all, why should we want to make it better? Some reasons for pursuing improvement beyond achievement to specification are given in Part 1 Chapter 1 on the subject of quality goals.

The simple answer is therefore, if you won't make it better, someone else will and take business away from you. Making it better does not only mean making better "mouse-traps" by improving the specification, it also means using less resources to make the same mousetrap. Much of the improvement potential does not require large injections of cash. It requires the right attitude – seizing opportunities from observed weaknesses – it requires a change in culture. When your management has the right attitude then and only then can you declare your policy on continual improvement. Cultural changes arise through awareness, experiences, and training that become embedded in the behavioral patterns of the organization. Cultural change requires an understanding of human psychology and requires you to overcome the inertia of the human mind. Whilst human psychology is beyond the scope of this book, a continual improvement philosophy will be evident in your organization when:

- People question the status quo

- Ideas for improvement, no matter how bizarre, are given serious attention

- Resources are allocated to studies which may yield improved performance

- People are not willing to accept the inevitable

- The "good enough is near enough" attitude is outlawed

- People accept constructive criticism of their performance

- There is a desire to excel and not be satisfied with mediocrity

- There is sharing of ideas and information

- There is trust in management, trust in the workers, trust in suppliers, and trust in the customer

- There is a team approach to solving the organization's problems

- There is an absence of fear

- People are empowered to act within mutually agreed boundaries

An excellent treatment of the subject in the context of continuous improvement is given in John Oakland's book *Total Quality Management*.

Once your corporate continual improvement policy is declared, you can then deploy it – spread the gospel to all concerned and teach by example, through your actions and decisions – your new system of values.

Improvement on price

One aspect of these requirements that may cause concern is the requirement for continual improvement on price. Continual improvement on price will need to be documented to demonstrate it is happening. However, the confidentiality of such information will need to be safeguarded as only your customer need know this information. The price charged for products is a function of cost, profit, and what the market will pay. Sometimes price is much higher than cost and in other cases only slightly higher.

Sloan in the early 1930s recognized that management should direct its energies towards increasing earning power through improved effectiveness and reduced expense. This strategy is today being pursued through QS-9000 by requiring improvement on price. In your particular business, it may be profitable to sell some products below cost in order to capture other business where you can make more profit. This will create a force to drive down costs. Remember that if you control change you control cost so the more stable your processes the less they cost.

If you find that you cannot absorb increases in labor and raw material costs, then you may either have to look for alternative approved sources, alternative materials, alternative methods or consider alternative designs. By including price in the improvement formula, it will act as a driving force.

Improvement on timing

One factor given some prominence in the standard is time. Note that in the following clauses timing is emphasized:

- Clause 4.1.5 – prompt solutions to customer related problems

- Clause 4.4.7 – performance activities shall be tracked to monitor timely completion

- Clause 4.5.2 – procedure to ensure the timely review of all customer engineering specifications

- Clause 4.6.2 – suppliers shall require 100% on-time delivery performance from subcontractors

- Clause 4.9 – predictive maintenance methods should include monitoring of uptime

- Clause 4.15.3 – inventory management systems shall optimize turnover time

- Clause 4.15.6 – systems to support 100% on-time shipments to meet customer production and service requirements

- Clause 4.17 – management shall take timely corrective action on deficiencies

- Section II-2.2 – unscheduled downtime

- Section II-2.2 – excessive cycle time

With a developed quality system you can monitor the cycle time for each process and not just the production processes. Often the administration and design processes are a source rich in cycle time improvements such as the time taken to change a document, a design, a policy etc.; the time taken to place an order, arrange a training course, authorize budgets and expenditure etc. Reaction time is also important in servicing, maintenance, customer support etc. You will collect masses of data, do the analysis, show that there is a problem to be solved. How long does it take to get management to react to a situation that requires their attention? There are priorities of course, but question these priorities if you believe they hinder continuous improvement.

Action plans for continuous improvement

The standard requires *specific action plans to be developed for continuous improvement in processes that are most important to the customer.*

Not all your improvement initiatives will need specific action plans. Many initiatives may require action only by local supervision. Where the initiatives require a multidisciplinary approach then formal action plans should be prepared in order to commit each discipline to provision of resources. Although the processes will be under statistical control and capable of yielding product within specification limits, the standard does require that you reduce variation around the target values. Such stability will improve the reliability and durability of equipment, providing of course these target values will deliver optimum performance. Design experiments should enable you to establish whether you have the right target values.

Quality and productivity improvements

The standard requires *opportunities for quality and productivity improvement to be identified and improvement projects implemented*.

Your general aim should be to improve product quality, increase productivity, and reduce the cost of development and manufacture. However, productivity is not easy to measure unless you have one product on one production line. With multiple products on multiple lines each at a different stage of maturity, it makes comparisons to detect changes in productivity difficult, if not impossible.

Opportunities for improvement can be identified by several means:

- Through process and product measurement systems

- Through system audits

- Through customer and supplier surveys

- Through suggestion schemes

- Through research

- Through experiments

- Through benchmarking

The examples given in the standard can all be placed in one or more of the above categories. However, a major source of improvement will arise by analyzing metrics produced using product and process data.

You need an improvement system that causes improvement opportunities to be identified. Relying on chance encounters will not create the conditions needed for continuous improvement. The data that needs to be analyzed will be generated by a particular process and this process governed by particular documented procedures. By placing instructions in these procedures for certain data to be transmitted to your data analysts, you can cause opportunities to be identified. Other opportunities that are less dependent on product or process data may arise from the audit process and particular projects such as benchmarking, customer and supplier surveys.

Productivity improvement may arise from making your standards difficult to achieve but possible to attain, as Sloan remarked. In this way it has the effect of encouraging initiative and resourcefulness and using the capabilities of your personnel. Many improvement opportunities will be identified by those who are eager to seek easier ways of doing things.

Techniques for continuous improvement

The standard requires *knowledge of certain techniques and methodologies for continuous improvement to be demonstrated and those that are appropriate to be used*.

There is no measurable criteria in the standard to judge whether you have sufficient knowledge of these techniques. All staff should know:

* Where to locate the authoritative texts

* What each technique is used for

* The benefits of using each of the techniques

* Who in the organization is the expert on using the technique

Apart from the above only those personnel who use the techniques need have an in-depth understanding and be able to apply the techniques.

The other requirement is to apply the techniques that are appropriate. Appropriate in this context means appropriate to your business and the type of improvement identified. It will therefore be necessary in your improvement plans to indicate which techniques will be used to analyze data, resolve concerns etc. and assign tasks to personnel who have the necessary understanding of the chosen techniques to be able to demonstrate that they are competent to apply them. The techniques listed in the standard are defined in Appendix A.

Chapter 23

Manufacturing capabilities

Scope of requirements

The requirements of this additional element of the standard relate to the development and management of manufacturing capability rather than process capability addressed in element 4.9. The APQP manual addresses the development of particular products whereas the requirements of this element deal with the manufacturing facilities in which these products will be produced. Unless products, processes, and facilities are developed in parallel, the product will be unlikely to reach the market when required. This requires product and process development to proceed simultaneously with facility development and hence the term "simultaneous engineering" or "concurrent engineering" has emerged to optimize the relationship between design and manufacturing functions. It is not a case of designing only those products for which facilities exist, but designing those products that will give you a competitive edge and laying down facilities that will enable you to fulfill that promise.

Omitted from element 4.9 are any requirements on plant design, tool design, material flow, and human factors and these are covered here. In this element are requirements for tool maintenance as well as those addressed in element 4.9 and for mistake proofing which is addressed briefly in clause 4.10.3. The emphasis on manufacturing capability is consistent with the intended application of the standard to sites where production parts are manufactured, which is why the standard does not apply to design centers or test houses.

The requirements in Section II-3 are linked with other elements of the standard even when there is no cross reference. This relationship is illustrated in Figure 23.1.

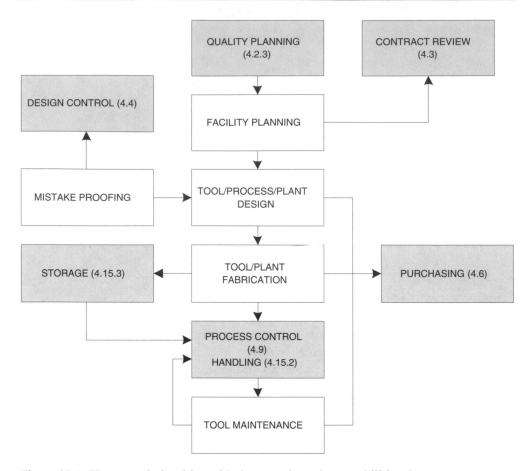

Figure 23.1 Element relationships with the manufacturing capabilities element

Using cross-functional teams for manufacturing capability development

The standard requires *the use of cross-functional teams for developing (manufacturing) facilities, processes, and equipment plans.*

The manufacturing facilities required to produce the product and achieve the production quota, cycle time, and process capability need to be planned, organized, and controlled since it won't happen by chance. Manufacturing facilities need to be designed in conjunction with product design. The characteristics of the process and the process flow will be developed during the product design and development phase with the facilities to realize the product being developed in parallel. The multidisciplinary team therefore needs to consist not only of those concerned with product and process design, but also those concerned with plant and facility design and maintenance. This is illustrated by the list of disciplines given in clause 4.1.2 under *Organizational interfaces*.

Plant and facilities planning

The standard requires *plant layouts to minimize material travel with synchronous material flow with methods for evaluating the effectiveness of existing operations*.

The term *plant* relates to the collection of buildings and equipment designed for a particular industrial purpose, whereas the term *facility* is a smaller collection of machines, equipment, and tools within a plant to facilitate particular operations or processes. Plant design cannot commence until conceptual design of the product and the process flow have been worked out and the planned production targets determined. You need to know what quantities of material and product need to be stored and moved plus the limitations on your current layout and determine whether changes are needed to minimize material travel and handling. This can create some difficult decisions since plant design decisions tend to be long term and cannot be implemented without considerable disruption to existing facilities. This is one advantage of cellular manufacturing where a complete cell can be redesigned without affecting other cells.

You should develop a documented procedure for this planning activity that will ensure the provision of adequate information on which to base plant design decisions. The procedures should provide for a separate development plan with allocation of responsibilities for the various tasks to be undertaken and cover the layout, specification, procurement, installation, and commissioning of the new or revised plant. The procedures should detail your evaluation methods and require consideration to be given to the overall plan of the plant, automation, ergonomics, operator and line balance, inventory levels, and value added labor content. Reports of the evaluation should be required so that they facilitate analysis by management and auditors.

The layout of your plant and facilities should be documented to facilitate its analysis. Detailed installation drawings and commissioning procedures should be prepared in order to ensure completion on time. Dimensions and movement times should be recorded and constraints imposed by handling equipment, safety and environmental regulations registered. The documents should be brought under document control since their revision is necessary whenever the layout is changed. Out of date plans will hinder future planning activities so their maintenance is a preventive action (clause 4.14.3).

During the product design and development phase, the plant and facility engineering staff serving on the multidisciplinary teams should undertake to complete the floor plan check list in Appendix A-5 of the APQP manual.

Mistake proofing

The standard requires *a mistake proofing methodology to be used to address potential sources of nonconformity.*

Mistake proofing is a means to prevent the manufacture or assembly of noncon-forming product. All people make mistakes. Mistakes are inadvertent errors and arise through human fallibility. We all forget things occasionally and we can either make things mistake proof so that they can only be performed one way or provide signals to remind us of what we should be doing. The terms foolproofing and Poka-Yoke (coined by Shigeo Shinto) are also used to describe the same concepts.

Mistake proofing can be effected by product design features so that the possibility of incorrect assembly, operation, or handling is avoided. In such cases the requirements for mistake proofing need to form part of the design input requirements for the part. The Design FMEA should be analyzed to reveal features that present a certain risk that can be contained by redesign with mistake proofing features.

Mistake proofing can also be effected by process design features such as sensors to check the set-up before processing, audible signals to remind operators to do various things. However, signals to operators are not exactly mistake proof; only mechanisms that prevent operations commencing until the right conditions have been set are proof against mistakes. In cases where computer data entry routines are used, mistake proofing can be built into the software such that the operator is prompted to make decisions before irreversible actions are undertaken.

In both cases the Design FMEA and Process FMEA should be analyzed to reveal features that present a certain risk that can be contained by redesign with mistake proofing features.

Provision of tool design, fabrication, and inspection resources

The standard requires *appropriate technical resources for tool and gage design, fabrication, and inspection to be provided.*

Element 4.9 requires the use of suitable production equipment and the approval of processes and equipment. Nowhere in ISO 9001 does it require you to design tools, or if you do design tools, that you need to control such activities. ISO 9001 imposes minimum controls which ensure that (in the case of tools) the right tool is selected and the selected tools are approved. In the automobile industry, the nature of the parts is such that special tools will inevitably be needed. Apart from general purpose cutting tools, hand tools, and gages, most of the shaping, forming, pressing, molding tools and inspection gages etc. will need to be especially designed and fabricated. This will probably require a tool design office where the tools, jigs, fixtures, and gages are designed and a toolroom where they are manufactured and inspected.

An item is a tool when it comes into contact with the part and produces a change to the part. Other items that do not perform this function are governed by the requirements of Section II clause 3.1.

Control of tooling is extremely important as in some cases you are reliant on the contour of the tool to form the part and cannot check the part economically. In such cases it is simpler to check the tool for wear providing you do so often enough to detect wear before it produces a nonconforming part.

Appropriate technical resources in this context means that you need to possess the necessary competence to design and make the tools you need and/or you need the ability to control any subcontractors you employ to do this work for you. You need appropriate numbers of staff to do the job, equipped with design and manufacturing resources that enable them to deliver effective tools when needed by the project team. Tooling engineers should serve as members of the multidisciplinary teams during the product design and development phase and undertake completion of the tooling checklist in Appendix A-3 to the APQP manual. They should also evaluate the DFMEA and PFMEA for opportunities for introducing mistake proofing measures.

Identification of customer owned tooling

The standard requires that *customer owned tooling be permanently marked so that ownership of each item is visually apparent.*

The reason for this provision is to safeguard customer supplied product. Whilst element 4.7 deals with the controls to be applied to customer supplied product, there is no requirement for specific identification and of course element 4.7 only relates to the product, not the support equipment. A cross reference in element 4.7 to this clause would help. Permanent marking should be applied by the customer before delivery of the tools. However, if permanent marking is not applied, then you have to apply it. Indenting the tool with markings may be an option but clear it with the customer first. Alternatively you can attach, through mechanical means, a metal label embossed or indented with the part number, version, and customer name. Make the name stand out so that there is no doubt as to whom the tool belongs.

Tooling management

The standard requires *a system for tooling management to be established and implemented*.

As stated in other parts of this book, when the standard requires a system to be established it means set up on a permanent basis, planned, documented, organized, and controlled. The tooling management system is a subsystem of the quality system so all the common elements apply, such as document control, corrective/preventive action, records, training etc.

Certain tools are perishable; that is, they are consumed during the process. Others are reusable after maintenance and this is where adequate controls need to be in place. The system needs to cover tool selection, set-up, tool change, and tool maintenance. You will need procedures for withdrawing maintainable tools from service, performing the maintenance, and then putting the tools back into service. Quite simple really, but you need to build in safeguards that prevent worn tools being used and to replenish tools when their useful life has expired.

If you do subcontract tool maintenance then you need to keep track of assignments so that you are not without vital tools when you need them.

Appendix A

Glossary of terms

This appendix contains a glossary of over 100 common and uncommon terms and phrases used in the ISO 9000 series of standards. It contains many terms and phrases not defined in ISO 8402 or ANSI/ASQC A3. Many terms are defined in QS-9000 and the five reference manuals and in general have not been repeated here. However, some alternative definitions are provided for clarification. The explanations are given for the context in which the terms are used.

Acceptance criteria
The standard against which a comparison is made to judge conformance.

Activities affecting quality
Any activity which affects the determination of product or service features and characteristics, their specification, achievement, or verification or means to plan organize, control, assure, or improve them.

Adequate
Suitable for the purpose. The term "adequate" appears several times in the standard allowing the assessor to vary the criteria for adequacy and hence not use a finite process to verify that the requirements have been met.

Adequacy audit
An audit carried out to establish that the quality system documentation adequately addresses the requirements of a prescribed standard; also referred to as a *documentation audit*.

Accreditation
A process by which organizations are authorized to conduct certification of conformity to prescribed standards.

Appropriate	Appropriate means "appropriate to the circumstances" and requires knowledge of these circumstances. Without criteria, an assessor is left to decide what is or is not appropriate.
Approved	Confirmed as meeting the requirements.
Assessment	The act of determining the extent of compliance with requirements.
Assurance	Evidence (verbal or written) that gives confidence that something will or will not happen or has or has not happened.
Audit	An examination of records or activities to verify their accuracy, usually by someone other than the person responsible for them.
Authority	The right to take actions and make decisions.
Authorized	A permit to do something or use something which may not necessarily be approved.
Benchmarking	A technique for measuring an organization's products, services, and operations against those of its competitors, resulting in a search for best practice that will lead to superior performance.
Calibrate	To standardize the quantities of a measuring instrument.
Capability index C_p	The capability index for a stable process defined as the quotient of tolerance width and process capability where process capability is the 6σ range of a process's inherent variation.
Capability index C_{pk}	The capability index which accounts for process centering for a stable process using the minimum upper or lower capability index.
Capability index P_{pk}	The performance index which accounts for process centering and defined as the minimum of the upper or lower specification limit minus the average value divided by 3σ.
Certification	A process by which a product, process, person, or organization is deemed to meet specified requirements.

Certification body	See *Registrar*.
Clause of the standard	A numbered paragraph or subsection of the standard containing one or more related requirements, such as 4.10.3. Note that each item in a list is also a clause. (See also *Quality system element*.)
Codes	A systematically arranged and comprehensive collection of rules, regulations, or principles.
Commitment	An obligation a person or organization undertakes to fulfill i.e. doing what you say you will do.
Comparative reference	A standard used to determine differences between it and another entity.
Compliance audit	See *Implementation audit*.
Concession	Permission granted by an acceptance authority to supply product or service that does not meet the prescribed requirements. (Note: the term *waiver* is used in the USA and has the same meaning.)
Concurrent engineering	See *Simultaneous engineering*.
Conformance audit	See *Implementation audit*.
Conforms to specified requirements	Meets the requirements that have been specified by the customer or the market.
Contract	An agreement formally executed by both customer and supplier (enforceable by law) which requires performance of services or delivery of products at a cost to the customer in accordance with stated terms and conditions.
Contractual requirements	Requirements specified in a contract.
Control	The act of preventing or regulating change in parameters, situations, or conditions.
Control charts	A graphical comparison of process performance data to computed control limits drawn as limit lines on the chart.
Control methods	Particular ways of providing control which do not constrain the sequence of steps in which the methods are carried out.

Control procedure	A procedure that controls product or information as it passes through an organization.
Controlled conditions	Arrangements which provide control over all factors that influence the result.
Corrective action	Action planned or taken to stop something from recurring.
Criteria for workmanship	Acceptance standards based on qualitative measures of performance.
Cross-functional team	See *Multidisciplinary team*.
Customer complaints	Any adverse report (verbal or written) received by a supplier from a customer.
Customer supplied product	Hardware, software, documentation, or information owned by the customer which is provided to a supplier for use in connection with a contract and which is returned to the customer either incorporated in the supplies or at the end of the contract.
Data	Information that is organized in a form suitable for manual or computer analysis.
Define and document	To state in written form, the precise meaning, nature, or characteristics of something.
Demonstrate	To prove by reasoning, objective evidence, experiment, or practical application.
Design	A process of originating a conceptual solution to a requirement and expressing it in a form from which a product may be produced or a service delivered.
Design and development	Design creates the conceptual solution and development transforms the solution into a fully working model.
Design of experiments	A technique for improving the quality of both processes and products by effectively investigating several sources of variation at the same time using statistically planned experiments.
Design review	A formal documented and systematic critical study of a design by people other than the designer.

Disposition	The act or manner of disposing of something.
Documentation audit	See *Adequacy audit*.
Documented procedures	Procedures that are formally laid down in a reproducible medium such as paper or magnetic disk.
Effectiveness of the system	The extent to which the (quality) system fulfills its purpose.
Employee empowerment	An environment in which employees are free (within defined limits) to take action to operate, maintain, and improve the processes for which they are responsible using their own expertise and judgment.
Ensure	To make certain that something will happen.
Establish and maintain	To set up an entity on a permanent basis and retain or restore it in a state in which it can fulfill its purpose or required function.
Evaluation	To ascertain the relative goodness, quality, or usefulness of an entity with respect to a specific purpose.
Evidence of conformance	Documents which testify that an entity conforms with certain prescribed requirements.
Executive responsibility	Responsibility vested in those personnel who are responsible for the whole organization's performance. Often referred to as top management.
Failure modes and effects analysis	A technique for identifying potential failure modes and assessing existing and planned provisions to detect, contain, or eliminate the occurrence of failure.
Final inspection and testing	The last inspection or test carried out by the supplier before ownership passes to the customer.
Finite element analysis	A technique for modeling a complex structure.
First party audits	Audits of a company or parts thereof by personnel employed by the company. These audits are also called *internal audits*.
Follow-up audit	An audit carried out following and as a direct consequence of a previous audit to determine whether agreed actions have been taken and are effective.

Functions	In the organizational sense, a function is a special or major activity (often unique in the organization) which is needed in order for the organization to fulfill its purpose and mission. Examples of functions are design, procurement, personnel, manufacture, marketing, maintenance etc. Departments may perform one or more functions but a department is a component of the organization, not a function.
Geometric dimensioning and tolerancing	A method of dimensioning the shape of parts that provides appropriate limits and fits for their application and facilitates manufacturability and interchangeability.
Identification	The act of identifying an entity, i.e. giving it a set of characteristics by which it is recognizable as a member of a group.
Implement	To carry out a directive.
Implementation audit	An audit carried out to establish whether actual practices conform to the documented quality system; also referred to as a *conformance audit* or *compliance audit*.
Importance of activities (in auditing)	The relative importance of the contribution an activity makes to the fulfillment of an organization's objectives.
In-process	Between the beginning and the end of a process.
Indexing	A means of enabling information to be located.
Inspection, measuring, and test equipment	Devices used to perform inspections, measurements, and tests.
Inspection	The examination of an entity to determine whether it conforms to prescribed requirements.
Inspection authority	The person or organization who has been given the right to perform inspections.
Installation	The process by which an entity is fitted into a larger entity.
Issues of documents	The revision state of a document.

Major nonconformity	The absence or total breakdown of a system to meet a requirement of QS-9000.
	Any noncompliance that would result in the probable shipment of a nonconforming product.
	A noncompliance that judgment and experience indicate is likely either to result in the failure of the quality system or to materially reduce its ability to assure controlled processes and products.
Minor nonconformity	A failure in some part of the supplier's documented quality system relative to a QS-9000 requirement.
	A single observed lapse in following one item of a company's quality system.
Manage work	To manage work means to plan, organize, and control the resources (personnel, financial, and material) and the tasks required to achieve the objective for which the work is needed.
Management representative	The person management appoints to act on their behalf to manage the quality system.
Master list	An original list from which copies can be made.
Measurement capability	The ability of a measuring system (device, person, and environment) to measure true values to the accuracy and precision required.
Measurement uncertainty	The variation observed when repeated measurements of the same parameter on the same specimen are taken with the same device.
Modifications	Entities altered or reworked to incorporate design changes.
Monitoring	To check periodically and systematically. It does not imply that any action will be taken.
Multidisciplinary team	A team comprising representatives from various functions or departments in an organization, formed to execute a project on behalf of that organization.
Nationally recognized standards	Standards of measure which have been authenticated by an accredited national body.

Nature of change	The intrinsic characteristics of the change (what has changed and why).
Objective	The result that is to be achieved, usually by a given time.
Obsolete documents	Documents that are no longer required for operational use. They may be useful as historic documents.
Operating procedure	A procedure that describes how specific tasks are to be performed.
Organizational goals	Where the organization desires to be, in markets, in innovation, in social and environmental matters, in competition, and in financial health.
Organizational interfaces	The boundary at which organizations meet and affect each other, expressed by the passage of information, people, equipment, materials, and the agreement to operational conditions.
Plan	Provisions made to achieve an objective.
Planned arrangements	All the arrangements made by the supplier to achieve the customers' requirements. They include the documented policies and procedures and the documents derived from such policies and procedures.
Policy	A guide to thinking, action, and decision.
Positive recall	A means of recovering an entity by giving it a unique identity.
Positively identified	An identification given to an entity for a specific purpose which is both unique and readily visible.
Potential nonconformity	A situation which if left alone will in time result in a nonconformity.
Pre-launch	A phase in the development of a product between design validation and full production (sometimes called pre-production) during which the production processes are validated.
Predictive maintenance	Work scheduled to monitor machine condition, predict pending failure, and make repairs on an as-needed basis; e.g. monitoring machine vibration.

Prevent	To stop something from occurring by a deliberate planned action.
Preventive action	Action proposed or taken to stop something from occurring.
Preventive maintenance	Maintenance carried out at predetermined intervals to reduce the probability of failure or performance degradation; e.g. replacing oil filters at defined intervals.
Procedure	A sequence of steps to execute a routine activity.
Process capability	The ability of a process to maintain product characteristics within preset limits.
Process	A sequence of tasks which combine the use of people, machines, methods, tools, environment, instrumentation, and materials to convert given inputs into outputs of added value.
Process parameters	Those variables, boundaries, or constants of a process which restrict or determine the results.
Product	Anything produced by human effort, natural or man-made processes.
Production	The creation of products.
Proprietary designs	Designs exclusively owned by the supplier and not sponsored by an external customer.
Prototype	A model of a design that is both physically and functionally representative of the design standard for production and used to verify and validate the design.
Purchaser	One who buys from another.
Purchasing documents	Documents which contain the supplier's purchasing requirements.
Qualification	Determination – by a series of tests and examinations of a product, related documents and processes – that the product meets all the specified performance capability requirements.

Qualified personnel

Personnel who have been judged as having the necessary ability to carry out particular tasks.

Quality activities

Any activity that affects the ability of a product or service to satisfy stated or implied needs or the organization's ability to satisfy those needs. If the quality system defines the activities that need to be executed to achieve quality then any activity specified in the documented quality system is also a quality activity.

Quality conformance

The extent to which the product or service conforms with the specified requirements.

Quality costs

Costs incurred because failure is possible. The actual cost of producing an entity is the no-failure cost plus the quality costs. The no-failure cost is the cost of doing the right things right first time. The quality costs are the prevention, appraisal, and failure costs.

Quality function deployment

A technique to deploy customer requirements (the true quality characteristics) into design characteristics (the substitute characteristics) and deploy them into subsystems, components, materials, and production processes. The result is a grid or matrix that shows how and where customer requirements are met.

Quality plans

Plans produced to define how specified quality requirements will be achieved, controlled, assured, and managed for specific contracts or projects.

Quality planning

Provisions made to prevent failure to satisfy customer needs and expectations and organizational goals.

Quality objectives

Those results which the organization needs to achieve in order to improve its ability to meet current and future customer needs and expectations.

Quality problems

The difference between the achieved quality and the required quality.

Quality records	Objective evidence of the achieved features and characteristics of a product or service and the processes applied to its development, design, production, installation, maintenance, and disposal as well as records of assessments, audits, and other examinations of an organization to determine its capability to achieve given quality requirements.
Quality requirements	Those requirements that pertain to the features and characteristics of a product or service which are required to be fulfilled in order to satisfy a given need.
Quality system	A tool for achieving, sustaining, and improving quality.
Quality system assessments	External audits carried out by second or third parties. They include a documentation audit, implementation audit, and the determination of the effectiveness of the system.
Quality system element	A distinct part of the system which is governed by a set of requirements.
	A subsection of the standard identified by a two-digit number, such as 4.1, 4.2, 4.3 etc.
Quality system requirements	Requirements pertaining to the design, development, implementation, and maintenance of quality systems.
Quarantine area	A secure space provided for containing product pending a decision on its disposal.
Registrar	An organization that is authorized to certify organizations. The body may be accredited or non-accredited.
Registration	A process of recording details of organizations of assessed capability which have satisfied prescribed standards.
Regulatory requirements	Requirements established by law pertaining to products or services.

Related results	Results that arise out of performing an activity or making a decision. In the context of quality activities they may be documents, records, approval and acceptance decisions, disapproval and reject decisions, products, processes.
Remedial action	Action proposed or taken to remove a nonconformity (see also *Corrective and preventive action*).
Representative sample	A sample of product or service which possesses all the characteristics of the batch from which it was taken.
Requirement of the standard	A sentence containing the word *shall*. Note that some sentences contain multiple requirements such as "to establish, document, and maintain". This is in fact three requirements.
Responsibility	An area in which one is entitled to act on one's own accord.
Review	Another look at something.
Scheduled maintenance	Work performed at a time specifically planned to minimize interruptions in machine availablility; e.g. changing a gearbox when machine is not required for use (includes predictive and preventive maintenance).
Second party audits	Audits carried out by customers upon their suppliers.
Service	Results that do not depend on the provision of products.
Service reports	Reports of servicing activities.
Servicing	Action to restore or maintain an item in an operational condition.
Shall	A provision that is binding.
Should	A provision that is optional.
Simultaneous engineering	A method of reducing the time taken to achieve objectives by developing the resources needed to support and sustain the production of a product in parallel with the development of the product itself. It involves customers, suppliers, and each of the organi-

zation's functions working together to achieve common objectives.

Specified requirements Requirements prescribed by the purchaser in a contract or requirements prescribed by the supplier in a market requirement or design brief as a result of an analysis of the market need.

Status The relative condition, maturity, or quality of something.

Status of an activity (in auditing) The maturity or relative level of performance of an activity to be audited.

Subcontract requirements Requirements placed on a subcontractor which are derived from requirements of the main contract.

Subcontractor A person or company that enters into a subcontract and assumes some of the obligations of the prime contractor.

Subcontractor development A technique for promoting continuous improvement of subcontractors by encouraging customer-supplier relationships and communication across all levels of the involved organizations.

Supplier A person or company who supplies products or services to a purchaser.

System audit An audit carried out to establish whether the quality system conforms to a prescribed standard in both its design and its implementation.

System effectiveness The ability of a system to achieve its stated purpose and objectives

Technical interfaces The physical and functional boundary between products and services.

Tender A written offer to supply products or services at a stated cost.

Theory of constraints A thinking process optimizing system performance. It examines the system and focuses on the constraints that limits overall system performance. It looks for the weakest link in the chain of processes that produce organizational performance and seeks to eliminate it and optimize system performance.

Third party audits	External audits carried out by personnel who are neither employees of the customer nor the supplier and are usually employees of certification bodies or registrars.
Traceability	The ability to trace the history, application, use, and location of an individual article or its characteristics through recorded identification numbers.
Unique identification	An identification which has no equal.
Validation	A process for establishing whether an entity will fulfill the purpose for which it has been selected or designed.
Value engineering	A technique for assessing the functions of a product and determining whether the same functions can be achieved with fewer types of components and materials and the product produced with less resources. Variety reduction is an element of value engineering.
Verification	The act of establishing the truth or correctness of a fact, theory, statement, or condition.
Verification activities	A special investigation, test, inspection, audit, review, demonstration, analysis, or comparison of data to verify that a system, product, service, or process complies with prescribed requirements.
Verification requirements	Requirements for establishing conformance of a product or service with specified requirements by certain methods and techniques.
Waiver	See *Concession*.
Work instructions	Instructions which prescribe work to be executed, who is to do it, when it is to start and be complete, and how, if necessary, it is to be carried out.
Workmanship criteria	Standards on which to base the acceptability of characteristics created by human manipulation of materials by hand or with the aid of hand tools.
Zero defects	The performance standard achieved when every task is performed right first time with no errors being detected downstream.

Appendix B

Procedures required by QS-9000

In this appendix each requirement in QS-9000 that requires, implies or suggests that a procedure is necessary is identified. Where a procedure is specifically required, usually by the clause "... *the supplier shall establish and maintain documented procedures for* ...", this is specifically stated in the list. Where there is a general requirement for documented procedures, such as that in clause 4.4.1 on design control, there is an implication that the procedures should address each of the subclauses, by virtue of clause 4.2.2 which states: "*The supplier shall prepare documented procedures consistent with the requirements of the standard.*" However, where there is no general requirement for procedures, as in clauses 4.1, 4.9, 4.12 etc., procedures are optional. Although there are 68 subjects requiring procedures and 53 subjects implying that procedures are required, with a further 52 optional procedures, it should not be construed that separate documents are required, several subjects may of course be addressed in one document. There are 173 subjects that require some form of documentation, either policy or practice or both. The list is therefore a good guide to the subjects that should be addressed in the quality manual where they are appropriate to your business. Even if they are not appropriate, it is good practice to declare this, so as to avoid misleading assessors and reviewers.

No.	Procedure Title/Subject	QS-9000 Clause	Status
1.	Formulation, promulgation, and maintenance of quality policy	4.1.1	Optional
2.	Formulation, promulgation, and maintenance of quality objectives	4.1.1	Optional
3.	Preparation and maintenance of job descriptions	4.1.2.1	Optional
4.	Project management	4.1.2.3	Required

No.	Procedure Title/Subject	QS-9000 Clause	Status
5.	Resource planning	4.1.2.2	Optional
6.	Conduct and recording of management reviews	4.1.3	Optional
7.	Business planning	4.1.4	Required
8.	Determination of customer expectations	4.1.4	Required
9.	Company data analysis	4.1.5	Optional
10.	Benchmarking	4.1.5	Optional
11.	Determination of customer satisfaction	4.1.6	Required
12.	Preparation and maintenance of the quality manual	4.2.1	Optional
13.	Preparation and maintenance of quality system procedures	4.2.2	Optional
14.	Preparation and maintenance of quality plans	4.2.3	Optional
15.	Resource acquisition	4.2.3	Optional
16.	Selection of standards	4.2.3	Optional
17.	Measurement capability assessment and development	4.2.3	Optional
18.	Advanced product quality planning	4.2.3	Required
19.	Establishing special characteristics	4.2.3	Optional
20.	Feasibility reviews	4.2.3	Optional
21.	Process Failure mode and effects analysis	4.2.3	Optional
22.	Control plans	4.2.3	Optional
23.	Conduct and coordination of contract reviews	4.3	Required
24.	Amendments to contract	4.3.3	Implied
25.	Design control	4.4.1	Required
26.	Design verification	4.4.1	Required
27.	Design and development planning	4.4.2	Implied
28.	Allocation of development and verification work	4.4.2	Implied
29.	Identification, transmission, and review of technical interfaces	4.4.3	Implied
30.	Identification, transmission, and review of organizational interfaces	4.4.3	Implied

No.	Procedure Title/Subject	QS-9000 Clause	Status
31.	Identification and review of design input requirements	4.4.4	Implied
32.	Computer aided design/engineering	4.4.4	Implied
33.	Conduct and recording of design reviews	4.4.5	Implied
34.	Design failure modes and effects analysis	4.4.5	Implied
35.	Documentation of the design solution	4.4.6	Implied
36.	Design output documentation review	4.4.6	Implied
37.	Design verification planning	4.4.7	Implied
38.	Design verification testing	4.4.7	Implied
39.	Design verification by demonstrations	4.4.7	Implied
40.	Design verification by calculation	4.4.7	Implied
41.	Design verification by similarity analysis	4.4.7	Implied
42.	Design stage documentation review	4.4.7	Implied
43.	Prototyping	4.4.7	Implied
44.	Design validation	4.4.8	Implied
45.	Identification and proposal of design changes and modifications	4.4.9	Implied
46.	Review and approval of design changes and modifications	4.4.9	Implied
47.	Production part approval submissions	4.4.9	Implied
48.	Document and data control	4.5.1	Required
49.	Review and approval of documents and data	4.5.2	Implied
50.	Document indexing	4.5.2	Implied
51.	Use of obsolete documents	4.5.2	Implied
52.	Control of customer engineering standards	4.5.2	Required
53.	Document withdrawal	4.5.2	Implied
54.	Document change control	4.5.3	Implied
55.	Purchasing	4.6.1	Required
56.	Selection and evaluation of subcontractors	4.6.2	Implied

No.	Procedure Title/Subject	QS-9000 Clause	Status
57.	Preparation and maintenance of assessed suppliers list	4.6.2	Implied
58.	Assessment of subcontractors	4.6.2	Implied
59.	Subcontractor development	4.6.2	Implied
60.	Subcontractor delivery performance monitoring	4.6.2	Required
61.	Preparation, review, and approval of purchasing documents	4.6.3	Implied
62.	Control of restricted substances	4.6.3	Required
63.	Verification at supplier's premises	4.6.4.1	Implied
64.	Verification of supplies by the customer	4.6.4.2	Implied
65.	Verification, storage, and maintenance of customer supplied product	4.7	Required
66.	Product identification	4.8	Required if appropriate
67.	Product traceability	4.8	Required if specified
68.	Production planning	4.9	Optional
69.	Installation planning	4.9	Optional
70.	Servicing planning	4.9	Optional
71.	Production procedures	4.9	Required
72.	Installation procedures	4.9	Required
73.	Servicing procedures	4.9	Required
74.	Selection and use of production, installation and servicing equipment	4.9	Optional
75.	Specification of working environments	4.9	Optional
76.	Process control and monitoring	4.9	Optional
77.	Control and monitoring of product characteristics	4.9	Optional
78.	Approval of processes	4.9	Optional
79.	Approval of equipment	4.9	Optional
80.	Specification of workmanship criteria	4.9	Optional
81.	Maintenance of equipment	4.9	Optional

No.	Procedure Title/Subject	QS-9000 Clause	Status
82.	Qualification of special processes	4.9	Optional
83.	Monitoring and control of special processes	4.9	Optional
84.	Safety procedures	4.9	Required
85.	Environmental procedures	4.9	Required
86.	Preventive maintenance	4.9	Required
87.	Process monitoring instructions	4.9.1	Required
88.	Operator instructions	4.9.1	Required
89.	Process capability studies	4.9.2	Optional
90.	Job-setup verification	4.9.5	Optional
91.	Appearance item controls	4.9.7	Optional
92.	Inspection and test requirements	4.10.1	Required
93.	Receipt inspection	4.10.2	Required
94.	Positive recall	4.10.2.3	Implied
95.	In-process inspection and test	4.10.3	Required
96.	Product release	4.10.3	Optional
97.	Quarantine areas	4.10.3	Implied
98.	Final inspection and test	4.10.4	Required
99.	Dispatch inspection	4.10.4	Implied
100.	Layout inspection and functional testing	4.10.4	Implied
101.	Preparation and maintenance of inspection and test records	4.10.5	Implied
102.	Control of inspection, measuring, and test equipment	4.11.1	Required
103.	Calibration of inspection, measuring, and test equipment	4.11.1	Required
104.	Maintenance of inspection, measuring, and test equipment	4.11.1	Required
105.	Control and maintenance of software	4.11.1	Required
106.	Qualification of reference material	4.11.1	Implied
107.	Qualification of test software	4.11.1	Implied

No.	Procedure Title/Subject	QS-9000 Clause	Status
108.	Preparation and maintenance of measurement design data	4.11.1	Optional
109.	Qualification of jigs, tools, and fixtures	4.11.1	Implied
110.	Determination of verification requirements	4.11.2	Optional
111.	Selection of inspection, measuring, and test equipment	4.11.2	Implied
112.	Handling, preservation, and storage of inspection, measuring, and test equipment	4.11.2	Implied
113.	Preparation and maintenance of calibration instructions	4.11.2	Implied
114.	Calibration invalidity recovery routines	4.11.2	Implied
115.	Specification and maintenance of inspection and test environments	4.11.2	Optional
116.	Measurement system analysis	4.11.4	Optional
117.	Indication and maintenance of inspection status	4.12	Required
118.	Registration and control of inspection stamps	4.12	Optional
119.	Control of nonconforming product	4.13.1	Required
120.	Identification of nonconforming product	4.13.1	Implied
121.	Nonconformance recording and reporting	4.13.1	Implied
122.	Evaluation of nonconforming product	4.13.1	Implied
123.	Review and disposition of nonconforming product	4.13.2	Required
124.	Processing concession applications to the customer	4.13.2	Optional
125.	Repair and rework of nonconforming product	4.13.2	Required
126.	Rework control	4.13.3	Implied
127.	PPAP change control	4.13.4	Optional
128.	Corrective action programs	4.14.1	Required
129.	Problem solving methods	4.14.1	Optional
130.	Collection and analysis of customer complaints	4.14.2	Required
131.	Collection and analysis of nonconformance reports	4.14.2	Required

No.	Procedure Title/Subject	QS-9000 Clause	Status
132.	Nonconforming product and process investigation and correction	4.14.2	Required
133.	Quality system nonconformity investigation and correction	4.14.2	Required
134.	Post corrective action audits	4.14.2	Required
135.	Returned product analysis	4.14.2	Optional
136.	Monitoring and analysis of processes and work operations	4.14.3	Required
137.	Collection and analysis of quality records	4.14.3	Required
138.	Collection and analysis of service reports	4.14.3	Required
139.	Preventive action programs	4.14.3	Required
140.	Post preventive action audits	4.14.3	Required
141.	Product handling	4.15.1	Required
142.	Product storage	4.15.1	Required
143.	Product packaging, packing, and marking	4.15.1	Required
144.	Product preservation and segregation	4.15.1	Required
145.	Product delivery	4.15.1	Required
146.	Control of storage areas	4.15.3	Implied
147.	Receipt and release of items from storage areas	4.15.3	Implied
148.	Stock condition audits	4.15.3	Implied
149.	Inventory management	4.15.3	Required
150.	Preparation and maintenance of packaging specifications	4.15.4	Optional
151.	Delivery performance monitoring	4.15.6	Required
152.	Shipment notification	4.15.6	Optional
153.	Identification of quality records	4.16	Required
154.	Collection of quality records	4.16	Required
155.	Indexing, filing, access, storage, and maintenance of quality records	4.16	Required
156.	Disposal of quality records	4.16	Required
157.	Planning internal quality audits	4.17	Required

No.	Procedure Title/Subject	QS-9000 Clause	Status
158.	Conduct of internal quality audits	4.17	Required
159.	Training strategy	4.18	Optional
160.	Identification of training needs	4.18	Required
161.	Training of personnel	4.18	Optional
162.	Maintenance of training records	4.18	Optional
163.	Evaluation of training	4.18	Optional
164.	Servicing equipment	4.19	Required
165.	Servicing reporting	4.19	Required
166.	Servicing verification	4.19	Required
167.	Application and use of statistical techniques	4.20.2	Required
168.	Continuous improvement	II-2.1	Required
169.	Facilities planning	II-3.1	Required
170.	Mistake proofing	II-3.2	Optional
171.	Tool design	II-3.3	Optional
172.	Tool fabrication	II-3.3	Optional
173.	Tooling management	II-3.4	Required

Appendix C

Bibliography

The last 50 years has produced some remarkable books on quality and management. Some of these have been a constant source of information and inspiration, and have helped form many of the ideas and beliefs presented in this book.

Armstrong, Michael. *How to be a Better Manager* – Kogan Page, London 1985

Chruden, Herbert J. & Sherman, Arthur W. Jr. *Personnel Management* – South-Western Publishing Co., Cincinnati 1976

Crosby, Philip B. *Quality Is Free* – McGraw-Hill Book Company Inc. 1979

Drucker, Peter F. *The Practice of Management* – Pan Books Ltd., London 1972

Feigenbaum, A.V. *Total Quality Control, Engineering and Management* – McGraw-Hill 1961

Goldratt, Eliyahu M. *The Goal* – North River Press, New York 1992

Gluckman, Perry *Everyday Heroes of the Quality Movement* – Dorset House Publishing, New York 1993

Hammer, Michael & Champy, James *Reengineering the Corporation* – Harper-Collins 1993

Hodgetts, Richard M. *Management Theory, Process and Practice* – W.B. Saunders Company, Philadelphia 1979

Imai, Masaaki *KAIZEN, The Key to Japan's Competitive Success* – McGraw-Hill Publishing Company 1986

Juran, J. M. *Quality Control Handbook* – McGraw-Hill Book Company Inc. 1974

Juran, J. M. *Managerial Breakthrough* – McGraw-Hill Book Company Inc. 1964

Juran, J. M. *Juran on Leadership for Quality – An Executive Handbook* – The Free Press, a division of Macmillan, Inc., New York 1989

Oakland, John S. *Total Quality Management* – Butterworth Heinemann Oxford 1993

Price, Frank *Right First Time* – Wildwood House Limited, Aldershot England 1984

Sayle, Allan J. *Management Audits* – Allan J. Sayle Ltd. 1988

Scott, John & Rochester, Arthur. *Effective Management Skills – What Is a Manager* – Sphere/British Institute of Management 1984

Sloan, Alfred P. *My Years with General Motors* – Currency and Doubleday, New York. First published 1963. Reprint with a new introduction by Peter Drucker 1990.

Appendix D

List of related standards

ANSI/API Spec Q1-1992	Quality Programs
ANSI/ASQC A1-1987	Definitions, symbols, formulas, and tables for control charts
ANSI/ASQC A2-1987	Terms, symbols, and definitions for acceptance sampling
ANSI/ASQC B1, B2, B3-1995	Guide for Quality Control Charts, Method of Analyzing Data and Controlling Quality during Production
ANSI/ASQC C1-1985	Specification of general requirement for a quality program
ANSI/ASQC D1160-1995	Formal Design Review
ANSI/ASQC E2-1995	Guide to inspection planning
ANSI/ASQC M1-1987	Calibration systems
ANSI/ASQC Q1-1986	Generic guidelines for auditing of quality systems
ANSI/ASQC Q2 1990	Quality Management and Quality System Elements for Laboratories – Guidelines
ANSI/ASQC Q3-1988	Sampling Procedures and Tables for Inspection of Isolated Lots by Attributes
ANSI/ASQC S1-1995	An Attribute Skip-Lot Sampling Program
ANSI/ASQC S2-1995	Introduction to Attribute Sampling
ANSI/ASQC Z1.4-1993	Sampling Procedures and Tables for Inspection by Attributes
ANSI/ASQC Z1.9-1993	Sampling Procedures and Tables for Inspection by Variables for Percent Nonconforming
BS 3811-1993	Glossary of maintenance management terms in terotechnology

BS 4778 Part 2-1991	Quality concepts and related definitions
BS4778 Part 3.1 1991	Availability, reliability and maintainability terms – Guide to concepts and related definitions
BS4778 Part 3.2 1991	Availability, reliability and maintainability terms – Glossary of International Terms
BS 4891-1972	A guide to quality assurance
BS 5179-1974	Guide to the operation and evaluation of quality assurance systems
BS5729 Part 5 1993	Guide to stock control – Storekeeping
BS5760 Part 0 1993	Introductory guide to reliability
BS5760 Part 1 1993	Guide to reliability and maintainability program management
BS5760 Part 2 1994	Guide to the assessment of reliability
BS5760 Part 3 1993	Guide to reliability practices: examples
BS5760 Part 5 1991	Guide to failure modes effects and criticality analysis (FMEA and FMECA)
BS5760 Part 7 1991	Guide to fault tree analysis
BS 5760 Part 14-1993	Guide to formal design reviews
BS 6143-1992	Guide to the economics of quality (Parts 1 & 2)
BS 7373-1991	Guide to the preparation of specifications
BS 7000 Part 1 1989	Guide to managing product design
BS7000 Part 3 1994	Guide to managing service design
BS7000 Part 10 1995	Glossary of terms used in design management
BS7750 1994	Specification for environmental management systems
Electronic Engineering Association	Guide to software quality audit
EN 45001-1989	General criteria for the operation of testing laboratories
EN 45002-1989	General criteria for the assessment of testing laboratories
EN 45003-1995	General criteria for laboratory accreditation bodies
EN 45004-1995	General criteria for the operation of various types of bodies performing inspection
EN 45011-1989	General criteria for certification bodies operating product certification
EN 45012-1989	General criteria for certification bodies operating quality system certification

EN 45013-1989	General criteria for certification bodies operating certification of personnel
EN 45014-1989	General criteria for supplier's declaration of conformity
ISO/IEC Guide 25 1990	General requirements for the competence of calibration and testing laboratories
ISO IEC Guide 40-1983	General requirements for the acceptance of certification bodies
ISO IEC Guide 48-1986	Guidelines for third-party assessment and registration of a supplier's quality system
ISO 2859	Sampling procedures for inspection by attributes
ISO 3951	Sampling procedures for inspection by variables
ISO 8402	Quality vocabulary
ISO 10011	Guidelines for auditing quality systems (Parts 1, 2 & 3)
ISO 10012	Quality assurance requirements for measuring equipment (Parts 1 & 2)
ISO 10013	Guidelines for developing quality manuals
ISO 10014	Guide to the economic effects of total quality management

Note: ANSI standards are issued by the American National Standards Organization
ASQC standards are issued by the American Society for Quality Control
BSs are British Standards issued by the British Standards Institution (BSI)
EN standards are European Norm standards obtainable from BSI
ISO standards are issued by the International Organization for Standardization

Appendix E

Relationship of clauses

Some clauses of QS-9000 address particular phases in the quality loop and others are independent of any phase. It should not be assumed that, for example, all the requirements that apply to purchasing are in clause 4.6. This matrix should help identify which requirements apply to any given phase.

PHASE INDEPENDENT	PHASE DEPENDENT						
	Contract Review 4.3	Design 4.4	Purchasing 4.6	Production 4.9	Delivery 4.15	Installation 4.9	Servicing 4.19/4.9
4.1 Management Responsibility	X	X	X	X	X	X	X
4.2 Quality System	X	X	X	X	X	X	X
4.5 Document and Data Control	X	X	X	X	X	X	X
4.7 Customer Supplied Product		X	X	X	X	X	X
4.8 Product Identification & Traceability		X	X	X	X	X	X
4.10 Inspection & Testing		X	X	X	X	X	X
4.11 Inspection, Measuring & Test Equipment		X	X	X	X	X	X
4.12 Inspection & Test Status		X	X	X	X	X	X
4.13 Control of Nonconforming Product		X	X	X	X	X	X
4.14 Corrective and Preventive Action	X	X	X	X	X	X	X
4.15 Handling, Packaging Preservation & Storage		X	X	X	X	X	X
4.16 Control of Quality Records	X	X	X	X	X	X	X
4.17 Internal Quality Audits	X	X	X	X	X	X	X
4.18 Training	X	X	X	X	X	X	X
4.20 Statistical Techniques		X	X	X	X		
II-1 PPAP		X		X			
II-2 Continuous improvement	X	X	X	X	X	X	X
II-3 Manufacturing capability	X	X		X			

Index